PRAISE FOR *ECSTATIC PESSIMIST*

"Czeslaw Milosz is that rare poet whose work has crossed seemingly impassable boundaries of place and time. Peter Dale Scott and Milosz were colleagues at Berkeley, and Scott, who had been a Canadian diplomat in Poland, became one of Milosz's first translators into English. From the unique perspective of a complex friendship, Scott is able to show us, as almost no one else can, the vatic, prophetic role Milosz had in Poland, how it was transformed by war and decades in the United States and emerged again triumphant in his late years. Learned and beautifully written, *Ecstatic Pessimist* takes us on a journey to the heart of Milosz's poetry, vibrant with the contradictions that make him a prophet of the postmodern age."

—**Robert Faggen, Claremont McKenna College**

"Czeslaw Milosz, with his unblinking witness to horror and his insistence on hope for humanity, has never seemed more relevant. To meet this moment, Peter Dale Scott simultaneously illuminates the arc of Milosz's oeuvre and narrates a passionate reader's lifelong relationship. A major contribution to Milosz studies."

—**David Shaddock, author of** *Poetry and Psychoanalysis*

"Of all the great poets of the late twentieth century, Milosz is the most multifaceted, even self-contradictory. Scott's own dialectical thinking makes him a perfect guide to Milosz, especially to the texts less well known in America."

—**Alan Williamson, University of California, Davis**

"*Ecstatic Pessimist* is the culmination of decades of Milosz and Scott's thought, study, and friendship. 'I have tried to be true to the Milosz I knew and loved,' Scott writes. He has succeeded. We are fortunate to have Scott as a guide to one of the greatest poets of our times, offering us a wise, insightful, and deeply learned journey through Milosz's poems and life in these pages."

—**Cynthia L. Haven, author of** *Czesław Miłosz: A California Life*

Ecstatic Pessimist

WORLD SOCIAL CHANGE

Series Editor: Mark Selden

Titles Published

The Economic Aspect of the Abolition of the West Indian Slave Trade and Slavery, by Eric Williams, edited by Dale W. Tomich with an introduction by William Darity Jr.

China: An Environmental History, Second Edition, by Robert B. Marks

Engaging Adversaries: Peacemaking and Diplomacy in the Human Interest, by Mel Gurtov

The Origins of the Modern World: A Global and Environmental Narrative from the Fifteenth to the Twenty-First Century, Fourth Edition, by Robert B. Marks

America in Retreat: Foreign Policy under Donald Trump, by Mel Gurtov

Ecstatic Pessimist

Czeslaw Milosz, Poet of Catastrophe and Hope

Peter Dale Scott

ROWMAN & LITTLEFIELD
Lanham • Boulder • New York • London

Published by Rowman & Littlefield
An imprint of The Rowman & Littlefield Publishing Group, Inc.
4501 Forbes Boulevard, Suite 200, Lanham, Maryland 20706
www.rowman.com
86-90 Paul Street, London EC2A 4NE

Copyright © 2023 by Peter Dale Scott
All rights reserved. No part of this book may be reproduced in any form or by any electronic or mechanical means, including information storage and retrieval systems, without written permission from the publisher, except by a reviewer who may quote passages in a review.

British Library Cataloguing in Publication Information Available

Library of Congress Cataloging-in-Publication Data

Names: Scott, Peter Dale, author.
Title: Ecstatic pessimist: Czeslaw Milosz, poet of catastrophe and hope / Peter Dale Scott.
Description: Lanham: Rowman & Littlefield, [2023] | Series: World social change | Includes bibliographical references and index.
Identifiers: LCCN 2022045578 (print) | LCCN 2022045579 (ebook) | ISBN 9781538172438 (cloth) | ISBN 9781538172445 (paperback;
) | ISBN 9781538172452 (epub)
Subjects: LCSH: Miłosz, Czesław—Criticism and interpretation. | LCGFT: Literary criticism.
Classification: LCC PG7158.M5532 S36 2023 (print) | LCC PG7158.M5532 (ebook) | DDC 891.8/58709—dc23/eng/20220923
LC record available at https://lccn.loc.gov/2022045578
LC ebook record available at https://lccn.loc.gov/2022045579

When I wrote in the introduction to Rescue that I accepted the salvational goal of poetry, that was exactly what I had in mind, and I still believe that poetry can either save or destroy nations.
—Czeslaw Milosz, "A Semi-Private Letter about Poetry," 1946

How to combine "transcendence" and "devenir" has always been my main question.
—Czeslaw Milosz, letter to Thomas Merton, 1959

The poetic act both anticipates the future and speeds its coming.
—Czeslaw Milosz, *The Witness of Poetry,* 1983

Contents

Acknowledgments	ix
Abbreviations	xi

PART I: MILOSZ, POETRY, AND POLITICS — 1

Chapter 1: Introduction: My Years with Milosz (1961–1967) — 3

Chapter 2: Milosz, Solidarity, and "Unpolitical Politics": Or, Poetry and the Liberation of a People — 17

Chapter 3: Looking "From Above": Milosz, Catastrophe, and "Doubleness" — 27

PART II: MILOSZ'S POETRY OF THE WAR — 43

Chapter 4: Milosz's Wartime Poem-Sequence, *Ocalenie*: Part I: Overview: The Structure of the Book — 45

Chapter 5: *Ocalenie* Part II: "The World" as Hub of the Book — 57

Chapter 6: *Ocalenie* Part III: "Voices of Poor People" — 67

Chapter 7: *Ocalenie* Part IV: "Flight" and the Flight from Warsaw — 81

Chapter 8: *Ocalenie* Part V: The Three Final Poems — 93

PART III: MILOSZ AFTER THE WAR (1946–1960) — 103

Chapter 9: Milosz, Auden, and "A Treatise on Morals" — 105

Chapter 10: Milosz the Émigré: "The Eternal Moment" — 123

Chapter 11: The Poetic Hegelianism of *A Treatise on Poetry* — 137

Chapter 12: "A Treatise on Poetry," Part IV: "Natura" — 155

PART IV: MILOSZ AS TRANSNATIONAL AUTHOR — 179

Chapter 13: Milosz in Berkeley, 1961: "Throughout Our Lands" — 181

Chapter 14: Milosz as a Poet in Later Years (1964–2004) — 189

Chapter 15: Milosz's Mature Prose: The Marriage of Blake and Eliot — 207

Chapter 16: Saning Insanity: Milosz as Healer of a Post-Secular Era — 231

Appendix: Three Poems to Czeslaw Milosz: Introduced by a Personal Memoir — 243

Appendix B: Three Poems to Czeslaw Milosz — 249

Permissions — 265

Notes — 267

A Short Milosz Bibliography — 341

Index — 345

About the Author — 361

Acknowledgments

This book has been so long in the making that I fear I shall omit some of the many people who have helped me fashion it.

Above all I must thank Robert Hass, for years of advice and discussion about Milosz, and specifically for his invitation to give a talk at a panel on Milosz, rewritten here as Chapter 2. My thanks to Michael Ondaatje, who heard that talk, and arranged for its original publication.

I profited greatly from a short course, "Reading Milosz," taught by Hass online in 2022. Among the discussants in that course was Renata Gorczyńska, some of whose valuable reminiscences are incorporated here.

I should also thank Robert Faggen, for the years of encouragement and guidance he has given me, for sponsoring two talks incorporated here, and also for transmitting an important question to Adam Michnik. Special hanks to Cynthia Haven, whose researches, discussions, and book on Milosz opened up fruitful new sources of information for me. And thanks to Rodric Braithwaite, who a half century ago helped introduce me to the brilliance of Polish intellectual life during the so-called Polish thaw of 1959 to 1961.

Out of the many people with whom I have had fruitful discussions of Milosz, I would like thank in particular his son Anthony Milosz, John Peck, David Frick, and the members of my poetry reading group and writing groups in Berkeley, in particular David Shaddock, Anita Barrows, Dawn McGuire, Murray Silverstein, Marsha Silverstein, and Alan Williamson. My thanks also to Caria Tomczykowska, for help with Polish. Once again, as with previous books, I am deeply indebted to PJ Heim for this book's Index.

Three other people have helped in ways too numerous to describe. One is my co-author Freeman Ng, who first encouraged me to write books about the interaction of poetry and politics, the two chief aspects of my divided life. Another is my long-time editor and friend Mark Selden, who has fostered this recent development of my prose in diverse ways. My children, Cassie. Mika, and John, have supplied needed technical assistance at crucial moments.

I also owe a great debt to Milosz's biographer Andrzej Franaszek and to his Miłosz: Biografia, Kraków, Znak, 2011, translated as *Milosz: A Biography* by Andrzej Franaszek, edited and translated by Aleksandra and Michael Parker, Cambridge Mass.: The Belknap Press of Harvard University Press, Copyright © 2017 by Andrzej Franaszek. Used by permission. All rights reserved.

My most important debt, as always, is to my wife Ronna Kabatznick, and far beyond what can be encompassed in words.

Abbreviations

ABC	Czeslaw Milosz. *Milosz's ABC's*. New York: Farrar, Straus and Giroux, 2001.
HPL	Czeslaw Milosz. *The History of Polish Literature*. Berkeley: University of California Press, 1983.
LU	Czeslaw Milosz. *The Land of Ulro*. New York: Farrar, Straus and Giroux, 1984.
NCP	Czeslaw Milosz. *New and Collected Poems: 1931–2001*. New York: Ecco Press/HarperCollins, 2003.
NR	Czeslaw Milosz. *Native Realm: A Search for Self-Definition*. New York: Farrar, Straus and Giroux, 1968.
SS	Czeslaw Milosz. *Second Space: New Poems*. New York: Ecco, 2004.
TP	Czeslaw Milosz. *A Treatise on Poetry*. New York: Ecco Press/HarperCollins, 2001.
Visions	Czeslaw Milosz. *Visions from San Francisco*. New York: Farrar, Straus and Giroux, 1975.
W	Czesław Miłosz. *Wiersze*. Kraków: Wydawnictwo Znak. 2001–2003. Volumes 1–3.
WP	Czeslaw Milosz. *The Witness of Poetry*. Cambridge, MA: Harvard University Press, 1983.
YH	Czeslaw Milosz. *A Year of the Hunter*. New York: Noonday Press, Farrar, Straus and Giroux, 1995.

PART I

Milosz, Poetry, and Politics

Chapter 1

Introduction: My Years with Milosz (1961–1967)

> We are, I know not how, double in ourselves, so that what we believe we disbelieve, and cannot rid ourselves of what we condemn.
>
> —Montaigne[1]

> Denying, believing and doubting are to man what running is to a horse.
>
> —Pascal[2]

Perhaps the most important and happiest surprise of my life was the chance, in the 1960s, to meet and work for six years with Czeslaw Milosz, when we translated Polish poetry together into English.

I met him in Berkeley in 1961, soon after arriving from my two years as a Canadian diplomat in Warsaw, where I had known his brother Andrzej. Czeslaw had long been famous in Poland, despite being officially banned. But elsewhere he was known then chiefly as author of *The Captive Mind*, rather than as a poet.

Having come from France only a year before me, Milosz like myself had few friends then in Berkeley, even in the Slavic Department. As I look back now on the six years we translated Polish poetry together, once or twice a month, I realize now how lucky I was to have met so regularly with him.

I may have been the first published poet to work with him in Berkeley. (His other friends and translators in those days were mostly his students.) In 1964, our first joint translation to be published, his early Berkeley poem "Throughout Our Lands," appeared in the CIA-subsidized journal *Encounter*. It was a happy moment for both of us; and, if I am not mistaken, it was the first of his many poems to be published in an English translation.

We shared more than being strangers in Berkeley, far from the cold climates of our youth. We both, for example, had been born in liminal lands where our own language—Milosz's Polish in Lithuania, my English in Quebec—was spoken only by a privileged minority, surrounded by an allophone countryside where faith in local miracles had in some places changed little since the Dark Ages.[3]

His childhood city of Wilno (now Vilnius)—hyperborean, multilingual, and distinguished by choruses of Sunday church bells, in streets crowded with Yiddish-speaking Jews—was comparable to the ghetto streets of my childhood Montreal. To the naked eye, the two cities might seem dissimilar. But the condition of being part of a dominant minority class aroused similar questions of identity and alienation (i.e., doubleness) in each of us.

Nevertheless, there were also significant differences between us. Most significantly, I had been too remote and too young—by a couple of years—to experience the war that had so devastated his life and environment.

My youth was an advantage. It made me happy to adopt Czeslaw as a mentor, and to listen without serious interruption as he shared with me his concerns for Poland and its intellectuals in that time of Cold War, or his theories about poets as diverse as Ovid, Blake, Jeffers, and Mandelstam.

Milosz soon had me assisting him on two much larger translation projects: poems by Polish contemporaries (which appeared in 1965 as *Postwar Polish Poetry*), and of earlier poets, going back to the sixteenth-century giant Jan Kochanowski (for his *History of Polish Literature*, 1969). And together we produced the first book in English of the poetry of Zbigniew Herbert (who I had also met and first translated when in Warsaw).[4]

The historical project opened for me a window into European history as seen from a Polish perspective. For example, Milosz, then at work on his *History of Polish Literature*, told me about the Arian (Socinian) College of Raków, whose books, as he recorded in his *History*, had been a major, if unacknowledged, influence on John Locke.[5] This was only one of the many examples he gave me of the Polish "Golden Age," when Poland was a leading source and refuge of Renaissance scholars. (Some of these scholars, forced to flee from the Catholic Counter-Reformation, later became a major influence on seventeenth-century English thought.)

Our work together as translators helped me develop a more direct and less self-indulgent style in my own poetry. His deep pessimism, in part the product of his grim wartime exposures to human brutality, was also an important balance to my naïve faith (inherited, I now see, from my father) in the human capacity for global community.

I believed then and believe still that poetry can and should reinforce this faith. So, at times (but more tentatively), did Milosz himself, who back in 1946 had written, "I still believe that poetry can either save or destroy nations."[6]

Milosz's awareness of the social function of poetry was not surprising in a man who came from a region where national frontiers slipped periodically east and west, and where both Poland and Lithuania had vanished at times from the map. As he wrote later, "My faithful language, / I have served you. / Every night I have set before you little bowls with color / . . . You were my homeland because the other one had gone missing" (NCP, 245).

As a Canadian, I too was attuned to the importance of poetry in confirming the cultural identity of an insecure, almost artificial nation. Thus, on my side, I had already felt somewhat estranged (like Milosz) from the historical mindlessness of postwar American poets I had met, like Richard Wilbur. My hope was for a poetry in English not numbed by ideologically motivated clichés like "A poem should not mean, but be."

Milosz encouraged me to think of a different tradition, where poets, by default, became repositories and promoters of people's hopes. (It was only later that I learned of his contributions in the 1950s and 1960s to what became the intellectual culture of Solidarność.)

THE EXPANDING PURPOSE OF THIS BOOK

That hope underlies the original agenda for this book, to look, in the context of biographical and historical events, at how the horrors of war augmented Milosz's poetic voice, and empowered him, in the tradition of Polish bards (*wieszcze*) like Mickiewicz, to explore his belief that poetry can serve as an "unpolitical politics," critiquing and redirecting our embattled twentieth-century culture.

(I will let Milosz explain the Polish notion of *wieszcz* [bard, *vates*] to those unfamiliar with it: "In Central and Eastern Europe," Czeslaw Milosz proclaims, "the word 'poet' has a somewhat different meaning from that which it has in the West. There a poet does not merely arrange words in beautiful order. Tradition demands that he be a 'bard,' that his songs linger on many lips, that he speak in his poems of subjects of interest to all the citizens.")[7]

Parts I and II of the book explore the context of his audacious challenge to poetry in 1945: "What is poetry that does not save Nations or people? A connivance with official lies" (NCP, 77). (I was electrified with excitement when I first saw his draft translation of these lines, not yet published in English. Unfortunately for me, Milosz, as we shall see, was at that point far more ambivalent about their suitability outside Poland.)[8]

This belief was echoed a half-century later in the lecture he delivered upon receiving the Nobel Prize in Literature in 1980: "Only if we assume that a poet constantly strives to liberate himself from borrowed styles in search for reality, is he dangerous. In a room where people unanimously maintain a conspiracy of silence, one word of truth sounds like a pistol shot."[9]

This was the first purpose of my book, to describe a Milosz who is unfamiliar to an American audience and who had a significant influence on the Polish Solidarity movement that led to the liberation of Poland and break-up of the Soviet Union.

But as I described Milosz's successive adjustments to life in exile, first in Paris (1951–1960) and then in America (1960–1989), I came to have increasing admiration for his expanded thinking in an expanded milieu.

In Parts III and IV of this book, I describe Milosz's reassessment, partly under the influence of Auden, of his (and any poet's) vatic role. In particular, I recall how, after arriving in America, Milosz, over my objections, rewrote his wartime poems in English, in order to downplay prophetic overtones that he rightly recognized to be less appropriate outside Poland.

Milosz thus became the Polish-American poet made familiar by critics like Helen Vendler, Seamus Heaney, and Robert Hass. I also discuss his period of activity with the Congress for Cultural Freedom, actions that, at first, I simply forgave but that I eventually came to admire.

Milosz was not writing now as a romantic bard, but as a specialist in a team of nonviolent Cold Warriors. Though he never ceased in his poetry to write of the ambitious goal of *salvation* (*ocalenie*, the appropriate title of his wartime book of poems), he came also to use more modest metaphors like "rescue" (*ratunek*, TP, 52) and "healing" (NCP, 50).

After winning the Nobel Prize in 1980, and especially after returning to Poland in 1984, Milosz returned to a modest reformulation of the vatic role he had earlier backed away from. Here I deal chiefly with Milosz's prose, where he developed, to a global rather than a Polish audience, his belief that "The poetic act both anticipates the future and speeds its coming" (WP, 109). I conclude that Milosz is indeed a new and innovative presence in the generative global canon enriched in the past by Virgil, Dante, Blake, Shelley, and Eliot.

I further believe that in his mature prose he presented what we can now call a post-secular critique of both modernism and postmodernism, one that is gaining in contemporary relevance and also strength. Finally, I see him as not just a critic but as a healer of a modern and postmodern world that is badly disrupted by failure to recalibrate the aging insights of the eighteenth-century Enlightenment.

Let me dare to be more specific. Milosz shares with most other great historical speculators of recent history—such as Hegel, Marx, Freud, Foucault—the belief that our cultural evolution (or what I call *ethogeny*) tends toward emancipation.[10] But where most modernists follow Marx in inverting Hegel's idealist claim that ideas shape societal institutions, Milosz restores and refines Hegel's claim: "The poetic act both anticipates the future and speeds its coming" (WP, 109). This was a rebuke, not just to Stalinist dialectical materialism but also to American poets who accept, with Auden, that "Poetry makes nothing happen."[11]

A key to this relevance is his frank acceptance and exploration of his human doubleness. I admire his acknowledgment and coming to terms with two conflicting urges in himself—one rational, one irrational. The world, also, is profoundly divided between neoliberal nations privileging freedom and rational inquiry (often at the expense of justice), versus authoritarian nations emphasizing solidarity and blind acceptance (often at the expense of freedom).

Recently, many countries committed to the freedom path have regressed toward the authoritarian model under leaders like Boris Johnson, Orbán, Putin, Modi, Duterte, and Trump. This worldwide trend is a symptom, I believe, of the increasing dysfunction of neoliberal values that have become fetishes.

And I believe that the works of Milosz, in which (as we shall see) he strove to reconcile the conflicting voices of freedom and authority inside himself, is a guide for renegotiating the conflicting forces of reason and unreason that are threatening the security of the world.

His legacy is timely. A recent dialogue, between post-secular thinkers like Habermas and Charles Taylor, has already begun, in diverse ways, to reconsider the Enlightenment legacy of materialism and secularism. In my last three chapters, I shall suggest how Milosz, as the poet of doubleness, contributes a poetic energy to this philosophic discourse. Philosophers analyze and critique; poets, speaking to our hearts, can heal.

MILOSZ'S CONGENIAL DOUBLENESS

With his admixture of gloom and hope, Milosz in the 1930s was recognized as one of the leading Polish catastrophist writers (NR, 116). But throughout his life, Milosz continued to struggle with two conflicting elements in himself, the self-described "ecstatic pessimist" (LU, 163). One was his conservative nostalgia for the relatively uncorrupted pre-Enlightenment culture of his birthplace in rural Lithuania. The other, inspired in part by his urbane Parisian relative Oscar Milosz, nursed radical liberationist hopes for a post-Enlightenment less class-bound society.

This doubleness underlay every stage of his long development. Starting with the id-ego conflict in all of us, he experienced sexual turmoil as an adolescent influenced by the tutelage of both his puritanical theology teacher and his enlightened science teacher. A little later he identified this pair, and also their conflicting influences inside himself, as avatars of the opposing characters in Thomas Mann's *The Magic Mountain*, "the Jesuit. Naphta, and the humanist, Settembrini" (NR, 71, 76).[12]

In his prime, Milosz came to see himself and mankind as torn between the conflicting claims of *esse*, or *being* (permanence, nature, God), and *becoming*, or history (NR, 275; cf. TP, 35, 106–7).[13] And when I met him, he was striving to reconcile the conflicting critiques of Enlightenment liberalism that he had learned from the conservative Eliot, on the one hand, and the radical Blake (and his distant cousin Oscar Milosz), on the other.[14] As he wrote, in 1959, to Thomas Merton, "How to combine 'transcendence' and 'devenir' has always been my main question."[15]

In short, Robert Hass is quite right to celebrate Milosz as the "complicated and many-sided" poet who "valued *being*."[16] But I believe he must also be recognized as the vatic poet whose quarrel with *becoming* is celebrated in this book.

Overall, this doubleness in Milosz seemed very congenial to me, also struggling to reconcile my love of my new home in America with my concern at its foreign policy. Unfortunately, my memories of our many long conversations are now lost in a haze of too much bourbon. But I do remember that my most dominant impression of Milosz was as a figure of post-secular enlightenment, showing me the chance of a third and more spiritual path beyond both the godless communism of the Iron Curtain countries and the godless capitalism of the United States.[17]

I saw in him a stubborn oppositional heroism in an enduring tradition of untraditional Catholics such as Pascal, or Simone Weil (who never quite joined either the Communist Party or, until just before her death, the Catholic Church). As a medievalist but not a Catholic, I shared with him in particular an interest in Greek Fathers such as St. Gregory of Nyssa.

We had both been profoundly influenced by the poetry of Eliot, but for different reasons. Milosz, who translated *The Waste Land* while Warsaw was being destroyed around him, had first admired Eliot for his "oppositional stance" in an age of alienation and decay.[18] But by the time I knew him, he was distinguishing himself from Eliot's focus on a lost past and "renouncing the world for the sake of 'the still point' outside time" (TP, 123).[19] I at that time, in contrast, was both a radical in search of a more just society and also a self-educated medievalist in pursuit of Eliot's "lost past" (an *ignis fatuus*, I soon decided, even as I drew closer to his critique of Enlightenment liberalism).

This doubleness, in both Milosz and myself, could perhaps have strengthened a bond between us. Unfortunately, it did not. Instead, it contributed to our disagreements. I need to say a few words about these, because they throw light on the structure of this book.

Introduction: My Years with Milosz (1961–1967) 9

OUR DISAGREEMENTS OVER VIETNAM, THE STUDENTS, THE COUNTERCULTURE

Our differences probably began tacitly, in 1964, over the Free Speech Movement (FSM) on our Berkeley campus; I soon respected and supported it; while Czeslaw later dismissed it as "a pitiable spectacle. . . . Mario Savio working the students into a fanatical, hysterical trance" (YH, 220).[20] But when we first began to discuss our differences, it was not about the FSM, but about Vietnam. Not so much the war itself, which had been gradually escalating since our first meeting back in 1961.[21] Nor was it the fact of my antiwar activities, which had become energetic after the escalations of early 1965.[22]

But by 1967, the war was becoming a direct confrontation between America and the Soviet Union; in June of that year, two American fighter planes, not for the last time, strafed a Soviet freighter that was anchored in Haiphong harbor.[23] Fearful of a wider war, I as an ex-diplomat became a vigorous defender of East-West détente. But as a Pole, Milosz, quite understandably, had an implacable hatred of the Soviet Union, as well as of its domination of Eastern Europe.

Finally, in the fall of 1967, Milosz saw me on an antiwar platform with Noam Chomsky. At our next meeting, he said stiffly that he could understand my remarks, but he could not forgive Chomsky's—meaning, I suppose, Chomsky's broad-brush denunciation of all American foreign policy. Chomsky, he said, was "the kind of intellectual who destroyed Weimar."

In those days, I still believed in the robustness of American democracy; thus, to compare America with Weimar seemed far-fetched to me; and I brashly said so. Very soon afterward, the invitations to work with him ended, abruptly, forever.

I see now how Milosz, ambivalently grateful to America for having accepted and supported him in a way that France never did, was becoming more and more impatient generally with those less grateful than himself—and impatient above all with those who underestimated what he saw as the Soviet threat to the world.[24]

This disagreement was related to another that we never discussed: the developing counterculture of the 1960s, which expanded the gap between us. Like the young Wordsworth in revolutionary Orleans, I briefly participated in the heady euphoric aspirations of that short-lived era, but Milosz soon denounced them as "Maoist madness" (ABC, 230).[25] His distaste led him at that time to prefer Robinson Jeffers's "inhumanism" and rejection of hopes for collective humanity. As he wrote in his one published poem written in English, "To Raja Rao" (1969):

> I hear you saying that liberation is possible
> and that Socratic wisdom
> is identical with your guru's.
>
> No, Raja, I must start from what I am.
> I am those monsters which visit my dreams
> and reveal to me my hidden essence.
>
> If I am sick, there is no proof whatsoever
> that man is a healthy creature.
> (NCP, 255)

Underlying all these differences, paradoxically, was what was perhaps our most striking similarity: we had both briefly served in the diplomatic corps of our separate nations, and subsequently each of us had reacted quite radically against the policies we had briefly served. As our respective countries had been on opposite sides in the Cold War, so also the arcs of our alienation moved us in opposite directions—to the left in my case, to the right in his.

Thus, at the time, I considered Milosz to be too unconcerned by an unjust Vietnam War; while Milosz probably rebuked me for being too accommodating toward the Soviet Union. As I wrote in my tribute to him in my trilogy *Seculum*:

> We are divided
>   by our separate gratitudes
>   each wanting to atone
>
> for years of well-meaning service
>   with opposing governments
>   in the name of peace.[26]

(Separate gratitudes—both of us were glad to be in Berkeley: Czeslaw to have tenure on the faculty, I to be learning from the protesting students.)

I suspect that some of my initial disagreements with Milosz's pessimism, quasi-Manicheanism, and ambivalence about nature (discussed later) will be shared by many North Americans. Nevertheless, I was so happy in our fortnightly encounters that I hoped they would continue indefinitely. But in 1967, unfortunately, the issues between us, long in the making, emerged into edgy debate. Soon, to my distress, our sessions, quite unexpectedly, came to an abrupt end.

In the appendix to this book, I give my version of our break-up, along with my 1982 "Letter to Czeslaw Milosz," which led to our partial reconciliation.

I had at least two more hours-long discussions with him before he left Berkeley. But my inspiring sessions of translation with him were over.
I have since come to attribute this shattering end to a second and probably more serious falling out. I, a passionate admirer then of his earlier and more radical poems, wanted very much to translate them literally, whereas he was now determined to rewrite and tone down their bardic claims, appropriate for a Polish but not for an American audience (details in chapter 4).

WHAT WE ALMOST NEVER DISCUSSED: THE COLD WAR ITSELF

Milosz may have noticed that I never said anything to him about the book for which at that time he was most famous, *The Captive Mind*. I had read it while in Poland during the last years of the "Polish thaw" (1959–1961). It was of course obvious that Polish intellectuals and poets had to dissemble and conceal their inner thoughts in public discourse (what Milosz referred to as the practice of *ketman*).

But Milosz had charged that by playing this role, "a man grows into it so closely that he can no longer differentiate his true self from the self he simulates, so that even the most intimate of individuals speak to each other in Party slogans."[27] I was willing to concede that this might have been generally true in the Stalin era, just as I felt it to be also true of my more ambitious fellow-diplomats, American and Canadian. And I believed it to be true of some of my Polish *apparatchik* acquaintances, such as the editor Mieczysław Rakowski, who later became Poland's last Communist prime minister.

I was also certain it could not have been less true in 1959 of the intellectuals and poets in Warsaw I was so stimulated by—men like the philosopher Leszek Kołakowski, the sociologist Zygmunt Bauman, the poets Zbigniew Herbert, Antoni Słonimski, and Artur Międzyrzecki, the novelist Leopold Tyrmand, the writer and composer Stefan Kisielewski, the filmmaker Andrzej Munk.[28] I had never met such a brilliant concentration of intellects in my life—certainly not at either Oxford or Harvard.

The "captive" intellects that I knew in Warsaw delighted in trenchant aphorisms, such as "Analfabecy muszą diktować" (Illiterates have to dictate). On a more serious level,

> Leszek Kołakowski's numerous essays on a reformed state socialism during the "Thaw" period, and particularly his influential [and controversial] "Kapłan i błazen" ("The Priest and the Jester") examined contemporary Marxism precisely in terms of its "theological" outlook, that is the justification of present human sacrifice in expectation of future goods (the utopian social order).[29]

But I badly underestimated the relevance of *The Captive Mind*. The Polish thaw I observed was short-lived. Within a decade of my meeting Milosz in 1961, a government crack-down in Poland had forced almost all of the men I have just mentioned (along with others I knew) to emigrate to the West.[30]

More importantly, my eccentric reservations about the *The Captive Mind* were not shared by the Poles themselves, some of whom, like Solidarność leader Lech Wałęsa, were imprisoned for distributing it. According to Andrzej Walicki, "a generation of young Poles, the generation of Solidarity, celebrated Miłosz as a great exposer of the totalitarian system."[31]

But on a deeper level, I was misled by my own brief experience as a participant in the Cold War, beginning in 1957. By then it was beginning to be true that, as Christopher Lasch would later scathingly state: "the campaign for 'cultural freedom' revealed the degree to which the values held by intellectuals had become indistinguishable from the interests of the modern state—interests which intellectuals now served while they maintained the illusion of detachment."[32]

But this was not true of the campaign for cultural freedom in 1951, when Milosz became influential in it. Only by writing this book have I now come to appreciate the integrity and importance of the cultural cold war in its earliest days, when Communism was contained behind the Iron Curtain in part by the self-motivated efforts of free-thinking left-wingers like Arthur Koestler, Dwight Macdonald, Mary McCarthy, and Nicola Chiaromonte—people who, in 1951, were joined by, and became friends with, Milosz himself.[33] These people, who founded the Congress for Cultural Freedom, accepted CIA funding but not direction; and I belatedly see how important it was that their insights and courage helped save Western Europe from the fate of, say, East Germany.[34]

This appreciation only came to me in when I was finishing this book, when I finally began to understand and appreciate the capacious historic vision of Milosz in his epic masterpiece, "A Treatise on Poetry."

Meanwhile Milosz did disagree in a friendly way with my avid support, especially after the Cuban Missile Crisis, for two memes of that era, "peaceful coexistence" and "détente." I will never forget him saying in his gruff Polish accent—"Peter, you speak of the Soviet Union as if it is a country. It is not. It is a cancer!"

I did internalize some of Czeslaw's rebuke to my earlier enthusiasm for détente. There are also signs that Czeslaw (though not because of me) retreated somewhat from his earlier vigorous condemnation of the hippie counterculture he seemed to take me as representing. In the late book *Milosz's ABC's*, he describes how a car breakdown in the Sierras led him by chance to spend time in a hippie commune where his car was fixed without charge.

We found ourselves in a land of gentleness. No one was in a hurry; no one raised his voice.... The men and women bathed together, absolutely naked, and even when they moved around the building or sat at the table to eat, most of them were naked or barely covered by a piece of cloth.... In the way they treated each other and in their behavior toward us they seemed completely tolerant and laid-back. How they would get on in the long run one could only surmise, but their little community in which no one, neither man nor woman, tried to impose on anyone else ... struck me as worthy of admiration, the exact opposite of the Gombrowiczean theater. (ABC, 253–54)[35]

For anyone familiar with Milosz's earlier fulminations against the counter-culture (Visions, 146–47),[36] this idealized bucolic episode, akin in tone to his idylls of childhood in Lithuania, is ample evidence of a counter-current inside himself.

Milosz himself captured this inner doubleness—arguably a chief theme of this book—when he wrote, in language suggestive of that other war poet, Whitman, "I was always an ecstatic pessimist" (LU, 163). One can see in him two currents—not only the Manicheanism, which Milosz frequently acknowledged in himself, but also what he called a countervailing "arcadian element in my poetry."[37] Most commonly this was nostalgic, but on occasion (as in this passage I helped translate), it was also lyrically prospective, utopian:

> umysł ludzki jest wspaniały, usta potężne,
> i wezwanie tak wielkie, że musi otworzyć się Raj.
>
> the human mind is splendid, lips powerful,
> and the summons so great, it must open Paradise.
> (NCP, 184)[38]

His experience in the Sierras indicates that his balancing of these two currents—the arcadian versus the Manichean—continued to evolve over time.[39]

I believe that the chapters of this book will progressively reveal these two currents within him and their expanding scope. In chapter 2, my focus is on what he helped achieve for Poland; by the end of the book, I am focusing on the "sense of open space ahead," which he believed (citing the example of Whitman) poetry could and should restore to the world: "The fate of poetry depends on whether such a work as Schiller's and Beethoven's 'Ode to Joy' is possible. For that to be so, some basic confidence is needed, a sense of open space ahead of the individual and the human species" (WP, 14).

Yeats once memorably wrote, "We make out of the quarrel with others, rhetoric, but of the quarrel with ourselves, poetry."[40] I am attempting to describe two closely related debates between myself and Milosz in which each of us, to some extent, was on both sides. Milosz himself confessed to the "two tendencies" within himself, "struggling with each other" (WP, 69, 72). I suspect many poets today, perhaps all great ones, share this expanded and conflicted sensibility.

In my own case, Milosz so influenced me that he brought out in me beliefs of which I had not yet been wholly aware. It is sad for me that most of that influence, and my concomitant interest in his work and that of Mickiewicz, occurred after we ceased to be in regular contact.[41]

The Milosz who is my model in this book is not the sometimes bitter and slightly angry pessimist who dropped me in the later 1960s but, rather, the Milosz of two decades later, emboldened by his Nobel recognition to revive the hopes and ambitions of his wartime poetry. Thus, for example, he said to a 1985 interviewer that "I believe firmly that the planet moves toward unification and the emancipation of human masses"—a hope I do not recall him expressing with such confidence back when we regularly met.[42] And in *The Witness of Poetry* (1983), he described how a poet can and should contribute to this movement, while criticizing that contemporary poetry in which "it is difficult to find any tomorrow" (WP, 14).

HOW AMERICA AND THE WORLD CAN LEARN FROM MILOSZ

My increasing interest in him, both during and especially after our time of collaboration, is reflected in the expanding scope of this book. I very much hope that the reader's interest in Milosz's Polish antecedents like Mickiewicz and Brzozowski will, like my own, develop incrementally from chapter to chapter.

By the time I wrote chapter 14, I had become excited by Milosz's prose critique of both the eighteenth-century Enlightenment and nineteenth-century romanticism. Milosz, in the wake of other writers as diverse as Alfred North Whitehead and Erich Heller, argued that the world today suffers from a distortedly materialistic view of reality—one that art, and particularly poets, must correct.

I take from Milosz's difficult work *The Land of Ulro* the sense that, like Blake, he sees mind evolving in time through and beyond the scientific intellect of Blake's enemies: Bacon, Locke, and Newton. Ulro is not so much a space as an age, a time of the Urizenian fall between the time of innocence lost and the time of innocence regained (WP, 25). A step toward that recovery is the recognition that there are limits to how much Reason can supplant the role in our outlook played by faith. Thus it is time now for the poet, and no longer just the philosophers, to struggle to gain access again to that ideal which, as Plato said in his *Republic*, is "laid up in Heaven for those who have eyes to see."[43]

It can be said that, after winning a Nobel Prize, Milosz became more famous in America than influential. Both his poetic and his prose writings have barely begun to reach the audience I believe they deserve. For example, his one-time best-seller, *The Captive Mind*, a historically important work but in my opinion his most journalistic, continues to outsell both his poetry and his more mature prose.

A few excellent book-length appreciations of Milosz have appeared recently in English, but nearly all of them (e.g., *The Eternal Moment* by Aleksander Fiut, or *Miłosz and the Problem of Evil* by Łukasz Tischner) are written by Poles for Poles.[44] To judge by their Amazon rankings, these books are reaching Slavicists rather than the general American public. And *The Witness of Poetry*, which I expect to be ranked someday with (if not above) the prose of Sydney, Shelley, and Eliot, is not widely read now either.

The critic Robert von Hallberg has written that the works of Milosz, like those of Ginsberg, Plath, and Celan, "migrate across political and linguistic boundaries."[45] Indeed some of the most important poets to be influenced by him are fellow Nobel Prize winners from other countries, notably Seamus Heaney, Derek Walcott, and Joseph Brodsky, as well as his compatriot Wisława Szymborska. Meanwhile, according to Robert Hass, Milosz's works "have been translated into almost every language in the world."[46]

A global, or at least pan-occidental, literary culture continues to evolve, in which US-born authors are today far less influential than in the days of Whitman and Eliot. It is significant to me that, of the nine US residents to have won the Nobel Prize for Literature in the last forty years (Bellow, Singer, Milosz, Brodsky, Walcott, Morrison, Heaney, Dylan, and Glück), only three (Morrison, Dylan, and Glück, one Black and two Jewish with immigrant grandparents) were born in America.[47]

(More pertinently to my argument, of the four immigrant poets, all of them from what the Irish poet Derek Mahon once called "the circumference," only two, Milosz and Brodsky, became US citizens; and ironically these two non-Anglophones continued to write poetry primarily in their native Polish and Russian. Both, furthermore, are now buried abroad, although neither in the country of their birth.[48] There is, in short, at present a separation, even a gap, between the mental realms inhabited by these world-minded poets and the more introspective concerns, whether national or personal, of most contemporary American poets.)[49]

Of all the transnational poets here mentioned, I suspect Milosz is the most likely to be remembered someday as part of the American canon. To begin with, his poetic style matured over three decades in this country so that, for three decades, although written in Polish, his poetry developed more and more features that could be called American.[50]

But Milosz's greatest work, including wartime poetry before he had ever visited America or England, had already internalized the diction and outlook of major writers in English that he had first translated into Polish—notably the poetry of Milton, Blake, Wordsworth, Whitman, Eliot, and Auden. His own poetic voice so thoroughly assimilated these influences that, even before he had been driven into exile, he was no longer writing just as a Pole but as part of a transnational literary canon.

In so doing, he acted not just as a participant but as a renovator. In this book we should distinguish between *culture*, the habits, mindset, and attitudes of a people, *counterculture*, the attitudes and beliefs working to modify the prevailing culture, and *generative culture*, the creative activity of a few individuals like Milosz (or Blake, or Eliot), which contributes, counterculturally, to the advancement of culture as a whole.[51]

As a first step to understanding Milosz's generativity, we shall look in the next chapter at how Milosz's writings, or what he called his "unpolitical politics," became a major factor in the formation of Solidarność in Poland. In the course of this book, I shall have more to say about this important distinction between political and cultural evolution.

Recently the term *socio-poetics*, describing various aspects of the interactivity between poetic creation and social change, has begun to attract scholarly interest. Socio-poetics can refer to the influence of social conditions on individual poetics,[52] or alternatively it can also refer to "works of art seeking to heighten awareness or create social change."[53]

In this book, I offer a larger term, *ethogeny*, to describe the dialectical process[54] of cultural evolution, embracing both the creative and the social aspects of this huge interactive process—one that embraces all artistic creativity, regardless of conscious intention.

Introducing this term in *Poetry and Terror*, I referred to the role of *Paradise Lost*, acknowledged by historians, in helping to generate the radical middle-class consciousness that produced the American Revolution.[55] I can think of no more hopeful example of ethogeny since Milton than that of Milosz's writings and Solidarity.[56]

But this book does not see Milosz's generativity as limited to Poland. On the contrary, I shall argue that he advanced a poetic development toward postmodernism and post-secularism, one that was also stirring in response to the needs of other countries.

He may have written in Polish. But to understand his greatness, we must see him as far more than just a Polish poet.

Chapter 2

Milosz, Solidarity, and "Unpolitical Politics": Or, Poetry and the Liberation of a People

Not by might nor by power, but by My Spirit," saith the Lord of hosts.

—Zechariah 4:6

Neither a shield nor a sword, but a masterpiece, is the people's weapon.

—Cyprian Norwid[1]

I remember that when I once was arrested the police found a box of treatises by Miłosz in my apartment. And during the interrogation the officer was saying, "Mr. Michnik, do you believe that with the help of this little poetry you are going to win against Communism?" And we won.

—Adam Michnik[2]

Stalin once famously asked a question—"How many divisions has the Pope got?"—to which the Polish Revolution of the early 1980s supplied a striking answer. The success of the nonviolent Solidarność (Solidarity) movement in compelling a peaceful transition away from Communist and Soviet domination of Poland is only one example of an emerging new reality—that, in the right circumstances, military and political power can be no match for cultural solidarity.

But this ultimate victory was not the pope's alone. Solidarność was a tripartite alliance dominated by organized labor, led by Lech Wałęsa, and the largely rural Polish Catholic church, headed after 1978 by the Polish Pope John Paul II.[3] Mediating between them was the Committee for Workers'

Defense (KOR), a group of writers and other intellectuals born out of a successful worker-intellectual protest in 1976. In the eyes of the KOR spokesman, Adam Michnik, describing it, Solidarność was inspired chiefly by three men: Pope John Paul II, Lech Wałęsa, and Czeslaw Milosz.[4]

Why Milosz? Because, as Michnik wrote elsewhere, "Poland's peaceful transformation . . . was preceded by an almost two-decade effort to build institutions of civil society."[5] This closely parallels John Adams's observation that the American Revolution was not the war: "It was in the minds of the people . . . in the course of fifteen years, before a drop of blood was shed at Lexington."[6] The remarks of Michnik and Adams confirm the importance of envisioners, like Milosz and the Polish Pope John Paul, in creating and consolidating *people power*.[7]

Even in exile, according to Michnik, Milosz was an inspiration to the slow build-up of an alternative Polish society. In Michnik's words: "For 30 years, his books had circulated in *samizdat* copies and been published either underground or abroad. He was an icon of the democratic opposition."[8]

(Michnik is not alone in singling out Milosz as inspiration; Michel Masłowski, pointing to Milosz's emphasis on human dignity and inter-class collaboration, writes that this is "why he was later considered the spiritual father of 'Solidarność.'")[9]

Unquestionably, Milosz's prose and his poetry contributed significantly to this Polish counterculture. Wałęsa was imprisoned for "distributing clandestine copies of *The Captive Mind*," and there was also a black market for the Polish émigré magazine *Kultura* from Paris containing Milosz's articles and poetry.[10] Even the primate of Poland, Cardinal Wyszyński, smuggled tapes of Milosz reading his poetry into Poland.[11]

At the time, Milosz was listed in the Polish encyclopedia only as "the enemy of the People's Republic of Poland." Thus, as Michnik recalled, Milosz's poems

> were like forbidden fruit, as they were very hard to come by, and thus had an extraordinary flavor. Familiarity with those poems was like a password among Polish dissidents. We recognized each other through quotations from Miłosz: without fear one could have a beer with someone who knew Miłosz's poetry. His books . . . were our required reading, devoured and read to the last page in the milieu of the democratic opposition.[12]

Other historians point out that Milosz's influence was largely confined to the KOR intellectuals in Solidarność. In the words of Adam Zagajewski, Milosz was an intellectual leader in this era, but "a leader for few; he was not a popular writer." His importance was to represent a very rare combination of radically ontological and religious interests—which would otherwise be linked to a conservative if not rightist political stance—fused with democratic, liberal, and very vocal anti-nationalistic political views. This is a salutary, original, and stereotype-breaking combination, opening new prospects for younger generations.[13]

The innovative prospects, in short, of what became Solidarność.

Meanwhile, Milosz's own experience of the 1950s was one of relative isolation, shunned in France both by leftists, East and West, and also by many in the Polish *emigracja* who could not forgive his years with the postwar government.[14]

At the time, propagandists in Poland called him a "traitor" and a "deserter" who had sold himself to powerbrokers of various ilks, including neo-Nazis. Meanwhile, to the "unreconciled" in London, he was first a "sellout" and then, even after his defection, a subversive "cryptocommunist" and agent of the regime. In the intellectual atmosphere of France, in which French intellectuals enjoyed a long intoxication with leftist ideologies, Milosz was a "renegade" dishonoring a "progressive system" and thus someone unclean.[15] His close circle of friends there were chiefly other Polish exiles connected with the *émigré* journal *Kultura*. He was, however, helped by another isolated intellectual, Albert Camus.

In America his status was more secure and comfortable, but at first also more isolated. Thus, in his 1968 poem, "My Faithful Mother Tongue," he writes as a solitary, involved in a dialogue alone with his language, a dialogue in which he fears he has lost touch with like-minded Poles:

> My faithful language,
> I have served you.
> Every night I used to set before you little bowls of colors,
> so you could have your birch, your cricket, your finch
> as preserved in my memory.
>
> This lasted many years.
> You were my native land; I lacked any other.
> I believed that you would also be a messenger
> between me and some good people,
> even if they were few, twenty, ten
> or not born, as yet.
>
> Now I confess my doubt.
> There are moments when it seems to me I have squandered
> my life.
> For you are a tongue of the debased,

> of the unreasonable, hating themselves
> even more than they hate other nations,
> a tongue of informers,
> a tongue of the confused,
> ill with their own innocence.
> (NCP, 245)[16]

In 1976, eight years after this poem of exile was written, Milosz and Michnik met for the first time in Paris and dined together. As Michnik remembered,

> The conversation was long and fascinating. At one point—more or less after the third bottle of wine—I began, without too much stuttering, to recite his poems from memory. I knew quite a few of them. Soon, to my great surprise, I saw that tears were running down Miłosz's cheeks. Astonished, I stopped the recitation, and heard the moved voice of the poet: "I didn't know that young people in Poland knew my poems by heart. I thought I had been cursed."[17]

More may have emerged from this meeting. One year later, in 1977, Milosz's Paris publisher (the émigré Instytut Literacki of Jerzy Giedroyc) published what has been called "a manifesto of the . . . Solidarity movement,"[18] Michnik's *Church, Left, Dialogue* (*Kościół, lewica, dialog*; published in America as *The Church and the Left*).

To understand the importance of this work and its radical proposal, one must understand that Michnik was a former Marxist of Jewish origin, just as Milosz was a Catholic. With the hindsight of victory, Michnik's call for a Church-left dialogue seems obvious. At the time, it may have seemed wildly utopian, somewhat as if one were to call on Noam Chomsky to enter into a constructive dialogue with America's Southern Baptists.

Milosz himself said of this book, in 1985, that Michnik's proposed alliance between the Church and the dissidents marked "a decisive turn in the political climate of his country."[19] Michnik, in response to a question, has noted that "the intellectual inspiration for the book was Simone Weil."[20]

Weil was known in Poland because of the 350-page volume of her works that Milosz translated selectively into Polish in 1958, after first encountering her works in Dwight Macdonald's New York journal *Politics* (YH, 118). Milosz had been encouraged to translate Weil by two of his few friends in Paris: Albert Camus and Józef Czapski.[21] Of this translation Milosz wrote two years later:

> My aim was utilitarian. . . . I resented the division of Poland into two camps: the clerical and the anticlerical, nationalistic Catholic and Marxist. . . . I suspect

unorthodox Marxists (I use that word for lack of a better one) and nonnationalistic Catholics have very much in common, at least common interests.[22]

In these words, he envisioned Solidarność, two decades before its creation. Milosz's architectural master-stroke in redesigning Polish culture was successful in both directions, not just with Jewish ex-Marxists like Michnik but also with the Catholic Church. As he later told Michnik in an interview, "I had the satisfaction of being told by Bishop Kominek of Wrocław—he was in Paris in 1971, I think—that the book was compulsory reading in all the seminaries in his diocese."[23]

When the dockyard workers of Solidarność in Gdańsk planned the Three Crosses Monument, to honor those who had been killed in the December 1970 massacre, they asked the celebrated Polish filmmaker Andrzej Wajda to contact his friend Milosz for an inscription. Milosz chose lines from a poem he had written in 1950, "for the drawer" (i.e., not for publication, he was still working for the postwar government):

> You who wronged a simple man
> Bursting into laughter at the crime. . . .
>
> Do not feel safe. The poet remembers.
> You can kill one, but another is born.
> The words are written down, the deed, the date.
>
> And you'd have done better with a winter dawn,
> A rope, and a branch bowed beneath your weight.
> (NCP, 103)[24]

"Do not feel safe. The poet remembers. You can kill one, but another is born." It took an act of faith to write those lines in 1950, when Stalin was still alive. This warning to ephemeral dictators perfectly complements and anticipates what Pope John Paul would say in 1979 to the Polish people, "Be not afraid." It exemplifies what Michnik meant by Milosz's "destiny which endowed him with the voice of a witness and the vision of a prophet." The poem reached far beyond the Gdańsk monument. As Jerzy Illg recalls, "Milosz's poem, 'You Who Wronged,' became the hymn of Poles oppressed for decades, and was reprinted on Solidarity flyers, posters, calendars and pennants."[25]

But a larger inspiration to many intellectuals of Solidarność was the whole body of Milosz's poetry, including the famous poem "Dedication" ("Przedmowa") that is at the heart of this book:

> You whom I could not save
> Listen to me.
> Try to understand this simple speech as I would be ashamed
>   of another.
> I swear, there is in me no wizardry of words.
> I speak to you with silence like a cloud or a tree.
>
> What strengthened me, for you was lethal.
> You mixed up farewell to an epoch with the beginning of a
>   new one,
> Inspiration of hatred with lyrical beauty,
> Blind force with accomplished shape.
>
> Here is the valley of shallow Polish rivers. And an immense
>   bridge
> Going into white fog. Here is a broken city,
> And the wind throws the screams of gulls on your grave
> When I am talking with you.
>
> What is poetry which does not save
> Nations or people?
> A connivance with official lies,
> A song of drunkards whose throats will be cut in a moment,
> Readings for sophomore girls.
>
> That I wanted good poetry without knowing it,
> That I discovered, late, its salutary aim,
> In this, and only this, I find salvation.
>
> They used to pour millet on graves or poppy seeds
> To feed the dead who would come disguised as birds.
> I put this book here for you, who once lived
> So that you should visit us no more.
> (NCP, 77, modified)

This poem was written in the wake of the partitions that twice extinguished the free Polish state, leaving culture, in the largest sense, as the sole vehicle to save and preserve the Polish people. Writing after the debacle of the 1944 Warsaw uprising, and the certainty of a third Russian occupation, Milosz felt acutely this responsibility, which was also an opportunity.

Then why does Milosz place his book for the dead hero, "so that you should visit us no more"? I shall explore this question at length in a later chapter, but want to deal here with the political relevance of the poem and this stanza, both at the time and since.

Milosz was a great admirer of the Polish national bard Mickiewicz, but not of his "Ode to Youth," where he encouraged young Poles to die for their country's name.[26] The futile Polish uprisings of the nineteenth century, inspired by this ideal, had repeatedly proved to be both heroic and a disaster.

During World War II, Milosz joined the Polish resistance, and worked with his brother Andrzej to help Jews escape Warsaw. But unlike the addressee of the poem, he did not join the mainstream Home Army (*Armia Krajowa*, or AK), which Milosz saw as yet another "disaster."[27]

Already in 1946, he wrote of "all our national manias, which always yield the same results."[28] Later, in *Native Realm*, Milosz clarified his dislike of the Home Army and its ill-fated Uprising: "I did not join the A.K.; nor were my literary colleagues, on the whole, eager to rush into the fray, gun in hand. . . . Not only did I now lack the impulse, but I was restrained by my passionate hostility to the leaders of the Home Army [in London] . . . the whole conspiratorial apparatus fed on an illusion, pumping into itself a gloomy national ecstasy" (NR, 242).

The poem's wish, that this spirit (of mixing up "Inspiration of hatred with lyrical beauty") "should visit us no more," was controversial: more than one Warsaw critic faulted Milosz's book of poetry for failing to celebrate "fighting, heroism, or sacrifice."[29]

The issue was a matter of some political urgency in 1945, when the poem was written; and it continues to afflict Polish politics today. The Armia Krajowa officially disbanded in January 1945, to avoid a civil war with the now dominant Soviet Army. However, many units, knowing that they were now targets of the new regime, continued their resistance. Thus began the sporadic attacks of the so-called Doomed or Cursed Soldiers (Żołnierze wyklęci).[30] (Though the movement was soon infiltrated, resistance of a sort continued into the 1950s.)[31]

Milosz himself made clear, in *The Captive Mind*, his contempt for the fruitless violence of the Doomed Soldiers: "To kill Party workers, to sabotage trains carrying food, to attack laborers who were trying to rebuild the factories was to prolong the period of chaos. Only madmen could commit such fruitless and illogical acts."[32]

In contrast, he strove for sanity and sobriety, the qualities that he praised in the otherwise quite different poet Zbigniew Herbert: "We feel that Herbert's poetry is eminently sane. . . . Everything he writes testifies to his refusal to be carried away by language conceived as a universe of its own, or to abandon logical structures for the sake of the ineffable. . . . In these times sanity may become as much of a corrective to normalcy as the absurd was in an earlier era."[33]

Milosz's sane admixture of vision and moderation also characterized Solidarność, a model for the unfinished revolution in Poland, and in the world. And I agree with this claim of his that his poetry constitutes "a kind of higher politics": "The Home Army . . . advanced toward its unhappy fate. . . . I perceived a wall. . . . And I realized . . . that we do not necessarily have to bloody our fists on that wall or to bow down before it in humility. . . . Right or wrong, I considered my poetry a kind of higher politics, an unpolitical politics" (NR, 246–47).[34]

Milosz saw that poetry, by contributing to cultural evolution, can change society—an insight that contributed to what Michnik called "the new evolutionism" of Solidarność and is an underlying theme of this book.

Milosz's insight, that the persuasive power of poetry can have the strength to counter the repressive power of tyranny, is a theme running through all of his major works I will discuss, including both his poetry and his prose. It closely mirrors Hannah Arendt's distinction between "coercion by force" and what she calls true power ("persuasion through arguments").

In her words, "Power corresponds to the human ability not just to act but to act in concert."[35] She contrasts power with the coercion of people by higher authority. The latter is violence: "Power and violence are opposites; where the one rules absolutely, the other is absent."[36] This recalls the distinction John Adams made, between the true revolution "in the minds of the people," and the shedding of blood.

Starting with his "Treatise on Morals" (1947), Milosz offers a long-term view of history in which two shaping forces are at work, with repression from above (or enforcement) slowly but inevitably modified, and eventually supplanted by persuasion from below (empowerment).

MILOSZ AND SOLIDARNOŚĆ IN 1980/1981

In 1980, after Milosz won the Nobel Prize, the failing Polish government, for its own reasons, invited Milosz to Poland. There Milosz made a point of meeting publicly with Lech Wałęsa, the head of Solidarity, and of being photographed with him.

A year later, after the imposition of martial law by General Jaruzelski, Milosz wrote an op-ed in the *New York Times*, indicating both his support for the embattled movement, and also a little of his reserve:

> The Solidarity movement is without precedent in modern history. . . . What they represented was hope. If the leaders of Solidarity proved to be naive—after all, the ruling party did not want to share power with anybody, least of all with workers—they sinned by hoping. Thus, they deserve sympathy and help from all men of good will . . . I do not believe that the democratic movement in Eastern Europe, of which Solidarity became the spearhead, is a transitory phenomenon.

On the contrary, its open or latent presence will prove more durable than all the juntas of our century taken together.[37]

Milosz had not been impressed by all that he saw of Solidarność in Poland. He was astute enough to detect in the movement the latent "danger of the re-emergence of nationalistic, right-wing tendencies"—the tendencies represented by the Law and Justice (PiS) Party today.[38] Thus he had striven in Poland to adhere to an agreed-upon non-political agenda for his visit and disappointed "the crowds of people . . . waiting expectantly" for something more. It was hardly surprising, therefore, that to many "he gave the impression of a man who was arrogant, off-putting, and lacking in empathy."[39]

With respect to politics, Milosz cherished his personal power as a poet; he never sought the people power of an activist. In addition, his perspectives by now were no longer exclusively Polish; and his concerns had moved beyond politico-cultural polemics to an anxiety, already expressed in *The Land of Ulro* (1977) about modern civilization in its entirety, East and West.[40]

But there was a deeper reason for Milosz's apparent lack of empathy. Six years later, in a year-long journal, he recalled his "return to Poland in glory" and commented that it should have been "the acme of my life. And yet it wasn't, because I was preoccupied with and protected by completely different problems, very private, very personal" (YH, 173). As will become clearer in this book (starting in the next chapter), he was obsessed by feelings of both grief and guilt.

Nevertheless, his concern for Poland never died. The last time I ever spoke to him, at a memorial dinner for Denise Levertov in 1998, he spoke in detail and at great length about his concerns about current Polish developments—not so much in the state, however, as in the Church.

POSTSCRIPT: THE DOOMED SOLDIERS, SOLIDARNOŚĆ, AND POLAND TODAY

The issue concerning the Doomed Soldiers, of whether to pursue violent or nonviolent resistance, divided Solidarność in the 1980s; and it continues to divide Poland today. Though the vast majority in Solidarność were committed to nonviolent social evolution without politically challenging the Third Republic, a minority faction, the Confederation for an Independent Poland (KPN), saw the movement differently, as a stepping stone to political rebellion.[41]

Those in the PiS Party governing Poland today have made a point of honoring the "Doomed Soldiers" (now renamed *Żołnierze niezłomni*, or

"Indomitable Soldiers"); and have instituted a National Memorial Day to celebrate their memory.

A website in their honor shows a picture of Adam Michnik, the KPN's enemy in Solidarność, together with Czesław Kiszczak of the Communist secret police, and explains:

> The term "Doomed Soldiers" is also an indictment against the media elites of the III Republic of Poland; an indictment for their conscientious omission, and elimination of this dramatic and heroic chapter of our history—an indictment for amputating history, written in blood and suffering by those who fought and died for [Poland's] freedom.[42]

The same page opens with an extract from a militant poem by the martyred wartime poet Krzysztof Kamil Baczyński (d. 1943), whom I shall suggest may be the anonymous fallen hero to whom "Dedication" is addressed.[43]

In short, the myth of the "Indomitable Soldiers" is to the Polish right-wing what the myth of Masada is to the Israeli right-wing. It is a myth used as a weapon, against the nonviolent, antiracist memories of Solidarność and against Milosz, who called the Doomed Soldiers "madmen."

Chapter 3

Looking "From Above": Milosz, Catastrophe, and "Doubleness"

I am a man of contradictions, and I do not deny that.

—Czeslaw Milosz[1]

Do I contradict myself?

Very well then I contradict myself,

(I am large, I contain multitudes.)

—Whitman, "Song of Myself"

In this world

we walk on the roof of hell

gazing at flowers.

—Issa (1762–1826)[2]

"Between the ages of seven and ten," Milosz recollected, "I lived in perfect happiness on the farm of my grandparents in Lithuania."[3] He had been born there to impoverished Polish gentry (*szlachta*), in his mother's parents' manor house, Szetejnie (in Lithuanian, Sjetenie), near Kowno (Kaunas). At that time this was in tsarist Russia, in an area that, only after World War I, became part of Lithuania. (Milosz, "as a child, had only Lithuanian citizenship.")[4]

The pastoral tranquility recollected by Milosz was far from the full story of his childhood. By his tenth year in 1920, when his family moved to Vilnius

27

(Wilno), his family had survived more violent historic changes than most Westerners can imagine. The Germans had ousted Russia in 1915; the tsars had fallen two years later; and with the withdrawal of the Germans in 1918, the region was contested in a series of moves between the new Lithuanian Republic, the new Polish Republic, and the new Soviet Army. The upshot was an award of Vilnius to Lithuania by the new League of Nations, followed by a supposed "mutiny" in 1920 by Polish troops that, for the next two decades, returned the city again to Poland.

Amid this tumult, the Milosz family, fleeing the Germans, followed Milosz's father, Aleksander, as he built roads and bridges for the Russian army from Latvia to the heart of Russia (NR, 41).[5] Young Czeslaw found it easy to befriend soldiers of different nationalities and languages, including, when he was still only three, "a young good-looking Cossack." But "Then a tragedy occurs. I was very attached to a little white lamb. Now the Cossacks are running him into the green grass, heading him off. To slaughter him. My Cossack tears off to help them. My desperate cry, the inability to bear irrevocable unhappiness, was my first protest against necessity" (NR, 41).

Two years later, during the Russian Revolution, a Russian army friend, Seryozha, came to Milosz with his shirt "spattered all over with blood"; in the general drunken uproar, "Seryozha . . . had diligently slain his own buddy."

Recalling the terror-stricken faces of women who expected to be robbed and murdered, Milosz concluded, "all this was not healthy for the heart of a child" (NR, 44–45). Perhaps not, but undoubtedly it fortified Czeslaw to deal with the greater disruptions of World War II and after.

The manor house was damp and chill, so the Milosz family lived in a nearby farmhouse. According to Milosz's biographer Andrzej Franaszek, relying on one of Milosz's poems, "The family lived upstairs, and farm-workers downstairs. . . . On the upper floor Polish was spoken, on the lower, Lithuanian."[6]

In his Nobel Prize lecture, Milosz recalled reading there Selma Lagerlöf's *Wonderful Adventures of Nils*, "who flies above the earth and looks at it *from above* but at the same time sees it in every detail." In his words, this "double role" of Nils "influenced to a large extent, I believe, my notions of poetry. . . . This double vision may be a metaphor of the poet's vocation."[7]

Later, after he had experienced the horrors of World War II and the Stalinist takeover of Poland, Milosz would defend this habit of looking down as the only way, albeit a conflicted one, to deal with a reality that was otherwise intolerable.

> An insoluble contradiction appears, a terribly real one, giving no peace of mind. . . . Reality calls for a name, for words, but it is unbearable, and if it is touched, if it draws very close, the poet's mouth cannot even utter a complaint of Job: all art proves to be nothing compared to action. Yet to embrace reality in such a

manner that it is preserved in all its old tangle of good and evil, of despair and hope, is possible only thanks to a distance, only by soaring above it—but this in turn seems then a moral treason.[8]

In a powerful late poem, "Treatise on Theology," Milosz wrote how, at Mass with Lithuanian peasants, he had already experienced twinges of culpable egoistic disdain:

> A poet who was baptized
> in the country church of a Catholic parish
> encountered difficulties
> with his fellow believers.
>
> He tried to guess what was going on in their heads.
> He suspected an inveterate lesion of humiliation
> which had issued in this compensatory tribal rite.
> And yet each of them carried his or her own fate.
>
> The opposition, I versus they, seemed immoral.
>
> It meant I considered myself better than they.
> (SS, 47)

This tension in him, caused by his inability to identify fully with those around him, was painful, and contributed to his many later confessions of pain and self-alienation.[9] But it also strengthened his self-identification as a poet, and even his sense of having been chosen to be a poet.

It is relevant that all four of the greatest Polish poets in the last two centuries—first Mickiewicz and Słowacki, and more recently Milosz and Zbigniew Herbert, shared this condition of having been born in the *kresy* or outlying eastern districts where Polish was not the only language in use. This may have left all of them feeling both somewhat isolated and also chosen, singled out from, and with a perspective on, the rest.[10]

THE TROUBLING MOVE FROM COUNTRYSIDE TO POLAND

As the world slowly returned to peace after the war, an end came to Milosz's life at Sjetenie. His father had been involved in the Polish Army's "mutinous" efforts to seize the disputed region for Poland, and the new Lithuanian government was aware of this.[11] In consequence, his mother "could no longer risk staying with her parents on an estate which at any moment might be subject to confiscation"; and the family settled in what was now Polish Wilno.[12] In old age, Milosz would remember this displacement as an archetypal expulsion out of Eden: "Walking to school in the morning, I would look at the hills beyond the Wilia [river] and in my thoughts I would journey to my lost paradise. Szetejnie; in other words, already then . . . I was oriented toward the past" (YH, 84).

That this expulsion was the consequence of his father's illegal military campaign might help explain both why Czeslaw "never held [his father] in high esteem,"[13] and also his deeply felt antipathy to honored Polish traditions of military revolt.[14] More clearly, it looms in the background of his wartime poems "The World" (with a very idealized father), and later "Flight" ("Ucieczka").

In *Native Realm*, Milosz voices the discomfort he felt on leaving the Lithuanian countryside for an urban school with Poles. Here, for the first time, he encountered and was offended by anti-Semitic Polish nationalism. Jews had formed part of his country background; in Vilnius, as he wrote later, they formed "almost half the population,"[15] and 80 percent of the post-Enlightenment intelligentsia with whom he soon identified (YH, 5). This Jewish presence "helped to form a complex in me" which divided him forever from the Polish "other side, right-wing tendencies, ritual Catholicism, an absence of intellectual interests" (NR, 95; cf. YH, 5).

Milosz later confessed another relevant reason for his alienation at school: he was bullied. "I had been living a happy and autonomous life until then. I thought that everything was just as it should be. In general, I didn't even think about it. And then all of a sudden there I was, the youngest boy in the class. Some of the students were awfully big, because that was the period after the wars. They sat in the last row. I was weaker than they were, and that was when I began to feel the cruelty of the world."[16]

MILOSZ'S AMBIVALENCE ABOUT CLASS, NATIONALITY, AND RELIGION

The doubleness that we encounter in so many poets was radical in Milosz: as a practicing Polish Catholic, part of him was now also anti-Polish and anti-Catholic.[17] This prominent self-contradiction would come to define his poetic style, even more prominently than the poetic distance of which he spoke in his Nobel Prize lecture. We shall see it in his 1936 poem "Slow River" (NCP, 18–20), in which, as he told Renata Gorczyńska, "various characters" speak in the poem, while the poem is "far from polyphonic. . . . A great many voices really can emerge at times when a person has a great many conflicts and contradictions. A person is never all of a piece."[18]

Late in life, Milosz published "Two Poems," with a prefatory note: "The two poems placed here together contradict each other. . . . But let it be, the two poems taken together testify to my contradictions, since the opinions voiced in one and the other are equally mine" (NCP, 542). Milosz told an interviewer that he learned "to live with contradictions . . . from the French philosopher Simone Weil" (i.e., after the war).[19] But it is clear that in the 1930s he had already learned it from his early model Whitman, along with his use of Whitman's capacious long line.

Milosz's doubleness extended also to ambivalence about his background as a descendant of families from the Polish *szlachta*, or gentry. "Gentry" did not connote wealth in Poland: a member of the *szlachta* might find employment as a taxi driver. In the 1950s, Milosz described his background as that of "impoverished gentry. . . . Born without the security that comes with inherited money, I had to make my own way in the world. . . . My material existence was so primitive that it would have startled proletarians in Western countries" (NR, 31–32).[20] Shortly afterward he explained to Thomas Merton, "I come from a country gentry, in the second generation, as my father belonged already to landless intelligentsia."[21] We must remember, however, that Milosz spent three of his early years in the manor of Szetejnie, in the possession of his mother's parents.[22] Milosz's own poverty did not diminish his sense of self-alienation from both the bourgeoisie of Vilnius and also the privilege of his own class. "My shame that I came from a family which had lived for generations off the labor of the common people (and had been involved in the Polonizing of those people) drove me to the left" (ABC, 204).[23]

But Milosz also explained his "distrust of 'trueborn' Poles" by referring to the traditions of his family. They in turn identified with their ancestors in the days of Polish-Lithuanian collaboration in the Grand Duchy of (Poland and) Lithuania, which in the fifteenth century had been the largest state in Europe.[24] To quote Milosz, "Our Grand Duchy of Lithuania was 'better' and Poland was 'worse,' for what would she have accomplished without our kings, poets, and politicians? In that local pride which was very widespread in our corner, the memories of a fame long past persisted. Poles 'from over there' (that is, from the ethnic center) has a reputation for being shallow, irresponsible, and, what is more, impostors" (NR, 96–97).[25]

Something of this family tradition remained in Milosz. It "counteracted the influences from school," and helped him to perceive that the textbooks there "had been put together by nationalists." In the history of literature, for example, "The only writing worthy of attention was in Polish. Nothing was said about the rich and beautiful Lithuanian folklore, although the pagan past survived in it" (NR, 97). Such a bias would of course make it difficult, for example, to fully appreciate Mickiewicz; and Milosz later wrote of "the extent to which we were served a Mickiewicz tamed by clichés, a cotton-wrapped

Mickiewicz" (LU, 99). Small wonder, then, that Milosz did not identify with the Poles he now, for the first time, went to church with—

> "good society" who, after Mass was over, would parade down the front walk: officers saluted, lawyers and doctors dispensed bows, women displayed their smiles, furs, and hats. As I moved out with this crowd, or watched them from the nearby square, I was nearly bursting with hatred. . . . These people were apes. What meaning had they? What did they exist for? I was soaring at some sort of divine height, poised over them as if they were specimens under a microscope. . . . I treated these people, in other words, as things. (NR, 80)

His early stance of self-hating condescension continued. But in Vilnius it became far more explosive, even though he later realized that "it was not as personal as I thought and that it was called 'hatred of the bourgeoisie.' That type of contempt, although intellectually useful, led me into many errors later on" (NR, 80).

In the short run, "brimming over with the spirit of protest," he rebelled in class against the theological teachings of his dogmatics teacher, Father Chomski, who he remembers in his memoir by the students' nickname, "Hamster" (*chomik*; NR, 72, 81).[26] Very soon, he publicly refused to go to Mass, but this crisis was short-lived. "When [Hamster] stopped pressuring me, I went to confession. But because the act of humbling oneself before Existence ought to be a strictly voluntary, personal thing, beyond social convention, I swore never to form an alliance with Polish Catholicism. . . . I would not submit to apes" (NR, 88).[27]

Although Milosz was spiritually inclined, this stance of his persisted into the 1930s: "I did not consider myself a Catholic, because that word had such a definite political coloring in Poland" (NR, 175).[28] Polish Catholicism had become identified with Polish nationalism, in which, especially after a century of foreign oppression, "if you were not a Catholic (let us say a Jew) you could not be a nationalist, or even a genuine member of the Polish nation."[29] (When right-wing Polish nationalists fomented anti-Jewish riots in 1931 at Wilno University, Milosz was among the few who defended their Jewish fellow-students.)[30]

MILOSZ'S AMBIVALENCE ABOUT HIS YOUTHFUL IDENTITY AS A LEFTIST RADICAL

As a preface to this section, I should warn that Milosz's doubleness and complexity make him an unreliable narrator about himself. We can believe what he told Robert Faggen in 1994, "When I was a [university] student I was very much impressed by *The Magic Mountain*"—Thomas Mann's novel with two opposing characters, Naphta, a Jesuit, and Settembrini, a secular humanist.[31] Milosz then continued,

> There is a character in it, Naphta, who is a Jesuit priest, a totalitarian, an enemy of the Enlightenment. I was fascinated with him. I had strong leftist totalitarian tendencies myself and was drawn to Naphta's skepticism of the Enlightenment. Today though, I would side with Naphta's antagonist in the novel, Settembrini, who represents the spirit of the Enlightenment. But my vision of humanity is much darker than Settembrini's.[32]

Again in *Native Realm* (1927), Milosz identified Naphta with his high school enemy, Father Chomski, and Settembrini, like himself, with his more friendly Latin teacher, a Socialist: "The mere presence of such a Naphta and such a Settembrini gave us an option. My rebellion against the priest weighted the scale in favor of the Latinist [i.e., Settembrini!]" (NR, 71, 76).

But amid the violent culture conflicts of the 1930s, Milosz now also identified his own progressive disengagement to that of Castorp, the hero of Mann's novel, who had fled from the conflicts in Germany:

> As our group moved further to the left, my own feeling toward it became tacitly more and more disaffected . . . now, however, I can see that my personal problems were a disguise for the collective uncertainty: Did not Hans Castorp fabricate his fever so that he could stay in Davos on the Magic Mountain, far removed from the world, because the world terrified him?" (NR, 118, 190)

In *Native Realm*, Milosz presented this doubleness in himself as a personal feature. However, just as in Mann's allegorical novel the yang/yin figures Settembrini and Naphta represented the humanist and totalitarian ideologies fighting for the future of the Weimar Republic, so Milosz in *A Treatise on Poetry* would enlarge his personal yang/yin conflict to encapsulate the destiny of Poland and indeed Europe (TP, 35, 106–8), as well as the conflicting postwar strains "toward *movement*" (dissent from America) and "back toward *being*" (dissent from postwar Poland) in himself (NR, 275).[33]

Milosz's writings about human duality or doubleness, so central to this book, inspired me to write an unpublished companion volume of larger scope, *Enmindment—A History: A Post-Secular Poem in Prose*. That book, largely inspired by my reflections on Milosz, focuses on the dialectic of yin and yang in both each individual person and the history of our cultural development (ethogeny).[34] And from time to time in that book I speculate whether this doubleness derives from the bilaterality of the human brain's two hemispheres.

I cite various texts based on neuroscience in that book. But only after I finished it did I discover corroboration in a book by Iain McGilchrist, *The*

Master and His Emissary: The Divided Brain and the Making of the Western World.[35] McGilchrist's unscientific survey, using much recent neuroscientific data, roughly validates my own linking of human doubleness to cultural development; as well as some of Milosz's claims in *The Land of Ulro*, as I shall discuss in chapter 15.

Milosz continued to write about "two equally strong and antithetical forces" (LU, 262) in himself. (McGilchrist claims that "The divided nature of our reality has been a consistent observation since humanity has been sufficiently self-conscious to reflect on it.")[36] In *The Witness of Poetry* (1983), Milosz ventured that "these two opposed tendencies [of 'classicism'—pursuit of ideal form, *esse*—and 'realism'—commitment to the historical world around us, *devenir*] usually also coexist within one person" (WP, 69).

Through writing *Enmindment—A History*, I have come to see this last simple but profound *aperçu* of Milosz as an aspect of the dual strains of yang and yin in both ourselves and also the DNA of global literate culture. In the final chapters of this book, I shall expand on Milosz's *aperçu* that we are all self-divided, to suggest how Milosz has not only analyzed the malaise of contemporary modernism and postmodernism, but offers a path beyond it, toward what he calls "the other shore" (LU, 270) of "a renewed civilization" (LU, 274).

From early on, Milosz had exhibited outwardly aspects of both Mann's characters. The French poet Oscar Milosz saw this doubleness on first meeting his distant cousin in 1931, writing to a friend approvingly that Czeslaw was "loyal to the monarchic, Catholic, and aristocratic tradition in its more intelligent and nobler aspects, with enough of the communist in him to be of service in this incredible age of ours" (LU, 90).

It is clear that Milosz's alienation from both his class and his nationality drove him, as a student, into association with Poland's non-communist left. He was at that time obsessed by "Poland's split, as an under-developed country, into a handful of rich—no more than a few tens of thousands—and millions of poor" (NR, 121).

Starting while he was still in high school, he joined a series of secret societies, at least one of them "conspiratorial," that were part of "the great if short-lived swelling of the leftist wave in the early 1930s."[37] At least two members of his tiny group, Stefan Jędrychowski and Jerzy Putrament, soon joined the Communist Party. (Later both were senior officials in the postwar government, as well as members of the party's ruling central committee. Putrament is portrayed as "Gamma" in *The Captive Mind*.)

Milosz was less clear as to whether he himself had ever been a Marxist. In 1958, he wrote that "While I was at the university, I did not call myself a Marxist out of modesty, because I had not read *Das Kapital* (NR, 115).

Furthermore, "Our cell . . . was certainly no conduit for Marxism. Marxists were Russia's spokesmen, and no Polish patriots who were patriots . . . would have trusted them" (NR, 108–9). This would seem to be confirmed by a letter he wrote in 1931 to his mentor Jaroslaw Iwaszkiewicz: "Theoretically, we are tired of the whole morass of capitalism, but we cannot be communists, nor, needless to say, members of any silly socialist movements."[38]

But in a letter to Andrzejewski in 1962, Milosz described himself as having once been "one of those who became a Marxist writer by a reflex-reaction."[39] Some of his private communications from that era sound Marxist in a dated sense, as when he wrote in a 1931 letter to Iwaszkiewicz, "The only criterion for evaluating a piece of art is its social role. . . . Enough of this liberal equality in everything. We need to rehabilitate fanaticism."[40]

Franaszek writes of Milosz in this era as "an impassioned artist who wanted to destroy the old order but had no proposals to put forward as to what an altered, improved structure might look like."[41] And Milosz has described his youthful destructive impulse in response to fellow churchgoers in Vilnius: "Religion, insofar as it was a social convention and a constraint, ought to be destroyed" (NR, 81).

MILOSZ'S VISITS TO PARIS AND HIS KINSMAN OSCAR MILOSZ

We shall see that, when Soviet armies of cultural destruction swept into Poland, Milosz re-identified with his Catholic background. But a major step in this return was his meeting in Paris in 1931, at age twenty, with his distant cousin, Oscar Milosz, whose two books (he wrote later) "decided my intellectual career."[42]

From him, as also from Mickiewicz, Czeslaw acquired a lifelong interest in Jewish Kabbalah, Jacob Boehme, and Emanuel Swedenborg. The special qualities that Milosz discerned in Oscar's poetry—"distance," "irony," "a nostalgic return to the past, poetry as memory, an abhorrence for twentieth-century realities, a sense of humor verging on the sarcastic"— would increasingly emerge in his own poetry and prose (LU, 77, 84; cf. WP, 23–25).

Above all, Czeslaw was both influenced by, and also skeptical of, his cousin's

> millenarianism, his belief in the advent of a new epoch—whatever name we may give it—Blake's New Jerusalem or the Epoch of Spirit of the continental Romantics. According to Oscar Milosz's philosophical writings, this new age would occur after an apocalyptic catastrophe, which he placed around 1944.

What he called "la conflagration universelle" perhaps signified the explosion of atomic weapons, an event unimaginable in the 1920s and 1930s. As to the new epoch, we are still [in 1982] waiting for it." (WP, 24)[43]

"THREE WINTERS" AND CATASTROPHISM: "HYMN"

After meeting Oscar in 1931, the year of his first visit to Paris, Czeslaw and his friends founded a Vilnius literary group called Żagary,[44] whose expectation of inescapable political breakdown led them to be called "catastrophists." Poland in the thirties was drifting towards a catastrophe, one which for Milosz slowly reinforced the futility of merely taking political sides: "I felt the future very keenly. On one side were the Germans. . . . On the other was Russia. In the middle was the Polish Right, which, in the perspective of time, was doomed to failure" (NR, 121).

After his second return from Paris in 1936, Milosz in his poetry still "needed to be of use" (NCP, 150; TP, 60). But from now on he would seek a more philosophical and spiritual poetry, that rose above the journalistic propaganda needs of revolution. He wrote at that time that "Reading articles by young Polish Marxists, one suspects that they really wish for this period to herald a future which sees the total demise of art and artistry. They are preoccupied solely with sniffing out betrayal and class desertion."[45] From this awareness Milosz began to write about "calamities of cosmic amplitude" in his book *Three Winters* (*Trzy Zimy*, 1936), which his critic friend Kazimierz Wyka considered "the most representative work of 'catastrophism'" (HPL, 413).

In his *History of Polish Literature*, Milosz wrote of other catastrophists' "foreboding of a universal conflagration" (Josef Czechowicz), and sense of a "doomed world" (Stanislaw Ignacy Witkiewicz; HPL, 412, 416). As Milosz himself wrote in his untranslated poem, "To Father Ch[omski]," "a stream of boiling lava / will extinguish the cities and Noah will not escape in his ark" (W 1:108).[46]

At the same time, just as in the poetry of Oscar Milosz, catastrophism hoped for renewal beyond the inevitable disaster. As Milosz would write in *The Land of Ulro*, "In a cruel and mean century, 'catastrophists' entertained dreams of an idyllic earth where 'the hay smells of the dream'; where tree, man, animal are joined in praise of the Garden's beauty" (LU, 275).

The stimulus Milosz received from his 1935 visit with Oscar in Paris is reflected in a major poem he wrote there, "Hymn":

> There is no one between you and me.
> Neither a plant drawing sap from the depths of earth
> nor an animal, nor a man,

nor a wind walking between the clouds.

The most beautiful bodies are like transparent glass.
The most powerful flames like water washing the tired feet of
travelers.
The greenest trees like lead blooming in the thick of the night.

Love is a sand swallowed by parched lips.
Hatred is a salty jug offered to the thirsty.
(NCP, 13)

Like much of his early verse, the poem is influenced heavily by the surrealism then fashionable in Paris. Within its refrain ("There is no one between you and me"), its catastrophist expectation of "demolished streets," and its transcendence of time, we see the stirrings of a voice, confident in its inspiration, that anticipates the prophetic authoritative voice of renewal in his last wartime poems.

> as if my life had not been,
> as if not my heart, not my blood,
> not my duration
> had created words and songs
> but an unknown, impersonal voice. . . .
>
> I have no wisdom, no skills, and no faith
> but I received strength, it tears the world apart.
> (NCP, 13)

This first acknowledgment of the presence of "an unknown, impersonal voice," or what decades later he would call his "daimonion" (NCP, 240), marks his entry into a lifelong mission that would distinguish him from his fellow poets in Wilno. "Hymn" reflects Oscar's alienation from the present, but without affirming his hopes for the future. The poem ends:

> The sound of the horn still is not heard
> Calling the dispersed, those who lie in the valleys.
> On the frozen ground as yet no rumble of the last cart.
> There is no one between you and me.
> (NCP, 15)

Asked by his friend Renata Gorczyńska to comment on "Hymn," Milosz replied: "There is no one between you and me" is addressed to God. Quite shameless. . . . I was ashamed after it was published—the immodesty of it."[47] And a little later, he added: "the poem was almost *écriture automatique*, written under the daimonion's influence. I clearly remember how I wrote the poem. In one go. The daimonion dictated it and I wrote it. In any case, this is the ecstasy of union with God, who is also the world, a feeling of special relationship with God."[48]

In his maturity, Milosz defined the poem as "pantheistic." From the internal evidence of the poem itself, I would add that the "you" of the poem is not clearly defined as a personal "God," only as the more powerful voice within himself that Milosz felt possessed by. We shall have much more to say about Milosz's wartime poems, some also written "in one go," in which he is again possessed.

There was also a dark side to Milosz's 1935 visit to Paris and his cousin. In accepting the scholarship to Paris, Milosz abandoned a young woman, Jadwiga Waszkiewicz, whom he had loved for perhaps three years, and whom, more importantly, he had gotten pregnant.

A half century later, after winning the Nobel Prize, Milosz would belatedly write to Jadwiga, saying that "for many, many years there was not a single day that I did not think about you."[49] Six years later, he would confess to her that "my crazy love for Jadwiga W was my main calamity, causing every inner torment . . . a lack of Christian love for W, you might say, was the greatest sin of my life."[50]

This partial reconciliation, however, was a half century late. At the time, Milosz appears to have essentially walked away from the messy situation, like Aeneas escaping from Dido at dawn.

As we shall see in chapter 14, after another similar abandonment, this guilt would return to haunt him.[51]

"THREE WINTERS" AND HOPE: "SLOW RIVER"

One year later, in Vilnius, Milosz's poem "Slow River" exhibits the yearning for harmony he would write of in 1974: "In the poetry of the catastrophists, every so often a note of irony toward their fate that befell them can be heard, but there is also a yearning for harmony, for beauty, which ought to be the lot of a saved man."[52]

In this poem an idyllic rural opening—

> There has not been for a long time a spring
> as beautiful as this one: the grass, just before mowing,
> is thick and wet with dew. . . .
> (NCP, 18)

—is contrasted with a contemptuous derision of an urban culture not worthy of it:

> Ah, dark rabble at their vernal feasts
> and crematoria rising like white cliffs
> and smoke seeping from the dead wasps' nests.
> In a stammer of mandolins, a dust-cloud of scythes,
> on heaps of food and mosses stomped ash-gray,
> the new sun rises on another day.
> (NCP, 19)

These lines, spoken in a different voice,[53] define not only the "rabble" (*tłuszcza*, "a very Eastern European form of contempt"),[54] but also the self-hating speaker of the poem, who asks himself in the midst of beauty,

> Why do your eyes hold an impure gleam
> like the eyes of those who have not tasted
> evil and long only for crime? Why does this heat
> and depth of hatred radiate
> from your narrowed eyes?
> (NCP, 18)[55]

The poet contemplates his own hand, for which great tasks await. But the hand is quickly weakened, and in the end "spattered" (*zbroczoną*), leading to a prophetic closure:

> And he didn't know if this is the new sign
> that promises salvation [*zbawiać*], but kills first.
> Three times must the wheel of blindness turn,
> before I look without fear at the power
> sleeping in my own hand, and recognize spring,
> the sky, the seas, and the dark, massed land.
> Three times will the liars have conquered
> before the great truth appears alive
> and in the splendor of one moment
> stand spring and the sky, the seas, the lands.
> (NCP, 19–20)

Much later Milosz explained to Renata Gorczyńska that the ending is one of catastrophism but not despair . . . that's the eschatological pattern—first you have to descend to the bottom so that some rebirth can take place later on. . . . Perhaps there'll be something like what Oskar Milosz foresaw in his vision of a theocratic society, a government of philosophers."[56]

Indeed, it is clear that Oscar Milosz helped orient Czeslaw in this direction, by his predictions (as Czeslaw summarized it) of an "apocalyptic catastrophe," to be followed by "the advent of a new epoch . . . a time when harmony between man and the universe had been recovered" (WP, 24).

MILOSZ, BRZOZOWSKI, AND WAR

But the poem's focus on the responsibility of the individual hand also reflects the influence on Milosz of the neo-Marxist Viconian Stanisław Brzozowski (d. 1911), a precursor of Lukács and Gramsci. Eschewing the scientific determinism of the later Marx (which he blamed on Engels), Brzozowski wrote in the spirit of Marx's early writings; and emphasized the role of human activity in shaping history.[57]

Thus I see the "slow river" of history, with its "tasks" for a human hand, as exemplifying, and perhaps inspired by, a line Milosz quotes from Brzozowski, "Whoever is a creator and inventor of value, whoever conceives of the future not as a stream carrying strengthless human puppets but as a task, connects everything with value" (HPL, 377–78).

Brzozowski was also a literary critic, one who had read and quoted Blake, Coleridge, and Cardinal Newman. He admired early romantics like Mickiewicz for their engagement with history; and he also detested the decadence and aestheticism of his Polish romantic contemporaries ("Young Poland"), in which he detected, as Milosz put it, "a decay of the will" (HPL, 378). For engaged romanticism Brzozowski had one memorable aphorism, "the revolt of the psyche against the society that produced it." For decadent romanticism he had a second, "Romanticism is the revolt of the flower against its roots."[58] This vital distinction between actively engaged and passive romanticism helps clarify Milosz's own startling ambivalence toward romanticism in the immediate postwar years.

Not for the first time in Polish history, the radically inadequate reality confronting interwar poets helped define more clearly their sense of the importance of what Milosz would later call "the objective reality situated beyond our perceptions" (SS, 3; cf. WP, 66). And his quality of detachment for which he had once reproved himself, his habit of looking down ironically from above, was now becoming an asset, helping him to deal with a world in which immersion was increasingly intolerable.[59]

This habit was reinforced in him by his move in 1937 from Vilnius to Warsaw (a "Babylon of depravity"), an emigration that he later described as "not necessarily easier than getting used to France or America."[60] But it was reinforced far more by the German/Russian occupation of Poland in 1939, making Poland (in a Latin phrase that Milosz adopted) *anus mundi*, the "cloaca of the world." Milosz wrote of the vital urgency of art in such a crisis:

> Gentle verses written in the midst of horror declare themselves for life; they are the body's rebellion against its destruction. They are *carmina*, or incantations deployed in order that the horror should disappear for a moment and harmony emerge. . . . They comfort us, giving us to understand that what takes place in *anus mundi* is transitory, and that harmony is enduring—which is not at all a certainty.[61]

Milosz, who had been so afflicted by shame and self-recrimination in his relatively peaceful childhood, now saw himself more and more fitted, by his detachment, to deal with disasters of apocalyptic magnitude.

PART II
Milosz's Poetry of the War

Chapter 4

Milosz's Wartime Poem-Sequence, *Ocalenie*

Part I: Overview: The Structure of the Book

The world need not always be like this, it can be different.

—Czeslaw Milosz[1]

During the Nazi occupation of Poland, while some poets became guerrillas and others wrote rhetorical exhortations to resist, Milosz, to the disapproval of some, dealt with wartime horrors with increasing detachment and perspective. This emergence to perspective marks the carefully structured contents of his 1945 book *Ocalenie* ("Salvation," or, in Milosz's less ambitious translation, "Rescue"), a roughly chronological postwar collection of his wartime poems.[2]

The book, like most of the poems in it, is structured about an increasingly prominent doubleness. This is much less clear at the beginning of the collection, containing miscellaneous poems written mostly between 1937 and Easter 1943. Milosz said later of these years: "I don't like that period. It seems to me there are times of search. You search blindly; you try one thing, then you try another; but there's a great underlying sense of being unsettled, lacking the knowledge of what you really want to do. . . . Something gets written, and it seems to be a crystallization. But actually, it's all a great inner chaos."[3]

But the structure of the book emerges with greater and greater clarity in the two following and contrasting sequences of poetry written in 1943: the idyllic mid-book Blakean series "The World," evoking the Lithuania of his childhood, and the subsequent "Voices of Poor People," an Eliotesque sequence set mostly in wartime Warsaw.[4]

In fact, it is not enough to say that the two sequences—one Blakean, romantic, straightforward, the other Eliotesque, classicistic, heavily ironic—are "contrasting." They are each shaped by the presence of the other; and the full gravity of *Ocalenie* is the worldview that emerges from their interaction. I am not alone in seeing this. In the words of the Polish critic Magda Heydel, "Jan Błoński, one of Miłosz's most important interpreters, sees the two cycles as a unity of contradictions, for both are curiously similar in some respects while entirely different in terms of theme, style, and poetics."[5]

It is striking that, in the same period but quite independently, W. H. Auden was also striving to reconcile Blakean and Eliotesque perspectives in his neglected major poem *The Double Man*. As we shall see, Auden's long poem became a model for Milosz's later efforts at classicist-romantic integration in his "Treatise on Morals" (1947) and "Treatise on Poetry" (1957).

Within this capacious structure of opposites from 1943, *Ocalenie* works toward a visible unity not perceptible in the book's earlier pages. What explains this visible enhancement of scope and style in 1943? Milosz himself later commented that, in that year, "Something very complex happened within me. . . . I had the sense that something was being revealed to me. . . . For various complex reasons, the pre-war period ended for me in 1943."[6]

When I come to describe the striking differences between his two poems about the Warsaw Ghetto Uprising of April through May 1943, "Campo dei Fiori" (before "The World") and "A Poor Christian Looks at the Ghetto" (after it), I think we shall see that witnessing the uprising engaged and changed both him and his poetry in a way that merely experiencing the German occupation of Poland had not.

Milosz himself pointed to another factor in his stylistic development: his reading and translation at the time of English poetry, including Thomas Traherne. In fact, one way of characterizing the striking stylistic evolution in *Ocalenie* is to say that, as we progress through the book, we see in his work the increasing influence of the English poets he was then translating: Shakespeare's *As You Like It*, the close of Milton's *Paradise Lost*, Traherne, Blake, Wordsworth's *Tintern Abbey*, Browning, and T. S. Eliot's *The Waste Land*. This was partly for an anthology of Anglo-American poetry in translation that Milosz edited in the spring of 1945; and "hoped—in vain, as it turned out—to publish in People's Poland at the war's close."[7]

Milosz's translation became integral to his own writing: he later wrote that "The English language is the language of poetry par excellence and every poet should be familiar with it."[8] In particular, the integration of voices he found in *The Waste Land*, from colloquial to spiritual, helped him move from a poetry of plural voices, such as we saw in "Slow River," to a more secure and confident interactive register. As he put it later, "I had written poems on 'social' themes and had been bothered by their artificiality. I had practiced 'pure' poetry and been no less irritated. Only now had the contradiction vanished. Now even the most personal poem . . . contained a streak of irony that made it objective" (NR, 247).

Another way to put it is that the book reflects a maturation, toward a register that embraces both the earthly and the ideal. In this process, "The World" in 1943, at the book's center, represents a poetic breakthrough. As Milosz explained, "The key to 'The World' is that it's a poem about the way the world should be. It was written in terrible circumstances. Warsaw in 1943—that was hitting bottom. But all it took was an act of magic to depict the exact opposite."[9]

This was a strong dissent from the militant poetry of resistance poets like Krzysztof Kamil Baczyński: "Their poetry was condensed, a magma of images, because of the enormous pressure of nightmarish reality. . . . But I was striving for a pure calligraphic line. . . . I rebelled strongly against being swept away by events. They were all submerged, but I didn't want to be."[10]

"The World" was followed by the second breakthrough, "The Voices of Poor People," a series of persona poems in which the voices, in contrast to that of the spectator in "Campo dei Flori," are themselves trapped by history in a devastated world. This separation of real and ideal is finally overcome in a third climactic breakthrough, beginning with "Flight" ("Ucieczka") and ending with "Dedication" ("Przedmowa").

As we shall see, Milosz later wrote that "By fusing individual and historical elements in my poetry, I had made an alloy that one seldom encounters in the West" (NR, 246–48). And in the book's last poems, the individual and the historical, the catastrophic and the transcendent, are indeed fused in a single confident voice.

This fusion is most complete in "Przedmowa" ("Dedication"), a poem we have already looked at, and shall consider again. It was perhaps the last to be written, and forms the end and climax of the poems he selected and translated into English in his *Collected Poems* as "Rescue." However, *przedmowa*, both etymologically and normally, means "foreword"; and Milosz placed "Przedmowa" as a frame (along with another poem, "Flight") at the beginning of *Ocalenie*, the book in Polish, leaving a very closely related poem, "In Warsaw," at the end.

THE INTEGRITY AND DEVELOPMENT WITHIN *OCALENIE* AS A WHOLE

Thus *Ocalenie* evolves, dialectically but methodically, toward "In Warsaw"'s pastoral (or as Milosz says, "arcadian") hope for a poet's "greenwood . . . moment of happiness," without which this "world will perish" (NCP, 76).[11] As we read the book from beginning to end, we become more and more aware of such polarities between ideal and actual, not just in the book, but in each poem.

As a "Foreword," "Przedmowa" does indeed introduce and organize elements of *Ocalenie* as a whole. The puzzling lines,

> That I wanted good poetry without knowing it,
> That I discovered, late, its salutary aim,
> In this and only this I find salvation [*ocalenie*]
> (NCP, 77)[12]

anticipate, I believe, the slow evolutionary development toward salutary insight in the late poems of *Ocalenie* the book.

That "salvation" should consist in wanting good poetry, "without knowing it" ("nie umiejąc"), points (I shall argue) to a profound mystery, as does the lover's healing his heart "without knowing it" ("choć sam o tym nie wie") in the book's pivotal central poem, "Love" (NCP, 50).[13] "Love"'s last line ("Nie ten najlepiej służy, kto rozumie"—literally, "He does not serve the best, who understands") is, I shall argue, a clear allusion to the occult romanticism we will see also in Mickiewicz ("faith and love are more discerning / than lenses or learning").[14]

In all Milosz's late prose non-fiction, but most specifically in *The Land of Ulro*, Mickiewicz's message—"to trust in 'faith and love' rather than in 'lenses and learning'" (LU, 99)—is seen as the way to heal the current "dichotomy between the world of scientific laws—cold, indifferent to human values—and man's inner world" (LU, 94). To correct the decaying legacy of the Enlightenment, in short.[15]

And that the poet "discovered, late," good poetry's "salutary aim," is a gesture toward *Ocalenie*'s final poem, "In Warsaw," with its epiphanic pastoral glimpse I have already mentioned, and shall discuss in more detail later:

> I want to sing of festivities,
> The greenwood into which Shakespeare
> Often took me. Leave
> To poets a moment of happiness,
> Otherwise your world will perish.

It's madness to live without joy. . . .
(NCP, 76)

To repeat, the poem "In Warsaw" is "late," not just in its book location, but also in order of composition. Just as many of the poems use Eliot's device of a persona, so also *Ocalenie* as a whole, and "The World" at its center, should be read on one level as a unified poem composed of sections, in the way we read Eliot's *The Waste Land* (translated by Milosz at this time) as a unified poem composed of fragmented sections in different voices.[16]

No one should doubt that Milosz composed and arranged his late wartime poems in serial relationship to each other, for only in this way could their doubleness and development be appreciated. As he told Renata Gorczyńska, "I get very irritated when the poems 'Faith,' 'Hope,' and 'Love,' [central to both 'The World' and to *Ocalenie* as a whole] are selected from 'The World' and published separately in anthologies. That takes them out of context. *It is precisely in an ironic context that they have their meaning.*"[17]

Irony, indeed, is a tone unifying the later parts of *Ocalenie* as a whole, particularly the sequences "The World" and "Voices of Poor People," in other respects so markedly opposed.[18] But the Arcadian ambiance of "The World" is ironic, not just in the context of the book, but also in contrast to the conditions of wartime Warsaw when the poem was written.[19]

I intend to show, however, that the condition of ironic contrast in "The World" is increasingly internal as well as external. As "The World" progresses, the poems in the sequence, as generally through *Ocalenie*, acquire increasingly ironic dualities, typically a sense of security challenged by a counter-sense (or at least trace) of violence or doubt.

In the earlier poems, the dualities are usually within time, or horizontal. From the middle of "The World" on, the dualities are increasingly vertical, between what happens within time, and something else. This will be illustrated later by the difference between Milosz's two poems about witnessing the destruction of the Warsaw ghetto. The first is "Campo dei Fiori," the last and strongest of the poems before "The World." The second is "A Poor Christian Looks at the Ghetto," among the later "Voices of Poor People." Both poems, written in 1943, express the guilt of the narrator. But the first does so in a context that is secular; the second is in a context that is otherworldly, or what Milosz calls "eschatological space."[20]

Towards the climax of *Ocalenie*, these internal dualities disappear; and Milosz writes for the first time in a powerful unified, almost prophetic voice. These latest poems are not beyond irony, but the ironic contrast is now one between a heightened, liberated voice and an alien world the speaker is breaking free from. In "Farewell," the last *persona* poem, the speaker, having rejected "youth and spring," asks in a semi-biblical voice (whose sources I shall explore in chapter 7):

> From life, from the apple cut by the flaming knife,
> What grain will be saved?[21]
> (NCP, 73)
>
> Z życia, z jabłka, które przeciął płomienisty nóż.
> Jakie ocali się ziarno?
> (W 1:228)

And "Przedmowa," also spoken in an inspired voice, shocks the reader with its audacious (and to some Catholics, perhaps almost blasphemous) question about salvation:

> What is poetry which does not save
> Nations, or people?
> (NCP, 77)
>
> Czym jest poezja, która nie ocala
> Narodów ani ludzi?
> (W 1:139)

The breaking free can be said to have begun with "The World." But it was with the concluding poems that Milosz truly reached that level where, as he wrote, "By fusing individual and historical elements in my poetry, I had made an alloy that one seldom encounters in the West" (NR, 246–48).

Therefore, to appreciate the breakthrough in "The World" and the final poems, I will lead up to them by considering the poems of *Ocalenie* as a single opus, in their order of composition and original presentation.

DEEP STRUCTURE IN THE POEM ORDER OF *OCALENIE*

In addition to "Przedmowa" and "Flight," Milosz in *Ocalenie* used the early poem "In My Homeland" (1937), the first of these poems written in Warsaw, to frame the ensuing chronological wartime sequence that ends with "In Warsaw."[22] (It pointedly thinks back to "my homeland / [Lithuania] to which I will not return," thus beginning a process of establishing ironic distance on Warsaw's wartime destruction, one which will be enhanced in the book.) Like "Slow River" a year earlier, this poem begins with landscape evocative of his rural childhood, where there is a "wonderful [*cudowne*, also 'miraculous'] . . . forest lake." But here too nature produces ambivalence: it is "a lake of thorns . . . where there are thorny grasses, / The screeching of black seagulls." The poet stares at the bottom; "and the thing that scares me, / Is there, that death will realize my form for the ages."[23]

The polarities of the book are here, between the ideal and the actual, the vital and the deathly, the present and the perspectives of time. Perhaps the most powerful common denominator of all these earlier poems is the theme of time negating the ideal (a theme reversed toward the end of the book, where time provides the necessary perspective to deal with and escape from present horror). An even more important distinction between the earlier poems of temporal dualities, and the later poems, is that in the latter temporal reality is contrasted with a different reality.

Perhaps no early poem in the book illustrates its finitude more clearly than the 1943 "Song of a Citizen," sung by a "poor man" whose lack of doubleness disqualifies him even to be included among the later "Songs of Poor People":

> This I wanted and nothing more. In my later years
> like old Goethe to stand before the face of the earth,
> and recognize it and reconcile it
> with my work built up, a forest citadel
> on a river of shifting lights and brief shadows. . . .
>
> And I can think only about the starry sky,
> about the tall mounds of termites.
> (NCP, 58)

In the often-quoted "Encounter," written in 1936, the poet vividly depicts a scene from his youth,

> We were riding through frozen fields in a wagon at dawn.
> A red wing rose in the darkness.
>
> And suddenly a hare ran across the road.
> One of us pointed to it with his hand.

and then shifts from the objective details of that moment to pathos in later time; the possibility of another life is alluded to only in an unanswered question:

> O my love, where are they, where are they going
> The flash of a hand, streak of movement, rustle of pebbles.
> I ask not out of sorrow, but in wonder.
> (NCP, 27)[24]

(Defending himself against the charge of utopian escapism, Milosz noted the same lack of a happy life in his poem "Morning":

> In vain do you remember Italian vineyards
> The green of England, and the oceans' gleams.

"Exactly," wrote Milosz, "in vain."[25])

As noted, Milosz later attributed these earlier poems in *Ocalenie* to a period "that I dislike," a period of "great inner chaos."[26] But one mysterious poem, "Day of Generation," records a sense of something more generative about to be received:

> Abysses, struck, go out one by one,
> For the sake of the past small as a plaything. . . .
> Now somebody else calls you in,
> Now somebody else summons you
> Where you are both a self and not a self. . . .
>
> It is your destiny so to move your wand,
> To wake up storms, to run through the heart of storms,
> To lay bare a monument like a nest in a thicket,
> Though all you wanted was to pluck a few roses.
> (NCP, 32)[27]

Note the alien power that will possess the poet, reminiscent of the "strength [that] tears the world apart" in the early poem "Hymn" (NCP, 13).

Written in 1942, under the German occupation, the complex poem "Waltz" opens with a beautiful woman waltzing in the year 1910. The poet, born in a rural village and "not there yet," addresses her:

> You, beautiful, do not know you're swaying with him.
> And you will dance forever in the legend,
> In the pain of wars engulfed in the clash of battles and smoke.
> ("Walc," W 1:188)

Milosz later commented:

> The poem "Waltz" is very simple: a lady who is dancing the waltz in the year 1910 has, or could have had, a vision of the years of the Second World War. Two epochs: the first, during which what will destroy the existing order is still developing, and the second, during which the destruction is completed. The tragedy of ignorance of the future. When, toward the end of the poem, I say to her,
> Forget it. Nothing exists but this bright ballroom

And the waltz, the flowers, the lights and the echoes
that is my compassionate irony placing a blindfold over her eyes.[28]

All of these poems create a dialectic *within* time; any hint of possible transcendence is typically noted only to record its absence.
Toward the end of the book, we see more clearly defined transcendent dualities, between the world as it is and an alterity as it should be. Prior to "The World," the latter is barely evident. After "The World," as we shall see, both are present, but in ways that are at first confusing and disheartening.

"In Warsaw," the final climactic poem in *Ocalenie*, is structured about the sharp contrast between the "dark love / of a most unhappy land" ("How can I live in a country / Where the foot knocks against / The unburied bones of kin?"), and the pastoral "greenwood" without which "your world will perish." (NCP, 75–76).[29]

The unified voice that speaks so clearly of both is identical with that of "Przedmowa," published as the first poem in the book.

ORDER OF POEMS IN *OCALENIE* AND IN SELECTIONS FROM IT IN "RESCUE"

Ocalenie	Order in Polish (*Wiersze* I)	"Rescue"	Order in English (NCP)
I [OPENING FRAME]			
Przedmowa (Warsaw, 1945)	139–40	[Dedication	77]
Ucieczka (Goszyce, 1944)	141	[Flight	74]
II IUVENILIA			
III TRZY ZIMY		[THREE WINTERS]	
IV			
W mojej oczyźnie (Warsaw, 1937)	142	In My Homeland	
Fragment (Paris, 1935)	143		
Pieśń Levallois (Wilno, 1935)	144–45	Ballad of Levallois	25
Siena (Italia-Silesia, 1937)	146–47	Siena	
Spotkanie (Wilno, 1937)	148	Encounter	27
Książka z ruin (Warsaw, 1941)	165–67	A Book in the Ruins	28
Dzień tworzenie (Warsaw, 1942)	183–84	A Day of Generation	31
Ranek (Szlembark, 1942)	185–87	Morning	
Walc (Warsaw, 1942)	188–90	Waltz	
Campo dei Fiori (Warsaw-Easter, 1943)	191–93	Campo dei Fiori	33

V ŚWIAT (POEMA NAIWNE)	194–96	THE WORLD: A NAÏVE POEM	36
Droga	194	The Road	36
Furtka	194	The Gate	37
Ganek	195	The Porch	38
Jadalnia	196	The Dining Room	39
Schody	196	The Stairs	40
Obrażki	197	Pictures	41
Ojciec w bibliotece	197	Father in the Library	42
Zaklęcia ojca	198	Father's Incantations	43
Z okna	198	From the Window	44
Ojciec objaśnia	199	Father Explains	45
Przypowieść o maku	200	A Parable of the Poppy	46
Przy piwoniach	201	By the Peonies	47
Wiara	201	Faith	48
Nadzieja	202	Hope	49
Miłość	202	Love	50
Wyprawa do lasu	203	The Excursion to the Forest	51
Królestwo ptaków	203	The Bird Kingdom	52
Trwoga	204	Fear	53
Odnalezienie	205	Recovery	54
Słońce (Warsaw, 1943)	205	The Sun	55
VI GŁOSY BIEDNYCH LUDZI		VOICES OF POOR PEOPLE	56
Piosenka o końcu świata	207	A Song on the End of the World (Warsaw, 1944)	56
Pieśń obywatela	208	Song of a Citizen	57
Biedny poeta	209	The Poor Poet	59
Kawiarnia	212	Café (Warsaw, 1944)	61
Biedny chrześcijanin patrzy na getto	213	A Poor Christian Looks at the Ghetto (Warsaw, 1943)	63
Przedmieście	216	Outskirts (Warsaw, 1944)	65
Pieśni Adriana Zielińskiego (Warsaw, 1943–1944)	218	Songs of Adrian Zieliński	67
VII CONCLUSION			
Los (Goszyce, 1944)	223	Lot	
Życzenie (Goszyce, 1944)	224	A Wish	

Skarga dam minionego czasu	225	Complaint of Ladies		
(Goszyce, 1944)		from a Bygone Time		
* * * (undated)	226	* * *		
Pożegnanie (Kraków, 1945)	227	Farewell	72	
[Ucieczka (Goszyce, 1944)	141]	Flight	74	
W Warszawie ((Kraków, 1945)	229	In Warsaw	75	
[Przedmowa (Warsaw, 1945)	139–40]	Dedication	77	

POSTSCRIPT: *OCALENIE* AND "RESCUE": MILOSZ'S DIFFERENT ARRANGEMENTS OF HIS WARTIME POEMS IN POLISH AND IN ENGLISH

Ocalenie (the original book in Polish, 1945) and "Rescue" (excerpted poems from it in English for Milosz's *Collected Poems*, two decades later) are two different collections for different times and audiences, each with its own distinct "salutary aim." I believe that, in the spirit of Brzozowski, we can see *Ocalenie* as a conscious effort to restore postwar Polish culture, even under Soviet domination, to its healthy antecedents in the radical vision of Mickiewicz.

In contrast, English translations from *Ocalenie* as "Rescue" are only one chapter in the chronological sequence of Milosz's lifelong pursuit of salvation, more subdued while in America. Thus, the skillful framing of the sequence in *Ocalenie* is abandoned in the *Collected Poems* for a more or less chronological order, with "Przedmowa" ("Foreword") closing the sequence rather than opening it.

This fits "Rescue" into the larger chronological sequence of the *Collected Poems*. Both in translation and in arrangement, "Rescue" is less bardic, less climactic, but better adapted for both an American and a global public.[30]

Translating with Milosz in the 1960s, I was a young and overeager partisan for preserving, in translation, the exact meaning of "Przedmowa" and exact order of the more radical *Ocalenie*.

In general, I now see I was wrong to challenge Milosz's modifications; the poems were his. But I still cannot accept the secular term "Rescue," devoid of anticipation, as an adequate translation for the transcendental term *Ocalenie*. A cat can be rescued from a telephone pole. In *Ocalenie,* as we shall see, Milosz was not at all interested in "rescuing" the Poland of the Second Republic, but in guiding Poland toward a better future.

But after his exile, Milosz became determined to avoid any appearance of acting—in the Polish tradition—as a national bard:

It makes me extremely uneasy to be turned into a patriot-poet, abroad; somehow I wasn't prepared for that role. It is true, though, that historical circumstances have often wrung literary works out of me in which either I or some persona, usually a persona, spoke as the medium for certain collective feelings. My years in occupied Warsaw produced some poems of that type. I can't say I like those poems; they show me in a posture that isn't in keeping with my temperament or my main interests. . . . The point here is that every so often I get an itch and I write something [such as] "To a Politician" or "He Who Wronged a Simple Man," or my recent poem, "To Lech Wałęsa." I continually write that sort of thing, then afterward worry that it'll ruin my image as a philosophical poet.[31]

In separating himself from the role of a national bard, he was preparing, whether he was aware of this or not, for a higher and more demanding role.

Chapter 5

Ocalenie Part II: "The World" as Hub of the Book

I was stretched, therefore, between two poles: the contemplation of a motionless point and the command to participate actively in history; in other words, between transcendence and becoming.

—Czeslaw Milosz[1]

The most beautiful flowers sometimes bloom on the edge of the abyss.

—Czeslaw Milosz[2]

This doubleness in *Ocalenie* first emerges unambiguously in its pivotal central section, "The World." As often noted, the initial doubleness reflects that of Blake's "Songs of Innocence" and "Songs of Experience."[3] Indeed, two of the simple quatrains in "The World, "Fear" ("Father, where are you?") and "Recovery," are explicitly modeled on two of Blake's "Songs of Innocence": "The Little Boy Lost" ("'Father, father, where are you going?'") and "The Little Boy Found."[4]

All of the short poems of "The World," written like Blake's in the quatrains of hymns or folk nursery rhymes, use childlike diction to present, in various ways, serious perspectives separating two worlds. Like old photographs in a Victorian zoetrope, the sections, like *Ocalenie* as a whole, must be read in sequence to discern their dramatic development. At first shifts in perspective are *horizontal*, of this world. But in later sections toward the end, there is more and more *vertical* movement, from where "tiny people walk a path below," to a feast above the treetops, where "an airborne coach carries gifts / For the invisible kings or for the bears."[5]

As the sequence opens, we are barely aware of these horizontal shifts in perspective. In "The Road," the first section, the point of view zooms in from a "green valley," like a camera lens or a child walking home, toward the red roof of a country home "visible at the bend."⁶ But as successive sections move us inside the home, the contrasts between the peaceful world within it and of violent history elsewhere in time gently become more and more disjunctive.

Seated on "The Porch," brother and sister draw "scenes of battle. . . . And with their pink tongues try to help / Great warships, one of which is sinking" (NCP, 38). Looking at a book, the children see an illustration of Hector's death at Troy. But their own experience of death is when a moth, flitting over the picture of "a Greek army storming a city," is "pinned to the page by the slap of a hand, / Flutters and dies on the hero's body" (NCP, 41).

The contrast between the opening (horizontal and secular) and the closing sections of "The World" (vertical and transcendent) is occasionally reinforced by recurring images. In "The Gate" we are told that "a wild pigeon once perched" on the gate's sharp white pickets. Later, in "The Bird Kingdom," "a pigeon returns to its airy wilderness," from which a feather drops to our "lake of darkness . . . bringing news / From a world that is bright, beautiful, warm, and free" (NCP, 52).

Inside the house, hints of outside dangers are quickly and easily dispelled. In the dining room, where time is measured by clocks, there are devils, but these are only "sculpted heads . . . smiling" (NCP, 39). "The Stairs" transmits the small children's fear of the stuffed boar's head on the staircase ("The boar's head is alive, enormous in shadow"), before Mother comes down and is there, carrying "a flickering light" (NCP, 40).

But the second half of "The World" moves outdoors again, and now fear is not so instantly dispelled. In the later poem "Fear," the children are lost in a wild, dark wood, and Father is *not* there. The children cry out,

> Where have you gone, Father? Why do you not pity
> Your children lost in this murky wood?
> (NCP, 53)

What explains "The World"'s shift from the secular opening sections to the later glimpses of what Franaszek calls a "higher, divine reality"?⁷ The answer lies in the trinity of sections separating them: "Faith," "Hope," and "Love" (the only explicitly Christian reference in "The World").⁸

As we saw in chapter 3, Milosz in his Nobel lecture wrote that reality is unbearable, and that "to embrace reality in such a manner that it is preserved in all its old tangle of good and evil, of despair and hope, is possible only thanks to a distance, only by soaring above it."⁹

All three poems lead us gently into this poetic distance between the world and our perceiving of it. "Faith" separates the things of human dreams from the world that "will remain as it has always been" (NCP, 48). In "Hope," "all things you have ever seen here / Are like a garden looked at from a gate" (NCP, 49). And finally, in "Love," we learn that "Love means to learn to look at yourself / The way one looks at distant things" (NCP, 50).

In a companion volume inspired by writing this one, I write of the human craving for "moreness," the human need to be "more than we are."[10] This craving is often selfish, for more sex, more money, or more fame. But in "Hope" and especially "Love," Milosz encodes a disinterested selfless moreness that he sees as the key, not just for survival in a radially imperfect world, but also for making it better.

The openings of the three poems, in sequence, all point toward this liberated perspective from above—like that of Selma Lagerlöf's Nils—that Milosz viewed as necessary. But my deceptively simple distillation of them here is, when we look at the full texts of the three poems, much less than the full story:

"Faith"

Faith is in you whenever you look
At a dewdrop or a floating leaf
And know that they are because they have to be.
Even if you close your eyes and dream up things
The world will remain as it has always been
And the leaf will be carried by the waters of the river.

You have faith also when you hurt your foot
Against a sharp rock and you know
That rocks are there to hurt our feet.
See the long shadow that is cast by the tree?
We and trees throw shadows on the earth.
What has no shadow has no strength to live.
(NCP, 48)

"Hope"

Hope is with you when you believe
The earth is not a dream but living flesh,
that sight, touch, and hearing do not lie,
That all things you have ever seen here
Are like a garden looked at from a gate.

You cannot enter. But you're sure it's there.
Could we but look more clearly and wisely
We might discover somewhere in the garden
A strange new flower and an unnamed star.

> Some people say that we should not trust our eyes,
> That there is nothing, just a seeming,
> There are the ones who have no hope.
> They think the moment we turn away,
> The world, behind our backs, ceases to exist,
> As if snatched up by the hand of thieves.
> (NCP, 49)

"Love"

> Love means to learn to look at yourself
> The way one looks at distant things
> For you are only one thing among many.
> And whoever sees that way heals [*leczy*] his heart,
> Without knowing it, from various ills—
> A bird and a tree say to him: Friend.
>
> Then he wants to use himself and things
> So that they stand in the glow of ripeness.
> It doesn't matter whether he knows what he serves:
> Who serves best doesn't always understand.
> (NCP, 50)

The first clue that "The World" is more than an idyll is the anti-idyllic challenge of "Faith's" last line, "What has no shadow has no strength to live." Critics have given an optimistic Catholic interpretation to this line. Tischner, for example, writes of the shadow that "the feature is a basic feature of existence, which—according to Thomas's teachings—is ultimately good."[11]

Undoubtedly St. Thomas, in contrast to St. Augustine, did believe in the goodness of creation: he wrote in his *Summa* that *Gratia non tollit naturam, sed perficit* ("Grace does not destroy nature, but perfects it," *Summa Theologiae*, I, I, 8 ad 2).[12] Part of Milosz, however, did not share this easy certainty. He has written frequently about his "propensity for Manicheanism," his sympathy for the Albigensians who "did not take refuge behind some vague will of God in order to justify cruelty," and "called necessity, which rules everything that exists in time, the work of an evil Demiurge" (NR, 78). And the detail of hurting your foot "against a sharp rock" was no casual memory, but an unusually painful one from Milosz's childhood.

In this context, I see "Hope," the central poem of "The World" and of *Ocalenie*, as a surprising small step away from the pastoral mood hitherto prevailing. For it calls on us to trust, despite all contrary evidence, in a flawed temporal reality, and not take refuge in some idealistic alternative.

Milosz in prose suggested something very similar, four decades later.

Our hope lies in a heightened sense of history, not in an escape to Saint Thomas Aquinas. There's a static quality to Thomism, and it allots a very weak role to historical change. Medieval people had no feeling at all for that dimension.

Some claim otherwise and defend Thomas Aquinas. But, basically, that was a world of immutable essence and human nature. The historical dimension was very weak.[13]

I believe we will have a clearer view of these three poems, and of all of *Ocalenie*, if we see in them Milosz's struggle to resolve his own doubleness as believer and doubter, which he saw as not idiosyncratic but reflective of "the reality that things human not only are but become" (NR, 83).[14] As we shall continue to see, these two principles of being and becoming, *esse* and *devenir*, static essence and historical change, are frequently explicit in his poetry and prose, and I see them as clearly present here, even in "The World."[15]

ESSE AND *DEVENIR*: THOMISM AND DIALECTICS IN *OCALENIE*

Milosz insisted, speaking of "The World," that "The 'naïve poems' I wrote then have a somewhat deceptive simplicity; they are really a metaphysical tract, an equivalent, in colors and shapes, of the schoolboard on the Rue d'Assas where Father Lallemant drew his Thomistic circles" (NR, 248).

These circles represented, according to Franaszek, "a hierarchy of *being*."[16] In Franaszek's words, the allusion is to "Thomistic philosophy, in which the world is presented as it is in reality, independent of our perception, and at the same time allowing access to a higher, divine reality."[17]

But Milosz did not, and could not, suggest that *Ocalenie* as a whole was Thomistic. To the early emphasis on *being* in the first part of *Ocalenie* and of "The World," there is a counter-current, a developing emphasis on *becoming* in *history*, leading us, through the "Voices of Poor People," to the question in "Przedmowa":

> What is poetry which does not save
> Nations or people?
> (NCP, 77)

In asking this question, the poem is not thinking Thomistically at all. For St. Thomas believed that what was "necessary for salvation" was "to be subject to the Roman Pontiff."[18] He also, notoriously, considered poetry in particular to be "the lowest of all intellectual studies" (*infima inter omnes doctrinas*).[19]

Ocalenie, as a whole, exhibits the same "struggle between *être* and *devenir*, between *esse*, a static sense of existence, and *becoming*, a struggle which has its political equivalents," that Milosz saw in the whole history of Europe since the French Revolution.[20] *Esse*, in Milosz's mind, was the realm of Thomism: "The essence of Thomism, the essence of Scholastic philosophy, is ultimately meditation on the meaning of 'to be.' What does it mean that this table *is*? The attribute the French call *esséité* is attached to the table."[21]

But Thomism, fitted to our spiritual dimension, could not deal with mid-century Polish history. Here, as Milosz wrote in his major work, "A Treatise of Poetry" (1957)

> Amid thunder, the golden house of *is*
> Collapses, and the word *becoming* ascends.
> (TP, 35; NCP, 132)[22]

Citing the French Jesuit Father Gaston Fessard, Milosz would later write,

> In Saint Thomas Aquinas, affirms Father Féssard [*sic*], there are no traces of pronouncements on the historical dimension. He was interested only in the *order of reason* and in the *order of nature*. "If the historical, says Father Féssard, plays a capital role in Hegel, in Marx . . . in the opinion of good judges it is, or rather it seems to be, completely absent from the Thomist doctrine.[23]

History, while *Ocalenie* was written, had produced, after Hegel and Marx, a Nazi occupation, with the clear prospect of a Stalinist one after it. And yet Milosz, encouraged by his kinsman Oscar and later Simone Weil, wondered if there could not be a quite different alternative, an "immanent force located in *le devenir*, in what is in the state of becoming, a force that pulls mankind up toward perfection."[24] This led him to explore, in *The Land of Ulro*, the hopeful prospects envisaged by Blake.

ESSE AND *DEVENIR* IN "THE WORLD"

With this in mind, we see that the closings of the three poems also show a contrapuntal development, away from the Thomistic focus on *being* (*esse*) in the openings (as earlier in "The Gate"), and towards a Blakean emphasis on *becoming* and historical reality. They form a process, from the shadows that complicate reality in "Faith," to the intellectual negations of recent history in "Hope,"[25] to what I see as the abandonment (or transcendence) of Thomistic understanding in the closing of "Love."

Let me expand what I mean by "the abandonment (or transcendence) of understanding." The last line of "Love" ("Nie ten najlepiej służy, kto rozumie") means, literally, "He does not serve the best, who understands." Here Milosz, in his style of "simple speech" ("prosta mowa"), alludes, as I said earlier, to the message in Mickiewicz's seminal poem, "The Romantic" ("Romantyczność," literally, "Romanticism"):

> faith and love are more discerning
> than lenses or learning.[26]
>
> Czucie i wiara silniej mówi do mnie
> Niż mędrca szkiełko i oko
>
> (Literally, "Feeling and faith speak louder to me / Than a scholar's lens and eye.")

There are truths intellect blinds us to, and love discerns.[27] (The "love" or "feeling" in Mickiewicz's poem "is not mere emotion, romantic or otherwise; it indicates spiritual intuition, insight, and inspiration, the 'eyes of the soul' by which one experiences spiritual reality and truth directly.")[28]

Later, in *The Land of Ulro*, Milosz would develop his kinsman Oscar's notion that "The science and philosophy of the Age of Reason were to blame for the tragedy of modern man," and that writers of insight like Mickiewicz could guide us to a "future as both a radical renewal and a restitution of the past."[29] There, Milosz quoted Mickiewicz's poem "The Romantic" in full, as both a polemic against "the rationalism . . . of the Enlightenment," and also a corrective to the "Romantic schism" that had followed in its wake.[30] I see Milosz's greatest poems, and *Ocalenie* in particular, as seeking to fulfill the same mission in poetry, with a central role played by the insight of Mickiewicz embedded in "Love."

The insight goes hand in hand with the earlier line, "A bird and a tree say to him: Friend." Here again Milosz guides us to a state of mind and nonverbal communication more easily accessed by farmhands than by intellectuals.[31] It is relevant that (as one learns from Mickiewicz) "In Lithuanian folklore trees can talk."[32]

We verge on a real but ineffable state of mind: that of "whoever . . . heals his heart /, Without knowing it. . . . A bird and a tree say to him: Friend" ("Love"; NCP, 50). Milosz verges on it again with "simple speech" in "Przedmowa," when the poet (who "wanted good poetry without knowing it") says, "I speak to you in silence like a cloud or a tree." ("Without knowing it" translates "o tym nie wie" in "Love," and "nie umiejąc" in "Przedmowa."

Thus, in Polish, there is no verbatim echo linking the two poems. But Milosz himself is responsible for the identity of the two translations into English.)

At this level of artistic distance, "The World" can now allude more directly, in its secure pastoral setting, to the anxieties of those experiencing World War II. It does so in the linked (and most explicitly Blakean) sections "Fear" and "Recovery." In "Fear," when "The hot breath of the terrible beast / Comes nearer and nearer," the children cry out (as many Poles must have in 1943),

> Where have you gone, Father? Why do you not pity
> Your children lost in this murky wood?
> (NCP, 53)

But in the companion poem "Recovery," Father does appear ("Here I am— why this senseless fear?"). And he promises them release in time: "Here it is still dark . . . / But the dawn on bright stilts wades in from the shore / And the ball of the sun, ringing, rolls" (NCP, 54). In its simple way, the poem aligns both the Father and the sun with what he later called a positive "immanent force located in *le devenir.*"[33]

In this way the sequence is directed to the next and concluding section, "The Sun," with its explicit depiction of the dual reality of fact and mind (or creation and Creator) in which humanity lives:

> the whole earth is like a poem
> While the sun above represents the artist.
> (NCP, 55)

"Love" had concluded with the warning, "He does not serve best, who understands" ("Nie ten najlepiej służy, kto rozumie," NCP, 50). "The Sun" expands this warning: the seeker for absolute knowledge, looking "straight up at the sun . . . will lose the memory of things he has seen." But he who abandons intellectual *hubris,* and accepts a more naïve and humble role, will find what civilization loses sight of:

> Let him kneel down, lower his face to the grass,
> And look at light reflected [*odbity*] by the ground.
> There he will find everything we have lost:
> The stars and the roses, the dusks and the dawns.
> (NCP, 55)

A straightforward interpretation of this passage is that, in the words of Leonard Nathan and Arthur Quinn, "we, as creatures, must not attempt to see with the eyes of God. A godlike vision of the whole is beyond our capacity."[34]

There is more happening here, however. These lines, besides being the culmination of "The World"'s idyll, also signify a departure from it. This is evident by comparing "The Sun" with "By the Peonies," the last of the poems *preceding* "Faith," "Hope," and Love." Here is the middle stanza of that poem:

> Mother stands by the peony bed,
> Reaches for one bloom, opens its petals,
> And looks for a long time into peony lands,
> Where one short instant equals a whole year.
> (NCP, 47)

She sees things, in other words, *directly*, with the same naivete that Blake celebrated in "Auguries of Innocence":

> To see a World in a Grain of Sand
> And a Heaven in a Wild Flower
> Hold Infinity in the palm of your hand
> And Eternity in an hour.[35]

But the closure of "The Sun," climaxing a development in the closures of the poems just before it, returns us from idyllic contemplation of an ideal world to the *reflected* images we see in the Platonic cave of twentieth-century Europe, where, the poem promises, we will find again "everything we have lost."[36]

THE TRANSITION FROM ONTOLOGY TO HISTORY

The duality of *esse* and *devenir* in what is real is closely related to the doubleness Milosz sees in himself (and later in humanity).[37] We can see this duality developing through "The World," just as later in the subsequent pages of *Ocalenie*.

The Thomistic view of reality as *being*, *être*, is presented as stable in the first "horizontal" half of "The World," only to be balanced in the second "vertical" half by an increasing sense of reality as *becoming*, *devenir*. The poems in the first half, like many of their titles, concern objects: "The Gate," "The Stairs," and "Pictures." In the second half, the poems concern processes in time, as in "The Excursion to the Forest," or the paired sequence "Fear" and "Recovery."

In the final stanza of "The Sun," the last of these "naïve poems," the world of sublunary becoming is dramatically contrasted with the eternal being of the sun itself above; it thus provides a transition from "The World" to the alienated "Voices of Poor People" in ruined Warsaw. While in the first stanza, "the sun above represents the artist," we are nevertheless told that "to paint the variegated world," we should "never look straight up at the sun":

> Let him kneel down, lower his face to the grass,
> And look at the light reflected [*odbity*] by the ground.
> (NCP, 55)

(A decade later Milosz reiterated this contrast between being and reflected being in his frequently anthologized poem "Esse," where he describes his brief sight of a woman in the Paris metro, "as the lights of metro stations flew by: 'And so it befell me that after so many attempts at naming the world, I am able only to repeat, harping on one string, the highest, the unique avowal beyond which no power can attain: *I am, she is*. Shout, blow the trumpets, make thousands-strong marches, leap, rend your clothing, repeating only: *is!*' She got out at Raspail. I was left behind with the immensity of existing things. A sponge, suffering because it cannot saturate itself; a river, *suffering because reflections* [odbicia] *of clouds and trees are not clouds and trees*" (NCP, 249, emphasis added).[38]

This contrast mirrors Milosz's internal doubleness, caught in one reality and striving towards another. It is reflected in the maxim he later selected for quotation from the writings of Simone Weil: "The distance between the necessary and the good is the selfsame distance as that between the Creature and the Creator."[39] Thus the book progresses, from naivete at the beginning of "The World" to "A Song on the End of the World," the first of the mundane "Voices of Poor People."

Chapter 6

Ocalenie Part III:
"Voices of Poor People"

For Milosz, the person is irrevocably a person in history, and the interchange between external event and the individual life is the matrix of poetry.

—Helen Vendler[1]

The gradual process in "The World," from immersion in history to first an escape, "by soaring above it,"[2] and then to a return, replicates the process in the entire book *Ocalenie*. "The World" is the centerpiece of the book, both in its location and in chronological order of composition. And so "Faith," "Hope," and "Love" divide the poems, not just of "The World," but of the book as a whole.

The dualities in the earlier poems in the book (earlier both in presentation and in time of composition) are, although varied and difficult to summarize, chiefly secular, like the "horizontal" early poems of "The World." By secular, I mean that the dualities in them are both contained within the dimension of historical time. Indeed, the disjunctive superimposition of two disparate realms which we saw in "Pictures"—the moth slapped and killed on an image of Hector's corpse—is prefigured in "A Book in the Ruins" (one of the few earlier poems to allude to the early, pre-Uprising, bombing of Warsaw):

> in a book picked up
> From the ruins . . .
> . . . . You pick a fragment
> Of grenade which pierced the body of a song
> On Daphnis and Chloe. And you long,
> Ruefully, to have a talk with her.
> (NCP, 28, 29)

That longing is clearly circumscribed within this world, not salvational. And at the end of the poem, workers

> . . . have dragged out
> Heavy books, and made a table of them
> And begun to cut their bread. In good time
> A tank will clatter past, a streetcar chime.
> (NCP, 30)

Like the later, "vertical," poems of "The World," the poems of "Voices of Poor People," which immediately follow them, see the poverty of the poems' speakers from the perspective of an unattainable, more spiritual world, or what Milosz later called "the objective reality situated beyond our perceptions" (WP, 66).³ But the speakers are excluded from this better world; each is an inhabitant of Blake's Ulro as Milosz defined it, that "realm of spiritual pain such as is borne and must be borne by the crippled man" (LU, 32).

THE TWO POEMS FRAMING "VOICES OF POOR PEOPLE"

This expanded spiritual universe in which the "poor people" speak is emphasized by the two slightly less pessimistic linked poems which introduce and end the sequence: "A Song on the End of the [or 'a'] World" ("Piosenka o końcu świata"; dated 1944) and "Songs of Adrian Zieliński" (dated 1943/1944).⁴

(I will use the Polish title of the first, because it is significantly more ambiguous than the English. Because Polish does not need to use an article, there is no "the" in the Polish title. The translation could also be "Song About the End of *a* World"; and I believe this possibility fits the open-ended tone of both "The World" and the book's final poems. In particular it reflects Milosz's explicit belief that the world of interwar Polish culture was finished, deservedly so, and yet a future of unknown possibilities still lay ahead.)

In "Piosenka" (as earlier in "Campo dei Fiori") the speaker is not himself one of the "poor people," but distinguished from them. The poem contrasts those who

> Do not believe it is happening now,
> As long as the sun and moon are above,
> As long as the bumblebee visits a rose,

with

..... a white-haired old man, who would be a prophet
Yet is not a prophet, for he's much too busy,
Repeats while he binds his tomatoes:
There will be no other end of the world,
There will be no other end of the world.
(NCP, 56)[5]

Similarly, in "Songs of Adrian Zieliński," the somewhat Prufrockian or Castorpian *persona* still distinguishes himself from the "poor astronomers" who, unlike himself, see "the ass of a girl passing by, / A round ass carved in splendor" ("Okrągly tyłek rzeźbiony w blasku") as a "planet." Disobeying the warning in "The Sun," the latter look up at the "navy blue zone of the sky"; and "are overwhelmed by their fear,"

And they lower their heads again,
Because the construct is too high for them.

They see, as the ass goes swaying off
The bright planet Venus in a telescope

I znowu nisko opuszczają głowy,
Bo za wysoka dla nich ta budowa.

Widzą, jak tyłek chwiejąc się oddala:
Jasna planeta Wenus w teleskopie.
(NCP, 70; W 1:221–22)[6]

Miłosz later said of "Piosenka": "In Miłosz's short, ironic 'Song at the End of the World,' Armageddon is permanent, but it is always accompanied by trees in bloom, kisses of lovers, the birth of babies" (HPL, 459).[7] The irony he refers to is that he described also in "The World": the prodigious gap between the equanimity of perspective in the poem, and the contemporary horrors of life in subjugated Warsaw, including the destruction of the ghetto.

In discussing this poem, Aleksander Fiut commented: "In a rather baffling way the Last Judgment has not so much a moral meaning as an ontological one. More than a just assessment of human action it signifies a change in all reality."[8] This observation is in keeping with Miłosz's own explanation of the enhanced new voice which we hear in the end of *Ocalenie*: "For various complex reasons, the prewar period ended for me in 1943. Only then did I have a sense of a new beginning. That's how it was."[9]

But if old man's repeated "There will be no other end to the world" echoes, as Magda Heydel points out, Eliot's repeated "This is the way the world ends" in "The Hollow Men," the climax (or anticlimax) of Eliot's poem ("Not with a bang but a whimper") is stunningly rebuked by the open-ended "calm beauty" of Milosz's images:

> On the day the world ends
> Women walk through the fields under their umbrellas,
> A drunkard grows sleepy at the edge of a lawn,
> Vegetable peddlers shout in the street
> And a yellow-sailed boat comes nearer the island,
> The voice of a violin lasts in the air
> And leads into a starry night.
> (NCP, 56)

In Heydel's words, "This is not a world of lacking and longing, as it is in Eliot's vision, but the opposite."[10]

The "Songs of Adrian Zieliński" open with a similar hint of transcendent equilibrium:

> The fifth spring of war is beginning,
> A young girl is weeping for her lover.
> Snow is melting in the Warsaw streets.
> (NCP, 67)

Near the end of these Songs, the speaker again voices his apparent inner well-being:

> There is a whisper of night that breathes in me,
> Little voices like cats lapping at my days,
> And my profound subjugated storms
> Erupt in a song of gratitude and praise.
> (NCP, 70)

Thus the framing poems of this section of the book supply an apparent equanimity and perspective that the harried voices of the "poor people" lack. However, the tone of the lines just quoted is soon interrupted by an abrupt violent transition—

> Peace to the house of the sage.
> Peace to his prudent wonder.
>
> ———————————
>
> O black treason, black treason—
> Thunder.
> (NCP, 71)

Ocalenie Part III: "Voices of Poor People" 71

that we will discuss in a moment.

ANGER AND SELF-DIVISION AMONG THE "POOR PEOPLE"

Most of the "Voices of Poor People" are Eliotesque *persona* poems, in which the speaker defines, or is defined by, his own inadequacy in a broken city. But the limitations outlined in these poems can be seen as a message from Milosz to his contemporaries in Warsaw.

The first of these poems is "Song of a Citizen," which begins:

> A stone from the depths that has witnessed the seas drying up
> and a million white fish leaping in agony,
> I, poor man, see a multitude of white-bellied nations
> without freedom. I see the crab feeding on their flesh.
>
> I have seen the fall of States and the perdition of tribes,
> the flight of kings and emperors, the power of tyrants.
> I can say now, in this hour,
> that I—am, while everything expires,
> that it is better to be a live dog than a dead lion,
> as the Scripture says.
> (NCP, 57; cf. Ecclesiastes 9:4)[11]

(Here the persona quotes explicitly from scripture, I believe for the first time in *Ocalenie*. We shall see that, in the poems of the book's final section, the speaking voice itself becomes scriptural in tone.)

Fiut notes the recurring imagery in Milosz's poems of this era that reduce human corpses (a tragic if daily sight for contemporary Warsovians) to animal carrion.[12] And he observes: "Such comparisons challenged a literature then accustomed to a noble, martyrological tone. Polish war poetry either lamented the innocent victims or [as in the case of Baczyński and others] called for revenge, invoking hackneyed romantic stereotypes."[13]

Milosz himself in the 1980s observed how the next poem in this series, "The Poor Poet," develops this alienation from contemporary culture. It is, in his words, a "polemic," and not just against poetry "in the idolatry of country" (NCP, 59), but "a polemic with art, a constant turning against art."[14] To illustrate his point that the poem defined the search for beauty as an outrage in times of war, he then quoted his own lines:

> I poise the pen and it puts forth twigs and leaves, it is covered
> with blossoms

> And the scent of that tree is impudent, for there, on the
> real earth,
> Such seeds do not grow, and like an insult
> To suffering humanity is the scent of that tree.
> (NCP, 59)

Milosz commented, "This is the immorality of art."[15] He then interpreted the later line, "To me is given the hope of revenge on others and on myself," in terms of "what Gombrowicz praised me for, my self-contradiction."

> The revenge the poor poet plots is more or less the one Różewicz carried out. Except that I was never a consistent nihilist. This is part of the complex that turns against European culture, against art, which, if the truth be told, had a lot that needed throwing out, a great deal that was disgraceful.[16]

In *The History of Polish Literature* (461–62) Milosz also quoted "The Poor Poet" to illustrate "the doubt concerning the dignity of art," among those poets who (in contrast to Różewicz) tried "to maintain an equilibrium between the sense of tragedy and an approval of life. Their rage, often self-directed, was mitigated by a certain humanistic rationalism."[17]

However, the poem itself, which voices a "cynical hope" from "the glow of fires, massacres," may be closer to Różewicz's nihilism than Milosz's later comments.

> Some take refuge in despair, which is sweet
> Like strong tobacco, like a glass of vodka drunk in the hour
>   of annihilation.
> Others have the hope of fools, rosy as erotic dreams.
>
> Still others find peace in the idolatry of country,
> Which can last for a long time,
> Although little longer than the nineteenth century lasts.
>
> But to me a cynical hope is given,
> For since I opened my eyes I have seen only the glow of
>   fires, massacres,
> Only injustice, humiliation, and the laughable shame of
>   braggarts.
> To me is given the hope of revenge on others and on myself,
> For I was he who knew
> And took from it no profit for myself.
> (NCP, 59–60)

We should remember, however, that this nihilism, this cynical hope of revenge, is not attributable to Milosz himself, but to the self-conflicted personas who emerge, again and again, in the successive poems of this sequence.

For this theme of self-division, or what I have elsewhere called doubleness, becomes more and more explicit in "The Voices of Poor People," leading in the end to the dramatic climax of "Songs of Adrian Zieliński." We see it next in the survivor's guilt of the two poems "Café" (NCP, 61–62) and "A Poor Christian Looks at the Ghetto" (NCP, 63–64), far and away the most famous of these poems.

"A POOR CHRISTIAN LOOKS AT THE GHETTO"

A good way to see the development in *Ocalenie* as a whole is to compare "A Poor Christian" with the earlier "Campo dei Fiori" (NCP, 33–35), the powerful poem that immediately precedes "The World."[18]

Both poems contemplate the destruction of the Warsaw ghetto from the viewpoint of a spectator outside. "Campo dei Fiori" is realistic, describing "baskets of olives and lemons" in Rome, and a "sky-carousel" ("karuzeli," W 1:191)[19] just outside the ghetto wall in Warsaw.

> I thought of the Campo dei Fiori
> in Warsaw by the sky-carousel
> one clear spring evening
> to the strains of a carnival tune.
> The bright melody drowned
> the salvos from the ghetto wall,
> and couples were flying
> high in the cloudless sky.
> (NCP, 33)

It depicts a world far less shattered than the more surreal "A Poor Christian," where "roof and wall collapse in flame. . . . Now there is only the earth"— with a mole burrowing through the rubble.

The world that is being shattered in the "Campo dei Fiori" is only that of the Jews in the ghetto, in contrast to the Warsaw outside of the Poles, with its carousel and laughing crowds. More importantly, the guilt of carefree insouciance that is implied in the first poem is that of *others*—the shoppers in Rome, the carnival-goers in Warsaw—not, as in the second poem, the guilt of the narrator himself.

No two poems in *Ocalenie* are more easily compared, and no two exhibit more vividly the development in the book toward a spiritual self-questioning that is simultaneously a questioning of the speaker's guilty civilization.[20]

The response of the narrator in the first poem, as riders on a festival carousel outside the wall catch flakes of ash in the air from the burning ghetto, is purely secular:

> ... that day I thought only
> of the loneliness of the dying.
> (NCP, 33)

The narrator in the second poem, in contrast, is fearful, and fearful not just for his life but for his soul:

> I am afraid, so afraid of the guardian mole, ...
> What will I tell him, I, a Jew of the New Testament. ...
> (NCP, 63)

When asked by Renata Gorczyńska (in Polish) about the guardian mole (*strażnik-kret*), Milosz replied, "I don't know who the guardian mole is. The poem is simply an image of an earth full of ashes."[21] But he also refers to the poem's subterranean space as "eschatological"; and in his *History of Polish Literature*, where Milosz quotes it in full to represent his wartime poetry—it comes right before his reference just quoted, to the theme of "doubt concerning the dignity of art."

The guilt here is not just personal, as in the preceding poem "Café" ("Of those at the table in the café ... I alone survived," NCP, 61) but something much more: a questioning of Christian faith itself in a world of sectarian hatred, especially strong in Poland.[22]

In this vein, Milosz, according to Gorczyńska, once said that "Campo dei Fiori" was immoral, "because it was written from the point of view of an *observer* about people who were dying."[23] But to repeat, it is primarily a poem about the moral failure of ordinary people, *others*. In "A Poor Christian," in contrast, it is the poet himself, and what he believes in, that must fear condemnation for the horror: "the ghetto, for God's sake, and the liquidation of three million Polish Jews, a sin that cries out—on the earth, in all of Poland—to be absolved."[24] In the face of such monstrosity, art is not just an inadequate response, but (Milosz tells Gorczyńska) a culpable one: an argument developed in his essay, "The Immorality of Art."[25]

In 1983, in a brilliant essay, Robert Alter identified the "guardian mole" as "a kind of archetypal representative of the Jewish people through the ages, somehow stubbornly managing to survive underground with its special wisdom and its peculiar spiritual authority, even when total annihilation has seemed to have overtaken it."[26] The end of the poem strongly supports this reading:

> I am afraid, so afraid of the guardian mole.
> He has swollen eyelids, like a Patriarch
> Who has sat much in the light of candles
> Reading the great book of the species.
>
> What will I tell him, I, a Jew of the New Testament,
> Waiting two thousand years for the second coming of Jesus?
> My broken body will deliver me to his sight
> And he will count me among the helpers of death:
> The uncircumcised.
> (NCP, 63–64)

In 1987, Jan Błoński's seminal essay, "The Poor Poles Look at the Ghetto," discussed Milosz's "terrifying poem" in a way that set off a firestorm of controversy in newly liberated Poland:[27]

> It is as if two fears coexist here. The first is the fear of death; more precisely, the fear of being buried alive, which is what happened to many people who were trapped in the cellars and underground passages of the ghetto. But there is also a second fear: the fear of the guardian mole. This mole burrows underground but also underneath our consciousness. This is the feeling of guilt which we do not want to admit. Buried under the rubble, among the bodies of the Jews, the "uncircumcised" fears that he may be counted among the murderers. So it is the fear of damnation, the fear of hell. The fear of a non-Jew who looks at the ghetto burning down. He imagines that he might accidentally die then and there, and in the eyes of the mole who can read the ashes, he may appear "a helper of death." And so, indeed, the poem is entitled: "A Poor Christian Looks at the Ghetto." This Christian feels fearful of the fate of the Jews but also—muffled, hidden even from himself—he feels the fear that he will be condemned. Condemned by whom? By people? No, people have disappeared. It is the mole who condemns him, or rather may condemn him, this mole who sees well and reads "the book of the species." It is his own moral conscience which condemns (or may condemn) the poor Christian.[28]

The heated responses by Poles to Błoński's essay, in a controversy that drew global attention, illustrates how, almost four decades after Milosz had left Poland, his poetry continued to supply moral leadership to a generation that had known him only as an exile. And this happened in a decade when, as we shall see, an aging Milosz was now admittedly "not very eager to play such a role."[29]

As Poland gradually retreated from the inter-faith solidarity of the 1980s, Milosz and his poems, "Campo dei Fiori" in particular, were increasingly attacked for being "anti-Polish." Aleksander Szumański, for example, wrote that "Miłosz is not one of us, but a denationalized cosmopolitan, a foreign, external man, and even hostile to our entire national, historical and cultural heritage." In his denunciation of "Campo di Fiori," "in which the poet mocks us," he reported a claim that "the situation was the opposite of what Miłosz says, because although the carousel belonged to a Volksdojcza [*Volksdeutsch*, someone who was ethnically German but not a German citizen] . . . it was closed during the fights in the ghetto."[30]

These arguments are childish, and largely irrelevant. The poem is framed by the burning of Giordano Bruno in 1600 in Rome [where people "peddled their white starfish"], precisely to stress that the poem, as it explicitly states, is about "mankind," and "the passing of things human" (NCP, 34); it does not target Poles. The carousel is in the poem, not because of who owned it, but of those who rode in it. And it may well have been closed at some point during the 1943 Ghetto Uprising, but how likely is it that the closure was precisely coordinated to begin with the German attack?

THE CLIMAX OF "VOICES OF POOR PEOPLE"

The two last poems of the section use devices from Eliot's *The Waste Land*—broken imagery, debased amusement, and glimpses of sterile sexuality—to depict Hannah Arendt's "banality of evil." The evocation of *The Waste Land* is particularly strong in "Outskirts":

> A broken shadow of a chimney. Thin grass.
> Farther on, the city torn into red brick.
> Brown heaps, barbed wire tangled at stations.
> Dry rib of a rusty automobile.
> A claypit glitters.
>
> An empty bottle buried
> in the hot sand.
> A drop of rain raised dust
> off the hot sand.
> Frank holds the bank. Now Frank is dealing.
> We play, Julys and Mays go by.
> We play one year, we play a fourth.
> The glare pours through our blackened cards
> into hot sand.
> (NCP, 65)

As Fiut writes, "the epithets speak indirectly of lifelessness, uselessness, wreckage, and destruction. . . . In a word . . . the destruction of the world is described—but . . . without excessive emotional emphasis."[31]

In contrast to the tragic "Poor Christian," the persona in "Outskirts" is also, when he finally defines himself, as debased as Frank, or as Eliot's "young man carbuncular":

> Look, there she goes, a pretty girl,
> Cork-soled slippers and curly hair.
> Hello sweetheart, let's have a good time.
> A barren field.
> The sun is setting.
> (NCP, 66)[32]

(The comparison of "Outskirts" to *The Waste Land* is more obvious in Polish, because in one line, "A barren field," there is a verbal reminiscence—*jałowe pole*—to the Milosz's title in Polish for *The Waste Land*—*Ziemia jałowa*.)[33]

We begin to catch glimpses of a better world in the last poem of this section, "Songs of Adrian Zielinski."[34] His own world is both banal and dangerous:

> A carousel drones in the little square.
> Somebody is shooting at somebody out there.
> A light squall blows from the torpid river.
> (NCP, 67)

And yet he can imagine an altogether happier one.

> Somewhere there are happy cities.
> Somewhere there are, but not for certain.
> Where, between the market and the sea,
> In a spray of sea mist,
> June pours wet vegetables from baskets
> And ice is carried to a café terrace
> Sprinkled with sunlight, and flowers
> Drop onto women's hair.
> (NCP, 69)

At first, like Eliot's Prufrock, he laments the gap between such places and his own world,

> Somewhere there are happy cities
> But they are of no use to me.
> I look into life and death as into an empty winecup.
> (NCP, 69)

But facing his own sense of self-alienation and loss, he thinks for a while that he, unlike Prufrock, has the strength to overcome it.

> There is a whisper of night that breathes in me,
> Little voices like cats lapping at my days
> And my profound subjugated storms
> Erupt in a song of gratitude and praise.
> (NCP, 70)

For two and a half quatrains, he exults in the peace he has achieved:

> What a wise man you are, Adrian.
> For you, as for an old Chinese poet,
> Everything is the same, as for a millennium.
> You look at a flower and you smile.
> (my version, cf. NCP, 71)
> Jakże ty mądry jesteś, Adrianie,
> Że tobie jak staremu chińskie poecie
> Wszystko jedno, jakie tysiąclecie.
> Patrzysz na kwiat i uśmiechasz się.
> (W 1:222)

But then, in the last rhyming quatrain, this seeming equanimity is explosively disrupted, shattered.

> Peace to the house of the sage.
> Peace to his prudent wonder.
> ———————————
> O black treason, black treason—
> Thunder.
> (NCP, 71)

What explains this sudden interruption of Adrian's self-deluding reverie? Based on its location in the book, it has to be the sudden outbreak of the Warsaw Uprising, on August 1, 1944. For on that day the entire era of the "poor people," indeed of the world as Milosz had known it, came to an abrupt end.[35]

For Milosz himself and Janka the interruption of life was equally dramatic. The house they were living in was destroyed on the same day; and they were forced to escape on foot from the burning city, with no more than what they could carry on their backs. During their long trek to Kraków, most of their few belongings were taken from them by robbers.[36] The following January, when he first encountered an armed band of Russian soldiers, "the shabby worker's overall which I was wearing was all I possessed in the world."[37]

It is hard for those of us who have not endured such deprivation to realize the psychic shock involved. I had a tiny glimpse of it in 1991, when the house I was living in and all its contents burned to a fine ash. Even though my computer (which I consider the external hard-drive of my brain) was thankfully elsewhere, I still felt, as I wrote in my poetic response, *Minding the Darkness*,

> as if in one week
> we had lived two different ages
> two habits of living
>
> the comfort of Culture
>   *more easily destroyed than preserved*
>   versus *Dasein face to face*
>
> *with its original nakedness.*[38]

The loss of his environs, along with virtually all he possessed, must have been shattering for Milosz. It also produced in him an altered state of being, which liberated him to write the last poems of *Ocalenie* in a new style at an altogether higher level. These are not poems of witness any more.[39] They speak instead constructively of the most serious and timeless concerns, in what I have to call a bardic or even prophetic voice of engagement.

Chapter 7

Ocalenie Part IV: "Flight" and the Flight from Warsaw

Wo aber Gefahr ist, wächst das Rettende auch. (Where there is danger, there also what saves grows stronger.)

—Friedrich Hölderlin[1]

A poet repeatedly says farewell to his old selves and makes himself ready for renewals.

—Czeslaw Milosz[2]

When the August 1944 Warsaw Uprising suddenly erupted in their neighborhood, Milosz and Janka were caught by surprise as they were walking to a tram stop. "Machine guns fired at anything that moved. Not far away some friends lived. . . . Heavy fire broke loose at our every step, nailing us to the potato fields. In spite of this I never let go of my book. . . . *The Collected Poems of T. S. Eliot*, in the Faber & Faber edition" (NR, 249).[3]

Soon after their escape from Warsaw a little later, robbers "seized what little money and valuables they had with them."[4] Explaining later why he cared little about money, Milosz wrote, "I had walked out of too many burning cities (literally or figuratively) without looking back: *omnia mea mecum porto* [Everything I own I carry with me]" (NR, 264).[5] It was almost as if Fate used robbers to liberate Milosz from his last attachments to his prewar social identity, and to prepare him for a new mission.

That sense of a new mission closes his brief apocalyptic poem, "Flight" ("Ucieczka"), written that December about the grim escape. It is an astonishing diapason in eight lines, rising from a traumatic personal memory to an altogether higher level—identification as a prophetic actor in an apocalyptic moment:

81

"Flight"

> When we were fleeing the burning city
> And looked back from the first field path,
> I said: "Let the grass grow over our footprints,
> Let the harsh prophets fall silent in the fire,
> Let the dead explain to the dead what happened.
> We are fated to beget a new and violent tribe
> Free from the evil and the happiness that drowsed there.
> Let us go"—and the earth was opened for us by a sword of flames.[6]
> Goszyce, 1944 (NCP, 74)

"Flight" was written while Milosz briefly took refuge at Goszyce, a rural manor or court (*dwór*) near Kraków. There, as he waited for the arrival of the advancing Soviet troops, he completed his further traumatic break with his past. He reveals this in his conflicting accounts of the New Year's Eve party at the manor—a last celebration by a privileged Poland on the point of disappearing, in "the cyclone that ruined families, fortunes, and whole classes" (NR, 258).

In his words, written almost a half century later, in 1987:

> A Dante of Sarmatia was needed to portray a scene from this *Finis Poloniae* [End of Poland].... My experience not just of a few hours at a New Year's Eve party but also of what my imagination suggested to me right then, at that very moment, of being inevitable, and also my experience of what did happen a few days later, following the pattern of the 1918–19 dress rehearsal: "Bolsheviks in the Polish manor." The rounding up of cattle, horses, sheep, from the barns and stables, the catching and slaughtering of chickens, ducks, geese, a green light to looting, the end of the good life. (YH, 76)[7]

His poetic memory of the event in "A Treatise on Poetry" (1957) was less specific, but even more apocalyptic:

> When the pages of books fall in fiery scraps
> Onto smashed leaves and twisted metal,
> The tree of good and evil is stripped bare....
> Where wind carries the smell of the crematorium[8]
> And a bell in the village tolls the Angelus,
> The Spirit of History is out walking.
> He whistles, he likes these countries washed
> By a deluge, deprived of shape and now ready....
> Poplars, as tiny as rye plants in a gully,
> Conduct the eye to the roof of a manor

From the forest, and there, in the dining room,
Tired boys are lounging in officers' boots.
A poet has already recognized the walker,
An inferior god to whom time and the fate
Of one-day-long kingdoms is submitted.
His face is the size of ten moons. He wears
About his neck a chain of severed heads.
(NCP, 127–28; TP, 29–31)

What happened at Goszyce was at a turning point, not just throughout the country for Poland, but for himself and his poetry. And we can see evidence of this also in his changing accounts over time to what happened to him there. In his 1958 memoir *Native Realm* (*Rodzinna Europa*), Milosz recorded his alienation from the New Year's Eve party:

> For them culture had come to a standstill in the Sistine Chapel, in Leonardo da Vinci's *Last Supper*, in good manners and brilliant conversation. . . . Now, as they nursed their myths for a while longer before they went down to ultimate defeat, I asked myself if my resentment towards them did not arise out of my own wounded self-love: they recognized only those who were already esteemed. But to demand that they know how to appreciate worth in someone less crowned by success would have been futile. One gained their recognition by flattering conventions, by lowering oneself and pretending to be more stupid than really was the case. Everything essential was too difficult for them. I shook them off me gently: let the dead bury their dead. Free to face tomorrow, I repeated to myself: they should worry, not I. (NR, 255–56)

But thirty years later Milosz, with greater candor, blamed his discomfort at Goszyce not on his hosts, but on himself. And he revealed that what really tormented him there was less his knowledge of its imminent destruction than that in the end he no longer desired it: that his 1930s public stance of radical alienation from gentry culture masked a deeper ambivalence, a belated acceptance that he too was a child of the manor and of Poland's past.

> That New Year's Eve was a descent into hell, into the bottom of a historical nightmare: I drank and behaved like a buffoon in order to extinguish thought, but in vain. . . . Eternal Polishness, the Polish manor, Nawłoć one minute before the day of reckoning, before its disappearance forever, and I, with my shame and my ambition to escape from the manor, thrust back into it once again as a sign that, like it or not, here is where I belong, that I had tried in vain to escape from the traditionalism that I disliked and the religion of absolutized values. (YH, 75–76)

(The translator, Madeline Levine, explains in a footnote that "In Żeromski's novel *Przedwiośnie* [*Early Spring*, 1925], Nawłoć is a manor presented satirically as the epitome of the gentry's carefree life, in contrast to the miserable life of the peasants.")

One factor forcing Milosz into this painful self-recognition may have been finding a new spiritual friend there in the host, Jerzy Turowicz. Turowicz was a long-time devout and observant Catholic, and a fellow reader of Jacques Maritain. A writer and intellectual, he would quickly become close to Milosz.[9]

This latest blow to Milosz's surrogate identity as an alienated radical was, he came to recognize, another painful disruption from his past, but also another necessary step in his liberation. He was moving toward a new stage where he would write neither "social" nor "pure" poetry, but focus on the world as it is ("in all its old tangle of good and evil") with both detachment and a deeper awareness of an alternative reality.[10]

MILOSZ'S "DESIRE TO SAVE THE CULTURE"

What was disturbing and exciting for Milosz in late 1944 was not just the destruction of Warsaw, but what in retrospect he called "the end of Europe" (YH, 238).[11] To quote Franaszek, "Driving him on was . . . the desire to save the culture [*chęć do ratowania kultury*] while it was still possible, and a strong sense that he was participating in events of an apocalyptic character, comparable to that which witnessed the fall of the Roman Empire."[12]

The idea that one as an individual might feel the responsibility to save a culture is alien to most American readers; it may come only to those born in smaller nations. We need to recall how it was literature, and above all poetry, that had preserved Polish culture through its previous loss of independence, and that Milosz was by this time recognized as a leader among Polish poets. It is clear from the poems written at Goszyce, and for a decade afterwards, that Milosz now felt the mantle of Mickiewicz, Słowacki, and Norwid on his own shoulders.

It is also evident in his efforts at this time to complete and publish an anthology in Polish of translations from English and American poetry. It represented, according to Franaszek, an effort to "present the culture of the West in the face of approaching barbarity, and also suggested an attempt on Miłosz's part to re-orient Polish culture away from its strong traditional ties with France towards the Anglo-Saxon countries."

The book was actually accepted for publication by the leading Warsaw publisher Czytelnik, but "due to the rapidly deteriorating political atmosphere between the USSR and the West, it never appeared."[13]

GOSZYCE: MILOSZ FINDS HIS BARDIC VOICE

Milosz's new poems in *Ocalenie* from this period reflect this excitement of historic mission. They are framed, and their tone set, by "Flight," which moves rapidly away from his and Janka's escape from Warsaw to intimations of a new era. In eight short lines, his voice inflates and becomes resonant with a newfound authority and prophetic voice—"We are fated to beget a new and violent tribe"—a voice echoing such previous authorities as Milton, Virgil, and above all Genesis.

To see this, let us look again at the poem more closely:

"Flight" ("Ucieczka")

> When we were fleeing the burning city
> And looked back from the first field path,
> I said: "Let the grass grow over our footprints,
> Let the harsh prophets fall silent in the fire,
> Let the dead explain to the dead what happened.
> We are fated to beget a new and violent tribe
> Free from the evil and the happiness that drowsed there.
> Let us go"—and the earth was opened for us by a sword of flames.
> (NCP, 74)[14]

As mentioned earlier, Milosz wrote this poem after he and Janka had escaped from the rubble of a Warsaw that the Germans would soon systematically destroy. But in this brief poem the speaker is escaping not just a city but its moribund culture, and pronounces himself "fated" (*znaczono*, designated) to beget a wholly new one, free from "the evil and the happiness" that had sedated the past.

To speak this way in ordinary tones would invite disbelief, perhaps derision. But Milosz in this brief poem, having lost his last Warsovian attachments, has acquired in their place the extra-temporal Tiresian voice of *The Waste Land* he carried with him out of the burning city.[15]

To begin with, I sense here a repeat of the uncertain optimism, seeing possible hope in violent and disruptive invasion, that marks the finale of Mickiewicz's *Pan Tadeusz*, as described by Milosz himself in his *History of Polish Literature*: "*Pan Tadeusz* is also a vast panorama of gentry society at the moment it is living through its last days. . . . The element of politics is not lacking. . . . At the end of the poem the young generation dons the uniform of the Polish Napoleonic army and in response to the spirit of the day proclaims the peasant a free citizen" (HPL, 228–29).

In four Polish words, "the happiness that drowsed there" ("szczęścia, które tam drzemało"), Milosz similarly turns away from the Nawloć of prewar Polish culture, all of it: from the gentry elegance of Iwaszkiewicz and the Skamander group to the card-playing workers in "Outskirts." In the last line, now freed from that culture, the Milosz persona finally uses six Polish words—"Idźmy. A miecz płomieni otwierał nam ziemię" (verbatim: "Let us go"—and "a sword of flames opened for us the earth")—to claim, and describe, an experience of biblical portent.

Especially in that last line, the poem carries echoes of Genesis 3:24 ("flaming sword"), Virgil's *Aeneid* (2:705ss: "Haste, goddess-born, and out of yonder flames, / achieve thy flight"), Milton's *Paradise Lost*, (12, 645–46, see below), Eliot's *Waste Land* ("Burning burning burning burning / O Lord Thou pluckest me out") and perhaps even Blake and Oscar Milosz.[16]

Some of these observations are not new. Critics have long recognized that the speaker in "Flight" evokes the fated escape of Aeneas from burning Troy (*Aeneid* 2:705ss), but without acknowledging the daring of Milosz's superimposing, on this escape to a new culture, the expulsion of Adam and Eve from Eden.

In the words of George Gömöri, "Here the poet is not unlike Aeneas carrying Anchises out of Troy on his back. In following years, the function of the myth changes: it is no longer a forecast but a point of reference belonging to the past. After all, Warsaw *did* suffer the fate of Troy, the end of the world *did* take place, and nobody took notice of it."[17]

Aleksander Fiut, Milosz's best Polish critic, has a deeper appreciation of the allusions in the poem: "The flight from Warsaw in flames recalls the scene of Adam and Eve's expulsion from Eden, Lot's escape from Sodom and Gomorrah [Genesis 19:15–23], and the rescue of Aeneas."[18]

But in the poem's close—with its biblical flaming sword, and the last surprising verbs, "drowsed" and "opened"—the poem is also apocalyptic, even prophetic, in a way that suggests (to Anglophones more clearly than to Poles) Milton and perhaps Blake. Clearly Milosz is thinking of the close to *Paradise Lost*, which he translated into Polish at this time:

> Som natural tears they drop'd, but wip'd them soon;
> The World was all before them, where to choose.[19]

Milosz later commented,

> There was pleasure in translating Milton in the summer of 1945 in Kraków.
> ... We were *in partibus daemonis* [in the regions of the devil], and tied to our fate. Milton's cosmic visions suited, I would say, as our key to experience.[20]

But the violence in the poem's close—

> We are fated to beget a new and violent [*gwaltowne*] tribe,
> Free from the evil and the happiness that drowsed there,

suggests, and may remember, the way that Blake took up and developed Milton's depiction of Adam and Eve's catastrophic expulsion, from limited consciousness to an open future:

> The ancient tradition that the world will be consumed in fire at the end of six thousand years is true, as I have heard from Hell.
> For the cherub with his flaming sword is hereby commanded to leave his guard at the tree of life, and when he does, the whole creation will be consumed and appear infinite and holy whereas it now appears finite & corrupt. . . .
> If the doors of perception were cleansed everything would appear to man as it is, infinite.[21]

The "world" in Blake's passage is, as others have noted, the world of Ulro, "the distracting illusion we have of the material world that is not God, not imagination."[22] (It is possible also that Milosz was influenced in this line by his cousin Oscar, Milosz informs us that his cousin Oscar Milosz had not read Blake; but Oscar's prediction of a fortunate destruction and violent rebirth was remarkably similar.)[23]

The most audacious feature of Milosz's new undivided voice here, no longer that of a "crippled man" like the "Poor Poet" or the "Poor Christian," is that, after two lines in the voice of a Pole fleeing Warsaw, he assumes, more confidently than his model Eliot before him, the authority of a prophet foretelling a liberated future.[24]

In thus freeing himself from a nationalistic Polish culture, Milosz has now participated for the first time in the on-going discourse of the western canon, and this not by just echoing the great voices of the past, but by fusing them into a prophetic view of the future, in a novel and generative way.

Just how unique this fusion is can be seen by comparing this short poem with the opening of Wordsworth's *Prelude*. There too Wordsworth dares to invest his leaving a city (Goslar) with biblical overtones: having already invoked Exodus by declaring his escape from "a house of bondage" (Exodus 20:2), he then quickly invokes the passage already quoted from Milton:

> The earth is all before me . . . and should the guide I choose
> Be nothing better than a wandering cloud
> I cannot miss my way
> (*Prelude* [1805], I, 5, 14, 16–17)

But Wordsworth here is not yet claiming any other role than that of his personal adventure. What Milosz claims here is so audacious, so unlike his usual previous style, that we have I think to attribute it to forces from outside his normal presentational self, whether we choose to think of the caldron of disruption around him, or the inner domain of what Milosz calls his *daimonion*.[25] From a merely human speaker, the effect would suggest satire, or invite it.

Milosz indicates that in "In Warsaw," the final poem of *Ocalenie*, he was indeed "possessed" in this external way:

> I did not want to pity so.
> That was not my design. . . .
> I hear voices, see smiles. I cannot
> Write anything; five hands
> Seize my pen and order me to write
> The story of their lives and deaths.
> Was I born to become
> a ritual mourner?
> I want to sing of festivities. . . .
>
> (NCP, 75–76)

As we shall see, further evidence that "In Warsaw" was dictated to him, rather than composed by him, is his remark to Renata Gorczyńska, that it was "a moral reaction . . . that poem was jotted down on a scrap of paper in half a minute."[26]

Other such generative poems—poems that defined their era and thus inaugurated a new one—were similarly composed by poets who at that moment were similarly "possessed" and not their normal selves. I am referring above all to Wordsworth's "Tintern Abbey" and Eliot's *The Waste Land*. And I find it no coincidence that Milosz in this period, having already translated *The Waste Land* for his intended anthology, now translated "Tintern Abbey" as well.[27]

One could say much more about the relevant content of these poems, and the tradition to which they both belong. Here I wish to focus on the way these poems imposed themselves on their authors, all three of whom had witnessed major social breakdowns.

I have already described Milosz's own psychic confusion at Goszyce. Seamus Heaney has written about Wordsworth's "breakdown in the early 1790s because of emotional crises (the outbreak of war between England and France separated him from his French love and mother of his child) and political confusions (the reign of Terror had dismayed supporters of the Revolution) [followed by] the 1798 edition of *Lyrical Ballads*, the epoch-making volume that initiates modern poetry."[28]

"Lines Written a Few Miles Above Tintern Abbey," the climactic finale to that volume, was in fact (according to Wordsworth's diary) composed on the road as he walked back to Bristol with his sister: "Not a line of it was altered, and not any part of it written down till I reached Bristol."[29]

Eliot, after losing a close friend in World War I, wrote *The Waste Land* in 1921–1922 in a condition of nervous exhaustion, for which he took three months' leave from his job at the bank. (The poem was completed while Eliot was receiving psychiatric treatment in Lausanne.)[30]

What is striking is here is that all three poets, suffering acute mental stress themselves in response to social breakdown, produced great works, in styles novel for them, that had a healing influence on those who came after them. This topic will be developed in my last chapter.[31]

Both Wordsworth and Eliot, as they healed, developed a sense of responsibility for correcting the culture of their times. Milosz, sensing the vacuum after the tragic fiasco of the Warsaw Uprising, moved to fill it with what Poland needed. "Flight," in eight lines, provided Poles with a memory of their rich cultural past—Biblical, classical, and romantic—to preserve in a violent and uncertain future. More than this, it did so by wedding, for the first time, the Polish vision of Mickiewicz to the complex western canon of Milton, Blake, and Eliot.

This was an achievement of major cultural significance, as Poland was about to enter a half-century of Soviet domination.

POSTSCRIPT: MILOSZ'S MINOR GOSZYCE POEMS

At Goszyce, Milosz wrote three other short poems for *Ocalenie*, all minor and never translated, but nonetheless interesting as evidence of his altered state at this crucial moment.[32] Each of them, in its own way, looks expectantly to the future. "*Los*" ("Lot," in the sense of either "Fate" or "Luck"), the first, asks cosmic questions in the style of Blake—"Are they the same—the acorn and hoary oak?"—and then ends,

> Let my poems go whatever way they want,
> Let my girls give birth to other children,
> To me is given coal, oak, and a ring, and the foamy wave.
> (W 1:223)[33]

Milosz later commented to Renata Gorczyńska that the poem "is based on cutting oneself off from the past, on forgetting, making a new beginning, which was nothing unusual in those circumstances."[34]

"Lot" is followed by another short lyric, "A Wish." Addressing his wife Janka, it recalls their shared escape, and ends with an even more resounding affirmative:

> Dear companion of our bloody trek
> Through the land of fire and war, air and hunger,
> May our hearts not be crushed by the call of anyone! . . .
> So that . . .
> They said, from the heavens . . .
> "Listen, humanity lives, our joy lives."
> (W 1:224)

These Goszyce poems have as context the Soviet future that was replacing a German present, but none as directly as the last:

> "Complaint of Ladies from a Bygone Time"
>
> Our flowing dresses fell on the road
> Pearls fell into the deep historical abyss,
> Wind chased flakes of burnt ribbon across the waters
> And in the dark people yanked the rings from our fingers.
>
> Our ornate coiffures, which the skill of a master
> Had woven with silver nests, flowers, paradisal feathers,
> Crumbled, and fell in ash into the dark.
>
> And when the dawn rose transparent from the sea,
> We walked naked on the walls of the new Babylon
> Trying to remember something with wrinkled brows.
> (W 1:225)

As so often in *Ocalenie*, there are two conflicting ways to read this poem. The stripping naked of the women can be seen as referring to their destitution and helplessness but also to their liberation from their oppressive past. Milosz wrote later of the same ambivalence, speaking of just this period: "What appeared to be the end was not the end of either tradition or literature or of art. . . . To track down and root out of oneself all vestiges of the past—what disruption and what temptation to regret! But also what purity of air, what nakedness, what readiness to face the future" (NR, 247).

Milosz later told Gorczyńska, "One way or another, the poem contains an awareness of enormous change. The Russians will be arriving any minute, there will be a new, different world."[35] This contrast between past and future must have been particularly vivid at the rustic manor (*dwór*) of Goszyce, in the last hours of a privileged lifestyle about to disappear forever.

When I first read this poem, I was startled and offended by its apparent indifference to the Soviet armies' orgy of mass rapes, gang-rapes, and rape-murders that had immediately begun with their arrival.[36] The poem is indeed suggestive of violation and rape, and can be read as accepting the yanking of rings from fingers as the inevitable cost of a violent transition to a new era.

(The problem of rape was enormous but also unmentionable directly in Polish media—unmentionable, indeed, until after the withdrawal of the Soviet army four decades later. It certainly could not be brought up overtly in a poem that was published in Warsaw in 1945.)

My reaction was and remains that mass rape is perhaps too overwhelming to be dealt with in poetry, even obliquely by allusion; and that "Complaint" was too light a lyric to deal with such a tragedy. But on re-reading, I see that the last two lines ("We walked naked on the walls of the new Babylon / Trying to remember something with wrinkled brows") are not light. On the contrary, they contain the distinctive admixture of catastrophe and hope at the end of "Flight" ("We are fated to beget a new and violent tribe, / Free from the evil and the happiness that drowsed there"). The two closures to "Flight" and "Complaint"—"drowsed," "trying to remember"—share a sense of awakening from a dreamy past to a violent new Babylon, one in which we are naked and free.

Nevertheless, in my view, this poem, in its uncomfortable proximity to the women's actual fate, strikes me as hollow and insensitive—reflective of a misogynistic streak one can detect elsewhere in Milosz's poetry.[37] Its hollowness is of course radically reinforced by the failure of postwar Poland to provide anything like the new society Milosz's poems hinted at.

Late in life, after winning the Nobel Prize, Milosz wrote that "The poetic act both anticipates the future and speeds its coming" (WP, 109). In describing "Complaint," Milosz spoke of its "awareness of enormous change [to], a new, different world."[38] But the world foreseen in this poem would soon be foreseeable in Poland no more.

Chapter 8

Ocalenie Part V: The Three Final Poems

After "Flight," Milosz wrote three more poems, "Farewell," "In Warsaw," and "Przedmowa," that were all included in *Ocalenie* and then translated into English for the climax of "Rescue."[1] I believe that, along with "Flight," they represent Milosz's first full performance as what Pablo Neruda, in his *Memoirs*, called a "social poet . . . still a member of the earliest order of priests."

All three poems still focus on the legacy of the war, but from a new and different perspective: after the war and in retrospect, among ruins. They now also have to deal with the new reality of a Stalinist Poland, whose condition was less violent than the recent past under Nazi occupation, but also far more certain to be long-lived and deeply invasive. This further intensification of catastrophe, like the destruction of Warsaw preceding it, also served to concentrate and intensify Milosz's poetic response.

The first is "Farewell" ("Pożegnanie"), which Milosz composed in Kraków in early 1945. Kraków was then a nightmare city. In Milosz's words, "The security police's building was right there, and it was filled with the young people [the Doomed Soldiers] Wajda tried to portray in the movie *Ashes and Diamonds*. The scenes at the rain station were straight out of Dante. It was a migration of nations. Millions of homeless people coming from the east and the west. The terrible world of the spring of 1945. That reality is reflected in this poem."[2]

Along with "Songs of Adrian Zielinski," "Farewell" in *Ocalenie* immediately follows the *persona* poems of "Voices of Poor People." It is not itemized among them, however. Instead, somewhat like Eliot's "Gerontion," the persona is a tragic transitional figure of stature, rather than a "poor" one, lamenting his doomed culture—that of the doomed Second Polish Republic. Like Moses on Mount Nebo, he sees a future he cannot enter, and says "Farewell" also to those who are moving on. The poem is one of great dignity and authority; and, for the first time in the book, makes references to salvation, and a saving power that is not for the speaker.[3]

The speaker is in Verona, a screen for Warsaw. The city now "is no more," gone with the nationalism for which it suffered:

> Verona is no more.
> I crumbled its brickdust in my fingers. That is what remains
> Of the great love of native cities.
> (NCP, 72)[4]

But the loss is not total:

> I hear your laughter in the garden. And the mad spring's
> scent comes toward me across the wet leaves.
> Toward me, who, not believing in any saving power [*zbawczą moc*]
> outlived the others and myself as well.

A discrepancy has emerged in the gloom. The "mad spring" disturbs the old man, even more than "depraved May" disturbed Eliot's "Gerontion."

> Children's laughter in the garden. A first clear star
> above a foam of buds on the hills
> and a light song returns to my lips
> and I am young again, as before, in Verona.

But this jolt from his past energizes him only to reject it. "A nightingale is singing," but its song is as alien to the speaker as the mermaids were to Prufrock:

> To reject. To reject everything. That is not it.
> It will neither resurrect the past nor return me to it.
> Sleep, Romeo, Juliet, on your headrest of stone feathers.
> I won't raise your bound hands from the ashes.
> Let the cat visit the deserted cathedrals,
> its pupil flashing on the altars. Let an owl
> nest on the dead ogive. . . .
> I won't return. I want to know what's left
> after rejecting youth and spring. . . .
> (NCP, 72)[5]

The oxymoron "stone feathers" recalls the oxymoron "feather of lead" spoken by Romeo after learning that his cousin, Benvolio, has fought with the Capulets ("Feather of lead, bright smoke, cold fire, sick health," *Romeo and Juliet*, I.i.173). Romeo's oxymoron reflects his ambivalence about the love and violence of Verona; Milosz's old man reflects his ambivalence about a lost era.

At the end of the poem the persona returns to the question of salvation, alluding again to Eden in the manner of "Flight"

> From life, from the apple cut by the flaming knife,
> what grain will be saved [*Jakie ocali się ziarno*]?[6]

—only to close the door on such hopes for himself—

> My son, believe me, nothing remains.
> Only adult toil,
> the furrow of fate in the palm.
> Only toil,
> Nothing more.[7]

The poem, in Milosz's words, "contains both despair and an acceptance of the new world."[8]

THE COMPOSITION OF "IN WARSAW" AND OF "PRZEDMOWA"

The stage is thus set for the last two poems to be written, "In Warsaw" and "Przedmowa." These escalate to yet another new tone, daring to indicate precisely how good poetry might still save people in a hopeless time, for which no political solution was then visible.

My high esteem for "In Warsaw" has to deal with the low opinion expressed by Milosz himself.[9] Unasked, he volunteered to Gorczyńska: "that poem was jotted down on a scrap of paper in half a minute. And—as is often the case with my poems—I don't consider it a poem, just a note."[10] But Milosz, who frequently declined to anthologize both "In Warsaw" and "Przedmowa," is here downplaying the work that went into its composition. Franaszek clarifies that it was only the "outline" of the poem that was "scribbled . . . on small pages pulled from a notebook," in response to the shock of returning to the remains of Warsaw.[11] But that was only the beginning of the process.

Milosz himself once said, "I cannot imagine writing poetry without the first impulse coming from [my *daimonion*]—and then, after the first line of a poem is given, my hard work starts."[12] Here, as often, he attributes all of his poetry to daemonic inspiration. But it also clear that "In Warsaw," like "Hymn" earlier, was written in an outburst of possession—*furor poeticus*—that like "Flight" was a response to an overwhelming traumatic experience of destruction.

Importantly, that initial speed of the poem's composition explains its archetypal simplicity and epideictic clarity, what we saw earlier in "Flight." "In Warsaw" is not exactly unprecedented; it is rather a culmination of energies gathering in *Ocalenie* ever since "The World." But the diction, in both it and "Przedmowa," achieves a new and calm sublime, which has no more need to echo scripture for its elevation.

What do I mean by calm sublime? Here is the opening of "In Warsaw":

> What are you doing here, poet, on the ruins
> Of St. John's Cathedral this sunny
> Day in spring?

And here is the opening of "Przedmowa":

> You whom I could not save
> Listen to me.
> Try to understand this simple speech [*prosta mowa*] as I
> would be ashamed of another.
> I swear, there is in me no wizardry of words.
> I speak to you with silence like a cloud or a tree.

Blake knew how to write language that was both elevated and simple:

> And did those feet in ancient time
> Walk upon Englands mountains green.

But both of Milosz's poems address the agonies of war ("How can I live in a country / Where the foot knocks against / The unburied bones of kin?") in a tone that transcends agony, speaking in the end calmly of "joy" in the first poem, and of "salvation" in the second.

The opening of "In Warsaw"—despite the rapid composition of the poem's outline—is carefully composed, linking directly in its opening to both the pessimism of "Farewell," and the hope in "Przedmowa":

> What are you doing [*Co czynisz*] here, poet, on the ruins
> Of St. John's Cathedral this sunny
> Day in spring?
> What are you thinking here, where the wind
> Blowing from the Vistula scatters
> The red dust of the rubble?
>
> You swore never to be
> A ritual mourner.

Ocalenie Part V: The Three Final Poems   97

> You swore never to touch
> The deep wounds of your nation
> So you would not make them holy
> With the accursed holiness that pursues
> Descendants for many centuries.
> (NCP, 75)

The poet addressed here sounds very much like the speaker who in "Farewell" recalled the suicide of nationalism.

> Verona is no more.
> I crumbled its brickdust in my fingers. That is what remains
> Of the great love of native cities.

The parallels continue. Both poems are dominated by a tension between the reality of rubble and mourning, versus the human needs of spring, laughter and song. Both in this respect bring in Shakespeare: the tragedy of urban love gone awry in *Romeo and Juliet* ("Farewell") opposed to the pastoral "greenwood" of festivities in comedy ("In Warsaw"; Milosz at the time was translating *As You Like It* for Warsaw's Underground Theater Council).[13]

But the speaker and addressee in the opening of "In Warsaw" link also to those in the opening of "Przedmowa" ("Dedication"). In chapter 2 we considered this poem from a political perspective; it is time now to consider its poetry.

> You whom I could not save
> Listen to me
> Try to understand this simple speech [*prosta mowa*] as I
>   would be ashamed of another.
> I swear, there is in me no wizardry of words.
> I speak to you with silence like a cloud or a tree.
>
> What strengthened me, for you was lethal.
> You mixed up farewell to an epoch with the beginning of a new one,
> Inspiration of hatred with lyrical beauty,
> Blind force with accomplished shape.
>
> Here is the valley of shallow Polish rivers. And an immense
>   bridge
> Going into white fog. Here is a broken city,
> And the wind throws the screams of gulls on your grave
> When I am talking with you.

> What is poetry which does not save
> Nations or people?
> A connivance with official lies,
> A song of drunkards whose throats will be cut in a moment,
> Readings for sophomore girls.
>
> That I wanted good poetry without knowing it,
> That I discovered, late, its salutary aim,
> This is, and only this is, salvation.
>
> They used to pour millet on graves or poppy seeds
> To feed the dead who would come disguised as birds.
> I put this book here for you, who once lived
> So that you should visit us no more.
> (NCP, 77)[14]

The "dark love" contrasted to the "greenwood" in "In Warsaw" underlie, I believe, the difference between the poet and addressee in "Przedmowa"'s second stanza, which I will repeat here in a slightly more literal translation,

> What strengthened me, for you was lethal.
> You *took* [*brałeś*] farewell to an epoch *as* the beginning of a
>   new one,
> Blind force *as* accomplished shape [*ksztalt*]

The last line here is alluding to a choice in lifestyle that corresponds closely to a choice between romantic and post-romantic poetic style.

The poet addressed in "Przedmowa" (the "You" of the first line is in Polish "Ty," "Thou") is clearly someone who has perished in the Home Army's Warsaw Uprising, another of the doomed Polish revolts which Milosz (himself in a more left-wing resistance group) deeply regretted.[15] Over and over in his prose and interviews, Milosz described his "antipathy for Polish messianism" and its cult of "redemptive martyrdom."[16]

A clue to the dead addressee in "Przedmowa" can be found in Milosz's comment to Gorczyńska that his creation, in "The World,"

> of an artificial world against the horror . . . is a very strange work, because it lays the fullest possible emphasis on the basic disagreement that had come between me and the young Warsaw poets from the "Art and the Nation" group, and Krzysztof Baczyński's group as well . . . I rebelled strongly against being swept away by events. They were all submerged, but I didn't want to be.[17]

Art and the Nation was published by a handful of very young students and militants of the Resistance:

all four of its editors perished.... Curiously enough, the monthly was politically bound to Rightist circles.... A colleague of these young men, though he did not associate with them, Krzysztof Kamil Baczyński ... edited another literary monthly.... [W]hat was said about the recurrence of Romantic patterns applies particularly to Baczyński's poetry, whose rich imagery served more and more overtly, as he developed, to point up his central theme of self-immolation for the sake of an ideal Poland.[18]

One reason to see the addressee in "Przedmowa" as the Home Army poet and martyr Baczyński is that his thematic poetry "of self-immolation for the sake of an ideal Poland" made him for Milosz the chief contemporary exemplar of the romantic tradition of "redemptive martyrdom."[19]

But the poem applies equally to anyone who died as a left-wing partisan fighting to overthrow the past, and bring in a new Marxist utopia. All factions erred in accepting and glorifying "blind force" and the "inspiration of hatred" in the name of a new epoch. And the tradition of Polish poetry that could not free itself from such inspiration was indeed "A song of drunkards whose throats will be cut in a moment."

Both in "Przedmowa" and "In Warsaw," Milosz is reconsidering Mickiewicz's immensely influential "Ode to Youth." On the one hand he still keeps alive, albeit by questioning rather than effusive affirmation, Mickiewicz's hope that history leads to salvation:

> Youth! Your power is your eagles' flight,
> Like thunder is your arm. . . .
>
> The impassive ice is vanishing,
> So are the superstitions which dim the sun:
> Welcome, O morning star of liberty,
> What comes after you is the sun of salvation![20]

On the other hand, he is clearly condemning the Ode's call for heroic self-sacrifice:

> On! On! young friends, nor fear to fall!
> He too knows joy and gladness, he who fell . . .
> For, by his sacrifice,
> He helped attain his country's fame!"[21]

Milosz wants to save the Mickiewicz of non-verbal mystery from the Mickiewicz of suicidal nationalism. Thus the poet in the last stanza places his book *Ocalenie* on the grave of the dead militant, "so that you should visit us no more"—this gesture follows the Lithuanian folk ritual described in

Mickiewicz's "Forefather's Eve" of "calling on the dead and offering them food" (HPL, 215).

As I wrote in chapter 2, Milosz is hoping to rid Poland from its obsessive cult of martyrdom, But in doing so, by invoking the ritualistic Lithuanian life of his childhood, he is also celebrating a "pre-scientific" state of mind which for him was exemplified by Mickiewicz at his best: "Mickiewicz sprang from a hinterland untouched by the skepticism of the Age of Reason. . . . Indeed, Mickiewicz's imagination never divested itself of pre-scientific cosmologies. . . . In times of national and personal crisis, Mickiewicz would draw on beliefs that were the antithesis of modernity" (LU, 103–4).

This would later become Milosz's model for addressing, in *The Land of Ulro*, a crisis that was not just Poland's but the world's. But one can sense that, already in "In Warsaw" and "Przedmowa," Milosz's *daimonion* was moving him in this direction.

POSTSCRIPT: "TRUTH AND JUSTICE"—AND MADNESS

"In Warsaw"'s last stanza is easily misread:

> It's madness to live without joy
> And to repeat to the dead
> Whose part was to be gladness
> Of action [*czynów*] in thought and in the flesh, singing, feasts,
> Only the two salvaged [*ocalone*] words:
> Truth and justice. (NCP 76)[22]

The main clause of this stanza is "It's madness to live without joy and to repeat to the dead. . . . Only the two salvaged words: Truth and justice" ("Prawda i sprawiedliwość"). In the last stanza of the book *Ocalenie*, the poem (like "Przedmowa" at the book's opening) uses a form of the verb *ocalić*, "to save." But it does so in an ironic and surprising way.

Irony can also be found in Milosz's later poem "Incantation" ("Zaklęcie"), where "Truth" and "Justice" are more clearly identified as finite products of "Human reason":

> Human reason is beautiful and invincible. . . .
> It establishes the universal ideas in language,
> And guides our hand so we write Truth and Justice
> With capital letters, lie and oppression with small.
> (NCP, 239)

Adam Kirsch, generally a brilliant essayist, later wrote: "the title of the poem is 'Incantation.' In other words, these humane formulas are a spell, a chant we utter to give ourselves the illusion of potency. The belief in reason, the title implies, is unreasonable, and Milosz's experiences gave ample support for this idea."[23]

But Milosz wrote of the importance of incantations, not as temporary illusions, but as a necessary, albeit irrational, reassertion and promotion of harmony in the midst of unbearable horror:

> Gentle verses written in the midst of horror declare themselves for life; they are the body's rebellion against its destruction. They are *carmina*, or incantations [*zaklęcia*] deployed in order that the horror should disappear for a moment and harmony emerge.... They comfort us, giving us to understand that what takes place in *anus mundi* is transitory, and that harmony is enduring—which is not at all a certainty.[24]

In "The World" the father "murmurs his incantations" ("zaklęcia"), which elevate him through love:

> O sweet master, with how much peace
> Your serene wisdom fills the heart!
> I love you, I am in your power
> Even though I will never see your face.
> (NCP 42)

The end of "In Warsaw" warns that it is madness to pursue ideas "without joy." Gladness and singing [and love] are needed to humanize these ideas of "truth" and "justice." By themselves, as raw ideology deprived of their cultural origins, they could only, Milosz had every reason to believe in 1945, lead to a Stalinist nightmare. So Milosz's poem is not just a lament for the past, like "the lament of Antigone / Searching for her brother" Polynices, it is also a spell for a kinder, more humane future of human joy.

Milosz's rejection of Antigone's lament reflects his politics. Polynices died in a Theban civil war, occasioned by the fratricidal conflict between two brothers. As we have seen, in 1945 Poland also faced the beginnings of a fratricidal civil war between the Communist and anti-Communist (Doomed Soldiers) resistance factions that during the war had both fought the Nazis.

I believe that Milosz's spell is cast against both joyless factions in this conflict: on the one hand against Stalinist rationalism, but also against the messianic Polish nationalism that, following Mickiewicz, saw Poland as the "Christ of Nations" ("Polska Chrystusem narodów"). For Poles know that, in a famous passage, Mickiewicz had written (in capital letters) that Christ himself had said "I AM TRUTH AND JUSTICE."[25]

In other words, "Truth" and "Justice" were in 1945 Poland words that instead of uniting the country, were symptoms of its chaos. As I wrote earlier, Milosz wanted to save the Mickiewicz of nonverbal and nonrational mystery from the Mickiewicz of homicidal and suicidal nationalism. By this purification of the romantic tradition, Milosz hoped to help save Poland from itself. (That message is relevant for Poland today, as its governing party of Law and Justice [Prawo i Sprawiedliwość, PiS, "with capital letters"], distances itself from western Europe and struggles to revive the divisive nationalism that Milosz contested.)

If incantations are "unreasonable," as Kirsch avers, this only reflects the inadequacy of reason by itself, according to Milosz, to cope with an unreasonable world. The same spirit explains why Milosz' important book about nineteenth century thought, *The Land of Ulro*, ends with incantatory talk of "an idyllic earth where 'the hay smells of the dream'" (LU, 275).

It is important to keep this in mind when, in the next chapter, we examine Milosz's adoption of a superficially classical style in his "Treatise on Morals" ("Traktat moralny").

PART III

Milosz After the War (1946–1960)

Chapter 9

Milosz, Auden, and "A Treatise on Morals"

There is a place at the bottom of the graves where contraries are equally true.

—Blake, *A Vision*

In 1945, life began to be re-established in Poland under the new post-war government. So did literature, and even, after a while, literary presses and journals. *Ocalenie* was published in a 1945 Warsaw that was 96 percent destroyed, but also relatively calm. It was the beginning of the era described by Milosz in *The Captive Mind* (1953), when authors, determined that literature should survive, wrote cautiously in a manner calculated to get by the censors.

These authors included Milosz himself, still hoping to function in postwar and post-Yalta Poland. But for the years 1946 to 1951, Milosz was now stationed abroad as a diplomat for the new coalition government, first in New York, and then in Washington. So it was in a quite different intellectual environment that, in 1946/1947, he wrote both prose and poetry in defense of *Ocalenie*.

A decade later, safely in exile, Milosz summed up the complexity of his situation:

Many were amazed at my cunning or my insensibility to totalitarian atrocities; they saw my stance as the height of hypocrisy. But it was not, perhaps, hypocrisy. In the teaching of "Ketman" practiced by Mohammedan heretics in Persia [the act of paying lip service to Islam while concealing secret opposition] (it was not unlike the Jesuit *reservatio mentalis*), a distinction was made between the goal toward which we fervently and passionately strive and the veils by which the prudent screen it from view. . . . I praised my time and I did not yearn for any other. Nor did I pine for Poland's prewar social economic order; anyone

105

who dreamed of its resurrection was my adversary. In this sense, my service at the Embassy coincided with my conviction. However, I wished my country a considerably better fate than that of a Stalinist province. (NR, 269)

In *The Captive Mind*, Milosz devoted an entire chapter to the ways in which Polish writers under Stalin practiced Ketman. One of these was Aesthetic Ketman, the practice of escaping from an alienating present by focusing on the exotic or the past:

> Aesthetic Ketman . . . is expressed in that unconscious longing for strangeness which is channeled toward controlled amusements like theater, film, and folk festivals, but also into various forms of escapism. . . . Many choose university careers because research into literary history offers a safe pretext for plunging into the past and for converse with works of great aesthetic value.[1]

Milosz may have described his own Ketman in "Greek Portrait," a short poem he wrote "for the drawer" (a Polish term from that era, meaning "not to be shared") in Washington in 1948 (and one of the first poems he set me to translating).

> I keep quiet as is proper
> For a man who has learned that the human heart
> Holds more than speech does. I have left behind
> My native land, home, and public office. . . .
> My plain face, the face of a tax-collector,
> Merchant, or soldier, makes me one of the crowd.
> Nor do I refuse to pay due homage
> To local gods. And I eat what others eat.
> About myself, this much will suffice.
> (NCP, 166)

Milosz later said of this poem, "Yes, it's a mask. What can you do with a strange guy who doesn't understand himself?"[2] But a mask in a free country is normally associated with diversion, theater, carnival. When, however, the environment is hostile and treacherous, a mask is used for concealment and survival.

For the rest of his life, even after his return to Poland, Milosz would live among people with backgrounds so different that he would be mindful of, and write about, the difference between his public and his deep persona.[3]

Recalling that Ketman is the art of maintaining a gap between what our heart holds and what our speech shares, we should be reminded by this poem, in the course of this chapter about Milosz's mask of anti-romanticism, that Ketman was not and is not practiced only in Islam and Stalinist Poland.[4]

MILOSZ'S DEFENSE OF *OCALENIE* IN 1946

As soon as *Ocalenie* was published in 1945, a controversy arose over its rejection of Poland's long romantic tradition of lethal uprisings, including the Home Army's Warsaw Uprising. The book was criticized, even by friends like Kazimierz Wyka, for its "aestheticism" and detachment.[5] In particular, a review by Dominik Horodyński accused Milosz of escapism and an inability to participate in the fate of the nation. "The cause of this tragic climate is the way you lived through the war. There is not a single word about fighting, heroism, or sacrifice."[6]

Milosz took these reviews seriously, and responded to them at length twice in works that had to pass the watchful eyes of Polish censors. The first time was in his thoughtful prose "Semi-Private Letter [to Wyka] about Poetry." A year later he published, in response to Horodyński,[7] his even longer poetic "Treatise on Morals" ("Traktat moralny"). This opened with the question, "What's this, poet, about salvation [*ocalenie*]?" and concluded (as we shall see) with the answer that

> salvation [*ocalenie*] is only in you
> Perhaps it is simply a healthy mind
> And a balanced heart.
> (W 2:98–99)

Both works reflect the influence of two major thinkers who influenced Milosz at this time; The first was his Polish Hegelian friend "Tiger" (Julius Kroński), to whom Milosz dedicates two chapters in his memoir *Native Realm*. (Kroński, like other Poles in the aftermath of the war, was "closest in spirit to eighteenth-century Enlightenment rationalism.")[8] And the second was W. H. Auden, whom I suspect Milosz may have met at this time in New York.[9] In their very diverse ways, both Kroński and Auden, dealing with the disasters of war and its aftermath, sought equanimity in a longer and lighter perspective—a classical one, in short.

This is the remedy proposed by Milosz in his "Letter" to Wyka, which advocated moving from the French barricades poetry of Aragon and Eluard to "the different turn in the Anglo-Saxon countries"—the works of Eliot, Auden, and specifically Karl Shapiro's *Essay on Rime* (a long verse-essay heavily influenced by Auden's *The Double Man*). In Milosz's eyes, these poets provided "new tunnels" for poetry, by "turning back to before the nineteenth century in search of forms of expression" that "compel the contemporary artist to utter freshness and sensitivity."[10]

Milosz noted, "in sorrow," that "at the present moment Polish literature is entering upon a renaissance of Romanticism." Those critics claiming to be left-wing Humanists were (by defending heroic martyrdom) in fact "Romantic arsonists . . . convinced that civilization dates from the nineteenth century."[11]

He concluded by quoting the last two lines of a quatrain from Mickiewicz, which I give here in full to convey his intention:

> [But when the sun of freedom will shine
> What insect will fly out from that envelope?]
> Will it be a bright butterfly soaring over the earth,
> Or a moth, dirty tribe of the night?[12]

Milosz's answer to Mickiewicz's question: "It seems it will be a Romantic moth. For Poles . . . will become entangled in a web of lies, like the émigrés, in a slightly different, leftist nationalist mode, *which, in the final analysis, makes no difference*."[13] (Consider my comments above about "Truth" and "Justice.")

In his response, Milosz declared, "I prefer Krasicki's *Myszeis* [The Mouseiad] in which the phrase 'Sacred love of our beloved Fatherland' appears on the occasion of a war among mice."[14] Yet, after Milosz's praise of lightness, he concluded more seriously, in a Warsaw already governed and censored by the postwar government,

> Faith in an arcadian myth is by no means a crime. . . . Sometimes the world loses its face. It becomes too base. The task of the poet is to restore its face, because otherwise man is lost in doubt and despair. It is an indication that the world need not always be like this, it can be different. . . .
>
> When I wrote in the introduction to *Rescue* [i.e., in "Przedmowa"] that I accepted the salvational goal of poetry [*wybaczny cel poezji*], that was exactly what I had in mind, and I still believe that poetry can either save or destroy nations [*narody ocalać, albo gubić*].[15]

Milosz was writing for the censor in 1946, and to a culture for whose future he was gravely concerned. It is possible to see a touch of Ketman (for the censor), even of the incantatory (for the culture), in this conversion of "Przedmowa"'s open question into a bald statement. But it represents an aspect of Milosz's polyphonous genius, one that would assert just as baldly, in *The Witness of Poetry* (1982), that "the poetic act both anticipates the future and speeds its coming" (WP, 109).

MILOSZ, AUDEN, AND DOUBLENESS ("DOUBLE FOCUS")

This apparent endorsement of the hope raised in "Przedmowa" has to be tempered by his earlier comment in the Letter that the poems in *Ocalenie* employed "the stylistic methods of pamphlet writing, of 'persiflage [*persiflaż*], and even of a philosophical treatise.'"[16] To say that *Ocalenie* was written in the style of persiflage ('light and slightly contemptuous mockery or banter') can be attributed to Milosz's Ketman: mindful of the Polish censors, he had already put on a mask."[17]

However, the quote exactly describes Milosz's "A Treatise on Morals" ("Traktat moralny," 1947), a long semi-satirical poetic essay written in rhymed Swiftian couplets. This new style imitated the models of Karl Shapiro and W. H. Auden given in the "Semi-Private Letter," in particular Auden's *The Double Man*. (This is the under-appreciated original American edition of *New Year Letter*, more than doubled in length, scope, and depth by reflective endnotes).[18] In an essay that passed the censor in 1948, Milosz described *The Double Man* as "a great philosophical treatise written in verse."[19]

Milosz's reworking of Auden's work marks an important stage in his movement beyond romanticism, and also his transition from a Polish to a global poet. Though "A Treatise on Morals" is often described as untranslatable, its striking similarities and differences from *The Double Man* illustrate this development; so the two works will be discussed together.

These poems mark for both poets a very significant and similar transition in their lives. For the sake of this book, the transition may be summarized as a retrenchment of Blake's romanticist aspirations, in the light of Eliot's classicist critique of them, resulting in mental doubleness, or (Auden's term) "the gift of double focus" (v. 828).[20] In the spirit of Blake and Yeats, Auden added, in an endnote to this line, that "The Devil, indeed, is the father of Poetry, for poetry might be defined as the clear expression of mixed feelings."[21]

Stan Smith later defined "the gift of double focus" as "the ability to stand back from one's conditioned and conditional allegiances, and subject an insular inheritance to the look of the stranger."[22] In less idiosyncratic terms, I would see a "double focus" as the ability to understand and respond to both a held opinion and its contrary, or also the ability to look at the present up close and also from a distance. The ability to articulate one's inner doubleness, in short.

This marks an important phase in the evolution of postmodern literature "in its ironic self-undermining critical stance and in its commitment to doubleness."[23] In the words of Aidan Wasley, "Auden inaugurated a poetic vision of post-Modernist America as an open, inclusive text defined not in terms of shared ideals of national, ideological, or historical inheritance, but by the freedom, and necessity, to choose among the kaleidoscopic range of formal, cultural, or transnational poetic identities made available by the collapse of those earlier ideals."[24]

Auden's doubleness can perhaps be traced to his mixed impressions of the Spanish Civil War, where—unlike almost all other observers, including Orwell—he had the wisdom to perceive that there were rights and wrongs on both sides.[25] (This position resembled the plight of Milosz in 1940s Warsaw, both sympathetic to and alienated from both the nationalists of the right and the communists of the left.)

In Auden's resulting poem, "Spain 1937," History tells the poet that the choice "to build the Just City" is not made by surrender to one or another faction, but individually: "I am whatever you do."[26]

This agenda was repeated in his "September 1, 1939," which contemplated the dictators in the mad culture of Europe with the dispassionate wisdom of Thucydides. Inspired by the "Ironic points of light" that "Flash out wherever the Just / Exchange their messages," it prayed "May I," in the face of "Negation and despair, / Show an affirming flame."[27]

THE SEARCH FOR BALANCE IN AUDEN'S *LETTER* AND MILOSZ'S *TREATISE*

The agenda was more fully developed in *The Double Man* ("New Year Letter"), written in early 1940, during Auden's slow self-redefinition as a Christian rather than a Marxist. It can be described as a debate with himself, and has an epigraph from Montaigne that he found in a Christian book, *The Descent of the Dove*, by his friend Charles Williams: "We are, I know not how, double in ourselves, so that what we believe we disbelieve, and cannot rid ourselves of what we condemn."[28]

Central to both Auden's "Letter" and later Milosz's "Treatise on Morals" are the themes of dealing with the splitting into false absolutes bred by the master-servant relationship, which Auden discusses in terms of Blake's distinction between the Prolific and the Devourer. Both see doubleness as human, and also as diabolic.[29] For Auden, following his early mentor John Layard, the devil is the Ego's "lame fallen shadow" (v. 11), and also "the great schismatic who / First split creation into two" (vv. 559–60).[30]

Might Milosz be alluding to Auden's poem when he writes, in "A Treatise on Morals,"

> I'm just here to remind you,
> That the devil, as I know from reading,

is *séparé de lui-même?*[31]
(W 2:96)

For both poems see what Auden calls a resulting conflict between "PLATO's lie of intellect" and "ROUSSEAU's falsehood of the flesh" (vv., 1378, 1384).[32] This results in abuses of free will, in the Ego's

> ... cold *concupiscence d'esprit*
> That looks upon her liberty
> Not as a gift from life with which
> To serve, enlighten, and enrich
> The total creature that could use
> Her function of free will to choose
> The actions that this world requires
> To educate its blind desires
> But as the right to lead alone
> An attic life all on her own.
> (vv. 1400–09)

Developing a very similar argument against unfettered egoism in terms of recent cultural evolution, Milosz argues that survival depends on avoiding the freedom of choice that was favored in Paris, he suggested, by Sartrean existentialists:

> In spite of everything, the *Ding an Sich*
> Still lingers on in them
> So lost in the chaos
> They grasped at a new way,
> And still desiring something that would last,
> They found it: *Etre pour soi.*
> (W 2:90)

To escape this fallen condition, Auden sees us as climbing a "purgatorial hill" (v. 929) that has been "our residence since birth" (v. 949).

> Since over its ironic rocks
> No route is truly orthodox,
> O once again let us set out,
> Our faith well balanced by our doubt,[33]
> Admitting every step we make
> Will certainly be a mistake,
> But still believing we can climb
> A littler higher every time,
> And keep in order, that we may

> Ascend the penitential way
> That forces our will to be free,
> A reverent frivolity.
> (vv. 959–70)

This sense of purposeful freedom in Auden's poem is addressed to the individual. But in Milosz's poem Auden's "ironic rocks" play an opposite more positive role, helping not just to deal with the oppressive avalanche of twentieth-century history, but to mitigate it.

> And you float on this social fact
> Like a nut in a Nile cataract.
>
> But you are not so helpless,
> And even if you are but a stone in a field,
> The avalanche must alter its course
> By the stones over which it flows.
> And, as someone used to say,
> You can thus influence [*wpłyń*] the avalanche,
> Ease [*łagodź*] its savagery and cruelty,
> For this, one will need bravery.[34]
> (W 2:89)

A half-century later, in 1996, a much older Milosz commented that the avalanche and stones expressed "the philosophy of collaborators who joined the party while claiming they wanted to change it from the inside."[35] But the poem as a whole, appealing in the spirit of the rationalist Tiger[36] for the preservation of human values, suggests that Milosz himself at the time shared this quasi-Marxist belief in the role of human agency in cultural development (ethogeny). Already in his wartime writings (collected in *Legends of Modernity*), Milosz had suggested that amoralists like Nietzsche and Gide had contributed to the breakdown of twentieth-century culture. But if literature can be a force for evil, it can be a force for good as well.

Milosz's poem, like Auden's, seeks a remedy in equilibrium. Just as the pilgrimage in Auden's poem relied on a "faith well balanced by our doubt," so also Milosz suggests that perhaps salvation (*ocalenie*) consisted of an individual sense of balance:

> As you can see, I do not have a prescription,
> I do not belong to any sect,
> And salvation [*ocalenie*] is only in you
> Perhaps it is simply a healthy mind
> And a balanced heart [*serca równowaga*].
> (W 2:98–99)

Indeed, Auden also was seeking in his poem a balance between reason and love.

> O when will men show common sense
> And throw away intelligence. . . .
> Establish a real neighborhood
> Where art and industry and *moeurs*
> Are governed by an *ordre du Coeur*.[37]
> (vv. 518–19, 525–27)

I myself believe that the central axis or issue of cultural evolution can be summarized as precisely development in the task of reconciling *yin* (faith, heart) and *yang* (doubt, reason). And I see Auden and Milosz in these two works making remarkably similar contributions to that evolution.

FROM A BARDIC OR VATIC (ROMANTIC) TO A SATIRIC (CLASSICIST) VOICE

The two poets' movement away from excessively romantic content was accompanied by a shift to a more light-hearted and witty eighteenth-century neoclassic style. Both poets imitated the tone and metrics of Jonathan Swift, to whom Milosz also dedicated a poem.

The resulting tension between sprightly form and grave content was intended. In *The Double Man*, according to Edward Mendelson, "the conservative order of its syntax and metre struggled to restrain the anarchic whirlwind of its ideas,"[38] many of them inspired by Blake.[39] For Milosz the controlled formalism of eighteenth-century satire supplied a balanced perspective to dispel the chaos and late romantic over-commitment of postwar Europe.

Following Auden, Milosz uses Swiftian humor to mock the postwar socialist Polish planners (in a dig the slow-witted censors failed to catch):

> Into the pot goes an encyclopaedia
> Which they apparently intend to eat
> (W 2:87)

This is a sly allusion to Swift's flying island of Balnibarbi in *Gulliver's Travels*, where the "Academy of Projectors" planned ambitious labor-serving projects to increase production "an hundred-fold"; but, as none of these projects was completed, the land lay waste.[40]

A striking corollary to this shift to satiric style was the authors' renunciation of their earlier bardic or vatic ambitions. While one critic has written how, "Like Auden, Milosz inherited [the] vatic legacy from romanticism,"[41] another has noted that "Like Auden, Czeslaw Milosz sought to move beyond the vatic tradition and its praise of the poet as prophet."[42] Mendelson writes that Auden "was the first English writer who absorbed all the lessons of modernism, but also understood its limits, and chose to turn elsewhere. He successfully challenged the vatic dynasty after more than a century of uncontested rule."[43]

Auden, he said, turned instead to a more modest tradition of "civic poetry," in which poets write "as citizens, whose purpose is to entertain and instruct."[44] (In like fashion, Milosz is often referred to as a "social poet.")[45]

In *The Double Man*, Auden, who had already written that "poetry makes nothing happen," rejects simplistic ideas of poets as legislators:

> Art is not life and cannot be
> A midwife to society
> For Art is a *fait accompli*.[46]
> (vv. 78–80)

The poem nonetheless struggles to discern, from the past examples of masters from Dante to Rilke, to determine "what / Is possible and what is not, / To what conditions we must bow / In building the Just City now" (vv. 1521–24).

Key to this building is the "double focus" of seeing both sides and a rejection of absolute solutions, including vatic prophecies: "All are so weak that none dare claim / 'I have the right to govern,' or / 'Behold in me the Moral Law'" (vv. 1636–38).

This transition to modesty also distinguishes "A Treatise on Morals" from its predecessor, *Ocalenie*. We have already seen how, in "Przedmowa," Milosz wrote like a romantic so that late romanticism "should visit us no more." Then in his "Semi-Private Letter" he proposed, in Tischner's words, "the emotional restraint of classicism [as] a catharsis to Polish poetry, dragging it back to reality."[47] For there was the need, when facing a long and inescapable period of gloom, to do so with the calmness of a long perspective. This is established near the outset of the Treatise:

> With the knowledge that night will end
> Sit down and read Thucydides
> And distil the purple juice
> Until you touch the seeds of style,
> And seek out what will be then
> The human footprint in the legend.
> (W 2:86)

Milosz later explained that by "seeds of style" (*ziarna stylu*) he meant not just poetic style, but a social mindset: "Here the poem says that we are in the power of the *episteme*, in the power of the style in which we think, write, and feel, and which is characteristic of our era." We need, in short, the insight which Thucydides showed in chronicling the Peloponnesian War (WP, 81). And then, reflecting his friend Kroński's Hegelian belief in a veiled but rational historical process, Milosz added:

> But behind this style lies the "inviolable pupa of events" [poczwarka nietykalna dzarzeń, *Traktat moralny*, W 2:86]—the reality which conceals itself behind our thoughts and language, which are closely bound up with each other. . . . We must be able to separate the dictates of the form in which we live—the style, language, or episteme—from what I would call the raw reality. Through this distinction, we can get to the truth about reality.[48]

The human footprint in the legend will outlast what the poet now describes, with allusions to Noah, as the deluge of history:

> I invite you today into the ark
> Which across the swift current of time
> Will take us to new shores.
> You will land in a flooded forest.
> The mist will subside. A rainbow will rise,
> And a dove will bring a green leaf.
> (W 2:87)[49]

The flood may last centuries, but learning will survive.

> In a hundred, maybe two hundred years,
> Somewhere in Taormina or maybe Trieste,
> In France (the China of Europe),
> Or where the graves of capitals lie today—
> A little center of learning will shine
> And provide a banner for the new homeland.
> (W 2:87–88)

History today will be made by "barbarians," but in the future, one of their grandsons will think about "those who preserved and carried the treasure through the darkness." In correspondence with Kroński about this line (originally "those who preserved their humanity"), Milosz wrote: "I have toiled over this passage, but I will continue to toil over it and rewrite it. . . . I would prefer to use the word decency [*przyzuwoitość*], *decentia*, or something like that."[50]

In the context of this human treasure, the vatic voice of "Flight" is downgraded to one that is more diminished, even slightly comic:

> So remember—in a difficult time
> You are to be an ambassador of dreams,
> Of those dreams from the deepest darkness,
> Which bear the pudgy face of the Baroque,
> Or a gentle Etruscan joke
> (W 2:89–90)

(Decades later, in "Secretaries" [1975], Milosz, no longer a diplomat, would downgrade the poet's social status still further:

> I am no more than a secretary of the invisible thing
> That is dictated to me and a few others.
> Secretaries, mutually unknown, we walk the earth
> Without much comprehension. Beginning a phrase in the middle
> Or ending it with a comma. And how it looks when completed
> Is not up to us to inquire, we won't read it anyway.
> [NCP, 343])

AUDEN'S *LETTER* AND MILOSZ'S "TREATISE ON MORALS": DIFFERENCES

That there are striking *differences* between *The Double Man* and "Treatise on Morals" should be hardly surprising. Auden's poem celebrates in part his *escape* (like Castorp) from the European nightmare to a safe harbor for his self-redefinition among new friends. It ends hopefully:

> Instruct us in the civil art
> Of making from the muddled heart
> A desert and a city where
> The thoughts that have to labor there
> May find locality and peace,
> And pent-up feelings their release.
> (vv. 1876–81)[51]

Milosz's poem contemplates no such escape for "a hundred, maybe two hundred years" (W 2:87–88). Our present era is "one of death / A giant *Likwidation*, in which a gravedigger with a revolver [*nagan*] 'buries systems, faiths, schools'" (W 2:87).[52] Its closure is bleak:

> . . . you will not flee the life given you
> Through some magic gateway.
> Let us go in peace, simple people
> Before us awaits
> —the "Heart of Darkness"
> (W 2:100)

As Franaszek recognizes, Milosz envisages the "Heart of Darkness" here as a fate, not just on one side of the Iron Curtain, but looming "over the entire human race."[53]

(The poem's distinction between a present age of the gravedigger, and the "new shores. . . . In a hundred, maybe two hundred years," illustrates the distinction I made earlier in Milosz: between violent enforcement from above (the avalanche) and ultimately successful empowerment from below (the *ocalenie* or salvation of "a balanced heart" that "is you alone.")

Milosz's view of New York on his arrival was nothing like Auden's: "There is little to compare with the sadness of these districts, the horror of a civilization going Nowhere."[54] His alienation from both East and West is captured in his 1947 poem, "Central Park," where he says to his friend Kroński (then in Paris)

> Under foreign powers' armed feet. . . .
>
> Gazing calmly on what is force, we know
> That those who wish to rule the world will pass.
> And we do not believe that we will need
> forever to live with a knife or automatic.
> (W 2:49–50)

Milosz's bitterness about the Yalta agreement, often expressed, was in response to both of the forces wishing "to rule the world."[55] In contrast to such a gloomy vision, Auden's poem seems much less serious. At times it does not seem serious at all, more like an after-dinner speaker's witty repartee, as when (for example) he calls Rilke "the Santa Claus of loneliness" (v. 216).[56]

Auden was undoubtedly very intelligent, quick-witted. But in none of his long poems (a genre he eventually abandoned) did he show himself to be what Milosz was, a deep thinker, still less a coherent and consistent one. To sum up: Auden's flashes of epigrammatic brilliance blind us to his poem's coherent structure, if it has one. Milosz's poem in contrast strikes me as both programmatic and dialectical. It proceeds by the "discipline of Elimination" (W 2:85) to discard current fashionable beliefs such as Heidegger or existentialism (W 2:91–92), and instead return to "the common gift of modest wisdom" we start with—"a healthy mind, and a balanced heart"—as the *Ocalenie* ("Rescue," "Salvation," "Making whole") that "is in you alone" (W 2:98–99). With this equipment we can, as "simple people," face the immediate future: "The Heart of Darkness" (W 2:100).

Such a speedy survey of a sixteen-page poem can hardly do it justice. But it may help show how Milosz, despite a corrective stylistic shift from the mystical romanticism of Mickiewicz to the satiric neoclassicism of Jonathan Swift, remains true to a central message he developed first in *Ocalenie* (1945) and again later in "A Treatise on Poetry" (1957).

MILOSZ'S "TREATISE ON MORALS":
AND CULTURAL EVOLUTION

This may help explain why Milosz's "Treatise on Morals" was far more favorably received in Poland than Auden's "Double Man" was in America. In a conversation with Aleksander Fiut, Milosz recalled that after the Treatise was published in 1947, it "was copied by hand and was often quoted at different gatherings."[57] Adam Zagajewski wrote later that students "read his 'Treatise on Morals' like a modern-day 'The Consolation of Philosophy' [by Boethius] in the worst years of Stalinism."[58]

But the Treatise was not just a consolation in the face of a hostile history. It also contained hints on how, not just to survive history, but even to influence it:

> You can thus influence the avalanche.
> Ease its savagery and cruelty,
> For this, one will need bravery.
> (W 2:89)

That history is both tragic and yet contains a "human footprint in the legend," and is responsive to human endeavors, I consider a claim of the greatest seriousness. So I see this cultural response to history in Milosz's poem as more developed than that of Yeats's alien "rough beast" in "The Second Coming," or the ultimate escape to the mountains in Eliot's *The Waste Land*.[59] It anticipates the more fully developed notion of the poet in history in Part IV of Milosz's "Treatise on Poetry" (see chapter 12).

This residual optimism had been latent in Milosz's thinking since his encounters in 1935 with his cousin Oscar. It underlay the last poems of *Ocalenie*, but was reinforced in the "Treatise on Morals," for example (as we noted above) in his attention to (and later interpretation of) the "seeds of style," moderating the "inviolable pupa of events."

This is what might be called Milosz's poetic Hegelianism, the idea that history, the domain of what he called *le devenir*, contained a deep generative pattern or hidden pupa that was rational but not knowable, only discernible at moments by poetic intuition. This notion was developed in conjunction with his Hegelian friend Kroński, and later by his translations of Simone Weil. It led him in 1960 to ask: "Is there any immanent force located in *le devenir*, in what is in the state of becoming, a force that pulls mankind up toward perfection? Is there any cooperation between man and a universe that is subject to constant change?"[60] This question, latent in the structure of "A Treatise on Morals," became the agenda in Milosz's second and more articulate treatise, *A Treatise on Poetry* (*Traktat poeticzny*), which was published in Paris, in 1957. There Milosz, no longer subject to censorship, could be more explicit about the role of poets in the evolution of culture, or what I call ethogeny.

POSTSCRIPT: WHAT MILOSZ IN 1946 DID NOT EXPLAIN ABOUT *OCALENIE*

Milosz's posture as an anti-romantic strengthened his case with postwar Warsaw critics for his unpolitical politics, including its salvational belief "that poetry can either save or destroy nations."[61] But there was another dimension to *Ocalenie*, far from anti-romantic, that his essay left unexplored. This was its approach to the ineffable.

I have already noted how the speaking "with silence" in the first stanza of "Przedmowa" (and of *Ocalenie*),

> Try to understand this simple speech as
>   I would be ashamed of another.
> I swear, there is in me no wizardry of words.
> I speak to you with silence like a cloud or a tree
> (NCP, 77)

alludes to a paradox, a truth of silence, a communication beyond words, which was bruited in a line of simple speech—"A bird and a tree say to him: Friend"—in the first stanza of "Love."

But how could an anti-romantic defend the transition, in just two lines, from a poem spoken in "simple speech" to a poem spoken "with silence"? I have no idea if Milosz composed this paradox deliberately, or whether this too, like the poem "In Warsaw," was a gift from the *daimonion*. But I am convinced that here something of crucial importance is being said (or, better, "unsaid").

As to what is being unsaid by this speech "in silence," Milosz offers clues elsewhere from this period. One can be found in an undated wartime letter to Jerzy Andrzejewski, Milosz refers to "the hidden corners of the human soul, which are closer to Mystery than the intellect is."[62] I see this as a prose acknowledgment of the truth in the last line of "Love": *Nie ten najlepiej służy, kto rozumie*: "He doesn't serve the best, who understands."

In the midst of the suffering he beheld each day from the Nazi occupation, Milosz, while his friends were dying in guerrilla actions, was writing about the notion of *poésie pure*, as enunciated by l'abbé Henri Brémond. As Milosz explained years later in *The Witness of Poetry*, "Brémond declared that pure poetry consists of an ineffable combination of sounds as in magic incantations, regardless of their meaning" (WP, 28–29).[63] At that later time, Milosz used Brémond to elucidate the hostile criticism of Oscar Milosz, for whom the two words "'pure poetry' . . . if they have any meaning at all, . . . denote a poetry that would remove religion, philosophy, science, politics from its domain."[64]

Milosz's attitude toward "pure poetry" was already hostile in 1938, when he "published an article ['The Lie of Poetry'] that caused a considerable stir in the [Polish] literary world and . . . at the same time marked a new stage in the development of the . . . entire younger generation."[65] Attacking recent poetic developments, he wrote,

> I would like to be able to proclaim my disgust at all those sterile games called pure poetry. . . . Enough, enough—let's finish at last with all the "avantgardes," the "imagination," "autentism," with all this babble of the specialists of the new poetics. . . . In my opinion the word should be judged . . . not only for its relation to the words that surround it but also for its relation to what it is at the moment that I write it, what it is *as extra-aesthetic consciousness*, and how I judge myself, the phenomena of the world and other people.[66]

But in the chaos of wartime Poland, and in retreat from his earlier quasi-Marxist sympathies, Milosz had reason to appreciate pure poetry and Brémond more affirmatively:

> Bremond knows that pure poetry rarely appears. It is a flash of lightning shimmering across one or two lines of verse and suddenly dying out. . . . *Excellent poetry strives for silence; it exists beyond the boundaries of speech.* It is a mystical state (imperfect, to be sure), a communion, a presence; its sources are the same as the sources of prayer, which Bremond later demonstrated in his book *Prière et poésie*.[67]

Milosz then listed the noted difficulty of responding to the aspirations of pure poetry "without renouncing simplicity and the unique meaning of words." Dante reached Paradise "through Hell and Purgatory," and anyone detecting in this journey "a beauty separate from the ideas of his time . . . would be making a grave mistake." Nevertheless, Milosz wrote,

> If I seem to stand in opposition to the element Bremond called the ineffable, *that is only illusory*. Actually, I criticize Pure Form *out of love*, because although one is pining for paradise, one may refuse oneself permission to return, if that return would result only in corruption. There is danger in a programmatic recognition of Pure Form as the root of art . . . when one takes programmatic aim at pure form, one inflicts on it an incurable wound.[68]

This agenda flowered in two important poems written a decade later in exile—examined in the following chapters. We shall see that in "Notebook: Banks of Leman" (1953) Milosz firmly enounced the temptation of pining directly for paradise:

> But whoever in what *is*
> Finds peace, order, and an eternal moment
> Will vanish without a trace.

And in his related "Treatise on Poetry" (1957) he similarly rejected poetry that was simply "pure":

> For contemplation fades without resistance.
> For its own sake, it should be forbidden.
> (TP, 59)

(Richard Lourie translated the second line as "It must be forbidden *out of love for it*,"[69] a more literal translation of the Polish *Z miłości do niej* (W 2:248).

Also a decade later, in *Native Realm*, Milosz would recall the dialectic by which in wartime he came first to "social" poetry, then to "pure" poetry," and finally to the synthesis that I have been describing in *Ocalenie*.

> I had written poems on "social" themes and had been bothered by their artificiality. I had practiced "pure" poetry and been no less irritated. Only now had the contradiction vanished. Now even the most personal poem . . . contained a streak of irony that made it objective. . . . The "naïve poems" I wrote then have a somewhat deceptive simplicity; they are really a metaphysical tract. . . . I also accepted my none-too-enviable place on earth and the dark instinct that led me to Warsaw. . . . In 1943, I set down my future duties quit clearly: neither the "pure poetry" of Abbé Bremond and its later theoreticians, nor Russian Socialist realism. . . . By fusing individual and historical elements in my poetry, I had made an alloy that one seldom encounters in the West. (NR, 247–48)

This was the hidden background to Milosz's thinking when he returned to the issue of pure poetry in his 1946 response to the critics of *Ocalenie*. Taking issue with the then fashionable ideological poetry of Aragon and Éluard, who "were throwing themselves into patriotic themes with a degree of enthusiasm we could not match," Milosz contrasted them with "the theoreticians of pure poetry who, like Edgar Allan Poe, argued that poetry should not venture into the realm of passion or the field of virtue." And he added, "Perhaps in a stormier era such poetry has a chance of surviving, since a certain degree of insensitivity helps one keep one's sense of balance.... However,... that safe 'alcove for rent' becomes cramped."[70]

Milosz's anti-romantic Ketman could not fully acknowledge the importance in *Ocalenie* of both acknowledging and turning away from the ineffable. But he would return to this theme after recovering his own sense of balance, something which would only happen after he became an émigré.

Chapter 10

Milosz the Émigré: "The Eternal Moment"

Human beings . . . are created by what they themselves have created. In this earthly church the human spirit worships the interhuman spirit.

—Witold Gombrowicz[1]

What is a poet who has no longer a language of his own?

—Czeslaw Milosz[2]

MILOSZ'S DEFECTION TO THE WEST

In the spring of 1949, as the news from Poland and East Europe under Stalin deteriorated, Milosz returned on a holiday to Poland, in order to assess whether he and his family should return. He traveled alone—perhaps, Franaszek writes, because "Janka wanted to keep as far as possible from a politically unstable Europe." In both going and returning, Milosz arranged for stopovers in Paris, a detail to which we shall return.[3]

What he saw in Poland, both in general and among old writer friends, appalled him. As an old friend told him, "We are slaves here."[4] He later summarized what he saw in his memoir, *Native Realm*:

> The whole country was bursting with suppressed hatred for its rulers and their Russian employers. The Normans after the conquest of England could not have been more isolated from the population than the new privileged caste (I, by the very cut of my clothes, carried the mark of that caste), and more than once I

123

noticed fear in the eyes of those who passed me in the street. Terror . . . is abject, it has a furtive glance, it destroys the fabric of human society. (NR, 280–81)

Milosz was thus confronted with an urgent question: should he return or defect when his posting to Washington expired in 1950?

In *Native Realm*, Milosz wrote how on his return to the US, "I fell into a crisis that was to endure over whole months, made more painful because there was no one with whom I could share my burden" (NR, 281). In fact, he consulted with the French poet and former diplomat, Saint-John Perse (by then a voluntary exile in Washington), and with Albert Einstein. Perse was uninterested; Einstein, believing that humans are fundamentally rational and that their collective madness is only temporary, advised him to return (NR, 281–83).[5]

Milosz felt that neither man understood the "demonic powers" now controlling the world.

> Nevertheless, in the fall of 1950 I said farewell to America. That was probably the most painful decision of my life—though none other was permissible. . . . [E]ven if I had wanted to cancel my share in the community the easy way, old-fashioned honor would never have permitted me to flee [i.e., remain] in such a manner. (NR, 283)

Even as he sailed for Europe, Milosz was still beset by anguished uncertainties about his decision. As he wrote in *Native Realm*, "For an average American my behavior would look insane, but I did not deceive myself either, and when I embarked in New York my teeth were chattering" (NR, 284).[6]

Milosz's turmoil had personal as well as historical reasons. Although he does not mention it in *Native Realm*, Janka (by then in a difficult pregnancy with their second child) was deeply opposed to the decision, and wished him to remain in America.[7] Janka's first pregnancy in 1947, with their son Tony, had been difficult, ending with a Caesarean section.[8] Her second pregnancy was even more traumatic, and her physician advised her she should not travel at that time.[9]

In this period of time, she and Czeslaw "argued repeatedly, mainly about America." Janka, terrified of the westward spread of Communism, wanted Czeslaw to defect and stay in the United States, where the playwright Thornton Wilder had offered him a farm and a chance to write poetry (YH, 121; cf. TP, 118, 120).

For three decades, in his public accounts of his defection, Milosz would omit reference to his abandonment of his pregnant wife. But in a letter to Janka on January 15, 1951, written from Paris two weeks before his ultimate defection, Czeslaw was already remorseful: "We have made gross mistakes.

One should never . . . fall into pride neither be . . . sure of oneself. This is evil. . . . We shouldn't have parted."[10] We shall see that Milosz's guilt over his temporary abandonment of her would haunt him, and deepen his poetry, for years to come.

When he returned to Poland in 1950, Milosz was shocked by the "astronomical changes since 1949." A friend later recalled that "It was easy to discern that he was close to a nervous breakdown."[11] The biographer of Milosz's Parisian protector, Jósef Czapski, confirms that after Milosz's return, "The conflict in him. grew unbearable, the strain was enormous, yet he still doubted the wisdom of defecting."[12]

His alienation from the Stalinist scene was soon recognized by the authorities. He was first ordered to surrender his passport, and then told that he would not be allowed to leave Poland. But the Polish foreign minister, Zygmunt Modzelewski, an old and therefore principled rather than opportunist Communist, convinced the president, Bolesław Bierut, that it was in Poland's best interests to let Milosz determine his own future.[13]

Milosz later told Thomas Merton that "Nobody could understand how I escaped from Poland, in full Stalinism. . . . The secret is that I was helped by a very influential person who hated Stalin, as Stalin had destroyed that person's family."[14] The person was almost certainly Modzelewski, who in the great Stalinist purge of 1937 had been arrested and tortured in Russia by the NKVD.[15]

So Milosz's passport, which had been taken from him, was returned; and he was authorized to return to his new post as cultural attaché in Paris. There, despite being under surveillance, he managed to escape from the embassy.[16] A friend, Nela Micińska, was waiting at the curb to take him by taxi to the office of the CIA-funded Polish *émigré* journal *Kultura*, which would hide, house, and nourish him for the next three and a half months.

In *A Year of the Hunter* (1987), Milosz gave a quite different account, that on his arrival in Paris, "Instead of reporting at the embassy, I feigned illness and surfaced at Maisons-Laffitte at *Kultura*" (YH, 239).[17] But in Franaszek's more credible account, two weeks elapsed before Milosz left the embassy, during which time he was "clearly engaged in clandestine contact" with the chief editors of *Kultura*, Jerzy Giedroyc and Józef Czapski, and also with the American intellectual James Burnham, who then was a full-time CIA consultant.[18]

THE CLANDESTINE BACKGROUND
TO MILOSZ'S DECISION

The contacts with Burnham and the *Kultura* émigrés had actually begun in America, months before Milosz's departure. Giedroyc and Czapski would become in 1950, along with Milosz, participants in the CIA-funded Congress for Cultural Freedom (CCF), of which James Burnham, then a full-time CIA consultant, was one of the chief founders. Czapski's biography confirms that Czapski sailed west from Liverpool in November 1949 for a brief American visit, during which "In Washington, Czapski met twice with Czesław Miłosz."[19]

The second encounter with Milosz was very probably in the company of Czapski's CIA handler James Burnham, who at the time was shepherding Czapski around Washington.[20] In the same month of November 1949, the FBI, which for two years had been passively recording information about Milosz, now opened a one-hundred-series operational Internal Security file on him.[21] Subsequent entries are heavily redacted, sometimes on grounds of FOIA "Exemption One: Classified national defense and foreign relations information."

After this, "Behind the scenes, with his American contacts [i.e., Burnham], Czapski worked to stress the potential importance of Milosz as the first intellectual of his stature to consider fleeing from the Soviet bloc."[22] Franaszek confirms that "From their first encounter with him in Washington, Czapski and Giedroyc seriously considered the possibility of Milosz's escape, and tried [obviously along with Burnham] to prepare for it by promising him an escape route back to the United States."[23]

So Milosz was now faced with a choice where to defect: Should he do so in America, where he risked being forgotten as just one more defecting Pole among dozens? Or in Europe, where his public defection could have historical impact, in the mounting cultural war to deter France and Italy from electing Communist governments.

The full Polish biography by Andrzej Franaszek makes it clear that Milosz had decided in advance to defect, but only after he had returned to Europe. In speaking to Janka about his return to Warsaw, "he did not have to lie—he really wanted to avoid 'choosing freedom' in the United States. He even preferred to be 'caught,' but alone—without Janka. She did not want him to leave her alone, but she knew that if she forced him to emigrate, it would destroy their love."[24]

From Milosz's FBI file we learn that, on September 21, 1950 [one week before his departure], the FBI Washington Field Office reported, under the heading "possible defecting Polish official," that Milosz might not accept his new posting in Paris, but instead seek asylum. (The memo named his ship and reservation date.)[25]

MILOSZ, BURNHAM, AND THE CONGRESS FOR CULTURAL FREEDOM

Having now seen Milosz's FBI file, I think that the sources for the WAC memo were probably Milosz's personal colleagues. But at first, I suspected that the source of this early privileged information, about Milosz as a "possible defecting Polish official," was from Burnham's shop in the OPC/CIA.

A former Trotskyite, Burnham's hatred of Stalinism had led him to join the CIA's Office of Policy Coordination (OPC) as a full-time consultant in October 1949. By the time of his contact with Milosz in 1949/1950, he was helping to organize the CIA-funded Congress for Cultural Freedom (CCF); and in 1950 he joined its steering committee.

In May 1951 Nicolas Nabokov, Secretary-General of the Congress, presented Milosz at a press conference sponsored by *Preuves*, then the only publication of the Congress. At this event Milosz announced his defection and denounced his former employers, in a much-publicized manifesto entitled "Nie" (No): "I am not a reactionary. . . . My homeland . . . ought to belong to the Polish people and not to high officials . . . people should not lie. A lie is the source of all crime. . . . The paramount duty of a poet is to tell the truth"[26]

The statement was read on Voice of America radio. Four months later, according to the CCF's historian, "An initial move by the Congress to establish its intellectual agenda, inspired by the defection and writings of Polish cultural attaché Czeslaw Milosz, was attempted in September 1951 with the organization of a 'closed' intellectual symposium . . . in a castle in Andlau near Strasbourg."[27]

At the symposium, a select group of invitees "heard Milosz dissecting the nuances of Polish intellectuals' seduction by communism."[28] Unlike most Polish defectors who sank into obscurity at that time abroad (such as the poet Jan Lechoń, who, in 1956, committed suicide in New York City), Milosz was now about to become famous.

THE CAPTIVE MIND: MILOSZ'S PUBLIC SUCCESS AND PRIVATE DESPAIR

Someone interested only in Milosz's rhetorical prose might consider the early 1950s the period of his greatest achievements and success. His "Nie" attracted widespread media attention, partly because it attracted instant condemnation on all sides, from the new Polish government and Warsaw intelligentsia, to the Polish émigrés in London and America. The émigré factions took offense at Milosz's political position: that he had been happy "the semi-feudal social structure" of prewar Poland was being replaced by "the new Poland that was building socialism"—until he was commanded to be a propagandist for dialectical materialism.[29] (They also mistrusted him because of his service with the postwar Polish government, as did parts of the US government, including another branch of the CIA.)

At the same time, this confession fitted Milosz easily into the basic State Department and CIA strategy of promoting the so-called Non-Communist Left (NCL), which in the CIA became "the theoretical foundation of the Agency's political operations against Communism over the next two decades."[30] Franaszek writes how "subsequently, Milosz himself became one of the keenest contributors to [the Congress's] activities, co-organising meetings and conferences on their behalf."[31]

According to a doctoral dissertation on Milosz, citing Congress records, "The Congress supported Milosz's efforts to get an entrance visa to the USA, guaranteed him privileges, generous royalties, and financial support from the Fund for Intellectual Freedom led by Arthur Koestler, and from the International Rescue Committee."[32] But this account, based on Congress archives, gives a misleading picture of Milosz's financial situation. In 1951, at first with minimal resources, and hiding (to avoid possible retaliation by the Polish secret police) in *Kultura*'s suburban villa. There his new friend Zygmunt Hertz "would thrust a hundred francs into his pocket to cover the costs of a ticket into Paris and a glass of red wine."[33]

Even with funds from the Congress, "he was still far from having financial stability and lived from one publication to another"; his honoraria from *Preuves* and the BBC "barely covered the costs of the most basic things."[34]

Milosz could have greatly improved his situation by working full-time for Radio Free Europe (RFE), the standard reward for important defectors. But (in his words), "I was possibly the only émigré who refused to write for Radio Free Europe, because I didn't care for its beating of the patriotic drum" (ABC, 205).[35]

Milosz thought he had negotiated with Burnham a deal that would guarantee him "a prompt departure to the United States."[36] But despite Burnham's strenuous efforts both inside and outside government, this proved impossible, even with further support from the CIA-funded International Rescue Committee.[37]

The Internal Security Act of 1950 (the so-called McCarran Act) denied suspected Communists entry to the US. The London Poles, organized Poles in America, and even other more conventional socialist defectors all vigorously opposed giving him a visa.[38] And another CIA department was convinced that

Milosz was not an authentic defector but a Soviet agent.[39] Consequently, the Miloszes were not reunited until 1953, when Janka, overcoming her misgivings, joined Milosz in France.

Worst of all, as a poet writing in Polish, now cut off from his audience, Milosz was at first convinced his poetic career was over. The psychological costs of this abrupt severance from his friends, family, and public were so acute that he contemplated suicide.[40] A quarter century later, Milosz invited a friend to a café in the Latin Quarter, and said, "I used to come here in the early fifties, each time thinking that I would commit suicide that day."[41]

This mood of despair was broken by meeting and soon living with Jeanne Hersch, a Jewish-Swiss philosopher with whom, in March 1952, he moved into a Paris Left-Bank hotel. She persuaded Milosz to write a novel in Polish to compete for the Prix Littéraire Européen. The resulting novel, *The Seizure of Power*, won first prize and earned him 5,000 Swiss francs, thus ending his urgent financial worries.[42]

His success, along with his happiness with Jeanne Hersch, now enabled Milosz to come to terms with another source of his immediate past misery, a gnawing sense of guilt over parting with Janka.

> She [Hersch] elevated to the level of moral duty my abandonment of my wife and children for the sake of a literary career which threatened to become a complete fiasco if I did not do that. I am not saying that my friends in Warsaw were wrong in saying that I would end up committing suicide if I were to break ties with Warsaw. But it is difficult to exist in the reach of those extended claws and have to listen to her hissing, 'you will perish,' alongside the feeling of being a leper and rejected by the world.[43]

Meanwhile the resources of ironic detachment that saved him at Goszyce again eased him in his new poetry, perhaps unconsciously, towards a new role: as a bard, no longer just of Poland, but of the world.

THE EVOLUTION OF MILOSZ'S NEW POETIC ROLE

Especially after his catastrophic visit to Poland in 1949, Milosz had already emigrated in his heart, a year before his public defection. Like Herbert after him, he wrote a number of poems "for the drawer" that he could not then publish, such as his celebrated 1950 poem, "You Who Wronged."

In 1948 he had already expressed his alienation from both of the world's superpowers in "Central Park" ("Gazing calmly on what is force, we know / That those who wish to rule the world will pass," W 2:50). In the same year he wrote of America,

> This new Jerusalem of old Puritans,
> Their dream fulfilled, but in reverse,
> Is for me an oppressive, empty stage set
> As when asleep I want to scream and cannot.[44]

And we can sense the anguish tormenting him in the sardonic bitterness of his major poem "Toast" (1949):

> Strengthen your heart! Unite! And do not give up!
> Blur! Hide under the cloth (In short, lie).
> That is the whole program. Good. As for whom.
> Not for those who can imagine the results.
> (W 2:118)

But in his 1951 poem "Mittelbergheim," the last poem in his first post-exilic poetry book *Daylight*, we see Milosz in Alsace finding a new equilibrium in his émigré status. This is indeed, as Franaszek writes (311) a "recovery poem."

> You, fire, power, might, for it is too early.
> I have lived through many years and, as in this half-dream,
> I felt I was attaining (*sięgam*) the moving frontier
> Beyond which color and sound come true
> And the things of this earth are united.
> Do not yet force me to open my lips.
> Let me trust and believe I will attain.
> Let me linger here in Mittelbergheim.
>
> I know I should. They are with me,
> Autumn and wooden wheels and tobacco hung
> Under the eaves. *Here and everywhere*
> *Is my homeland, wherever I turn*
> *And in whatever language* I would hear
> The song of a child, the conversation of lovers.
> Happier than anyone, I am to receive
> A glance, a smile, a star, silk creased
> At the knee.
> (NCP, 104, emphasis added)[45]

Milosz was in Mittelbergheim because of the CCF conference that same month at the neighboring castle of Andlau. Though Milosz was treated by the Congress as a "prized possession,"[46] the new attention he was receiving was irrelevant to his poetic dreams of attainment in "Mittelbergheim." As he wrote later, "I was too besieged, pained, and suspicious, and above all, too poor to feel good in that company. Poverty sees right through the fatty tissue in which the rich encase themselves" (ABC, 88).[47]

The objects of Milosz's disdain here were the American bureaucrats "with good salaries" who set up "their posh offices in the most expensive district of Paris." Toward his fellow-artists in the CCF he was more ambivalent. One can detect a certain resentment in his new "aversion" toward Robert Lowell, whom he had first befriended on more equal terms before his defection (YH, 219).[48]

On the other hand, Milosz recalled "those moments of happiness" he shared with the Chiaromontes and Mary McCarthy in a seaside village, after a CCF conference in Milan in 1955 (ABC, 64–65; cf. YH, 272–73). At the same conference he met Dwight McDonald; and from this encounter issued an important and very relevant poem, "In Milan":

> He [McDonald, YH, 118]: That I was too politicized.
> And I answered him more or less as follows. . . .
> Yes, I would like to be a poet of the five senses.
> That's why I don't allow myself to become one.
> Yes, thought has less weight than the word *lemon*
> That's why in my words I do not reach for fruit.
> (NCP, 170)

In the Polish these lines were followed by another, quoting Mickiewicz: "'Whoever has not touched the earth . . .' / Few have understood / this" (NCP, 761). The full Mickiewicz line, from *Forefathers' Eve* (*Dziady*), is "Whoever has not touched the earth will never be in Heaven."[49]

This is the argument for doubleness that Milosz will develop in his Lake Leman Notebook and his Poetic Treatise: that a poet should only approach the "perfect stillness outside time" by engaging with this world (retaining "both ends of the contradiction"), not by simply renouncing the world (TP, 123, 122).

In these two later poems landscape has become a temptation to be turned away from. In "Mittelbergheim," it restored the poet to a needed health: "Let me linger here in Mittelbergheim. // I knew I should." The common aim in all three poems is balance.

The important point is that Milosz did not think for a moment of blending his poetic career with his new political one, as did, to his great detriment, his new friend Stephen Spender.[50] Milosz had learned, while serving the Communists, to keep his poetry quite separate; and that habit would continue, now that he was in effect working with and for the West. (In chapter 12 we shall recall this repeated service when discussing the two Faustian incantations to the devil in Part IV of the Poetic Treatise.)

Thus in "Mittelbergheim" he does not allude to his recent experience at Andlau Castle. Instead, still mindful of "attaining the moving frontier / Beyond which color and sound come true," he also accepts that he can be at home in a new, albeit foreign present, and also inspired by it.

THE CHOICE BETWEEN BEING AND BECOMING, NATURE AND HISTORY

Barely beneath this contrast in the poem, between lingering and attaining, is the enduring choice between the contradictory opposites of *being* and *becoming*, *esse* and *devenir*, nature and history, that will become the central theme of his most important work in the 1950s.[51]

In *Native Realm*, Milosz described how his different experiences in Europe and America made him more adept at shifting his commitment from *movement* to *being*, and back.

> In America, the contradiction inclined me toward *movement*, while in Paris, through my [1949] conversations with Tiger, it drove me back toward *being* [*esse*], and I tried to diagnose my case. Whoever commits himself to movement [*devenir*] alone will destroy himself. Whoever disregards movement will also destroy himself, but in a different way. This, I said to myself, is the very core of my destiny—never to be satisfied with one or the other, only at moments to seize the unity of these opposites. (NR, 275–76)[52]

When he returned to Paris in 1951, Milosz's closest friend was now no longer the Marxist Tiger (Kroński), who had returned to Warsaw to take up a teaching position, but two other Polish émigrés: first Zygmunt Hertz from the émigré *Kultura* circle, and then Stanisław Vincenz, an older writer then living in Grenoble. However, the geographical contrast between America and Europe continued to underlie the existential contrast of being and becoming, as we shall see when we consider "A Treatise on Poetry" (1957).

America, at least in Milosz's experience of it, represented Nature to him, *being*. (In 1947, he wrote to Paweł Hertz: "America has restored my ability to behold worldly phenomena.")[53] Europe in contrast represented history, *becoming*. Thus after his move to Berkeley, in "Bobo's Metamorphosis," the dream of *attaining* became occluded by an acceptance of the present (and its virtues):

> A woman . . . looked at me as if I were a ring of Saturn
> And knew I was aware that no one attains [*nikt nie dosięga*].
> Thus were affirmed humanness, tenderness
> (*człowiecznozść i tkliwość*, NCP, 196–97; W 3:13)

But in two great poems from the 1950s, the Leman Notebook and *A Treatise on Poetry*, Milosz explicitly, if ambivalently, subordinated the temptations of natural beauty (*being*) to a commitment to engage in history (*becoming*). Although Milosz chose not to include the first poem in his *New and Collected Poems*, I shall, like Aleksander Fiut, quote it in full:

"Notebook: Banks of Leman" [Lake Geneva]
["Notatnik: Brzegi Lemanu"]

Copper beeches, glistening poplars
And pine-trees steep above the October fog.
In the valley the lake steams. On the other side,
On mountain ridges, snow already lies.
What remains of life? Only this light,
Peculiar to sunny weather in this season,
Which makes you blink. People say: *this is*,
And there is neither skill nor talent
Able to reach beyond whatever *is*,
And unnecessary memories lose their strength.
A smell of cider in barrels. The priest
Mixes lime with a spade outside the school.
My son is running on a path there. Boys carry
Sacks of chestnuts they have gathered from the slopes.
If I forget thee, O Jerusalem
(Says the prophet) *let my right hand wither.* [Psalm 137:5][54]
Underground trembling shakes [*wstrząsa*] that which *is*:
Mountains crack, forests are rent asunder.
Touched by what will be and what was,
What *is* crumbles into dust.
Violent, clean, the world is again in ferment.
And neither ambition nor memory will cease.
Autumn skies, the same in childhood,
The same in manhood and old age, I shall
Not look at you. Landscapes,
Nourishing our hearts with gentle warmth,
What poison in you, muting our lips,
Makes us sit with folded arms, and the look
Of dreamy animals? But whoever in what *is*
Finds peace, order, and an eternal moment
Will vanish without a trace. Do you agree
To abolish [*niszczyć*] what *is*, and to pluck from movement,
An eternal moment, like a gleam
From a black river's water? Yes.

Bon [i.e., Bons], 1953 (W 2:162–63)[55]

Although Milosz is thanked for his assistance in translating this poem, he did not include it in his *New and Collected Poems*. Nor was it reprinted after its appearance in *Kultura* (1954) in any of his serial Polish collections before his collected poems (*Wiersze*). In it his family problems, and the one-sided conclusion he then drew from them, were perhaps too apparent.

Milosz and Janka had just been reunited in Le Havre after thirty-three months of separation. From Le Havre, they had come directly to Bons-Saint Didier, a small village on the French side of Lake Geneva.[56] This reunion (including his sight, perhaps for the first time, of his son running) moves him at the outset to paint a landscape portrait reminiscent of "Mittelbergheim," summarized as

> .... whatever *is*,
> And unnecessary memories lose their strength.

His most recent memories, in contrast, are indeed incompatible. They have been of his historical engagement, including the successes of *The Captive Mind* and his prize-winning novel *The Seizure of Power*, the latter inspired and promoted by the philosopher Jeanne Hersch with whom he had been living.

History and memory now disturb this tranquil poem, with the stern vow of the exiled psalmist in Psalm 137 ("By the waters of Babylon, we sat down and wept"):

> How shall we sing the Lord's song
> in a foreign land?
> If I forget you, O Jerusalem,
> let my right hand forget its skill!
> (Psalm 137:4–5)

(I suspect that for Milosz in 1953, Jerusalem would have suggested Blake's Jerusalem, or what Millosz called "the moving frontier" of the future, "beyond which . . . the things of this earth are united" [NCP, 104].)

I suspect also that Milosz, having already translated *The Waste Land*, was recalling Eliot's line "By the waters of Leman I sat down and wept." Note that the psalm itself, Eliot's adaptation of it, and Milosz's quotation from it, all concern the challenge of writing, or not writing, poetry in a foreign location. The psalm of exile, unique in acknowledging that it was written in exile, expresses a vow to remember Jerusalem, even while refusing to "sing the Lord's song in a foreign land." Eliot, in contrast, wrote the close of his description of social decay, *The Waste Land*, precisely *while* exiled to the shores of Lake Leman.[57]

In any case, Milosz's pastoral vista of what *is*, once jarred by the psalmist's vow, "crumbles into dust":

Mountains crack, forests are rent asunder. . . .
And neither ambition nor memory will cease.

Having used Eliot's (rather than the Polish) name for Lake Geneva ("Leman"), Milosz now rejects the gentle warmth of landscapes as "poison" (*trucizna*) "muting our lips." Confronted with the threat of vanishing into oblivion, the poet then agrees to "abolish what is" (*co jest, niszczyć*), and instead seek an "eternal moment" (*moment wieczny*) from a place in movement (*ruchu*)—that is, history, "like a gleam / From a black river's water."

Milosz later explicated this final paradox to Renata Gorczyńska: "Time is given to man for his use. But he should not allow himself to be completely carried away by time, because then he will be lost in relativism and utter fluidity and be smashed to bits. That motif also appears in my poem 'Bon on Lake Leman,' where I say, 'To pluck an eternal moment from movement.'"[58]

This stark Brzozowskian opposition of "what is" and "movement," and the decision to choose the latter, are at the heart of one of Milosz's greatest and most closely crafted poems, "A Treatise on Poetry" (1957).[59] So is the unstated, tragic choice between his self-appointed historic mission and caring for his wife, along with the unexplained reference (in translation) to an "eternal moment." Much later, in his expanded notes to his Poetic Treatise, Milosz will have this to say: "The eternal moment is the opposite of time. It is, if only for a second, outside the flow of time. T.S. Eliot in *The Four Quartets* speaks of 'the still point of the turning world.' This idea often appears in the writings of mystics from various civilizations" (TP, 121n; cf. NCP, 761). Without entering into details at this stage, it seems clear that the eternal moment (*moment wieczny*) refers to what Milosz a decade earlier had called "a mystical state . . . beyond the boundaries of speech."[60]

To make sense of Milosz's "intriguing and mysterious" statement about this "eternal moment,"[61] it helps to read the Bons poem in the context of the Treatise, where the dilemma of choosing between Nature (Being, "what is") and History (Movement, Becoming) is visited again. At Bons, it is now clear to me, Milosz is saying that to choose Nature, and afterward an eternal movement, is to lose the necessary tension between the two aspects of our existence.[62]

But to choose Movement, and from *there* pluck an eternal moment, is to achieve what Milosz desires in the Treatise: "to retain both ends of the contradiction" in a "search for equilibrium" (TP, 122–23n). This resembles what Milosz had to say of Brzozowski's pursuit of both Marxism and the

Catholicism of Cardinal Newman: "he wants to place everything in a balance of opposites."[63]

These issues are far more explicit in the Treatise, which Milosz, following the example of Auden in *The Double Man*, helpfully explicated four decades later with copious prose endnotes, longer than the poem itself.

Chapter 11

The Poetic Hegelianism of
A Treatise on Poetry[1]

I had gotten involved with Hegelianism, which was very unhealthy for me.

— Czeslaw Milosz[2]

Even in English, the *Treatise on Poetry* seems to me the most comprehensive and moving poem of this half-century.

— Helen Vendler[3]

A TREATISE ON POETRY AND SALVATION (*OCALENIE*)

A Treatise on Poetry (*Traktat poetycki*) is the second of Milosz's three poetic treatises (on morals, on poetry, and on theology). Considered together, the three form a quasi-Hegelian triad illustrating his spiritual evolution, into a historic mission, and then beyond it. But the *Treatise on Poetry* is far longer and more complex than the other two. Containing as it does a half century of Polish cultural history, it deserves close attention and can be described as a short epic.

The poem supplies a dialectical exposition of Polish cultural evolution, or ethogeny, one in which poetry is not just a by-product of historical forces, as in Marxism, but also a source contributing to them. (Just as Marx, in his materialist concept of history, claimed to have turned Hegelian idealistic dialectics "right-side up," so Milosz can be said to have restored *thought* to its original generative dominance in Hegelian dialectics—albeit poetic rather than philosophical thought.)[4]

In *A Treatise on Poetry*, Milosz called for a "new diction" that

137

> . . . might allow us to express
> A new tenderness [*czułość*] and save us from a law
> That is not our law, from necessity
> Which is not ours, even if we take its name.
> (NCP, 144; TP, 51–52)

(The second line, "Tę nową czułość, a w niej ocalenie," translates literally as "This new tenderness and in it salvation / [From a law that is not our law].")[5] In a note, Milosz explained that "'A new diction' and 'a new tenderness' are seen as the means of liberating man from fatalism and determinism, from the presumed law of historical necessity." In Polish terms, this "presumed law" would refer to Marxism, and Milosz added that "intense thinking . . . leads in a different direction from the Marxist theses" (TP, 117n).

Expanding on this message of "hope" in the Treatise, Milosz said to Renata Gorczyńska:

> Our hope is in the historical. That is what Brzozowski called "*storicismo polacco*," he thought that philosophy was given a new beginning in the work of Giovanni Batista Vico because history as time, but time remembered, is something different from nature's time.[6] Our hope lies in a heightened sense of history, not in an escape to Saint Thomas Aquinas. There's a static quality to Thomism, and it allots a very weak role to historical change.[7]

Milosz defined this "heightened sense" more precisely in *Native Realm*, as a rebuttal (in the spirit of Brzozowski) to the *diamat* (dialectical materialist) Marxists who reduced history to the "mathematical necessity" of nature.

> But nature's kingdom is not our own; we belong to it and yet we do not belong. In nature's kingdom necessity is the only good; not so for us. In our kingdom, the process of becoming is history, and it obeys quite different laws. It grows out of ourselves, out of even our smallest deeds. Unfortunately, our adaptation to historical fluidity has not passed beyond the stage of awkward beginnings, but to liberate ourselves from her magnetism we must reinforce her, not turn away from her. (NR, 295)

Explaining how he came to break with Kroński (Tiger), he presented this argument as "the most vital part" of his Poetic Treatise, while conceding that "poetry can never be reduced to prose" (NR, 294). In this vein, Milosz then quoted a couple of lines from the Treatise about "the Spirit of History . . . 'His face large as ten moons, a chain of freshly cut heads around his neck'" (NR, 295; cf. NCP, 128; TP, 31). His post-Marxist argument will become more tangible and concrete when we consider these lines below in greater detail.

A TREATISE ON POETRY, PART I, "BEAUTIFUL TIMES"

Milosz's *Treatise on Poetry* opens with a preface, in which poetry "still knows how to please," but is seen as "pushing thought aside, cheating thought." In contrast,

> ... serious combat, where life is at stake,
> Is fought in prose. It was not always so.
>
> And our regret has remained unconfessed.
> Novels and essays serve but will not last.
> One clear stanza can take more weight
> Than a whole wagon of elaborate prose.
> (NCP, 109; TP, 1)[8]

In the spirit of the Enlightenment, Auden's *The Double Man*, and "A Treatise on Morals," *A Treatise on Poetry* will attempt to restore serious thought to poetry. More specifically, it will assign to poetry a significant role in cultural evolution.

Milosz's dialectical sketch of Poland's cultural evolution begins in Part I, with what he ironically calls "Beautiful Times"/ Kraków 1900–1914." A Western reader needs to be reminded that at this time there was no Polish political state; and that, of the three regions into which Poland had been divided, the area of Galicia including Kraków, in the Catholic and multiethnic Austro-Hungarian Empire, was the only one which permitted the teaching of the Polish language and culture.

The section opens with a theme to be sustained throughout the poem: the separations by class of the elements of Polish culture. (In this case, the "ethereal" sound of a poet's "lyre from a garret window" is contrasted with that from the *Tingeltangel* or dance hall just below it.) "Our style," writes Milosz, "was born there. . . . Pure, forbidden the use of certain words: "toilet, telephone, ticket, ass, money" (NCP, 112–13; TP, 7). In one of his longest Notes to the poem, Milosz returns to his ambivalent obsession with "pure poetry." He detects in the Krakovian poets of Young Poland the influence of French poets like Mallarmé, who "favored the search for essence at the expense of range, and thus discouraged the kind of poetry that describes everyday life. The Polish language still bore the marks of the Romantic era, which left it somewhat ethereal and ill adapted to the reality of the twentieth century" (TP, 72n).[9]

To put it more bluntly: the special interests of Polish culture, which depended on literature for survival, were not being served by dependence on foreign models. This disjunction of literature from historical reality was first broken by Conrad, whose

> ... tale of a jungle river was a warning:
> One of the civilizers, a madman named Kurtz,
> A gatherer of ivory stained with blood,
> Scribbled in the margin of his report
> On the Light of Culture: "The horror." And climbed
> Into the twentieth century.
> (NCP, 114; TP, 9)[10]

These poets' shelter in the "somewhat ethereal" legacy of an earlier era, "ill adapted to the reality of the twentieth century" (TP, 72n), ended abruptly with the outbreak of World War I. Many of the poets now became "aesthetes in infantry boots" as members of General Piłsudski's army (NCP 115; TP, 10), "With the end of the war [and his army including 'poets and painters'], Piłsudski achieved his goal, an independent Poland" (TP, 78–79n).

A TREATISE ON POETRY, II, "THE CAPITAL"

In "Part II / The Capital / Warsaw 1918–1939," Milosz now addresses the "alien [i.e., Russified] city" of interwar Warsaw, until then a Russian garrison town, along "with your blackened ghetto / The somnolent anger of your unemployed" (NCP, 116–17; TP, 13–14). Presiding over these contradictions, Piłsudski, the head of the new state,

> could never believe in permanence.
> And would say again: "They will attack us."
> Who? He pointed to the East, the West.
> "I've stopped the wheel of history a moment."
> (NCP, 117; TP, 14)

Warsaw, in other words, was doomed to be destroyed,

> Till not one stone, O city, remains
> Upon a stone, and you too will pass away.
> Flame will consume the painted history.
> Your memory will become a dug-up coin.
> And for your disasters this is your reward:
> As a sign that language only is your home,
> Your ramparts will be built by poets.
> (NCP, 117; TP, 14–15)

As it had done for two centuries, Poland would survive through its enduring literature, rather than its ephemeral political structures. Milosz here reaffirms the quotation from Cyprian Norwid he had used in his "Semi-Private Letter": "Neither a shield nor a sword, but a masterpiece, is the people's weapon."[11] Milosz then discusses the major interwar poets of the Skamander group, noting first ironically of the need for a poet to "issue from good stock / To have a saintly tzaddic [Hebrew for 'righteous man'] in his lineage." This, he added later in his notes, was "a time when the leading figures in Polish literature and theater and art were Jewish" (TP, 109n). Of the poets named in Part II, the notes state that two (Tuwim and Słonimski) were indeed Jewish,[12] while Iwaszkiewicz, who was ethnically Polish, was "from the Ukraine." (Milosz did not need to point out to his audience how Skamander's Jewishness contributed to the gap between the poets and the Polish people, especially in rural areas.)

But the ramparts the poets erected were not just inadequate; in Milosz's eyes, they failed to address the problem:

> There had never been such a Pleiade!
> Yet something in their speech was flawed,
> A flaw of harmony, as in their masters.
> The transformed choir did not much resemble
> The disorderly choir of ordinary things.
> It was there everything sprouted, fermented,
> Deeper than a rounded word can reach.
> (NCP, 119; TP, 17)

The "flaw of harmony" was a sign that the disempowering gap marked earlier in Part I, between poetry and everyday Polish life, had not yet been overcome.

> In the absence of common values, the country fell apart . . .

> This was a time of schism
> "God and country" had ceased to be a lure.
> A poet despised a cavalry officer more
> Than bohemians had once despised a banker.
> He mocked national banners and a show of flag,
> Would spit when a crowd of screaming youths
> Marched, wielding canes, against a Jewish merchant.

> The end was prepared in advance. It was not
> For lack of armor and cannon that the Republic fell.
> In Poland a poet is a barometer,
> Even if he published in *Linia* or *Kwadryga*.

> A skein of common values came undone.
> No common faith bound our minds together.
> Those who saw took refuge in irony
> And lived in the crowd as on a desert island.
> (NCP, 121–22; TP, 20)[13]

A younger poet, Konstanty Galczyński, tried to pull things together (by incorporating into the cosmopolitan Skamander style elements of slang, kitsch, and street humor [HPL, 409]).

> One of those who understood pretended
> To worship the gods the nation worshipped.
>
> Galczyński wanted to fall on his knees.
> His story contains an elemental truth,
> Namely, that a poet without community
> Rustles in the wind like dry grass in December.
> (NCP, 122; TP, 20)

But the result was a faux nationalism that "resurrected the sword of Boleslaw the Brave . . . evoking Scythian/Virtues, penning a Polish Horst Wessel lied" (NCP, 122–23; TP, 21).[14]

At this point we first meet a "schoolboy," obviously Milosz himself, a "dreamer" entranced by the landscapes of the Amazon he has read in a book by the nineteenth-century Irish-American adventurer Thomas Mayne Reid (d. 1883). From his outside viewpoint "up some Amazon," he "will preserve with tenderness [*czułość*] his guides Iwaszkiewicz, Lechoń, and Słonimski. . . . As they lived in his young and ardent mind" (NCP, 124; TP, 23). (This is the "tenderness" that, as we have already seen, Milosz looks to in Part IV to save Poland from the rigors of Marxist thought.)[15]

But they have not addressed the weaknesses threatening the Republic, for which "Piłsudski should not shoulder all the blame" (NCP, 125; TP, 23). Instead, for the first time, the poet addresses his audience with an indication of what to do.

> Young reader, you won't live inside a rose.
> That country has its planets, its rivers,
> But it is as frail as the edge of the morning.
> It's we who create it every day anew,
> By respecting as real many more things
> Than are frozen between a noun and its sound.
> We wrest them into the world by force.
> If got too easily, they don't exist at all.

So, farewell, things gone. Your echo calls us,
But we need to speak gracelessly and roughly.
(NCP, 125; TP, 24; emphasis added)

As we shall see in Part IV, the "rose" is explicated there as "a sexual symbol / Symbol of love and superterrestrial beauty" (NCP 147; TP, 53)—living in it is, in short, an escape from history.

In a note to this passage, Milosz explicates even further:

We sustain the existence of the realm of poetry only through daily effort. It is wrested from the world not by negating the things of the world, but *by respecting them more than we respect aesthetic values.* That is the condition for creating valid beauty. If it is obtained too easily, it evaporates. This passage presents the principle of realistic poetics applied by the author in *A Treatise on Poetry.* (TP, 93n; emphasis added)

Milosz is repeating here, albeit with more tenderness, the message to ground poetry in "extra-aesthetic consciousness" that he expressed in his prewar manifesto, "The Lie of Poetry" (1938).[16]

Part II closes with an episode under the barrage balloons that were erected to protect Warsaw on the eve of World War II. Like the close of Part I, it is about mundane rather than "superterrestrial" sexuality. A watchman, identified, but in the English translation only, as Milosz himself (who briefly was an air raid watchman) hears the voices of "a little whore and a worker from Tamka" making love in the weeds nearby.[17] Perhaps aware as a catastrophist of imminent disaster, his response is, "I do not know how to bear my pity" (NCP, 126; TP, 25).

The end of Part II marks the beginning of the narrator's personal alienation from the world around him, which will become central to the poem's open closure. But it is also another sign of the gap between sentient thinkers and the Polish people—the underlying problem discussed in Part III.

A TREATISE ON POETRY, III, "THE SPIRIT OF HISTORY"

The opening of Part III collapses Poland's wartime experience into an apocalyptic epitome of destructiveness: not just of the art, institutions, and literature of civilization, but even of its moral and spiritual underpinnings:

When gold paint flakes from the arms of sculptures,
When the letter falls out of the book of laws,
Then consciousness is naked as an eye.

> When the pages of books fall in fiery scraps
> Onto smashed leaves and twisted metal,
> The tree of good and evil is stripped bare.
>
> When a wing made of canvas is extinguished
> In a potato patch, when steel disintegrates,
> Nothing is left but straw huts and cow dung
> (NCP, 127; TP, 29)

The third line once again evokes Heidegger's condition (quoted in chapter 6) of *"Dasein face to face with its original nakedness."* For a moment Milosz, recalling the catastrophe of Warsaw's destruction, has resumed the prophetic / vatic style that we saw him appropriate from Genesis in "Flight."[18] But there is a new influence in his style here: that of "Lord Weary's Castle" by Robert Lowell, whom Milosz first met when still a diplomat in America (YH, 219).

Calling Lowell a "new Keats," Milosz had translated and commented on "Children of Light" in 1947 for a Warsaw journal. There he found Lowell's dense clusters of consonants—"A brackish reach of shoal off Madaket"—congenial, comparing them to a line of Mickiewicz—"Zamek na barkach nowogrodzkiej" (A castle sits on Nowogródek hill)—that reappears in this part of the Treatise (NCP, 137; TP, 41).[19]

Milosz must have also felt close to Lowell's antinomies, and his outsider's ambivalence towards both the oppressive Christianity into which he was born, and the sterile materialism that was replacing it. In keeping with the heightened imagery, the structure of the Treatise now also changes, becoming like Lowell's more disjointed, dialectical, and ambivalent—reflecting both the lack of settled social traditions in America and also the poet's own internal turmoil.

We see this in the very next lines. Shifting to a more quotidian voice, Milosz describes how life in Warsaw was concentrated, after city life had been destroyed, into a struggle for survival. As the notes clarify, the poem "draws on scenes observed by the author. The death agony of an old man, Jewish, attracted no attention: that was part of the general callousness and indifference" (TP, 97n; cf. TP, 30).

Then once again in a vatic voice, Milosz speaks the lines I quoted earlier, describing his arrival at Goszyce:

> Where wind carries the smell of the crematorium
> And a bell in the village tolls the Angelus,[20]
> The Spirit of History is out walking.
> He whistles, he likes these countries washed
> By a deluge, deprived of shape and now ready. . . .
> He stretches his thick fingers toward the sky.

Under his palm, a rider on a bicycle:
The organizer of a security network,
A delegate of the military faction in London.
Poplars, as tiny as rye plants in a gully,
Conduct the eye to the roof of a manor
From the forest, and there, in the dining room,
Tired boys are lounging in officers' boots.
(NCP, 128; TP, 30)

In an important note to "the Spirit of History," Milosz raises the question he has raised in various forms so many times:

> Is history just a mass of facts, with no traceable logic or direction? Or is it subject to hidden laws? . . . According to Hegel, mankind, throughout its life in time, that is, in history, is pushed forward by the internal necessity of the human mind. History therefore is not chaos, and at every moment we may discern the actions of a Zeitgeist, a Spirit which pushes man to a higher stage of development. (TP, 97–98n)

But the elliptic reference to the bicycle rider of the secret Home Army, and "the tired boys . . . in officer boots" he had seen at Goszyce, evoke a note twice as long. It explains: "The poet . . . stresses the durability of prewar class divisions—the manor, the boys in officers' boots. . . . The poem takes as its subject poetry, not politics. Part three tries to answer the question of how to save poetry [*jak ocalić poezję*], save its very existence" (TP, 99n).

But to save poetry is also to save society, because the health of society depends on the health of its literature, and ultimately its poetry.[21]

> In the whole debate about the Spirit of History, it would seem that the following premise is detectable. Human societies live enveloped in myths and legends. Sometimes these myths and legends serve a positive function, but they become harmful when they obscure reality. History [*Historia*], its Spirit, does not favor those who refuse to examine reality in its nakedness (TP, 99–100n).

Milosz then points to Nazi Germany as "a society entangled in delusion," but in context it is clear that he extends that judgment as well to the Polish exile government in London and its Home Army.

> The narrator assumes that there is a certain level of reality below which no real poetry can be accomplished. A poet should not be the prisoner of national myths: . . . The government in exile in London and its underground state meant a continuation of prewar Poland, both its mentality and its poetry. A break with that poetry, a new beginning, amounted to distancing oneself from the rhetoric of the underground state. A new poetry, intellectual and ironic, might be able to

cope with atrocity and the sense of absurdity. So this chapter describes a breakthrough in Polish poetry which can be dated roughly to 1943. After the end of hostilities, that new poetry would play its own game, distancing itself from the language of the new rulers, that is, the Communists. (TP, 100n)

In this succinct exposition of what I call his poetic Hegelianism, poetry has supplanted and expanded the role that Hegel attributed to Reason (*Vernunft*). One might even say that for him the fundamental Hegelian premise—"the real is the rational"—has become "the real is the daemonic" (i.e., not the left-brain knowable, but that ineffable right-brain correspondence, between mind and the course of events, which in Milosz's view gives poets access to the mysteries of reality).[22]

Milosz has also reversed Hegel in a more hopeful way. For Hegel humans could see the reason for a historical event only after it had happened: "The owl of Minerva takes its flight only when the shades of night are gathering."[23] For Milosz in contrast, the poetic act does not just follow history, but also anticipates it.

Milosz's pursuit of the real would continue all his life; but as he matured, so would his notion of "reality." In this note, however, as in the poem, it is clearly Hegelian. What would not change for Milosz was what in "Przedmowa" and the "Semi-Private Letter" he called poetry's "salutary aim" (NCP, 77) or "salvational goal" (*wybawczy cel*).[24] The mysterious Hegelian link between history and consciousness (or here we should perhaps say the poetic mind) clearly survives in Milosz's 1982 statement, "The poetic act both anticipates the future and speeds its coming" (WP, 109).

Having recognized a discernible dialectic pattern in history, the poem then asks whether or not this pattern is inevitable (as Marxists would have it).

> A poet has already recognized the walker,
> An inferior god to whom time and the fate
> Of one-day-long kingdoms is submitted.
> His face is the size of ten moons. He wears
> About his neck a chain of severed heads.
> Who does not acknowledge him begins to mumble.
> Whoever bows to him attracts his scorn. . . .
> Who are you, Powerful One? The nights are long.
> Do we know you as the Spirit of the Earth,
> Shaking down caterpillars from an apple tree
> So that the thrushes have an easy gleaning?
> Who gathers beetles' legs for a fecund humus
> From which in time the hyacinth flowers?
> Are you and he the same, O Destroyer?
> (NCP, 128; TP, 31)

The Poetic Hegelianism of A Treatise on Poetry   147

Tischner rightly identifies the Destroyer (*Tępiciel*) with the destroying angel of Revelation.[25] But the poem will give us reason to see him also as a feature of modern literature, and notably of Dostoevsky's tale, "The Grand Inquisitor."

Milosz told Gorczyńska that this passage "is based on my question as to whether Hegel's Spirit of History is the same spirit that rules the cruel world of nature."[26] He later explained in a note that he is asking whether Darwinian necessity, which underlies late-Marxist materialism, "applies to history as well."[27] (Both in poetry and in prose, Milosz returned many times to this question, relating it to his later fascination with Manichaeanism.)[28]

This passage in Part III is the one which Milosz quoted in *Native Realm* when summarizing "the most vital part" of the poem; and we have already seen that his simple prose answer there to the question put here to the Destroyer is, no: "In nature's kingdom necessity is the only good; not so for us" (NR, 295). But we will see that the poetic answer in Part IV is far more complex and in the tradition of Brzozowski, who "in the same breath . . . would say 'yes' and 'no.'"[29]

PREWAR POLAND'S NEED FOR A "NEW DICTION"

Much of the remainder of Part III expands on the dilemma that the poet discerned when recognizing the Spirit of History:

> Who does not acknowledge him begins to mumble.
> Whoever bows to him attracts his scorn.
> (NCP, 128; TP, 31)

The former are those who cling irrationally to the myths and legends of prewar Poland; the latter are the Marxists for whom dialectical materialism becomes the New Faith. Both camps failed to find the "new diction" that will save.

Milosz returns to this dilemma two pages later:

> We do not know at all
> How to unite Freedom and Necessity.
>
> In a dream the mind visits two sharp edges.
> Woe to the unearthly [*nieziemskich*, i.e., "unworldly"], the radiant ones.
> While storming heaven, they neglect the Earth
> With its joy and warmth and animal strength.
> Woe to the reasonable [*rozważnych*], the heavy-minded.
> Their lies will extinguish the morning star,
> A gift more durable than Nature is, or Death. . . . [30]

> Poetry feels too much. Therefore its silence.
> Still it responds to a distant call,
> Not ready to bear the weight of something new.
> (NCP, 130; TP, 33)

The "unworldly" are addressed first:

> The twenty-year-old poets of Warsaw
> Did not want to know that something in this century
> Submits to thought, not to Davids with their slings.
> (NCP, 130; TP, 33)

In *Ocalenie* one of these young martyrs had been addressed and reproved for his "inspiration of hatred" ("It is madness to live without joy," NCP, 77, 76). Here they and their martyrdoms are remembered by name and described lovingly. But a note echoes the judgment in "Przedmowa" ("You took farewell to an epoch as the beginning of a new one," NCP, 77): "Their sensibility testifies to the survival of an eerie Polish romanticism from the beginning of the nineteenth century. . . . But postwar Polish poetry did not follow in their footsteps" (TP, 104n).

Milosz then turns to the "reasonable," those who were not unworldly martyrs in the Warsaw uprising, but survivors who

> ran through fields, escaping
> From themselves, knowing they wouldn't return
> For a hundred years.
> (NCP, 132; TP, 35)

They would have to deal with a world completely despoiled of past order.

> Before them were spread
> Those quicksands where a tree changes into nothing,
> Into an anti-tree, where no borderline
> Separates a shape from a shape, and where,
> Amid thunder, the golden house of *is*
> Collapses, and the word *becoming* ascends.
> (NCP, 132; TP, 35)

Milosz makes explicit here in poetry the distinction between *is* (JEST) and *becoming* (STAJĘ SIĘ, literally "becomes"),[31] which we saw underlies the structure and movement of *Ocalenie*. In a note Milosz identifies the collapse of the golden house with the displacement of the medieval world-view of St. Thomas by the "discovery of movement . . . culminating in the belief in universal evolution."

The clash between the static and dynamic principles acquired for some Polish thinkers a political meaning. That was the view of the philosopher Józef Maria Hoene-Wroński (1778–1853), according to whom the struggle between the conservative force of *être* (to be) and the revolutionary force of *devenir* (to become) had been tearing Europe apart since the French revolution. (TP, 107n)[32]

A succeeding note specifies that "the Polish government in exile and its army represented the principle of *être*, namely, a return to prewar Poland" (TP, 107n). The survivors

> . . . all of them
> Carried the memory of their cowardice,
> For they didn't want to die without a reason.
> (NCP, 132; TP 35)

Instead, they (i.e., "those who opted for the power of *devenir*," TP, 108n) crawl to the feet of the Spirit and sing to him:

> "King of the centuries, ungraspable Movement,
> You who fill the grottoes of the ocean
> With a roiling silence, who dwell in the blood
> Of the gored shark devoured by other sharks. . . .
> You without beginning, you always between
> A form and a form, 0 stream, bright spark,
> Antithesis that ripens toward a thesis,
> Now we have become equal to the gods,
> Knowing, in you, that we do not exist."
> (NCP, 132–33; TP, 36)

The singers' hymn to the Spirit of History reflects ideological aspects of our own age, from the Faustian element Milosz sees in contemporary literature (where "action creates Value, thus man becomes a god")[33] to, above all, the "dread spirit, the spirit of self-destruction and non-existence," in Ivan Karamazov's tale, "The Grand Inquisitor."[34]

Contained in this scene of idolatry is the germ of a cultural critique that Milosz, expanding on Dostoevsky, would develop at length in *The Land of Ulro*—a critique, once again, not limited in its thrust to those behind the Iron Curtain. But these "reasonable" survivors, like the "unworldly" martyrs before them, retain their humanity:

> . . . every one of them
> Kept hidden a hope that the possessions of time
> Were assigned a limit. That they would one day
> Be able to look at a cherry tree in blossom,

> For a moment, unique among the moments,
> Put the ocean to sleep, close the hourglass,
> And listen to how the clocks stop ticking.
> (NCP, 133; TP, 37)[35]

According to Milosz, "The ocean, the hourglass, clocks, they all represent the flood of time."[36]

THE FINAL PAGES OF PART III: BREAKDOWN

At this point, with Warsaw occupied and eventually reduced to rubble, and the voices of survivors either scattered, imprisoned in ghettos, or subverted to Stalinist idolatry, the coherent argument breaks down. The final eight pages of this section are a chaos in which the narrator's voice, except for brief moments, is replaced by the voices of those whom poetry failed to save. In this it is much like parts of *The Waste Land*, especially its closure. Eliot's fragmented voices caught the spirit of social breakdown after World War I; Milosz concentrates them here to correspond to the war phase in a larger arc of time.

The first speaker is a ghettoized Jew, robbed of the security of his faith:

> When they give me an injection of phenol,
> When I walk half a step with phenol in my veins,
> What wisdom of the prophets will enlighten me?
> (NCP, 133; TP, 37)[37]

The poem, now in fragments, lurches from the voice of the martyred Jew to "the awkward speech of Slavic peasants," "an anonymous song" for Jewish girls marching," and snatches from Mickiewicz. Poland "deprived of shape" and social organization, is characterized now only by its "Plains, empty and listless," that stretch from Skiernewice in Poland to the Urals (NCP, 136; TP, 40).[38]

We next hear the poet anticipating his own escape from this wreckage of history to the calm of nature in America (in Part IV):

> Wooded hills, clear waters are needed.
> A man can never be defended here. . . .
> The idea of a center slowly fades. . . .
> He who was not born on these level plains [that is, Milosz]
> Will sail the seas. . . .
> Or chase the reflection of his homeland

In the pines and black-green rivers of Maine.
(NCP, 137; TP, 41–42)[39]

The narrator at this point is about to escape from the Poland of

Pickled cucumbers in a sweating jar.
A sprig of dill. Cucumbers are eternal.
(NCP, 136; TP, 40)

According to Tischner, Słowacki once criticized Poles for their "taste for pickled cucumbers."[40] But Milosz is not being literary here; he is describing the farm house near Skierniewice where he stayed after being robbed on his way from Warsaw to Goszyce, and dug potatoes like a peasant (TP, 40; cf. 44). He then recalls the "'light' spirits" in Mickiewicz's *Forefathers' Eve*, "who cannot enter heaven because they were too happy on earth . . . ask for a mustard seed, and . . . recite. . . .

He who has never tasted bitterness
Will never taste sweetness in heaven.
(HPL, 215; cf. NCP, 136; TP, 41, 111n)

But even Mickiewicz's life "distilled from classical herbs," his castle "on the Nowogródek hill" (NCP, 137; TP, 41)—even that (Milosz told Gorczyńska) is "a luxury now." The new world is being prepared in which "The man not born to these level plains [i.e., but instead in hilly Lithuania] / Will sail the seas" to the Dordogne and Maine (NCP, 137; TP, 42).

The peasants in the treatise are also disaffected:

That Mickiewicz is too hard for us
What does the learning of lords [*szlachta*] and Jews have to do with us?[41]
We worked with a plough, with a harrow.
On feast days we heard another music.
(NCP, 137; TP, 42, adapted)[42]

Asked to explain the poem's erratic leaps here, Milosz explained,

That structure has the logic of historical events. . . . The dead man's poem refers to the final liquidation of the ghetto, the slaughter of the Jews. And then all that is left is an earth that is burdened, blood-stained, desecrated. . . . And the question arises, What will be left in the end? Grass, pickles, that's the essence of Polishness. The crime burdening the land was the crime against the Jews. The past is Mickiewicz, culture is Mickiewicz, but the reality is:

"Pickled cucumbers with a stalk of dill
Ferment in sweat-beaded jars."

That's the real Poland. Everything has been wiped out, but the pickles remain.
. . . A total mess.[43]

Not quite total. The peasants now turn to "another music": simple folk carols in old Polish.

> Hu du hu du
> We are playing too
> We sing to Christ the Lord
> Not for a reward
> Hu du
> (NCP, 138; TP, 42–43)

This first explicit reference to Jesus Christ in the poem (and in Milosz's entire corpus of translated poetry) is naïve but not trivial. Together with two earlier more oblique references—to the "Angel of the Lord" (*Anioł Pański*, "Angelus" in English, NCP, 128; TP, 30) and "Mother of God" (*Matka Boska*, "Madonna" in English, NCP, 131; TP, 34)—it completes the ironic framing of the "Spirit of History" section. In this way, the section acknowledges the enduring reality of Polish Christianity, which guaranteed, Milosz could rightly believe in 1956, that the "new faith" of Communism was superficial and would ultimately fail.[44] (1956 was the year of the Poznan riots in Poland and subsequent "Polish October," similar to if overshadowed by the major Hungarian uprising at the same time. These were the first major upheavals in the Soviet bloc. And they were harbingers of the overthrow two decades later, after Pope John Paul's victorious tour of his native Poland, with the simple message, "be consistent in your faith," became, as is widely recognized, a catalyst for Poland's successful revolution.)[45]

After pages of phantasmagoria, how can one establish closure? Eliot's solution in *The Waste Land* is for the return, in the first person, of the narrator's voice:

> I sat upon the shore
> Fishing, with the arid plain behind me
> Shall I at least set my lands in order?
> London Bridge is falling down falling down falling down
> *Poi s'ascose nel foco che gli affina*
> *Quando fiam uti chelidon*—O swallow swallow
> *Le Prince d'Aquitaine à la tour abolie*
> These fragments I have shored against my ruins. . . .

Milosz's similar closure to the section also sets his fragments in perspective:

> I rolled a cigarette and licked the paper.
> Then a match in the little house of my hand.
> And why not a tinderbox with flint?
> The wind was blowing. I sat on the road at noon,
> Thinking and thinking. Beside me, potatoes.
> (NCP, 139; TP, 44)[46]

The narrator, caught between thinking and potatoes, is once again in the gap we saw in the closures of sections 1 (between the fat singer[47] and her song of "a hero's grave"), and 2 (between the watchman and the little whore from Tamka).

But in this third closure the narrator speaks using the first person (for the first time in the Polish version, as opposed to the English). More than that, in thinking of potatoes, he is recalling the brief time of his peasant-like work in Skierniewice (a "return to an elementary existence," NR, 253) while escaping from Warsaw to Goszyce.[48]

Thus the stage is set for the very different, very personal narration in Part IV.

Chapter 12

"A Treatise on Poetry,"
Part IV: "Natura"

I left for America under the protection of Jerzy Putrament and Jerzy Borejsza. Putrament warned me: "Remember that you are signing a pact with the devil." And it was, no doubt, a pact with the devil, considering my consciousness of what had happened. . . . I suffered and accused myself of prostitution.

—Czeslaw Milosz[1]

The shift from impersonal to personal narration in Part IV is evident even in the title: "Part IV, "NATURA / Pennsylvania, 1948–1949." Though the section will make a general argument for choosing history (Europe) over nature (Pennsylvania), the *dating* (1948–1949) establishes that we have here an autobiographical account of Milosz's difficult personal choice at that time: what to do and where to go when his diplomatic posting to America ended in 1950.[2]

Even when he was sure he needed to break with Stalinism, he still faced two choices: whether to defect quietly in America (as Janka, now in a difficult pregnancy, urgently wished), or publicly in Europe, as part of the cultural cold war then waging over the uncertain political future of Italy and France. "Natura" develops, with misgivings, Milosz's elaborate philosophical argument for choosing the second option, concluding that "we needed to be of use" (NCP, 150; TP, 60).

Almost from the opening of Part IV, it is clear that the "nature" described in this section will be America as experienced from the European perspective of Milosz himself—sharing little or nothing with the "nature" of Frost or even Wordsworth:

155

> The garden of Nature opens.
> The grass at the threshold is green.
> And an almond tree begins to bloom.
>
> *Sunt mihi Dei Acherontis propitii!*
> *Valeat numen triplexJehovae!*
> *Ignis, aeris, aquae, terrae spiritus,*
> *Salvete!*—says the entering guest.
>
> Ariel lives in the palace of an apple tree,
> But will not appear, vibrating like a wasp's wing,
> And Mephistopheles, disguised as an abbot
> Of the Dominicans or the Franciscans,
> Will not descend from a mulberry bush
> Onto a pentagram drawn in the black loam of the path.
>
> But a rhododendron walks among the rocks
> Shod in leathery leaves and ringing a pink bell.
> (NCP, 140; TP, 47)

As Milosz explained later, the Latin text here is the diabolic incantation

> used by Faust in Marlowe's *Doctor Faustus*. Translated, it says: "May the gods of Acheron be friendly, praised be the triple name of Jehovah, welcome, spirits of fire, air, water, and earth." Nature here is magical, straight from a fairy tale. Ariel, who lives in a palace of apple trees, Mephistopheles, the pentagram, are connected with Faust and the forces of nature.[3]

This passage, like others in Part IV, is dense with possible and conflicting meanings; Tischner, for example, sees Goethe's *Faust II* being imitated here.[4] But why then would Milosz quote directly instead from *Marlowe's Doctor Faustus*? Because, I believe, he wishes us to think of the entire evolving Faustian tradition, and not least of Thomas Mann's novel, *Doktor Faustus* (1947). For the Faustian pact made by Mann's hero with the devil centers on sacrificing love for the sake of power. Similarly, Milosz, in "Natura," will turn away from the "rose" (TP, 55) of love (and the chance to experience a calm life in American nature) and choose instead a life in historical Europe, enabling him to become famous by writing *The Captive Mind* (TP, 119n, 121n).[5]

But in Milosz's passage I am more struck by two other powerful and antithetical allusions: the first being to innocence and the countryside of his childhood, and the second (to which we will return) to his self-damnation ("a pact with the devil").[6]

First, innocence. This magic scene evokes his native Lithuania, as he had described it in his autobiographical novel *The Issa Valley* (1955): a region that "has the distinction of being inhabited by an unusually large number of devils," making the peasant wives there set out milk by their door for the water snakes, and "recall the struggle being waged for dominion over the human soul."[7] It is also the homeland of Mickiewicz, who "sprang from a hinterland untouched by the skepticism of the Age of Reason," and thus was able to describe in *Forefathers' Eve* "the juncture of two historical epochs."[8]

In America, however, the narrator is, like Wallace Stevens in "Comedian as the Letter C" (TP, 113n), a *"Socrates of snails . . . musician of pears"* (NCP, 140; TP, 48)—that is to say, not an inheritor of shared myths but a creator of his own "supreme fictions."[9] Accordingly Nature "does not respond" (TP, 113n).

THE 2001 TRANSLATION: NATURE, MAN, AND "THE ETERNAL MOMENT"

As we might expect from a poet of doubleness, "Natura" has two competing nodes or foci of attention. One is philosophical, and we shall see that this is given great emphasis in the 2001 English translation by expansive notes about the "eternal moment" or *moment wieczny*, that Milosz said in his Leman Notebook poem should be sought, or plucked, from movement or history, not "in what is" (see chapter 11).[10]

The other focus is personal; it is about his dangerous decision in 1950 to abandon the safety of America and risk imprisonment by returning to Stalinist Poland. As we shall see, the original 1956 poem has more to say about the "gale" "in you and in me" (W 2:246) caused by his decision to travel to Europe alone. I shall argue that the "you" here can only refer to his wife, Janka, and that the original poem in Polish dealt in part with his having abandoned her in the midst of her difficult pregnancy.

We saw that, when translating *Ocalenie*, Milosz decided not to translate his poems literally, but to rewrite them slightly in the light of his changed American situation. The same has happened here in the 2001 translation, done in the 1990s when Janka was dead and Milosz was happily remarried.

The gale "in you and in me" does not appear in the 2001 English translation, having been replaced by the much less meaningful gale "in us" (NCP, 151; TP, 61). And the "eternal moment" in the 2001 translation (NCP, 149; T 58), commented on as a *moment wieczny* in the Polish version of the notes, is not really in the 1956 Polish poem at all. "The eternal moment" (NCP, 149; TP, 58) is used to translate "temat wieczny" (W 2:246), for which a more literal translation would be "the eternal topic," or "the eternal theme."

Both the early and the late versions of the poem are of great interest. And each version corresponds to part of his anguished mind in 1950, when faced with the difficult decision over how to defect from the Stalinist government in Warsaw. It was for him a tragic dilemma, between engaging with history in Europe, the only way he could see remaining in touch with his literary career and audience, and remaining in America with his wife Janka, in the midst of her difficult pregnancy.

We shall focus at first on the 2001 translation.

THE 2001 TRANSLATION: MILOSZ'S EPIPHANIC QUEST FOR A BEAVER

Nature's non-responsiveness to Man, who is "alien to Nature because of his mind" (TP, 113n) is the first subject of "Natura," and the first step in the poet's decision in it to turn away from Nature (in America) back to History (in Europe). Milosz repeatedly tells how painful this decision is (even though, in so doing, he fails to mention here that it led to disagreement with and separation from his wife): "This section of *Treatise on Poetry* is also very closely bound with my experience in America when I was here, in 1949, 1950. Very painful and difficult issues prompted these thoughts. Even if I had wanted to forget about my poetry, my language, America would have still been completely static for me."[11]

Therefore, as we have already seen, "in the fall of 1950 I said farewell to America. That was probably the most painful decision of my life—though none other was permissible" (NR 283).

This painful choice between nature and history repeatedly interrupts the poet's vivid personal narration of a night quest ("on a lake in northern Pennsylvania," TP, 114n) in search of a beaver:

> To keep the oars from squeaking in their locks.
> He binds them [in Polish, "I bound," *Zwijałem*][12] with a
>   handkerchief. . . . My boat
> Divides the aerial utopias of the mosquitoes
> Which rebuild their glowing castles instantly.
> A water lily sinks, fizzing, under the boat's bow.
> (NCP, 141; TP, 48–49)[13]

Milosz (now no longer an impersonal narrator) sees the beaver:

> . . . . I wait an hour
> In the silence, senses tuned to a beaver's lodge.
> Then suddenly, a crease in the water, a beast's

black moon, rounded, ploughing up quickly
from the pond-dark, from the bubbling methanes.
(NCP, 141; TP, 49)

His response to this epiphany is twofold. On the one hand he, just like the beaver, is part of Nature:

I am not immaterial and never will be.
My scent in the air, my animal smell,
Spreads, rainbow-like, scares the beaver:
A sudden splat.
(NCP, 141–42; TP, 49)

At the same time, this coming to consciousness (provoking the narrator's first use for himself in Polish of the first-person pronoun, *ja*, "I") "brings back a sense of the distance separating man from Nature" (TP, 114n):

.... I [*ja*] remained where I was
In the high, soft coffer of the night's velvet,
Mastering what had come to my senses:
How the four-toed paws worked, how the hair
Shook off water in the muddy tunnel.
It does not know time, hasn't heard of death,
Is submitted [*poddany*, i.e., subject] to me because I [*ja*] know
    I'll die.
(NCP, 142; TP, 49)

This second, opposite awareness of being in time (becoming) provokes an outburst of quite contrary memories from Europe: some of them historical and "from another epoch" ("That wedding in Basel," TP, 49), and some admittedly "personal" (TP, 115n). A key image is quaintly erotic ("Felt out the hooks and clasps of the silk / And the dress opened like a nutshell, / Fell from the turned graininess of the belly," NCP, 142; TP, 50; cf. 51). In this way the focus "shifts to personal matters. History and the personal flow into each other."[14]

(A clue to this mysterious reverie may perhaps be found in a line from his much later poem "The Hooks of a Corset": "I endow with a philosophical meaning the moment when I helped her to undo the hooks of her corset"; and his still later comment on this line in 1986: "I guess that if we are truly in love we don't have these thoughts.")[15]

This entry into reflection leads to what Milosz later called "the basic motif" of the poem: "the search for eternal values, eternal truths, by denying the flow of time."[16] Here is the passage he is referring to:

> Yesterday a snake crossed the road at dusk.
> Crushed by a tire, it writhed on the asphalt.
> We are both the snake and the wheel.
> There are two dimensions. Here is the unattainable
> Truth of being, here, at the edge of lasting
> and not lasting. Where the parallel lines intersect,
> Time lifted above time by time.
> (NCP, 143; TP, 51)

The last line ("Czas wyniesiony ponad czas przez czas" [W 2:237]) is clearly, as Milosz confirms, a reference to Eliot's "Burnt Norton" (TP, 116n).[17] We have now arrived in the poem to the lines about tenderness "with salvation in it" ("a w niej ocalenie" [W 2:238]) with which this analysis opened: Milosz calls for a "new diction" that

> ... might allow us to express
> A new tenderness [*czułość*] and save us from a law
> That is not our law, from necessity
> Which is not ours, even if we take its name.
> (NCP, 144; TP, 51–52)[18]

Milosz has experienced the Brzozowskian awareness that "We do not belong to it [the kingdom of Nature] / And still, in the same instant, we belong" (NCP, 144; TP, 51). From this mix of belonging and not belonging comes the hope that poetry, both grounded in a "heightened sense of history" and also outside history, can "unite the beaver's furriness and the smell of the bulrushes [nature] / And the wrinkles on the hand holding a pitcher from which wine trickles [remembered history]."[19]

THE 2001 TRANSLATION: BEING, BECOMING, AND AN "ETERNAL MOMENT"

This is what I mean by Milosz's poetic Hegelianism, the ambition to achieve, however briefly, a synthesis between our antithetic dimensions of nature and history, Being and Becoming, *être* and *devenir*, the eternal and the transitory. As he explains in his notes, the narrator in the poem "wants to retain both ends of the contradiction," and unite, "if only for a second," with the "eternal moment" (Eliot's "still point") "outside the flow of time" (TP, 122n, 121n; cf. NCP, 150; TP 58–59). Milosz expanded on this paradox to Gorczyńska: "Sufficiently intense thought about history leads to a dimension that is truly divine, because the entire idea of secular progress, dialectical movement, and in change is in fact taken from the Bible, modified and translated into secular language."[20]

As explained in the poem and notes, the "eternal moment [*moment wieczny*, W 2.246] "often appears in the writings of mystics from various civilizations" (TP, 121n). But when he links it to "the idea of secular progress," Milosz also gives it an entirely new and unprecedented relevance: that through what he calls historicity (a heightened and altered understanding of history), we can retain both the biblical awareness of the divine and the enlightenment sense of progress in human development, by freeing the latter from the Marxist "materialist concept of history." In other words, history, though it "grows out of ourselves" (NR, 295), has a pattern with a spiritual dimension, and it falls to the poet to restore that connection to the eternal. (The poem here begins to focus on Milosz's personal choice of a personal future.)

Milosz at this moment, as earlier in "Notebook: Banks of Leman," is once again speaking as a prophet—no longer just of Polish culture, but of what is increasingly being called a new, postmodern and post-secular age. His vision is clearly rooted in those of his cousin Oscar, as well as of Brzozowski, Weil, and Blake. But by relating it to both traditional and secular arguments, and then responding to them, Milosz's insight is also entirely new.

This denouement, of wanting "to retain both ends of the contradiction" [TP, 122n], allows us to see more deeply the dialectical development of the poem, between Part I (when tradition dominates, and Wyspiański "couldn't overcome the contradiction" between it and the dream of a new nation [NCP, 114; TP, 9]), and Part III, where tradition, "the golden house of *is*, / Collapses, and the word *becoming* ascends" [NCP, 132; TP, 35]. Where the previous sections ended in unresolved oppositions, Milosz now offers, from a fresh perspective outside history, a new poetic synthesis.

Milosz now asks, "Why cry out / That a sense of history destroys our substance?" (NCP, 144; TP, 52). "A sense of history" here translates the Polish *historyczność*, elsewhere translated as "historicity" (TP, 116–17n) or (more helpfully) *historicité* (TP, 116n), a term used by Sartre to denote a human's uniqueness and therefore freedom.[21] Though Milosz has contempt for the subjective "warmed-over Jacobin ideas" of the existentialists ("They were just talking in their sleep," NR, 274–75), he does see in *historyczność* an "instrument" (the "muse of our grey-haired father, Herodotus"), "like a plumb with a pure gold center," to restore our equilibrium and thus "rescue human beings" (NCP, 144; TP, 52).

A note here explains that historicity demands (*żąda*) a new skill in thinking, in which we become flexible, able both to react to the flow of time by a "retreat into the fortress of Being," and also to see that "clinging to *être* . . . is doomed to defeat" (TP, 117n). It is worth recalling here how, in *Native*

Realm, Milosz tells how his thinking profited by being ricocheted between the ahistoricism of Americans and the historicism of Kroński:

> I felt at home with his historicism, so I profited from those lessons. Yet my inner castle did not fade; on the contrary, it acquired clarity, thanks to the contradiction. In America, the contradiction inclined me toward *movement*, while in Paris, through my conversations with Tiger, it drove me back toward *being*, and I tried to diagnose my case. Whoever commits himself to movement alone will destroy himself. Whoever disregards movement will also destroy himself, but in a different way. This, I said to myself, is the very core of my destiny—never to be satisfied with one or the other, only at moments to seize the unity of these opposites. (NR, 275–76)[22]

Two years later, in 1959, Milosz would write to Thomas Merton, "How to combine 'transcendence' and 'devenir' [the spiritual and the progressive] has always been my main question."[23] He had no way of knowing yet that, thanks in part to his influence, the same formula would underlie the successful coalition of Solidarność.

INTERLUDE: THE ECSTATIC ODE, "O CITY"

After this elevated passage on *historyczność*—at the level of abstraction for which Karl Shapiro reproached Auden in *The Double Man*[24]—the poem returns to the scene with the beaver:

> With such reflections I pushed a rowboat. . . .
> Aware that at this moment I—and not only I [nie ja jeden]—
> Keep, as in a seed, the unnamed future
> (NCP, 144; TP, 52)

It would appear that "seed" (*ziarna*), coming after references to historicity and Herodotus, has the same metaphoric importance here as it did in the "Treatise on Morals," when it also came after a reference to Herodotus, and later to Thucydides:

> Sit down and read Thucydides
> And distil the purple juice
> Until you touch the seed of style
> (*ziarna stylu*, W 2:86)

As we saw, Milosz explained this as meaning not just poetic style, but a social mindset or episteme. Milosz counseled then to "seek out. . . . The human footprint in the legend." Now Milosz's break with the determinism of Krońskian *diamat* is far greater. We are no longer just "*in* the legend," presented then metaphorically as an "avalanche" (and earlier in "To Father Ch," 1934, as a "stream of boiling lava"); the whole unnamed future is now in us. In a note, Milosz compares this openness, from a broadened and deepened comprehension of human history, to the later pragmatism of Richard Rorty: "The narrator is convinced that his new, flexible way of thinking may serve to 'rescue human beings' [*uratowania ludzi*] and to anticipate [in Polish, 'allow us to have hope for,' *pozwoli mieć nadzieję na*] the future. 'Keep, as in a seed, the unnamed future'" (TP, 117–18n, W 2:239n).[25]

Now, as earlier, the confrontation with Nature in the rowboat provokes, *à rebours*, another empowering vision of History from an outside persective. This is in the form of an ode:

> O City, O Society, O Capital,
> We have seen your steaming entrails.
> You will no longer be what you have been.
> Your songs no longer gratify our hearts
>
> Steel, cement, lime, law, ordinance,
> We have worshipped you too long. . . .
> (NCP, 144–45; TP, 53)

In this Ode, the bourgeois city, alienated from the peasantry of the countryside, is destined to disappear, and be replaced by "an oeuvre of our own."

> Those walls of yours are shadows of walls,
> And your light disappeared [*zniknęło*, an adjective, i.e., "gone"] forever.
> Not the world's monument anymore, an oeuvre of our own
> Stands beneath the sun in an altered space.
>
> From stucco and mirrors, glass and paintings,
> Tearing aside curtains of silver and cotton,
> Comes man, naked and mortal,
> Ready for truth, for speech, for wings.[26]
>
> Lament, Republic! Fall to your knees!
> The loudspeaker's spell is discontinued.
> Listen! You can hear the clocks ticking.
> Your death approaches by his hand.
> (NCP, 145; TP, 53–54)

The Mickiewicz-inspired vision at Goszyce in "Flight," of the destruction of Warsaw as the dawn of a new era, is here universalized for humanity: with the death of the bourgeois city, man will emerge naked [*nagi*], like the ladies of "Lament" who walked "naked [*nago*] on the walls of the new Babylon" (W 1:225).

Milosz has offered conflicting interpretations of this memorable passage. In 1970, in the midst of what I consider his conservative decade, Milosz treated this hope of liberation as ironic: "Man liberated from all bonds is either a never-realized project or nothing: an anti-man." And he illustrated his point by paraphrasing Leszek Kołakowski's influential essay, "The Priest and the Jester" ("Kapłan i Błazen," 1959). "Were there no [dogmatic] priest, there would be no [liberating] jester."[27] The similarities between Milosz's thought and his friend Kołakowski's are arresting, but in my view more relevant to Milosz's 1961 poem "Throughout Our Lands," and will be discussed in chapter 13.

But in the 1980s, Milosz later explained to Gorczyńska that the function of this ode is to induce an altered way of looking at civic history from a "higher dimension":

> if one acquires a fuller historical vision, *and if historicism enters a higher dimension*, then all society, all service, the entire state that calls for our service, whether it be a socialist state or another sort, starts to fade for us. It no longer exists for us. A deeper historical vision gives us distance, and we search for something else . . . this is a higher dimension through the medium of intense reflection on history, the past.[28]

Milosz then illustrated this higher dimension by referring to the intersection of "the historical [urban intercourse] and the supernatural [peasant 'communion with the souls of our ancestors'] in Mickiewicz's *Forefathers' Eve*." What makes *Forefathers' Eve* such an unusual work is that intersection of the supernatural and the historical, ancestral rites and political action. And in the poem, "O City, O Society" I depict the relatively short-lived period in which society and the state are able to place unlimited demands on us."[29]

And in the 1990s, finally reestablished in Poland, Milosz abandons ironic reserve for a fully affirmative paraphrase of the ode, returning to the spirit in which I would like to believe he wrote it:

> O City, O Society: The song (in rhymed quatrains) is addressed to society with its oppressive power over the individual. The city invoked is Paris. The author had lived there and would often take the suburban train from the station St. Lazare. A girl in a window, seen from a passing train, unleashes in the narrator a desire to give human beings the freedom of which they are deprived, though

they are not aware of it. The narrator here shows his colors as a socialist, though in his prophecy liberation would not be the result of a revolution on Marxist lines. He envisages victory as the moment when "Man arrives, naked and mortal / Ready for truth, for speech, and for wings." (TP, 118n)

I will return in chapter 16 to Milosz's belittling of contemporary civilization and everyone in it ("We have worshipped you too long," TP, 53), in the light of "a higher dimension." I see this as a different level of history, often called the history of consciousness. I prefer to call it the history of cultural evolution (*ethogeny*), which is also the evolving history of what Burke called our own "second nature."[30]

Milosz sees great poetry, contributing to this cultural evolution, as arising out of what in a companion volume to this one I call our moreness, our human need "to be more than we are." For many, this can mean more sex, or more money. But to those guided as Milosz was by an inner daemon, it is the drive not just to excel in our civilization (our "second nature") but to further develop both ourselves and it (which might be called our third nature). More anon, starting with the next two sections.

INTERLUDE: "THE ROSE ... SYMBOL OF LOVE AND SUPERTERRESTRIAL BEAUTY"

After this peak, the poem plunges back again into what the poem twice calls subjective "grit" (or "dirt"—"brud subiektywny," NCP, 142, 151; TP, 50, 61). But the anticlimax of the return to the first person singular ("An oar over my shoulder, I walked from the woods," NCP 146; TP, 54)[31] is mild compared to the shock of his view of America, confessedly idiosyncratic, which follows:

> America for me has the pelt of a raccoon,[32]
> Its eyes are a raccoon's black binoculars. . . .
> America is for me the illustrated version
> Of childhood tales about the heart of tanglewood,
> Told in the evening to the spinning wheel's hum.
> And a violin, shivvying up a square dance,
> Plays the fiddles of Lithuania or Flanders.
> My dancing partner's name is Birute Swenson.
> She married a Swede, but was born in Kaunas. . . .
> Why not establish a home in the neon heat
> Of Nature? Is it not enough, the labor of autumn,
> Of winter and spring and withering summer?
> (NCP, 146; TP, 54–55)

In America, Birute the Lithuanian and Czeslaw the Pole can converse as equals—that is to say, not in the class-defining languages of Lithuanian and Polish, but in English. This American release from the oppressive divisions of class is expanded on in the lines which follow:

> You will hear not one word spoken of the court
> of Sigismund Augustus on the banks of the Delaware River.
> *The Dismissal of the Greek Envoys* is not needed.
> Herodotus will repose on his shelf, uncut.
> (NCP, 147; TP, 55)

In a note (TP, 129), Milosz tells us that *The Dismissal of the Greek Envoys* was a play by Kochanowski performed at the court of Sigismund Augustus (d. 1572).

It would be wrong to see these lines as a denigration of America. We saw that in Part III Kochanowski was remembered for his "belief that visible beauty / Is a little mirror for the beauty of being" (NCP, 132; TP, 35). But in his *Witness of Poetry*, Milosz will spend pages discussing this play as at the heart of his "Quarrel with Classicism," against the elite culture of a privileged class, not accessible to "the great human family" (WP, 65–67). So America's loss, seen this way, is actually a gain.

This European praise of America, for its lack of a class-bound culture, recalls Goethe's lines to "The United States":

> Amerika, du hast es besser
> als unser Kontinent, der alte.
> Hast keine verfallenen Schlösser
> und keine Basalte.[33]

> America, you have it better
> Than our old continent.
> You have no ruined castles
> and no basalts,—

a poem which Auden, then fresh off the boat, quoted in *The Double Man*, and then reproduced in full in his notes.[34]

LOVE, THE ROSE, AND MILOSZ'S PERSONAL DILEMMA

As we approach the close of "Natura," and the stressful dilemma over how to defect, the tone of the poem itself becomes less philosophical, and more self-questioning, even tormented. Facing an imminent end to his Embassy posting, this awareness of America's potential only enhanced Milosz's Lowellian anguish over what he should do next. A note expands on this dilemma:

> The narrator is obviously in love with American Nature, which he duly romanticizes.... He also loves the way of life in rural parts of the United States, square dances, for instance. Observing one, he asks himself: why not stay in America for good? The temptation is strong, yet it takes its shape exclusively from the American countryside, not its cities. To live on a farm somewhere? It would mean to isolate oneself from the affairs of the twentieth century and from the political and philosophical commitments of Polish poetry. (TP, 118n)[35]

We have turned from the enlightened perspective on history, to an exploration of the issue tormenting Milosz in 1950: whether to return to Europe and history or to remain in ahistorical America. We saw that in *Native Realm* (1958) Milosz called this "a crisis that was to endure over whole months, made more painful because there was no one with whom I could share my burden" (NR 281). But Milosz revealed later that this claim of isolation was not true, when he explained that this passage in the treatise "is connected to a very specific temptation. Thornton Wilder tried to convince me—we'd become very good friends—that I was totally wrong in wanting to return to Poland, that he had a clear vision of my future in America. He'd set me up on a farm where I'd sit and write poems."[36]

This temptation to "establish a home in the neon heat / of Nature" (NCP, 146; TP, 55) is then rendered metaphorically by a song of "the rose only, a sexual symbol, / Symbol of love and superterrestrial beauty," which

> Will open a chasm deeper than your knowledge.
> About it we find a song in a dream:
>
> *Inside the rose*
> *Are houses of gold,*
> *black isobars, streams of cold.*
> *Dawn touches her finger to the edge of the Alps*
> *And evening streams down to the bays of the sea.*

"All you have to do," Milosz later commented, "is take the rose and immerse yourself in it, take a journey of imagination—into the depths of everything."[37] The childlike simplicity of this song recalls, like the carols in Part III, Mahler's climax of his Fourth Symphony with *Des Knaben Wunderhorn*. It also invites comparison, as Tischner points out, to "By the Peonies" in "The World": ("Mother . . . looks for a long time into peony lands, / Where one short instant equals a whole year," NCP, 47).[38] But

> *If anyone dies inside the rose,*
> *They carry him down the purple-red road*
> *In a procession of clocks all wrapped in folds.*
> *They light up the petals of grottoes with torches.*
> *They bury him there where color begins,*
> *At the source of the sighing,*
> *Inside the rose.*
> (NCP, 147; TP, 55–56)

To be buried "inside the rose," here, means to be forgotten by history. But there is tragic irony in this naïve presentation. The saving simplicity of "The World" and the rose is what a divided Milosz will reject in 1950, when, just as later at Bons, he chose history and Europe over nature and America.

In his author's notes, written almost four decades later, Milosz himself gives a deceptively simple explanation of the song: "For the narrator the option of staying in America for good would mean choosing life on its biological level. . . . Though he admires American landscapes, he regards life in Nature as an impoverishment. What replaces history is sex, which becomes for people the main interest, the subject of their explorations" (TP, 119n). And he made a similar comment in the 1980s to Gorczyńska: "This is a song of temptation, because life, apart from history and historical thinking, offers a sufficient number of themes to be explored. . . . The world is full of mysteries . . . so why involve yourself in the history and immediate issues of the twentieth century."[39]

But in *The Year of the Hunter*, written in the year after Janka's death in 1986, Milosz revealed that this abstract contrast between history (*devenir*, Europe) and sex (*esse*, America) had to do with a painful disagreement between his wife and himself, forcing him to choose between love (the rose) and political engagement: "Common sense and decency were on Janka's side: we ought to have stayed in America. For me, however, to stay would have meant choosing birth, copulation, and death, and nothing more. Because I could not imagine any activity involving language here" (YH, 124). Milosz, here, accurately presents the seriousness of the decision being weighed, but the note in 2001 seriously underplays (as the poem does not) its tragic dimension. For the rose he is about to turn away from is not just a symbol of sex, but also of his love for Janka.

Love was at the very center of *Ocalenie*, and of "The World" within it. It was evident also in the two poems involving Janka ("Dear companion of our bloody trek") in *Ocalenie*'s closure. Here the poet-narrator mentions "love" (*miłość*) for only the second time, as what he must turn away from to fulfill a more urgent historical mission.[40]

The poem that calls for a new diction and a new tenderness is also a poem chronicling and explaining his personal suspension of tenderness. For in rejecting the offer of a farm, Milosz was saying no, not just to Wilder, but also to his pregnant wife, whose second pregnancy was then so difficult that her doctor, as I noted earlier, had advised her not to travel.[41] Her preference would have been to raise her children in the security of America, not under the shadow of Stalin in Poland or even France.[42] In leaving America, he would also be leaving, at least for a while, both her and his children.[43]

Milosz never spoke candidly about this marital disagreement until *The Year of the Hunter*, a meditative journal written in 1987 after Janka's death:

> After Tony was born [in 1947], Janka changed, or perhaps it was I who became jealous; whatever the cause, we argued repeatedly, mainly about America. She was an intelligent and loving person, and not the first woman who had to cope with a husband afflicted with philosophical or ideological madness, although my case was a particularly drastic one. . . . For her, America was not first and foremost a land of well-being and wealth; rather, it signified security and a homeland for the children. An ironist, but utterly lacking in cynicism, she wanted to believe, and . . . she believed in American democracy. That's why she found it so difficult to move to France. (YH, 120)

The rose in short, like the invocation of Mephistopheles earlier, becomes a symbol as complex as the decision the narrator makes at this point. It is like a hologram: you can see a positive thing tilting one way; and tilting another way, something quite different. In this way, it captures the torment of Milosz's difficult decision at the time.

THE ODE "O OCTOBER": POETRY AND FREEDOM

The ode, "O October," that follows is also subject to conflicting interpretations. It begins by celebrating an American autumn unburdened by history and the heavy memory of the Bolshevik Revolution ("Let names of months mean only what they mean" [NCP 147; TP, 56]).[44] But it ends by referring to the awesome decision that has just been finalized (October was the month of his return to Europe):

> O October
> Season of poetry, of the total daring
> Of starting one's life at every moment anew,
> You gave me the magic ring which, when turned,
> Sends down a gleam from your jewel of freedom,
> Oh October
> (NCP, 149; TP, 58)

The magic ring here evokes the ring of Gyges in Book Ten of Plato's *Republic* (359e); which, when its jewel was turned inward, rendered the bearer invisible and thus free from all external social restraints. Thanks to poetry, Milosz, having both completed his survey of historicity and also glimpsed the beaver outside it, is now theoretically free from the constraints of history. This ambitious hope ignores the extreme anxiety of Milosz when he set sail from New York, reaching Paris on October 5, 1950.[45]

(Note that the two preceding lyrics in Part IV also promised freedom of a sort, but at a tragic price: the death of the city [in "O City"] or of an individual's memory ["Inside the rose"]). Neither of these lyrics could transcend the dichotomy between the active and contemplative life, which Milosz would later comment on in "Heraclitus" (1960):

> Particular existence keeps us from the light
> (That sentence can be read in reverse as well).
> (NCP, 165)

In a 2001 note to the Treatise, Milosz recalls the significance of this liberation, achieved when still a Polish bureaucrat "writing for the drawer":

> *You gave me the magic ring which, when turned, / Sends down a gleam from your jewel of freedom*: Does not our author, who was in the service of the Polish Embassy in Washington, DC from 1946 to 1950, reveal here conflicts of his own? The magic ring he wears is poetry. It is writing poetry that gives him a hidden sense of freedom. (TP, 120n)[46]

But when he speaks of "starting one's life at every moment anew," Milosz clearly is not thinking of a return in Europe to his diplomatic career. The poem gives a sign of a more significant break from the past—that his historically significant and life-changing decision to defect has already been made, even if tentatively, before his return to Europe by ship.[47]

SECOND THOUGHTS ABOUT THE DECISION TO RETURN

No sooner has this fateful decision been made ("The narrator has said 'no' to a peaceful life on a farm somewhere in America," TP, 120n), then it is partially regretted and objectively criticized. (In doing so, the narrator now speaks again in the first-person plural, not used since Part III).

> There is much with which to reproach us.
> Given the choice, we rejected peaceful silence

And long meditation on the structure of the world
Which deserves respect. Neither the eternal moment
Attracted us as it should, nor purity of style.
We wanted, instead, to move as words move,
Raising the dust of names and of events.
(NCP, 149; TP, 58)

As Milosz comments, "This passage repeats . . . the basic dilemma that confronts the narrator throughout the poem: poetry as contemplation of being [*bytu*] or poetry as participation in movement [*ruchu*], that is, in history, and thus a poetry of commitments? The first choice seems more in harmony with the vocation of the poet; the second involves a departure from the rules of a perfected art in the name of moral (?) passion" (TP, 121n).[48]

But the next note, on "the eternal moment," lifts us to a less divided perspective: "The eternal moment is the opposite of time. It is, if only for a second, outside the flow of time. T. S. Eliot in *The Four Quartets* speaks of 'the still point of the turning world.' This idea often appears in the writings of mystics from various civilizations" (TP, 121n).

"The eternal moment" here ("moment wieczny") is not a translation but a late alteration in English (ca. 1996) of the poem's original Polish (1956): "temat wieczny" ("eternal topic or theme"). Few words could be more antithetical in meaning than "theme" and "moment." To catch the oxymoronic intersection of time and the timeless, "eternal moment" might be seen as an improvement, as well as a helpful allusion to the "moment wieczny" in the Leman Notebook. The Polish note, also from the 1990s, glosses "temat" as "moment" (W 2:246n).[49]

But the Polish word *moment*, which occurs four times in eight pages in the English translation of the poem (TP, 52–59), does not occur once in the Polish text, where one synonym and three unrelated words are used ("chwili," "sekundzie," "temat," "wszędzie," W 2:239–47). It seems clear that Milosz's decision in 1996 to translate and comment on *temat wieczny* ("the eternal theme") as "the eternal moment" was influenced by the English publication in 1990 of his friend Aleksander Fiut's major critical book, *Moment Wieczny— The Eternal Moment* (Berkeley: University of California Press, 1990).

The result is to incline "Natura," in translation, towards a calm philosophic meditation, and serve as a helpful guide to readers and critics. But what is lost from the original Polish is the angst of an imminent choice between "the rose . . . symbol of love" (TP, 55) and the call "to be of use" (TP, 60), the latter choice soon qualified not just as "sometimes burdensome," but "our foolishness" (TP, 60, 61). The interpolation of "eternal moment" in the translation matches, in short, the suppression of Milosz's pained appeal to Janka at the end to understand that their resulting separation, though stormy, will not be permanent.[50]

The remainder of the poem proceeds on the two levels. It both narrates the "subjective grit" of Milosz's decision to return to Europe without Janka, and also continues an objective "polemic with the T. S. Eliot of *The Four Quartets*" (TP, 123n). Between these two levels, the back and forth of the dialectic of the poem continues. He first returns to his desperate confusion at that time, while placing it in perspective:

> Many a man will concede, if he knows himself,
> That he was like one who hears a chorus
> Of voices and doesn't know what they mean.
> Thence, fury. A foot to the accelerator, as if
> Speed could save us from voices and phantoms.
> (NCP, 149; TP, 59)

But at the same time, he defends himself from the charge of conservative accusers from the right:

> And yet the accusers were mistaken, if,
> Shedding tears over the evils of this age,
> They saw us as angels, hurled into an abyss,
> Shaking our fists at the works of God.
> There is no doubt that many perished, infamously,
> Because, like an illiterate discovering chemistry,
> They suddenly discovered relativity and time.
> For others the very roundness of a stone
> Picked up on the bank of a river provided
> The lesson. Or the bleeding gills of a perch,
> Or—the moon rising over banks of clouds—
> A beaver ploughing the slumbering softness of water
> (NCP, 149–50; TP, 59)[51]

(The chorus of accusations from the world of *devenir* in the despondent first passage, and purity of the rising moon [*esse*] of the hopeful second, will be reunited in the transcendent line from Horace—

> Jam Cytherea choros ducit Venus imminente luna
> [Already Cytherean Venus leads her chorus under the rising moon]
> (NCP, 151; TP 61)

—that concludes the poem.)

"A Treatise on Poetry," Part IV: "Natura" 173

The Hegelian effort to reconcile opposites is now addressed, in a rebuke to Eliot on the one hand, and the prewar Cracovian poets of Young Poland in Part I on the other:

> For contemplation fades without resistance.
> For its own sake, it should be forbidden.
> And we, certainly, were happier than those
> Who drank sadness from the books of Schopenhauer,
> While they listened from their garrets to the din
> Of music from the tavern down below.
> (NCP, 150; TP, 59–60; cf. TP, 7)

Commenting on the line, "There is no doubt that many perished infamously," Milosz identified them as those who

> read the subverters of traditional values, Nietzsche and Marx, and are tempted by the nihilist denial of Being, which to medieval thinkers was another name for God. *The narrator advises against such an extreme; he wants to retain both ends of the contradiction.* According to him, the observation of tangible things (the roundness of a stone, the gills of a perch, a beaver) restores our reverence for the fundamental quality of the world, which is *esse*, "to be." Contemplation of that quality is a basic attribute, and the privilege, of poetry. Thus the narrator speaks here as a poet; he defends his craft against the encroachment of social and political duties. (TP, 122–23n, emphasis added)

Here Milosz shows once again the influence of Brzozowski, who, in his "Marxist-Catholic" reading of Hegel, "wanted to embrace everything, to place everything in a balance of opposites."[52] In the same spirit—of "a balance of opposites"—Milosz then expanded on the poetic passage: "*For contemplation fades without resistance*: This line is directed against purity in poetry, but it is also a polemic with the T. S. Eliot of *The Four Quartets*. By renouncing the world for the sake of 'the still point' of perfect stillness outside time, we may deprive contemplation of its intensity" (TP, 123n).

(I detect a similarity between the views Milosz ascribed here to Eliot, and the "Aesthetic Ketman" which in *The Captive Mind* he had described to Polish intellectual escapism—by "plunging into the past and . . . converse with works of great aesthetic value."[53] This attack on quiescence is in fact an attack on his own Ketman—as he later described it in *Native Realm*[54]—while serving the Polish government. And it summarizes his resolve not to return to the life of dissembling he had been practicing.)

All Milosz's arguments in "Natura" have reinforced him in his decision to engage in history rather than live on an American farm. The earlier anguish of the decision has been momentarily eclipsed by the joyous conclusion to the October ode. The decision he has made celebrates, at the end of the poem, liberation from his earlier duplicitous, historically constrained form of life:

> At least poetry, philosophy, action were not,
> For us, separated, as they were for them, [Young Poland]
> But joined in one will: we needed to be of use.
> And that is the—sometimes burdensome—recompense.
> (NCP, 150; TP, 60)[55]

Poetry and action "were not separated." As Milosz comments, "This is a bold statement, yet it is justified to some extent by the very fact of writing a work like *A Treatise on Poetry*. It is, after all, a poem of commitment, both to a vision of what poetry should be and to a non-totalitarian model of society" (TP, 124n).

THE OPEN CLOSURE OF "NATURA"

And now, at the conclusion of "Natura," Milosz invokes three of the four spirits he had prayed to in his Faustian invocation at the outset—"earth" now being omitted.[56]

> Spirits of the air, of fire, of water,
> Keep close to us, but not too close.
> The ship's propeller drives us from you.
> We pass the zone of gulls and dolphins.[57]
> It's not fulfilled: the old hope that Neptune
> Will show his beard, trailing a retinue of nymphs.
> Nothing but ocean which boils and repeats:
> In vain, in vain.
> (NCP, 151; TP, 50)[58]

Does Milosz merely wish here (by omitting the earth in his invocation) to acknowledge that he has renounced the peaceful option of the farm and nature? Or is he also suggesting, more ominously, the fear that he is abandoning his old "pact with the devil" (his communist government service) for a new pact with the devil (engagement—with the CIA-funded Congress for Cultural Freedom—in the anti-communist cultural cold war)?

It is relevant that Milosz at this time "felt increasingly trapped between two worlds, neither of which, to his mind, was manifestly superior to the other."[59] (It was in this period that Milosz composed "A Man from Detroit," a poem "so critical of America that, on Kroński's advice, he decided not to publish it, so that people in Poland would not presume that he had joined the anti-capitalist campaign.")[60]

One thing is certain: in "Natura" Milosz does not foresee a return to his life of dissimulation and writing for the drawer; something more exciting awaits. In the daring of starting his life anew, the classical myths of the past will not constrain, for the future is a *tabula rasa* that his poetry can help make "an oeuvre of our own."[61]

In a note from the 1990s, Milosz explicitly links his decision to leave America to his future role as a cultural warrior for the mind of the West:

> For the author, this was a very difficult option, slightly insane from a practical point of view, but not without a hidden existential logic. Staying in America, he might very well have written contemplative poetry, and he would probably not have produced prose like *The Captive Mind*, *Seizure of Power*, and *Native Realm*, books that arose from the circumstances to which he exposed himself: his feud with the Stalinists and his life as an émigré. *Treatise on Poetry*, written in France in 1955–56, traces a part of that journey. In succinct form, it explains why he could not, either philosophically or politically, be on the right, though he also rejected Communism. (TP, 124–25n)

The end of Milosz's epic sees in the "ship's body" (i.e., human civilization, TP, 125n) an epitome of the forces at work in the poem.

> The ship's body, creaking, carries the freight
> Of our foolishness, vagueness, and hidden faith,
> The dirt of our subjectivity, and the homeless
> White faces of the ones who were killed in combat.
> Carries it where? To the isles of bliss? No,
> In us storm winds drowned that stanza of Horace
> A penknife carved into a wooden bench at school.
> It [i.e., the verse] will not find us in this salt and void:
>
> *Iam Cytherea choros ducit Venus imminente luna*
> (NCP, 151; TP, 61)
> ("Already Cytherean Venus leads choruses [*sic*] under the rising moon." TP, 125n)

This, like the end of the Jewish Bible (with Cyrus saying he will rebuild a temple in Jerusalem, 2 Chronicles 36:23) is what we call an open closure: one that anticipates rather than concludes. After the triumphant prophecies of the poem's two odes, the closure (in the Milosz-Hass translation) is anticlimactically ambiguous, open-ended, unsure. Everything about it echoes Milosz's own uncertainty in 1950 about the journey: "When I embarked in New York my teeth were chattering" (NR, 284).[62]

THE PERSONAL CLOSURE OF 1956: THE GALE "IN YOU AND IN ME"

In the English translation of the Poetic Treatise, the last four lines (beginning with the inscrutable "In us a gale drowned that Horatian verse. ...") bear no clear relation to the poet's intense thoughts about nature and history in Part IV. But in the 1956 Polish version, these same four lines, translated literally, make sense if they refer to the poet's pursuit of history and temporary abandonment of Janka.

In you and in me ["W tobie i we mnie," (W 2:250), versus "in us"][63] a gale drowned that Horatian verse
A penknife carved into a wooden bench at school.
It [i.e., the verse] will not find us in this salty void:
Iam Cytherea choros ducit Venus imminente luna.
(Cf. NCP, 151; TP, 61)

Who is this "you" (singular)? Up to now this intimate pronoun has only been spoken in the poem's songs to abstract forces—to the king of movement (TP, 36), to the city (TP, 53–54), and to October (TP, 57–58). To me the ending on a line from Horace only makes sense if Milosz is speaking on a personal level to Janka, reassuring her that he will not abandon her after his return, the way Aeneas abandoned Dido, or Theseus Ariadne.

Milosz is lamenting that a gale (*wicher*) of turbulent events has drowned out the Horatian tranquility of their love. But we expect a gale to be impermanent (*becoming*), revealing in the end that Venus and the moon (*being*) are still there. So the ending, though fraught with uncertainty and pain, finishes with an *au revoir* to Janka, not an *adieu*.[64]

This personal reading of the poem may be perceived also in the memorable snake image, near the beginning of "Natura," which we considered earlier from a philosophic perspective:

> Yesterday a snake crossed the road at dusk.
> Crushed by a tire, it writhed on the asphalt.
> We are both the snake and the wheel.
> There are two dimensions. Here is the unattainable
> Truth of being, here, at the edge of lasting
> and not lasting. Where the parallel lines intersect,
> Time lifted above time by time.
> (NCP, 143; TP, 51)

Who are the "we" here? Is every human condemned to be a lethal tire, crushing snakes? Or is this someone who, answering the call of history, has abandoned his pregnant wife? Milosz makes no explicit distinction here. But he will return tacitly to his abandonment of a pregnant woman in "Bypassing Rue Descartes" (1980), where he will remember his adolescent murder of a snake "most vividly" among "my heavy sins" (NCP, 394). And the theme of being separated and reunited will supply an underpinning to the dialectical structure and development in Milosz's third treatise, the "Treatise on Theology." (See chapter 14.)

Milosz in 1980 gave Renata Gorczyńska a philosophic rather than personal reading to the poem's Horatian closure:
I describe my journey back to Europe from America, in a certain sense, [as] a farewell to that farm. That is the reason I conclude by quoting Horace: *Iam Cytherea choros ducit Venus imminente luna* . . .
A farewell to the farm, and to the rose as well. A very complicated poem.[65]
More complicated, indeed, than he was willing to share about Janka in 1980 with Gorczyńska.[66]

POSTSCRIPT: THE CLOSE OF "NATURA" AND MICKIEWICZ

Consciously or unconsciously, the conclusion of the treatise contains faint reminiscences of Mickiewicz's two great masterpieces, the drama *Dziady* (*Forefathers' Eve*) and the epic *Pan Tadeusz*. The two works were also published in France by a Polish publisher in exile, with the intention (and result) of strengthening the liberation movement in Poland.

Though I am no Mickiewicz scholar, I would like to think that he hoped to do this by proposing western (French) ideas of freedom, in the service of a non-Russian folk culture, against an alien and intolerant Russian tyranny. (The more permissive Austrian occupation of Poland was never his target.) That is analogous to what I see Milosz doing in Part IV of the poetic treatise, writing about American openness and equality for a Polish audience still subject to the same tyranny.

Dziady, like the treatise, was written in four parts, and has been characterized as combining elements of folklore, history, and personal love in a wholly new genre. It too, like the Treatise (and its quotes from *Dziady* in Part II, NCP 110–11, TP 42), struggles to deal with the Polish problem of consolidating a nation from an effete upper class and an unlettered peasantry:

> Our nation's like a living volcano:
> The top is hard and cold, worthless and dried,
> But boiling, fiery lava seethes inside.

Part III of *Dziady*, written after the failure of the 1830 Polish uprising, attempted to understand it in the perspective of a dialectical theory of history. Part IV of *Dziady*, in marked contrast, combined a disguised account (through a persona, Konrad) of Mickiewicz's own love for a woman, recounted in the context of his personal philosophy of life.[67]

The echo of *Pan Tadeusz* that I see in the treatise is less obvious, but equally important: the open closure of the ending. In chapter 7, I wrote how Milosz's poem "Flight" sees possible hope in a violent and disruptive invasion; and compared it to the finale of Mickiewicz's *Pan Tadeusz*, when the squabbles of the Polish *szlachta* (gentry) are violently disrupted by the Polish Napoleonic army; and "in response to the spirit of the day" (as I quote from Milosz's treatment of the poem in his *History of Polish Literature*) someone "proclaims the peasant a free citizen" (HPL, 229). Thus, in the case of *Pan Tadeusz*, the actual Napoleonic (French) presence creates what Milosz would later say was "needed, a sense of open space ahead" (WP, 14).

In the open closure of both "Flight" and the poetic treatise I see the dictum of Hölderlin (a possible response to the French Revolution), "Wo aber Gefahr ist, wächst das Rettende auch" ("Where there is danger emerges also what can save us"), a mantra that might serve very well for America in the year 2022.

As to the relationship of poetry to that "oeuvre of our own," Milosz would return in *The Land of Ulro* to demonstrating how poetry is needed to serve as a correction to the world's current scientific and deterministic *Weltanschauung*.

PART IV
Milosz as Transnational Author

Chapter 13

Milosz in Berkeley, 1961: "Throughout Our Lands"

In 1950, in Warsaw, I said to a friend of mine, "In ten years I shall write on God, but not earlier.

—Czeslaw Milosz[1]

Call it delusion, but a demonic presence can be felt on this continent.

—Czeslaw Milosz[2]

Religion used to be the opium of the people. To those suffering humiliation, pain, illness, and serfdom, religion promised the reward of an afterlife. But now, we are witnessing a transformation, a true opium of the people is the belief in nothingness after death, the huge solace, the huge comfort of thinking that for our betrayals, our greed, our cowardice, our murders, we are not going to be judged.

—Czeslaw Milosz[3]

In 1965, Milosz, after just five years in Berkeley and still spelling his name with a Polish "ł," published his first book in English, the influential anthology *Postwar Polish Poetry*. His prefatory manifesto provided a rationale for the book, by acknowledging the relocation of his past poetic agenda in a new episteme of dissent and negativity:

The underlying motive, as I see it, was my distrust of a poetry which indulges in negation and in a sterile anger at the world. Man confronted with mechanisms beyond his control is a loser until he learns that what seemed to crush him was, in fact, a necessary trial to open a new dimension and to prepare his mind to

cope with unheard-of circumstances. This, in my opinion, is what has happened
to contemporary Polish poetry. A historical steam-roller has gone several times
through a country whose geographical location, between Germany and Russia,
is not particularly enviable. Yet the poet emerges perhaps more energetic, better
prepared to assume tasks assigned to him by the human condition, than is his
Western colleague.[4]

One can see here the old dialectical European Milosz (who learned from torment to move into a new dimension) adjusting to America; and thus, at some distance from the historical steam-roller, receding from a radical attack on the status quo, to a more traditional defense of culture. The doubleness of his ambivalence at Goszyce, in short, but in a new and indeed global milieu.

Milosz's sentence about "sterile anger" might sound like a challenge to the Beat generation and Ginsberg's "Howl." But in fact Milosz, already an admirer of Henry Miller and Whitman's barbaric yawp, would in his late poem "To Allen Ginsberg" celebrate him as a "good man, great poet of the murderous century, who persisting in folly attained wisdom" (NCP, 611).[5] Writing in prose about the importance of a "leap" for generative poetry ("Either there's a leap or there isn't"), Milosz acknowledged that "Allen Ginsberg's *Howl* was a leap, but only owing to its somewhat hysterical American apocalypse and rage" (YH, 112, 113).

"THROUGHOUT OUR LANDS"
("PO ZIEMI NASZEJ"), 1961

Four years earlier, having just arrived in Berkeley, Milosz had written his first American long poem, "Throughout Our Lands" (NCP, 182–88).[6]

(A more literal translation of *Po ziemi naszej* [W 2:316–22], which I argued for vainly in 1961, would be "Throughout Our Earth," a title I shall use in this chapter.)[7] It records his response to Berkeley in its initial and relatively innocent sexual revolution of the early 1960s, inspired in part by Henry Miller, before the mass marketers of sex and drugs had taken over with their misnamed "Summer of Love."[8]

Milosz's European years had not prepared him for this freedom, and in "Throughout Our Earth" he records his bewilderment

> If I had to tell what the world is for me
> I would take a hamster or a hedgehog or a mole
> and place him in a theater seat one evening
> and, bringing my ear close to his humid snout,
> would listen to what he says about the spotlights,

sounds of the music, and movements of the dance.
(NCP, 182)

And we see, in the sequence, the doubleness of his manifesto. On the one hand he lets his id voice a European kinship with fantasies of nakedness and easy sex he associated with Whitman[9] and would in a decade attribute obsessively to the youthful rebels around him (Visions, 48, 98–100, 108, 130, 189; cf. ABC, 6):

> Who has not dreamt of the Marquis de Sade's chateaux?
> Where one ("ah-h-h!") rubs his hands
> and to the job: to gouge with a spur
> young girls drawn up in line for a footrace[10]
> or to order naked nuns in black-net stockings
> to lash us with a whip as we bite the bedsheets
> (NCP, 187)[11]

On the other hand, now a "catastrophist emeritus"[12] and also remote from the reactionary shadow of the Polish and Gallican churches, he dared (I believe for the first time in his translated works) to affirm Christian dogma to a modern audience:[13]

> And what if Pascal had not been saved
> and if those narrow hands in which we laid a cross
> are just he, entire, like a lifeless swallow
> in the dust, under the buzz of the poisonous-blue flies?
>
> And if they all, kneeling with poised palms,
> millions, billions of them, ended together with their illusion?
> I shall never agree. I will give them the crown.
> (NCP, 184)

This acceptance of Christian devotion as a human fact is echoed in a remarkable Milosz letter of October 5, 1961, to Thomas Merton (a Trappist monk!). Forwarding French translations of both the hedgehog and Pascal sections, Milosz commented on the Pascal section by admitting his own uncertainty and ambivalence: "Dear Merton, I cannot say I found my place in that world of contingencies. I cannot proclaim myself a Catholic, if I do not know whether I am one.... You know, I am thinking of writing on Swedenborg."[14]

In a more conflicted passage, he revealed how far he had receded, after coming to America, away from the search in the *Traktat Poetycki* for an "equilibrium" between Being and Becoming (TP, 122–23n):

What to do with one's Christianity? Why do I consider myself a Christian? Traditions, their pressure? But I feel strongly, as a poet, that all is futility except our striving towards Being. In spite of all my hatred for the Thomists (usually totalitarians); a vengeance of time for their being inheritors of that crazy St. Dominic; what saved the Church from Eastern elements, from gnosis, taking shape via Bulgarian Bogomils in the Albigenses, is an indelible stigma of blood at the same time), in spite of that, I know that the only subject for a philosopher and for a poet is the verb "to be."[15]

The poem echoes this final conviction: "Only this is worthy of praise. Only this: the day" (NCP, 184). But it links the fertility of the natural world to spiritual regeneration:

> Paulina, her room behind the servants' quarters, with one
> window on the orchard
> where I gather the best apples near the pigsty
> squishing with my big toe the warm muck of the dunghill. . . .
> Paulina died long ago, but is.
> And, I am somehow convinced, not just in my consciousness.
> (NCP, 185)

Milosz was, I think, quite mindful that to affirm traditional belief this way broke the new tabus of the 1960s. In "A Task" (1970) he wrote about the "sham" of the epoch: "We were permitted to shriek in the tongue of dwarfs and demons / But pure and generous words were forbidden" (NCP, 259).

"Throughout Our Earth" wanders between visions of California with its "spiraled freeways" and memories of his childhood in Lithuania ("a garden's corner / scaling white paint of wooden shutters, a dogwood bush and rustling of departed people" [NCP, 183]). Echoing his earlier globalist affirmation in "Mittelbergheim" ("Here and everywhere / Is my homeland" [NCP, 104]), Milosz wrote "Grateful for a rising and a setting sun / Wherever you are, you could never be an alien" (NCP, 186).

And at the end he identified himself, now transplanted among unsophisticated Californians, with the shipwrecked Spanish explorer Álvar Núñez Cabeza de Vaca (c. 1488–1560), who for some years was enslaved by Gulf Coast tribes, until he adapted to their lifestyle, and (in Milosz's account) on return to Europe, felt alienated from Western civilization:

> Seven years' march from the Mexican Gulf to California,
> the hu-hu-hu of tribes, hot bramble of the continent.
> But afterward? Who am I, the lace of cuffs
> not mine, the table carved with lions not mine, Doña Clara's fan, the
> slipper from under her gown—hell, no.
> On all fours! On all fours!

Smear our thighs with warpaint [*Farbą wojenną*].
Lick the ground. Wha ha, hu hu.
(NCP, 188)[16]

Though the speaker here is a persona, the voice here strongly echoes what we heard from Milosz's own id two pages before. We have seen other Milosz sequences end with a glimpse of a reality both beyond words and beyond the status quo. But this is the first where the search for the nonverbal has gone inward, not outward.[17]

What I find unique about "Throughout Our Earth" is that this vigorous expression of the Eros within us is no longer pessimistic, but seems to be entirely consonant with, even contributory to, the poem's optimism about Logos, human nature, and the future:

> The human mind is splendid; lips, powerful,
> and the summons so great, it must open Paradise.
>
> They are so persistent. that give them a few stones
> and edible roots, and they will build the world.
> (NCP, 184)[18]

This Rousseauian (or Blakean, or Rortyan) optimism sustained the hope we saw in the *Treatise on Poetry*, that the death of the city we would see "man, naked and mortal, / ready for truth, for speech, for wings" (NCP, 145; TP, 54).[19]

And the mixture in this sequence of traditional belief with antinomian revolt suggests the contesting attitudes in Kołakowski's ground-breaking essay "The Priest and the Jester" ("Kapłan i Błazen," 1959), which Milosz himself linked to the vision just quoted.[20] In that essay, Nina Witoszek noted, "Kołakowski proposed an innovative framing of an 'incurable' antagonism between a philosophy that perpetuates the absolute, and a [postmodern] philosophy that interrogates and detonates accepted doxa."[21] I remember well how Kołakowski's essay ignited not just avid discussion but hope in Warsaw from 1959 to1961, the years that I was there. And I see Milosz in this poem as hoping to do what he hoped to do in the *Treatise on Poetry*: "to retain both ends of the contradiction" between Being and history (TP, 122n).

"THROUGHOUT OUR EARTH" AS A GLOBAL POSTMODERN POEM

From one perspective, "Throughout Our Earth" can be seen as Milosz's first global poem, and the first time that he used a new prophetic voice as a bard of postmodern globalism. But from another point of view, the poem can be seen as deeply personal, his adaptation of the American genre of confessional poetry to his own Catholic needs.

For the poem, in Catholic terms, is doubly confessional: a confession both of sin (*confessio peccati*) and, for the first time, of his faith (*confessio fidei*). While still in France, Milosz had told Thomas Merton, "I have always been crypto-religious and in conflict with the political aspect of Polish Catholicism."[22] Now, far from Poland, it was safe to confess publicly his belief in an afterlife.[23]

I suspect it is no accident that Milosz's first published poem in English, his first as a legal resident and soon-to-be citizen of the new world, should also be one in which he first ceased to be "crypto-religious." Although he already developed from his first visit a stereotype of America as a mindless realm of "birth, copulation, and death" (YH, 124; cf. Visions, 101), this was now intensified by his sustained exposure to the banality of US television (which his children watched for hours, "to [his] impotent rage").[24] The barren concrete landscape that opens the poem—

> At noon white rubble of cemeteries on the hillsides:
> a city of eye-dazzling cements
> glued together with the slime of winged insects
> spins with the sky about the spiraled freeways.
> (NCP, 182)

must have presented a spiritual vacuum, one to which his *daimonion* responded with thoughts, strange in Berkeley, that would have been commonplace in the land of Paulina, with her "iron crucifix and images of the saints" (NCP, 185).

So the poem looks back in history to another "alien" from Christian Europe, Father Junipero Serra, and his struggle to convert natives (descendants of still earlier aliens) who, ignorant of history,

> had almost completely forgotten the Garden of Eden
> and had not yet learned the reckoning of time. . . .
> But, poor people, they had lost the gift of concentration
> and a preacher had to hang from his neck a roasted flank of deer
> in order to attract their greedy eyes.
> But then they slobbered, so loudly, he could not speak.
> (NCP, 186–87)[25]

Milosz makes no effort to emulate the Franciscan's attempts; instead, as already noted, he is briefly converted in the opposite direction, lapsing for a moment (like both the Indians and Cabeza before him) from *devenir* into *esse*, his animal nature:

> On all fours! On all fours!
> Smear our thighs with warpaint.
> Lick the ground. Wha ha, hu hu.
> (NCP, 186)

I see the poem's double confession—of sin and of faith—as at the core of his postmodern significance for a post-secular world in which the Roman Catholic church is just one of many religions, but the inadequacy of a purely scientific outlook is becoming more and more widely recognized as inadequate. The poem also represents for me what Seamus Heaney saw in Milosz's poetry of the 1960s: "the full summer of his poetic powers."[26]

POSTSCRIPT: "ELEGY TO N. N." (1962)

A year later, in 1962, Milosz wrote again of the huge gap between his two cultures, but without the same exuberance. Receiving news of the death of his mother's cousin Gabriela Kunat (whom he had once described as his "première passion d'amour"), Milosz composed "Elegy to N. N." (NCP, 267).[27] In the context of first the German and then the Soviet invasions, the poem describes her wartime expulsion as a Pole from Lithuania to settle later in the region around Danzig.

And the poet's reminiscences ("the horses standing by the forge," "the bath cabin where you used to leave your dress") are overshadowed by death on all sides in eastern Europe, from Kunat herself, her beloved (husband?),[28] a Jewish woman they knew, to the former German owner of her new home, whose blood "was washed from the wall."

In the close to this poem, the poetic distance established by "the Sierras and abandoned gold mines" of California gives the poet, instead of empowerment as before, a sense of loss:

> We learned so much, this you know well:
> how, gradually, what could not be taken away
> is taken. People, countrysides.
> And the heart does not die when one thinks it should. . . .
> No, it was not because it was too far
> you failed to visit me that day or night.
> From year to year it grows in us until it takes hold
> I understood it as you did: indifference."
> (NCP, 268)

Years later, Milosz first explained and then recanted the sad word "indifference":

> Upon my arrival in Berkeley in 1960 directly from Europe, I was for a long time visited by a thought that the distance separating me from the places of my childhood and youth had something eerie in it, that perhaps I found myself, if not in Hades, at least upon some unearthly fields among lotus-eaters; in other words, that I started to lead a sort of after-life.
>
> This found its reflection in the poem's last stanza. Which is invalidated by the rest of the poem. For N. N. visited me, after all. And by writing about her, I proved that I was not indifferent.[29]

Milosz would continue to assess and reassess his exilic condition, until he returned to Poland.

Chapter 14

Milosz as a Poet in Later Years (1964–2004)

In the next forty years, Milosz was at last (like so many American poets) financially secure as a university professor. Now over fifty, he proceeded to write more than 650 pages of poetry in the last four decades of his life. In this chapter, I originally gave only twenty pages to these (the space I devoted earlier to the eight-line poem "Flight").

That bias reflected my conscious intention to focus on his Polish role as a social or public poet, indeed a bard or *wieszcz*, to compensate for the many Western critics who focused only on his more personal poetry.[1] I believed (and still believe) that his voice had its fullest diapason when he was speaking close to the anguish of his country, and also to its people, not isolated half-way round the globe from them. But after hearing a memorable series of talks by Robert Hass about *his* Milosz, the self-doubting Milosz, I realized that this book also could not do justice to Milosz's equivocal diapason, until I acknowledged more fully the contribution to it of his rich American experience.

The American poems, the most accessible to a Western audience, are those most usually appreciated by critics like Donald Davie, Seamus Heaney, Helen Vendler, and Robert Hass. But after his return to eastern Europe in 1989, he recovered elements of the vatic voice that he, in conformity with American expectations, had largely eschewed while writing in America. We shall see this in two remarkable poems from his last years in Kraków: "Orpheus and Eurydice," and "Treatise on Theology," the Hegelian capstone to his two earlier treatises.

In short, they contribute to the Miloszian project of salvational poetry explored in this book. I at first saw the American poems, some of them majestic and deeply contemplative, as backing away from this project. But to fully appreciate his late achievements in both poetry (*Second Space*) and prose (*The Witness of Poetry*), one must take them into account.

MILOSZ'S SHIFT OF EMPHASIS FROM FUTURE TO PAST (1964–1980)

My blissful years together with Milosz began to be threatened by the outbreak in 1964 of student protests and Berkeley's Free Speech Movement. I myself was eventually converted, by campus police brutality, to the cause of the students.[2] But like other *émigré* professors on campus, notably Lewis Feuer, Milosz was reminded by the disturbances of the unpleasant student protests of the 1930s in Europe, that had been not only anti-intellectual but, in Wilno, anti-Semitic.[3]

Milosz wrote to Merton that "the very existence of our university is endangered," and predicted that if "it is closed down the majority of professors would migrate."[4] For the rest of his life, Milosz would attack what he (as opposed to myself) called the "utterly senseless demands" (Visions, 214) and "Maoist madness of the Berkeley revolution" (ABC, 230).[5]

This did not make him a simple reactionary. When asked to respond to the accusation of Solzhenitsyn and others that American writers lacked depth, Milosz responded

> My attitude toward Western writers is different than that of Russian writers. Being a Pole, I have the feeling of belonging to the West and quarreling with it at the same time. I imagine that Western literature holds for me a great source of reflection. I mentioned Walt Whitman; it would be very hard for me to name a poet with whom I feel a greater affinity.[6]

(And Milosz, always self-questioning, could later confess that—as noted earlier—he could see aspects of the hippie counterculture "as worthy of admiration,"[7] even of envy.[8])

I suspect that what most alarmed Milosz about the student revolution (if it was indeed that) was its challenge ("Never trust anyone over thirty") to the authority of the past.[9] This may have revived in him his moment of truth at Goszyce in 1939. Unquestionably we see a shift in his next books of poetry (1965 and 1969) and prose (*Visions from San Francisco*, 1969) away from opening the future, toward preserving the past.

In "Three Talks on Civilization" (1963), a poem with many echoes of *A Treatise on Poetry*,[10] Milosz revives the dichotomy in his earlier "Ode to the City" between state restraints and human freedom. Only this time he questions his own beliefs from the perspective of the oppressor: the voice speaking is a persona from the past, the preeminent statist Klemens von Metternich (d. 1859).[11] And it is now he who imagines twisting the magic ring of Gyges (cf. Plato, *Republic*, 359e; NCP, 149; TP, 58):

> Hermance, if at a twist of my ring
> those quarters vanished through which my retinue
> rushes forward not to see eyes fixed on nothing,
>
> if people . . . nibbled chocolates in a theater,
> if they were moved by loves of Amyntas
> and in the daytime read the Summa, luckily too difficult,
>
> none would be fit for the barracks. The State would fall.
> (NCP, 203)[12]

At the end of the poem, Metternich, shown by his henchmen "proofs of my crime . . . the forgotten knife," stares in the mirror at his swollen eyelids and concludes:

> I detested these pups of foolish Jean-Jacques
> And envied them their belief in their own noble nature.
> (NCP, 204–5)[13]

The poem as a whole offers no answer to Metternich's pessimistic assessment that states must be established at the expense of human freedom and culture. Aleksandr Fiut, who was close to Milosz, writes that the meaning "of this excursion into the past, the poet says, is that [Rousseauian] faith in man's goodness threatens every absolute order, for the foundation of such orders is the opposite conviction, that of the weakness and baseness of human nature, which is defenseless against the brutality of nature."[14]

But Fiut concludes his impressive book with a vision of Milosz's life work as "a series of versions of the same poem."[15] He does not note the absence in this poem of any hope of transcending this duality—in marked contrast to what we saw earlier in the ode to the city.

Nor does he observe the novelty of the poem's allying the cause of human goodness with the reading of St. Thomas's *Summa Theologica* and Virgil's *Eclogues*, two works from the past whose inadequacy for the present Milosz has noted elsewhere. (In *The Witness of Poetry*, when Milosz looks at literature again in the light of "the dialectic of master and slave," Virgil's poetry is faulted for its alliance with the masters; WP, 63, 66).

As an émigré in America, not yet even a citizen, Milosz has receded, both in poetry and in prose, from any pretense of writing bardic poetry with a "salvational goal."[16] As he asked in "A Magic Mountain" (1975)

> So I won't have power, won't save the world?
> Fame will pass me by, no tiara, no crown?
> (NCP, 335)

So also he answered in *The Land of Ulro* (1977), "One would like to astound the world, to save the world, but one can do neither" (LU, 9). (Such was his mood just before winning two major awards: the Neustadt [1978] and Nobel [1980] Prizes for Literature.)

MILOSZ'S SELF-REFLEXIVE POETRY IN BERKELEY (1964–1994)

What did not abandon Milosz was the need to write. John Updike noted that in the *New and Collected Poems 1931–2001*, "four-fifths of the pages were written after 1960, and, remarkably, nearly a third after 1991, in Milosz's eighties."[17] Other poets, notably Wordsworth and Tennyson, continued to swell the corpus of their work in their late years, long after their poetic fame had eclipsed the memory of the crises that had produced their earlier, generative work.

Milosz, in contrast, was in no such decline: he continued to write poetry that was generative, complex, and self-questioning. (And in the same period, Milosz also produced major seminal prose works; we will look at: his *History of Polish Literature* [in English, 1969], *The Land of Ulro* [1977], and *The Witness of Poetry* [in English, 1983]. Each of these books expanded his already imposing cultural legacy.)[18]

But he continued to write his poetry in Polish (unlike his friend Joseph Brodsky, he published only one poem written in English); and so he felt acutely his distance from a Polish audience. In "A Magic Mountain" (1975), a poem in English about a calm Berkeley without seasons, he mocked himself in his new role, so alien to his old one, as an academic in a hooded procession, who "wrote poems in some unheard-of tongue . . . "

> So I won't have power, won't save the world?
> Fame will pass me by, no tiara, no crown?
> Did I then train myself, myself the Unique,
> To compose stanzas for gulls and sea haze,
> To listen to the foghorns blaring down below?
> (NCP, 335–36)

But Milosz did not retreat into irrelevance. The 1970s, for Seamus Heaney, marked Milosz's change of status "from émigré writer to world visionary."[19] One sixty-page poem, "From the Rising of the Sun" (1973–1974), in particular, is considered by Joseph Brodsky and others to be his greatest achievement.[20] It certainly expanded his already capacious diapason. In it, Milosz, at last securely remote from both Catholic Poland and partially Catholic France, wrote his first doctrinally spiritual, and in part Catholic, long poem. The title, for example, is a translation of Psalm 113:3 (112 in the Vulgate), *Laudate pueri*, sung at Vespers High Mass.[21]

On the other hand, the poem is at times heterodox, with references to the Manicheans, Origen's doctrine of *apocatastasis*, and (at the end) Blake and Swedenborg. More importantly, the religious setting intensifies, rather than mitigates, his characteristic self-questioning. He drove to "the parking lot at Roc Amadour" (a former pilgrimage site in the Dordogne)

> And saw a wooden Madonna with a child in a crown,
> Surrounded by a throng of impassive art lovers.
> .... I hear no call.
> And the holy had its abode only in denial.
> (NCP, 290)[22]

The poem's last lines present even more vividly the tone of bewilderment I am trying to describe in his exilic poetry:

> Though not for certain, perhaps in some other year
> It shall come to completion in the sixth millennium, or next Tuesday.
> The demiurge's workshop will suddenly be stilled.
> .... Unimaginable silence.
> And the form of every single grain will be restored in glory.
> I was judged for my despair because I was unable to understand this.
> (NCP, 331)[23]

This is not the voice of someone wishing to "save nations, or people." Milosz has retreated from hopes of a public or bardic role—though not as much as a decade later, in his conclusion to *Unattainable Earth* (1984, 1986): "To find my home in one sentence, concise, as if hammered in metal. Not to enchant anybody. Not to earn a lasting name in posterity. An unnamed need for order, for rhythm, for form, which three words are opposed to chaos and nothingness" (NCP, 452).[24]

The psychology of this renunciation is more visible in a self-examining poem from the same book:

> One thing is certain: in you, there are two natures.
> The miserly, the prudent one against the generous.
> For many years you will attempt to reconcile them
> Till all your works have grown small
> And you will prize only uncalculated gifts,
> Greatheartedness, self-forgetful giving,

Without monuments, books, and human memory.
("A Boy," NCP, 422)

This transcendent escape from ego issues is even more explicit in the companion poem "Winter":

> I know what it means to beget monsters.
> And to recognize in them myself. . . .
> Not important whether the generations hold us in memory.
> Great was that chase with the hounds for the unattainable
> meaning of the world.
> (NCP, 420)

The American Buddhist poet Jane Hirshfield, whom Milosz befriended (and translated) about this time, explicated this transcendent note in Milosz's late poetry: "'Great was the [sic] chase with the hounds for the unattainable meaning of the world.' In such a statement, the energies move not toward ego and self but outward, accompanied by archetypal hounds. Leaping not after worldly success, but for what cannot be achieved—the only goal that holds its interest."[25] But this is not the goal of the bard who once aspired to "save nations, or people."

"BYPASSING RUE DESCARTES": MILOSZ DECONSTRUCTS HIS SENSE OF MISSION

1980 stands out as a major cusp in Milosz's life story, the year in which he definitively transitioned from isolation in exile to global fame as winner of the Nobel Prize in Literature. A little earlier, he wrote "Bypassing Rue Descartes" (in the Polish original, "Rue Descartes," the title I shall use).

He wrote it in the summer of 1980 when he returned to Paris, already aware that he was shortlisted for the Nobel. This return to the city of his past produced a poem remarkable on two levels. On the one hand, "Rue Descartes" revives his European bardic voice of "unpolitical politics"; and combines it, perhaps for the first time, with his American voice of self-doubt and guilt. Even more remarkably, the poem ends by calling "what I have met with in life" (international recognition, the fulfillment of his youthful ambition), as "just punishment" for his "heavy sins," as "the breaker of a taboo."

The first of the many times I finished this book, I thought I could just ignore this poem and its paradoxical conclusion. But after hearing a remarkable exposition of it by Robert Hass and Renata Gorczyńska, I am now forced to acknowledge a darker psychological aspect to Milosz's bardic voice, just as Milosz did, repeatedly, himself.

The political message, relatively clear and simple for Milosz, opens the poem.

> I descended toward the Seine, shy, a traveler,
> A young barbarian just come to the capital of the world.
>
> We were many, from Jassy and Koloshvar, Wilno and Bucharest,
>   Saigon and Marrakesh,
> Ashamed to remember the customs of our homes [*domowe*
> *zwyczaje*],
> About which nobody here should ever be told:
> The clapping for servants, barefooted girls hurry in,
> Dividing food with incantations,
> Choral prayers recited by master and household together.
>
> I had left the cloudy provinces behind,
> I entered the universal, dazzled and desiring.
> Soon enough, many from Jassy and Koloshvar, or
>   Saigon or Marrakesh
> Would be killed because they wanted to abolish the customs of their
>   homes [*domowe zwyczaje*] ...
> Soon enough, their peers were seizing power
> In order to kill in the name of the universal, beautiful ideas.
> (NCP, 393)

In sixteen lucid lines, Milosz ironizes his "dazzled" youthful naivete, simply by looking at its consequences around the world.[26]

But in the second half of the poem, what appears at first to be a happy resolution—"the abolished customs have recovered their good name"—soon moves in an unexpected direction to a guilty memory: a memory not from his youth in Paris, but from his childhood in Lithuania:

> Again I lean on the rough granite of the embankment,
> As if I had returned from travels through the underworlds
> And suddenly saw in the light the reeling wheel of the seasons
> Where empires have fallen and those once living are now dead.
>
> There is no capital of the world, neither here nor anywhere else,
> And the abolished customs are restored to their small fame
> And now I know that the time of human generations is not like the
>
>   time of the earth.

> As to my heavy sins, I remember one most vividly:
> How, one day, walking on a forest path along a stream,
> I pushed a rock down onto a water snake coiled in the grass.
>
> And what I have met with in life was the just punishment
> Which reaches, sooner or later, the breaker of a taboo.
> (NCP, 394)

We can hear in this the cry of a guilty conscience, even without the explanation Milosz once gave when reading at the Library of Congress: namely, "that killing a water snake represents a grave sin in some pagan religions, a remnant of which remains in his childhood home, Lithuania."[27]

But what Milosz had "met with" at this late stage in his life was international fame. Already the recipient of the Neustadt, he knew that he was a candidate for the world's most prestigious literary award, the Nobel Prize. How could this fame be construed as "just punishment" for his "heavy sins"?

And yet, as we saw in chapter 2, Milosz in these years was indeed conflicted in just this way: "I was preoccupied with and protected by completely different problems, very private, very personal" (YH, 139). And in a personal letter of 1978 he revealed how painful these problems were: "I was a recipient of many tributes; in 1977 an honorary degree from the University of Michigan with much celebration, in 1978 I was awarded the Neustadt Prize with an equally ceremonial event, television etc., and I only bow and smile like a puppet, maintain a mask, while inside me there is suffering and great distress. . . . I have run out of faith, hope, love."[28]

"Faith, hope, love"—the core of his wartime poem[s] "The World," and the source of the energy and confidence with which the wartime book *Rescue* [*Ocalenie*, "Salvation," "Making Whole"] dared to challenge received notions of both Poland's destiny, and poetry's.

Robert Hass, who was working closely with Milosz at this time, has confirmed the claim of Milosz's biographer, Franaszek, that Milosz at this time was painfully preoccupied with the crippling physical illness of his wife Janka and the mental illness of his son Peter (Piotr). Franaszek focuses particularly on Peter's decline into paranoia, stressing that Czeslaw responded to it with guilt as well as pain:

> [Peter] was filled with hatred towards the surrounding world. On one occasion, he opened fire from a motel window at an imaginary opponent, and was sent to prison. . . . The hardest moment came when the son saw in his father an enemy, threatened him and compiled lists of absurd grievances against him. . . . [Czeslaw] with his guilt complex, reproached himself for not being an attentive father, for not devoting time to his sons.[29]

But "Rue Descartes" (in the context of other poems) helps explain a sense of guilt both older and far deeper than just being an inattentive father. Let us begin with a poem from this period not translated until after Milosz's death:

> Forgive [literally, "Get away from"] me, dark spirit.
> Don't say that you are the truth of my being
> And that my whole life was only about concealing evil.[30]

Renata Gorczyńska, who was close to Milosz when "Rue Descartes" was written, supplies the biographical explanation for the young Milosz's sense of guilt in 1934/1935. It was that Milosz, by accepting the chance to visit the supposed "capital of the world" on a scholarship, had abandoned in Wilno his lover Jadwiga Waszkiewicz, whom he had gotten pregnant.[31]

The details of this abandonment are confirmed by the Franaszek biography (115–24). That the older Milosz felt guilt about this abandonment is confirmed by the fact that in the 1980s, after almost a half century of silence, he belatedly resumed contact with her, and was soon sharing details with her about his other, more recent infidelities.[32]

But the remorse Milosz felt over this early abandonment of a pregnant lover (in favor of Paris) would have been commingled with and overshadowed by what he himself (as we saw in chapter 10) called "my abandonment of my wife and children [in Washington] for the sake of a literary career [in Paris]."[33] (At the time, Janka, as we saw, was in a difficult pregnancy with their younger son Peter.) This was a painful choice that permanently and gravely impacted what Milosz in 1987 called "the central fact of my life story: Janka's and my marriage" (YH, 196–97). Milosz soon added that "a true marriage is heaven on earth. That is what I sought and that is what, but only briefly, I experienced with Janka" (YH, 216).

Part IV of *A Treatise on Poetry* described this difficult decision at length, as a principled and essentially selfless choice. He decided to be part of History because "we needed to be of use" (TP, 60); and in so doing he turned away from the "rose . . . of love and superterrestrial beauty" ("the option of staying in America for good would mean choosing life on its biological level. . . . What replaces history is sex," TP 55, 119). By the 1980s, as we saw, he had come to describe his historic ambitions as an affliction "with philosophical or ideological madness" (YH, 120).

In *Native Realm* (1959), Milosz reflected on his year in Paris in 1935; and he astutely wondered whether his shame over his egotistic pursuit of ambition, or what he vaguely referred to as "my sins," did not explain his appetite for what he called in "Rue Descartes" "the universal, beautiful ideas."

My intelligence remained disturbingly disproportionate to my development as a man, to my formation of character. I was like a child, in love with myself yet enough aware so that my conscience bothered me incessantly. Despair over my monstrous egoism—which I did not want to renounce—reached extremes of tension in Paris. It was not only adolescent Weltschmerz. My sins, after all, were not imagined. Who knows if it was not precisely this impossibility of bringing order to my personal problems that caused me to nourish myself so passionately for several years on catastrophic visions, borrowing from the Marxists little more than their belief in a spasm of history? (NR, 172–73)

By 1980, in "Rue [N. B.] Descartes," Milosz has lost faith both in his youthful dream of coming "to the capital of the world" and in his 1950 goal (as intimated in the Poetic Treatise) of rescuing Paris (Europe), with its past history of the St. Bartholomew's Day Massacre and the Terror of the Jacobins. Paris is in fact just a city, like the Florence of Giordano Bruno, behaving "in accordance with nature,"

> Buying fish, lemons, and garlic at street markets,
> Indifferent as it was to honor and shame and greatness and glory,
> Because that had been done already and had transformed itself
> Into monuments representing nobody knows whom.[34]

"There is," in short, "no capital of the world."

But why does this disillusion lead Milosz so quickly to talk of his heavy sins, and to describe "what I have met with in life"—the imminent award of the Nobel Prize—as

> ... the just punishment
> Which reaches, sooner or later, the breaker of a taboo.

A clue to the answer is in the 1979 letter that Milosz wrote to his sometime confessor in France, Father Jósef Sadzik, confessing to the priest about his repeated supplication in his prayers for the restoration of Piotr's [Peter's] sanity in exchange for the honor of the Nobel Prize.[35]

It seems to me inevitable that Peter and the Nobel would have been intimately associated in Milosz's mind, long obsessed by his "heavy sins." I know from the experience of friends how, when major mental illness occurs in someone born after a traumatic pregnancy, it is natural to fear that the trauma was a cause of it.[36]

UNATTAINABLE EARTH: MILOSZ'S RETURN TO THE EROTIC

Even after winning the Nobel Prize, Milosz continued to struggle to control the unruly poetic voices competing over the shattered terrain vacated by his vatic role. A new voice appeared in 1986 with the publication of his complex, self-reflective, late-erotic book, *Unattainable Earth*.
Milosz by then was seventy, with his wife now an invalid. Fresh with Blakean thoughts after writing *The Land of Ulro*, and also empowered by winning the Nobel Prize, he began an intense affair with a woman thirty-two years younger than himself whom he called "Eve." As we see from the book, the affair aroused in him both happiness and guilt, along with a need to self-investigate, exploring his "belief that the pulse of impatient blood / Fulfills the designs of an impatient God" (NCP, 440).
This need underlay a five-page poem of forgiveness to his high school prefect, Father Chomski ("Father Ch., Many Years Later," NCP, 446–40), who earlier he blamed for his contrary "almost [*sic*] unhealthy conviction that sexuality is evil" (NR, 272).[37] It may also explain why he went with Eve to Corsica and introduced her to Jeanne Hersch, the Swiss philosopher with whom he had had a similar affair in the 1950s, when Janka was still in America.[38] And why he took the occasion to discuss both of them, after a half-century of silence, with Jadwiga Waszkiewicz, the woman he had impregnated and then abandoned in the 1930s, when leaving for Paris:[39] "Jeanne could never get over the fact that I did not want to divorce Janka and marry her. And, let's be frank, I lost Ewa [Eve] for exactly the same reason, as I am absolutely incapable of leaving my wife."[40]
But was it just loyalty to Janka that made him reluctant to remarry? Or was it also his deep-rooted sense "that it is precisely sexuality that makes fools of adults . . . depriving them of the capacity for disinterested enthusiasm" (NR, 272)?[41] In "In Salem," an Eve poem addressed partly to Jadwiga, Milosz meditates on his divided condition:

> Now you must bear with your poor soul.
> Guilt only, where you proudly stood.
> Diplomas, honors, parchment, scrolls,
> Lectures at Harvard, doctor's hood:
> Tongues in which nothing loudly calls.

And he says to "J. W." (Jadwiga):

> Early I guessed what was my fate,
> The sentence was already signed

At Haven Street and the Outgate.
(NCP, 423)

Milosz has moved from suffering his guilty condition to contemplating it.[42]

MILOSZ'S RETURN TO POLAND (1991): *SECOND SPACE*

After the fall of the Communist government in 1991, Milosz began to return freely to Poland, and in 1993 he bought an apartment in Kraków. A distinctive if not fully definable energy, missing in his poetry after 1961, also began to return; a restored sense of higher purpose partially replaced the uncertainties of exile. I wish to give two examples of this from his final volume of verse, *Second Space* (*Druga Przestrzeń*, 2002).

It is interesting to compare the Berkeley poem, "On Parting with My Wife Janina" (1987, after the death of his Polish wife Janka), with the Kraków poem "Orpheus and Eurydice" (2002), after the death of his American wife Carol Thigpen. Both are memorable. Yet it is chiefly in their diametrically opposite endings that they give any indication that they are by the same author.

The Berkeley poem is personal and somewhat confessional—

> I loved her, without knowing who she really was.
> I inflicted pain on her, chasing my illusion.
> I betrayed her with women, though faithful to her only.
> (NCP, 469)

This sounds a little like an American poem, but is not quite in the style of the American poets whom Milosz (in the same year, 1987) mocked for having "nothing to write about" but their "life of lecturers on university campuses [and] their family-life complications" (YH, 111–12).

For those poets were "free of historical earthquakes"; while Milosz begins his elegy by evoking both their home life in Berkeley and also the burning city of Warsaw a half century earlier, from which the two had escaped together:

> Women mourners were giving their sister to fire.
> And fire, the same as we looked at together,
> She and I, in marriage through long years,
> Bound by an oath for good or ill, fire
> In fireplaces in winter, campfires, fires of burning cities . . .

At the end of the poem the poet shifts his thoughts from this world to the alterity of a "second space":

> .... Heraclitus, crazy,
> Sees the flame consuming the foundations of the world.
> Do I believe in the Resurrection of the Flesh? Not of this ash.
> I call, I beseech: elements, dissolve yourselves!
> Rise into the other, let it come, kingdom!
> Beyond the earthly fire compose yourselves anew!
> (NCP, 469–70)

The opening of "Orpheus and Eurydice," in contrast, melds the contemporary with the mythic ("the sidewalk at the entrance to Hades," SS, 99). And the author, back in Kraków, feels again empowered to speak in a mythic voice—as Orpheus—just as near Kraków a half century earlier he had written as Adam/Aeneas fleeing from Paradise or Troy.[43] Traces of the confessional are still present, but they are markedly less personal:

> He remembered her words: "You are a good man."
> He did not quite believe it. Lyric poets
> Usually have—as he knew—cold hearts.
> (SS, 99)

The mythic loss of Eurydice is narrated as a consequence of the poet's traditional doubleness—which can be read as intimately personal, but also as emblematic of modern, civilized, self-divided man:

> Under his faith a doubt sprang up
> And entwined him like cold bindweed.
> Unable to weep, he wept at the loss
> Of the human hope for the resurrection of the dead,
> Because he was, now, like every other mortal.
> (SS, 101)

But the consequent loss of Eurydice on the route from Hades is accompanied by a startling move to an alterity (in this case, a reverse of the Janka poem's move to a kingdom "Beyond the earthly fire"):

> It happened as he expected. He turned his head
> And behind him on the path was no one.
>
> Sun. And sky. And in the sky white clouds.
> Only now everything cried to him: Eurydice!
> How will I live without you, my consoling one!
> But there was a fragrant scent of herbs,
> the low humming of bees,
> And he fell asleep with his cheek on the sun-warmed earth.
> (SS, 102)

Milosz's last book (in its English version) closes with this magnificent reaffirmation of Milosz's core belief, that poetry, instead of indulging in negation, should in the end celebrate *Esse*, the miracle of life.[44]

I cannot close this chapter without a few words on Milosz's third and final Treatise, "Treatise on Theology." On a first reading, this is far and away the most personal of the three Treatises, focused on his inner conflict of belief and doubt. And at the same time, it is the most universal: in it he remembers both Lithuania and Poland, but this Treatise, unlike the other two, has no geographic confines. Nor is it precisely limited to the present era: the persona of the poem, after recognizing more and more clearly his identification with Mickiewicz, begins at one point to speak in Mickiewicz's voice:

> What a distance! And yet I was able to hear a driver's whip clacking as the carriage, with all of our company from Tuhanowicze, arrived at the front steps of the Chreptowicz's manor in Szczorsy.
>
> To read in the largest library in Lithuania books adorned with a picture of Cosmic Man.
>
> If, writing about me, they would mix up centuries, I could confirm that, yes, I was there in 1820, leaning over "*L'Aurore naissante*," of Jakob Boehm, the French edition of 1802. (SS, 53)

Milosz saw this Treatise, being about "first things," as logically prior to the other two, even though it was only with the approach of death that morals, poetry, and politics let theology take center stage. Now even poetry, in a vivid metaphor, fell short:

> A young man couldn't write a treatise like this,
> Though I don't think it is dictated by fear of death.
> It is, simply, after many attempts, a thanksgiving.
> Also, perhaps, a farewell to the decadence
> Into which the language of poetry in my age has fallen.
>
> Why theology? Because the first must be first.
>
> And first is a notion of truth. It is poetry precisely,
> With its behavior of a bird thrashing against the transparency
> Of a window-pane, that tells us
> That we don't know how to live in a phantasmagoria.
> Let reality return to our speech.
>
> That is, meaning. Impossible without an absolute point of reference. (SS, 47)

A tension throughout this Treatise arises from the doubleness of having both a sense of mission and a need for humility. On the one hand, he acknowledges his inheritance of a responsibility from Mickiewicz and the Masonic lodges of the Enlightenment's Age of Raptures (1780–1840s):[45]

> To present myself at last as an heir to mystical lodges,
> also as a man different from that of the legend. . . .
> Only a dark tone, an inclination toward a peculiar Manichean strain
> of Christianity, could have led one to the proper trail.
>
> And, we should add, an entanglement of that individual in the
> history of the twentieth century, the absurdity of some of his
> actions, his narrow, miraculous escapes [*cudownych ocaleń*].
>
> As if a substitute vocation had been confirmed, and the Good Lord
> had asked from me the completion of my oeuvre,
>
> I toiled, I looked for greatness, the failure of which, I thought, could
> be attributed to the meanness of the era.
>
> Finding greatness in others, sometimes in myself,
> I was grateful for the gift of participation
> In an extraordinary divine plan for mortals.
> (SS, 62–63)

On the other hand, is his struggle with the consequent sin of pride, the pride that tainted Mickiewicz's achievements, and in the end derailed him:[46]

> A poet who was baptized
> in the country church of a Catholic parish
> encountered difficulties
> with his fellow believers. . . .
> The opposition, I versus they, seemed immoral.
> It meant I considered myself better than they were.
> (SS, 47)

Separating from them, he moved from the world of ritual to that of Latin theology.

> Perhaps I became like a monk in a mid-forest monastery
> who, seeing from his window a river in flood,
> wrote a treatise in Latin, a language completely incomprehensible
> to peasants in their sheepskin coats.
> (SS, 48)

Taking a leading from Kabbalistic teachings about the Cosmic Man, Adam Kadmon, Milosz writes how this Adam

> ... lost his immortality.
>
> So it looks as if original sin
> is just a Promethean dream about man,
> a being so gifted that by the very force of his mind
> he would create civilization and invent a cure for death.
> And that a New Adam, Christ, assumed a body and died
> in order to liberate us from Promethean pride.
>
> Which pride, it is true, was most difficult for Mickiewicz.
> (SS, 57)

He sees, in himself as well, the need "to redeem himself from the sin of pride" (SS, 48);

> I feel in myself so much veiled evil
> That I do not exclude myself from the possibility of hell.
>
> It would probably be the hell of artists.
>
> I.e., people who valued the perfection of their oeuvre
> Over their duties as husbands, fathers, brothers, citizens.
> (SS, 61)

Years later, after his explorations of the mystical lodges of Mickiewicz, and "a peculiar Manichaean strain of Christianity," Milosz revived the tepidity of his own faith with the warmth and "vein of ecstasy" of those singing and praying at Lourdes.

> Naturally, I am a skeptic. Yet I sing with them,
> thus overcoming the contradiction
> between my private religion and the religion of the rite.
> (SS, 63)

After a lifetime of left-brain ideas, he is again, through the right-brain activity of singing, in community with those less educated than himself.

In my own old age, I see great wisdom in this enlargement of emphasis from theology to ritual. The value of theology can be questioned. But as humans, each of us is a social and ritual animal (*homo socialis et ritualis*), who can experience something beyond normal gratification when singing in community.[47] The wisdom of ages has adjusted the world's rituals to meet this need.

The Treatise ends, like Dante's *Paradiso*, with a final section in praise of the Virgin Mary:

> Beautiful Lady, you who appeared to the children at Lourdes and Fatima,
>
> What astonished these children was your loveliness, unsayable.
>
> As if you wished to remind them that beauty is one of the components of the world.
> (SS, 64)

The poet reaffirms both his identity as a poet needing to express from within, and also his commitment to the ineffable, the "unfathomable intention" of the Virgin:

> My presence in such a place [i.e., Lourdes] was disturbed
>
> By my duty as a poet who should not flatter popular imaginings,
>
> Yet who desires to remain faithful to your unfathomable intention
>
> When you appeared to children at Fatima and Lourdes.
> (SS, 64)

Once again, the conclusion of this Treatise, like the conclusion of so many of Milosz's greatest poems, points beyond words.

"TREATISE ON THEOLOGY" AND THE PARADOX OF SANITY

Only after I finished this book, and especially its final chapter, did I realize that the "Treatise on Theology" is far more than a personal poem. It is indeed a Treatise on Theology, that is to say, on "the science which treats of God," an oxymoronic attempt to understand what cannot be understood.

Milosz's career, in this poem, is seen as devoted to this pursuit, which elevated him simultaneously to the level of Mickiewicz, and also to "Promethean pride" (SS, 57). But theology (like poetry) is not just a vehicle for change and redirection in cultural evolution, it is simultaneously a flawed vehicle, preserving vestiges of class privilege. The "truth"—"I don't understand anything" (SS, 59)—leads him back to the "beautiful lady . . . who appeared to the children at Lourdes and Fatima."

> According to the testimonies, You stood above a little tree,
> Your feet about ten centimeters above the topmost leaves.
>
> You had the body not of an apparition, but of some immaterial matter
> so that one could see the buttons of your dress.
> (SS, 64)

In short, he becomes (to quote "Love") "like a lover able to see / he is only one among many," who thus "heals his heart / without knowing it" (NCP, 50). Theology, like the Buddhist ladder of the sutras, is no longer needed.

I see my initial suppression of this ambivalence about theology in the same light as my initial suppression of Milosz's "quarrel with classicism," for ignoring "centuries of ignorance and misery among serfs, peasants, and proletarians" (WP, 66–67; see chapter 15).

In my concluding chapter on Milosz as a healer, I will talk of his remedy of a paradoxical sanity so simple it risks eluding the college-educated. Just as there was sanity among Lithuanian peasants who believed that snakes were spirits, so sanity today is less likely to be found in seminaries or universities than in a simple community of faith.

Let me conclude with an anecdote about Milosz not available from Franaszek. Some years ago, I needed to have a jacket fitted; and I dealt with a seamstress in the suburb of Walnut Creek. She was Polish, and so I asked if she had heard of a poet called Czeslaw Milosz. "Heard of him?" she replied heatedly, "I knew him personally." Apparently, a church in Martinez, another suburb nearby, held a monthly Mass in Polish that both she and Milosz attended. Her tone implied that she shared with him an intimacy (as Polish-speakers in a largely Hispanic-American suburb) that I, as a professor, would not understand.

Chapter 15

Milosz's Mature Prose: The Marriage of Blake and Eliot

I would not like to create the impression that my mind is turned toward the past, for that would not be true. Like all my contemporaries I have felt the pull of despair, of impending doom, and reproached myself for succumbing to a nihilistic temptation. Yet on a deeper level, I believe, my poetry remained sane and, in a dark age, expressed a longing for the Kingdom of Peace and Justice.

—Czeslaw Milosz [1]

From where will a renewal come to us, who have spoiled and devastated the whole earthly globe? Only from the past, if we love it.

—Simone Weil [2]

With his 1961 arrival in Berkeley, Milosz, freed for the first time from financial anxiety and the need to write novels, entered the most productive period of his life. In the next forty-four years, as already noted, he wrote more than 80 percent of his total poetic output. He also produced three major books in prose, *The History of Polish Literature* (1969), *The Land of Ulro* (*Ziemia Ulro*, 1977), and *The Witness of Poetry* (1983). Of these three, the first and third were first written and published in English.

All three are inspired by the Viconian view of history as a coherent dialectical development that Milosz found in the writings of Norwid and Brzozowski, and then expounded in *A Treatise on Poetry*.

THE HISTORY OF POLISH LITERATURE (1969)

Milosz's *History of Polish Literature* grew out of lectures he delivered on the same subject, an ideal way for a literary historian to produce such an encyclopedic work. But I cannot think of any major contemporary poet who has undertaken a comparable task; nor can I contemplate an analogous *History of English Literature* by any serious poet. Milosz's achievement illustrates once again the mantle of social responsibility that is inherited only by those poets who come from smaller countries than Britain or the United States.[3]

Because written for a non-Polish audience, the history is also to some degree a history of Poland itself and, particularly in the first fifty pages, an ecclesiastical history. But because it covered a period when Poland disappeared twice from Europe's political map, it is clearly a cultural rather than a political history. As Milosz explained in his introduction to the second edition, "I am imbued, for better or worse, with the historicism typical of many European intellectuals. . . . Literature, to me, appears as a series of moments in the life of the species, coagulated into language" (HPL, xvi). The volume is in spirit a prose expansion of the *Treatise on Poetry*, where Milosz first offered "a sense of history" (*historyczność*) as an "instrument . . . to rescue human beings" (*ratunek ludzi*) (NCP, 144; TP, 52).[4]

Milosz also noted in his Introduction the *continuity* in Poland's cultural evolution (or what I have called *ethogeny*), despite the nation's political discontinuity, and its dialectical clashes between Protestant and Catholic, Latin and vernacular:

> The vernacular, stifled for a long time by Latin, the language of the Church, won its ascendancy in Poland primarily thanks to the religious controversies engendered first by the ideas of Jan Hus, then by Luther's and Calvin's. Poland of the "Golden Age" was largely a Protestant country, a "paradise for heretics." And despite the subsequent victories of the Counter Reformation, the heritage of intellectual rebelliousness has never been lost, and was transmitted through the publicists of the Enlightenment and the democrats of the nineteenth century to the liberal intelligentsia of our time. (HPL, xv–xvi)[5]

Unlike the selective excerpts which follow here, the book itself, though not unopinionated, is remarkably even-handed and objective. For example, Milosz devotes seven pages to the poetry of his contemporary Tadeusz Różewicz, who remained and won awards in the postwar regime Milosz defected from, and only four pages for his own.

Nevertheless, as elsewhere, Milosz is using the past to strengthen his hopes for the future. His own ideals, not surprisingly, influence what he chooses to emphasize from the past. It is important to him that Poland, leading up to the Reformation, was relatively tolerant; its rulers were under the spell of Erasmus (HPL, 27–28), and thus Poland became a haven for endangered Hussites and Humanists from elsewhere in Europe (HPL, 16–17).[6]

Partly as a consequence, Poland itself became a cockpit of Protestant intellectual ferment, particularly among the Arian Polish Brethren at Raków, who "went so far as to attempt communal living."[7] Dividing the history of Polish Arianism into two periods, Milosz emphasizes from the first period their pacifism ("A Christian cannot use the sword") and their egalitarianism ("Since all men are brothers, a Christian cannot own serfs nor profit from their labor, but should live by the work of his own hands," HPL, 33).

And in its second, more intellectually doctrinal Socinian period ("between 1602 and 1638"), the Raków School was "actually in advance of the intellectual trends in Europe":

> Such philosophers of the seventeenth century as Spinoza and John Locke borrowed many ideas from the Socinians, although Locke, when accused of this in his lifetime, denied it. As H. L. McLachlan says in his work *Socinianism in Seventeenth Century England* (Oxford, 1951): "He always repudiated his debt to the 'Racovians' even to the point of declaring, (in the *Second Vindication of the Reasonableness of Christianity*) that he had never read a page of Socinus or Crell." McLachlan goes on to prove that Locke had a rich collection in his library of "Rakovian" books whose margins were covered with notes in his own handwriting. (HPL, 115)

Milosz's excitement about the Raków School, which he shared with me when I first met him in 1961, had soured a decade later, in his more Blakean *The Land of Ulro*:

> The clergy of Western Europe, Catholic as well as Protestant, was horrified by the specter of the Antitrinitarian heresy, by the "monster of Socinianism." Their fear was fully justified, as a refutation of the Trinity reduced Christ to a moralist-teacher and God to an impersonal Clockmaker (Blake's Urizen). Paradoxically, sixteenth-century [*sic*, i.e., seventeenth-century] Poland, through the Socinian presses in Raków, became the exporter of ideas conducive to the spread of the heresy—of what was, initially, a "rational Christianity." (LU, 223)

In other words, conducive to the spread of the Enlightenment, of which I will say more in a moment.

Another pre-Enlightenment factor was the humanism of the first major writers in Polish, from what Milosz agrees is "the Golden Age of Polish letters" (HPL, 159). Chief of these was Jan Kochanowski (1530–1584). Milosz praises Kochanowski for his "classical, limpid" style—"a pure 'breathing' of Polish"—which he attributes to Kochanowski's "Latin and Italian sources," leading to a classical humanist detachment (HPL, 60).⁸ "In a period of violent religious disputes [Kochanowski] remained primarily a humanist who observed the golden mean. . . . Even more, the pagan element of Stoicism in [his] poetry, far from contradicting his deep piety, rendered his religious verse ecumenical, that is, acceptable to both Protestants and Catholics" (HPL, 62).

This shaping of a progressive inter-faith Polish culture was furthered by the "men of the Enlightenment with their broad vistas," open to the ideas of French writers like Voltaire and Rousseau (HPL, 159).⁹ Their "Camp of the Reform [followed] French philosophers who advocated the equality of man and the right of the individual to assess institutions by reason." Because they faced resistance, from both "the larger mass of the ruling class, the gentry," and also Russia and Prussia, "practically all" of these men met secretly in Masonic lodges, one of whose members, significantly, was King Stanislaw August Poniatowski, (1732–1798; HPL, 159–60).¹⁰

In 1773, a new Commission for National Education was founded, to supply classrooms and textbooks for a secular Polish education. Thanks to the Commission, "a new type of writer made his appearance: no longer a self-educated amateur but a man with a good humanistic training obtained in a high school and at the University" (HPL, 161–62). However, "the eighteenth century . . . was not only a century of rationalism . . . there was also a pronounced inclination toward the pietistic and mystical. Some Poles played a prominent part in the French 'mystical' lodges which proliferated in the last decades before the Revolution" (HPL, 163).

True to Milosz's already-noted ambivalence between eighteenth-century classicism and nineteenth-century romanticism, the *History* has praises for both. For example, Ignacy Krasicki (whose mock-heroic epic, *Myszeis* [*The Mouseiad*, 1775], Milosz had praised in 1946 for belittling the phrase "Sacred love of our beloved Fatherland") is praised in *History* for his "admiration for Erasmus" and his return to "the clear and simple language of Kochanowski" (HPL, 177).¹¹

A key figure in the transition from classical to romantic ideals is the writer Jan Śniadecki, already noticed here as the target of Mickiewicz's enormously influential polemical ballad, "The Romantic." Śniadecki is first honored in the *History* for his work with the Commission for National Education (HPL, 162), and then belittled for his very late critical essay (1819), "in which he called Romanticism 'a school of treason and plague'" (HPL, 207).

Mickiewicz's rebuttal to Śniadecki ("a man with a learned air") in "The Romantic"—by far the longest poem to be quoted in full, in both the *History* and *The Land of Ulro*—provides a fulcrum in both works for Milosz's treatment of competing currents in Polish culture and in himself. In the *History*, "The Romantic" is celebrated as a victory in terms of language. Classical poetry had been an exercise by the learned for the learned. Now, servant girls, valets, and people barely able to read suddenly found something close to their hearts and quite understandable without any recourse to learning. Hence the success of [Mickiewicz's] *Ballads and Romances* with the lower strata of the population. (HPL, 213)

It is safe to say that for Milosz no subsequent Polish poem was of equal moment, or received anything like equal attention in the *History*. Mickiewicz's legacy continued to overshadow the developments, already discussed, between Young Poland, Skamander, and himself.

Of great significance, however, are Milosz's expanded treatments of two later literary critics to whom he is indebted. The first is Mickiewicz's friend Cyprian Norwid (1821–1883), a poet so impoverished and neglected in his lifetime that he once had to live in a cemetery crypt. Milosz summarizes Norwid's thought in language that anticipates his notes to *A Treatise on Poetry*:

For Norwid, History was a continuity, a process ending in a certain direction, a constant accomplishment of God's hidden plan through mankind. A given civilization was just a phase between the past and the future: the present could not simply be cast aside, because it was the place where the future was being engendered. The materialistic civilization of the nineteenth century worshiped financial and political power, condemning those who were true to the conscience of history.... The goal of history, according to Norwid, was "to make martyrdom unnecessary on the earth," and the achievement of this was, therefore, the only criterion of progress. As he said himself: A man is born on this planet to give testimony to the truth. He should, therefore, know and remember that every civilization should be considered as a means and not as an end—thus, to sell one's soul to a civilization and at the same time to pray in church is to be a pharisee. (HPL, 272–73)

(Milosz does not mention Norwid's debt here to Vico, which has however been noticed by more recent commentators.)[12]

Milosz concludes his lengthy treatment of Norwid by saying that

Norwid's intense historicism, his refusal to practice a narrowly utilitarian poetry, and, at the same time, his rejection of "art for art's sake," paved the way for a specific kind of literature that meditates on history and art and that is, perhaps, uniquely Polish. His reflections on work inspired one of the most original Polish thinkers of the twentieth century, Staniislaw Brzozowski. (HPL, 279–80)

And although I have perhaps referred adequately to Brzozowski's influence on Milosz, I will conclude my summary of the *History* with one more quotation:

It would not be an exaggeration to say that the crux of Brzozowski's thought is his dialectical reappraisal of Romanticism, including Polish Romanticism. The latter, activist and voluntaristic, is, as redefined by Brzozowski, different from what is commonly signified by that term. Brzozowski, thus, revendicated certain of Mickiewicz's and Norwid's pronouncements (especially the latter's) whenever those writers contended against standard Romantic attitudes. He regarded the scientific *Weltanschauung* that infatuated the second half of the nineteenth century as the outcome of a duality born within the Romantic man. . . . How can the duality be overcome? Only through a denial, on the one hand, of the supposedly immutable laws in historical development which are indifferent to human values, and, on the other, of a shameful withdrawal into one's subjectivity. (HPL, 377)

NEUROSCIENCE ON HUMAN DUALITY: A LATE DIGRESSION

Milosz's writings about human duality or doubleness, so central to this book, have inspired me to write another, *Enmindment*, on the dialectic of yin and yang in both each individual person and also the dialectical history of our cultural development (ethogeny).[13] And from time to time in that book I ask if this doubleness is grounded in the bilaterality of the human brain's two hemispheres. I wish to digress for a moment on this topic, which I will return to when discussing Milosz's global legacy.

Only after I finished *Enmindment* did I discover a book by Iain McGilchrist, *The Master and His Emissary*. McGilchrist, using neuroscientific data, lends support to what I quote here from Milosz on Mickiewicz and Brzozowski (as well as his own book *The Land of Ulro*, which I am about to discuss).[14] McGilchrist begins by dispensing with "popular misconceptions" of left-brain right-brain laterality that for years tended to discredit this form of research: "Perhaps the most absurd of these popular misconceptions is that the left hemisphere, hard-nosed and logical, is somehow male, and the right hemisphere, dreamy and sensitive, is somehow female."[15]

In its place McGilchrist posits that the left hemisphere focuses on detailed methodical analysis, the right is concerned with perception of the whole:

> One of the more durable generalisations about the hemispheres has been that the left hemisphere tends to deal more with pieces of information in isolation, and the right hemisphere with the entity as a whole, the so-called *Gestalt*. The link between the right hemisphere and holistic or *Gestalt* perceptions is one of the most reliable and durable of the generalisations about hemisphere differences. The right hemisphere sees the whole, before whatever it is gets broken up into

parts in our attempt to "know" it. . . . On the other hand, the left hemisphere sees part-objects.[16]

McGilchrist attributes to the right hemisphere the Mickiewicz/Milosz critique of the Śniadecki Enlightenment ("faith and love are more discerning / than lenses or learning"):

> The successors to the Enlightenment, the Romantics . . . belonged to a world more dominated by the right hemisphere. . . . Romanticism is more inclusive. The best of Enlightenment values were not negated, but *aufgehoben* ["preserved, as well as transformed," a Hegelian term], by Romanticism. . . . The right hemisphere is grappling with experience, which is multiple in nature.., while the left sees only a vision or representation of that experience, in which, by contrast, the world is single, knowable . . . a world we can master—the Enlightenment world.[17]

And he warns that "built into the foundations of Enlightenment thought are precepts that are bound to lead eventually to a less flexible and humane outlook, that of the left hemisphere alone."[18]

Like Milosz, McGilchrist believes that the mind functions best when both hemispheres work in synergy. Though language is the special strength of the left hemisphere,[19] "many examples exist of famous scientific problems that were solved [with the help of the right hemisphere] without language."[20] The "rationality" of the left hemisphere is one-sided, unlike the "reason" of the right. For the right hemisphere recognizes

> that (in contravention of the consistency principle) a thing and its opposite may well both be true. . . . Reason is about holding sometimes incompatible elements in balance, a right-hemisphere capacity which had been highly prized among the humanist scholars of the Renaissance. Rationality imposes an "either-or" on life which is far from reasonable.[21]

In other words, McGilchrist's conclusions from neuroscience support Milosz's prose critique, in *The Land of Ulro*, of narrow post-Enlightenment scientism.

The left brain's substitution of parts for the whole can be seen elsewhere, as well—for example in Yeats's "The Second Coming" ("Things fall apart, the centre cannot hold / Mere anarchy is loosed upon the world"), in Eliot's "heap of broken images" in *The Waste Land*, and of lines in Milosz's *Treatise on Poetry*, already quoted:

> A skein of common values came undone.
> No common faith bound our minds together.
> (NCP, 122; TP, 20)

MILOSZ AND BLAKE: *THE LAND OF ULRO* (1977)

Milosz wrote about these concerns in *The Land of Ulro*, a more subjective and polemical book. It described our present era as flawed by the rationalism and "dread sleep" of Blake's Ulro, equated by Milosz with "Western civilization, which is the product of a scientific Weltanschauung."[22]

> The name Ulro is from Blake. It denotes that realm of spiritual pain such as is borne and must be borne by the crippled man. Blake himself was not one of its inhabitants, unlike the scientists, those proponents of Newtonian physics, the philosophers, and most other poets and artists of his day. And that goes for their descendants in the nineteenth and twentieth centuries, up to and including the present (LU, 32).[23]

However, the most important influence on the book is not Blake but, for better or worse, his cousin Oscar. And, persuaded that his cousin had shown fallible predictive insights into World War II, Milosz's book did not write, by Western standards, a critical study. It is perhaps better to read it, especially toward the end, as a poem in prose.

As a result of the existential deficiencies of the scientific world-view, according to Milosz, our modern episteme is divided between Darwinian reductionism on the one hand, and "Romantic and Modernist excesses" (LU, 92) on the other. The perspective on this duality was less that of Brzozowski than of Oscar, who in turn turned to three heterodox occult masters whom Mickiewicz had already named as "prophets": Jakob Boehme (1575–1624), Emanuel Swedenborg (1688–1772), and Claude de Saint-Martin (1743–1803) (LU, 108–9, 186, 193). Though Oscar blamed "the science and philosophy of the Age of Reason . . . for the tragedy of modern man," he could see in this "second, clandestine Renaissance . . . the promise of future reconciliation . . . hailed by him as the 'new Jerusalem.'" Swedenborg in particular was claimed by Oscar as his "'celestial master'" (LU, 192–93).

The Land of Ulro is a loose survey of authors, all of them influenced by Swedenborg, who envisioned an escape from Ulro: Blake, Goethe, Mickiewicz, Dostoevsky, and Oscar Milosz.[24] In this sequence, Mickiewicz's quarrel with Reason (Śniadecki) is again a fulcrum, but with the balance now tipped to the extra-rational. Milosz has more to say here than in the *History* about the impact on Mickiewicz's thought of the "pre-scientific cosmologies" in rural Lithuania (LU, 103),[25] and also Jewish influences, above all of the eighteenth-century antinomian Jacob Frank (1726–1791).[26]

Repeatedly in the book, Milosz attempts to put some distance between his cousin's ideas and his own, notably Oscar's millennial predictions: "The renewal I contemplate has none of the grandeur of a millennium, and yet I am prudent enough to place it beyond my own lifetime and that of my contemporaries" (LU, 272–73).[27] Yet many of Oscar's theosophist beliefs [e.g., "Dante's membership in the Order of the Templars," LU, 192][28] are presented uncritically; and his mystic writings like *Les Arcanes* are defended by a dubious distinction between them and what Milosz gratuitously describes as "cellophane-wrapped Buddhism," and "Eastern obfuscations" (LU, 198).

This casual dismissal of Buddhism, provoked by California feelgood practitioners of it during what he called the "revolt against authority" in the 1970s,[29] earned for the book the justified rebuke that "Since the land of Ulro is wholly a Western product, surely anyone aspiring to ascend it would benefit from a more open attitude toward what Milosz passes off as 'Eastern obfuscations.'"[30]

But Milosz, in time, would come to acknowledge the affinities between his own and the Buddha's preoccupation with suffering: "My attractions to the teachings of the Buddha is obvious, since what has troubled me throughout my life—the suffering of living creatures—is at the center of the all-embracing empathy of Prince Siddhartha" (ABC, 72).[31]

His treatment of Oscar, which I find unsatisfactory, is perhaps best seen as a transition to the conclusion of *The Land of Ulro*, where fact merges into myth. As he writes, memorably, in his final paragraph:

> how much of millenaristic yearning betrays a childish instinct. . . . In a cruel and mean century, "catastrophism" entertained dreams of an idyllic earth where "the hay smells of the dream," where tree, man, animal are joined in praise of the Garden's beauty. By recalling that the boy and the poet "catastrophist" and the old professor in Berkeley are the same man, I am merely observing the guiding principle of this book, a book both childish and adult, both ethereal and earthbound. (LU, 275)

In a generally astute review, Jaroslaw Anders saw how *The Land of Ulro* was a work in service of Milosz's lifelong salvational quest:

> His book can be read both as a story of European imagination exiled in the land of modernity, and as the story of the poet himself, who understands that a homeland is "very much a need and a product of the imagination," and that it is born "of the same realm as myth and fable. . . . The ability, and need, of the human animal to believe unverifiable truths is in Milosz's view identical with his imaginative ability. Thus for Milosz, theology and poetry often merge. Nobody lives in the "objective" world, only in a world filtered through imagination. Imagination can fashion the world into a homeland, as well as into a prison or a place of battle.[32]

But Anders's last sentence elides the radical hope of Milosz's dream in *Ulro*. People shape the world into a prison or a battleground by their own misguided thoughts. The imagination that guides us slowly and hesitantly toward "the other shore" (LU, 270) of an "idyllic earth" (LU, 275) is for Milosz that of our civilization itself, "shaped as it is," Milosz reminds us, "by the Bible and, for that reason, eschatological to the core" (WP, 37).

MILOSZ, ELIOT, AND THE GENERATIVE CANON: *THE WITNESS OF POETRY* (1983)

I feel about *The Land of Ulro* as I do about Blake's longer poems. I am more eager to read and reread it, than to write about it: it is a yin work for which yang analysis may not be fully appropriate. But four years later, luckily, many of Oscar's best ideas were concentrated, rationalized, and simplified by Czeslaw in *The Witness of Poetry*, a series of lectures first presented at Harvard in 1981. I have come slowly to appreciate their generative importance.

The difference in style between the two books can be attributed in large part to Milosz's Nobel Prize in 1980. In the mid-1970s, Milosz, still relatively unknown, decided to treat *The Land of Ulro* as an arcane topic for an arcane audience, "keeping only a few Polish readers in mind" (LU, 9).[33] After 1980, Milosz, now assured that he was world-famous, distilled the ideas inspired by his cousin to make them more easily accessible to his enlarged, transnational public.

Winning a Nobel Prize is not always good for poets. But in Milosz's case it revived for him the great ambitions for poetry that he had voiced earlier, with the Polish bard (*wieszcz*) Mickiewicz in mind.[34] He began to write in a style that was more confident, optimistic, and above all suited for a multinational rather than a narrowly Polish audience.

We see this change in the lectures published in 1983 as *The Witness of Poetry*. Here Milosz developed what he had said earlier about a poet's role in extracting the future from the past; in his words, "the poetic act both anticipates the future and speeds its coming" (WP, 109). Instead of merely hoping like Eliot to invigorate the canon, Milosz, like Blake, hoped for a literature that would supersede a prevalent pseudo-scientific "reductionist Weltanschauung," one afflicting the entire present era (WP, 109). The canon in short (in the spirit of Milosz's lecture-sequence) should help prepare for the future, not just restore and preserve the past.

Earlier, in his lecture accepting the Nobel Prize in 1980, Czeslaw Milosz acknowledged his debt to authors preceding him, and also his duty to maintain their tradition, by rescuing it from what was now dated: "Those who are alive receive a mandate from those who are silent forever. They can fulfill their duties only by trying to reconstruct precisely things as they were and by wresting the past from fictions and legends."[35] To do so, the poet must liberate his style from that of the past: "Only if we assume that a poet constantly strives to liberate himself from borrowed styles in search for reality, is he dangerous. In a room where people unanimously maintain a conspiracy of silence, one word of truth sounds like a pistol shot."[36]

In acknowledging a poet's obligation to what we now commonly call the literary canon, Milosz was following in the footsteps of T. S. Eliot. For Eliot, against the romantic prejudice of his era, also argued that great creativity came from incorporating tradition, not from breaking with it. In his seminal essay of 1919, Eliot saw tradition as an "ideal order," with new works rejuvenating a past: "What happens when a new work of art is created is something that happens simultaneously to all the works of art that preceded it."[37]

Eliot's praise of a Eurocentric "ideal order," has frequently been criticized as too static, underestimating the degree to which its tradition was dialectical and even anti-traditional, in what Octavio Paz once called "a tradition against itself."[38] But once we read Eliot from this perspective, we can see that Eliot's critique of moribund romanticism was itself a valid part of that anti-traditional tradition. And equally so, in the same spirit, was Milosz's later critique of Eliot's reactionary classicism.

Milosz in his Nobel speech endorsed what Eliot wrote about the need to learn from poets of the past. But Eliot was not concerned about revising and advancing the canon; he saw cultural change as a development which "never improves," and "which abandons nothing *en route*."[39] Milosz saw the past as a legacy to be learned from and reassessed, as a means to facilitate a better future.[40]

I consider Eliot, Milosz, and the tradition they both cared for, as not just a recuperative but also a generative tradition. And I see Milosz's Harvard lectures of 1982, later published as *The Witness of Poetry*, as a seminal correction to the reactionary polemics of Eliot's "Tradition and the Individual Talent"—just as Eliot's essay had been a seminal correction of the decadent romantic critic J. Middleton Murry.[41]

THE CONTEMPORARY EPISTEME AND HOPE FOR LIBERATION FROM IT

Milosz's progressive alienation from his great teacher Eliot, discernible already in the Poetic Treatise (TP, 59, 123), and later in an essay for *Kultura* (1965),[42] is expressed most strongly at Harvard in his repeated complaints that "in Eliot and to some extent in Pound a certain norm is placed in the past, the model of time is regressive, the future does not promise anything good" (WP, 34): "The expatriate poets hate the present and the future; they turn their eyes to the past. It is difficult to find any tomorrow in T. S. Eliot's *The Waste Land*, and where there is no tomorrow, moralizing makes its entrance" (WP, 14–15).[43]

Echoing a complaint voiced by his cousin Oscar Milosz, he attributed the loss of hope in contemporary poetry to a schism between the collective and individual imagination, the isolated poet of high culture and the public. He criticized the "pessimism, sarcasm, bitterness, and doubt" of twentieth-century poetry, which had withdrawn "from the domain common to all people into the closed circle of subjectivism" (WP, 14, 26).[44] And he saw this pessimistic failure of vision as in part a *cause*, rather than just a consequence, of the horrific wars of our century:[45] "This [pessimism] precedes the perception of specific reasons for despair, which come later. . . . It is possible that the gloom of twentieth-century poetry can be explained by the pattern that resulted from [here he quotes the other Milosz] the "schism and misunderstanding between the poet and the great human family" (WP, 14, 37).

I have suggested that, not long after arriving in Berkeley in 1961, he backed away from his earlier characterization of "poetry which does not save / Nations or people" as "A connivance with official lies" (NCP, 77). Yet he returns to it in his Harvard lectures after winning the Nobel Prize, in his critique of modern poetry for losing touch with the "aspirations of 'the great soul of the people'" (WP, 26).[46] In this Milosz is ambitiously following the path set out by the Polish *wieszcze* or national bards of the nineteenth century, above all Mickiewicz, whose work constituted "a home for incorrigible hope" (WP, 13).[47]

Thus the Harvard lectures exhibit what, in 1965, Milosz admired in Eliot: "the tension that derives from contradictions."[48] While criticizing the pessimism of Eliot, *Witness* extracts Blakean hopes from Eliot's generative canon. And while praising Blake, and "his prophecies on the victory of man against the night" (WP, 13), it also, in great contradistinction to Blake himself, praises the spirit of Blake's era as an "Age of Raptures," when people seemed "to breathe confidence and hope, as well as faith in the approach of a new era for humanity" (WP, 13, 12).

Milosz, the "ecstatic pessimist," is showing both sides of his own conflicted personality. While seeking to revive hope, he also, like both Blake and Eliot, sees his own age as one of cultural decline—indeed, of Ginsberg's "despair at the imprisonment of man in an evil civilization, in a trap without release" (WP, 15). True to his own doubleness (and successive debts to romanticism and classicism), he, perhaps for the first time, has fused Eliot and Blake in a single self-contradictory but nonetheless coherent contribution to tradition.

Milosz's message of hope (like Eliot's, I am tempted to add) starts from recognizing the importance of tradition to radical change, and the debt owed by the individual to the communal imagination. In *The Witness of Poetry*, he celebrates an art in which "the sacred and the rational are not separated." He attributes this art to the era of Blake and Mickiewicz, which he calls not the age of romanticism (a debased word, especially in English), but "the Age of Raptures" (WP, 13, 18). Milosz saw this age as an advancement from the earlier "Age of Reason," when the Enlightenment turned back to its sources in faith, rather than seeking to replace faith. Milosz cites the example of Mozart's *Magic Flute*: "The libretto of the Mozart opera deals with a struggle between the darkness of obscurantism and the light of reason; the sacred and the rational are not separated, for the Temple, in other words, the Freemasonic lodge, bestows sacral features on the human mind in search of Wisdom. That Wisdom, besides, was conceived in various ways, as exemplified by the proliferation throughout the eighteenth century of 'mystical lodges'" (WP, 11). That age is for Milosz an exemplar of the sense of how poetry, at its best, should supply hope not only to poets but through them to their community. "The fate of poetry depends on whether such a work as Schiller's and Beethoven's 'Ode to Joy' is possible. For that to be so, some basic confidence is needed, a sense of open space ahead of the individual and the human species" (WP, 14).

Speaking to an American audience, Milosz emphasizes the example— not of Mickiewicz, whom he sets aside as "untranslatable"—but of Walt Whitman, "a poet for whom the future was as open as it had been both in the Age of Reason and in the Age of Raptures" (WP, 14).[49] Milosz regrets that the forward-looking poetry of the Age of Raptures was replaced by pessimistic nostalgia, after the link between poetry and people had first been broken in the nineteenth century, by elitist aesthetes like Stephane Mallarmé, for whom the poem was an idiosyncratic, "peculiar anti-world" (WP, 46; cf. 18–19).[50]

In his Harvard lectures, Milosz developed further this notion (taken from Oscar Milosz) that poetry is "a passionate pursuit of the Real" (WP, 25, 66, 75). That Milosz means by "Real" here something Platonic is confirmed by his claim that the poet—transcending the powers of computers, remains "with his intuition . . . one strong, albeit uncertain, source of knowledge" (WP, 107).[51] Elsewhere he claimed that "every poet is a servant of Eros, who (and here he quoted from Plato's *Symposium*)

> interprets between gods and men, conveying and taking across to the gods the prayers and sacrifices of men, and to men the commands and replies of the gods; he is the mediator who spans the chasm that divides them, and therefore in him all is bound together, and through him the arts of the prophet and the priest,

their sacrifices and mysteries and charms, and all prophecy and incantation, find their way.

(WP, 74; cf. *Symposium*, 202–3a)

The same claim was made, quite independently, by Heidegger: "The poet stands between human beings and gods."[52]

Milosz's use of Plato is in a sense quite un-Platonic, since Plato mistrusted the truth-telling powers of poets, and banished them from his Republic. More relevantly, it is also quite un-Catholic: St. Augustine spent a whole chapter of the *Civitas Dei* attacking the idea that *daemones* (which we can translate here as "demons") "may carry to the gods the prayers of men, to men the answers of the gods."[53] And St, Thomas, as we saw earlier, believed poetry to be "the lowest of all intellectual studies" (*infima inter omnes doctrinas*).[54]

But I believe that the truth Milosz in our time was grasping for is the same that Plato and Augustine were grasping for in theirs. The difference is Milosz's belief that the vehicle of escape in our time is "poetry, precisely, / With its behavior of a bird thrashing against the transparency / Of a windowpane" (SS, 47).

In *The Land of Ulro*, Milosz identified with the alienated minds of Blake, Mickiewicz, and Oscar Milosz, poets who have rescued the contemporary imagination from a more lethal disease: "a multi-layered irony . . . stripped of any ontological support" (LU, 242; cf. 106). In *The Witness of Poetry*, he presents Oscar's "opinion that the future belongs to the workers," and that "the truly inspired poet of the future will transcend his paltry ego (his 'spectral self,' as Blake would say) and, in contrast to the poets of the elite, would voice the unconscious longings of downtrodden people who were now being emancipated" (WP, 28).

After the agonies of World War II, I do not consider our present era as significantly more fallen than others, or that it has been lost in the throes of a totalizing scientism since (in Milosz's words) the "Age of Raptures came to its close" in 1848 (18).[55] For example, I see Baudelaire, whom Oscar Milosz accused of impoverishing the role of poetry (WP, 26), as having preserved from Virgil and Dante, and perhaps from Homer, the eternal search for a higher human condition, like Yeats and Eliot after him.[56]

What now seems slightly dated about *The Witness of Poetry* is the hard line it draws between the West, with its "despair at the imprisonment of man in an evil civilization," and the East, where "utopian hope," captured by Marxism, has become murderous (WP, 15). The Cold War was already waning when Milosz wrote this, and I hope such distinctions may become even less relevant as the world addresses climate change.

Above all, we should not misunderstand the sharp contrast Milosz draws (in *The Witness of Poetry*) between the "open future" of the Polish romantics "and our future laden with catastrophe" (WP, 14). Drawing on what Milosz himself has written, I would say that poets, wherever they are, neither inherit nor fabricate an "open future." All great poets rediscover, for themselves and their era, the immediate possibilities for open space ahead latent in our past and our future, latent in what Milosz calls our "one universal civilization" (LU, vi), and perhaps ultimately in our biology.[57]

POETRY AND THE "REDUCTIONIST WELTANSCHAUUNG" OF SCIENCE

In *The Witness of Poetry* Milosz situated Polish poetry in the larger context of "our [European and American] civilization, shaped as it is by the Bible and, for that reason, eschatological to the core" (WP, 37). (The eschatological, Milosz wrote elsewhere, "rejects the present inhuman world in the name of a great change.")[58] Both here, as earlier in the more radical book *The Land of Ulro*, Milosz seriously redefined Eliot's classicist concept of the "simultaneous order" of European literature, much as Eliot had redefined the more romanticist notion of culture established before him by Matthew Arnold.

His redefinition is from a Polish perspective, above all that of his great mentor Mickiewicz. As Milosz explained in *Witness*, Poles, precisely because of their history "comparable only to violent earthquakes. . . . tend to view [poetry] as a witness *and participant* in one of mankind's major transformations" (WP, 4, emphasis added). Through two centuries of oppression from abroad, "Polish poetry became a home for incorrigible hope, immune to historical disasters" (WP, 13). In this way, Polish poetry preserved the spirit found in Blake's "prophecies on the victory of man in his struggle against the night" (WP, 13).

As Milosz noted in *The Land of Ulro*, Mickiewicz came from a region where the scientific spirit had barely penetrated, and his "imagination never divested itself of pre-scientific cosmologies" (LU, 103). Thus Mickiewicz's epic, *Pan Tadeusz* "seems to draw its strength from a belief in the basic goodness of the world sustained by the hand of God and by the poetry of country people" (WP, 13).[59] Its verse was marked, like the Enlightenment before it, by "a basic optimism toward the future, a millenarian faith in the Epoch of the Spirit" (WP, 13–14).[60]

Defending with Blake the naïve imagination, Milosz emphasized the importance of "saving" humanity from "images of a totally 'objective,' cold, indifferent world from which the Divine Imagination has been alienated"

(WP, 47). Echoing the end of *The Land of Ulro*, Milosz closes his chapter on "The Lesson of Biology" with the hope

> that technological civilization may begin to see reality as a labyrinth of mirrors, no less magical than the labyrinth seen by alchemists and poets. That would be a victory for William Blake and his "Divine Arts of Imagination"—but also for the child in the poet, a child too long trained by adults. (WP, 57)

MILOSZ'S "QUARREL WITH CLASSICISM"

A brief digression. We come now to a section of *Witness* which I initially skimmed through with impatience, almost distaste: Milosz's "Quarrel with Classicism," and specifically with Virgil, for ignoring "centuries of ignorance and misery among serfs, peasants, and proletarians" (WP, 66–67; see chapter 14).

Convinced as I was that Milosz, just like Virgil, was a culture-shaper, I at first dismissed this quarrel as a personnel eccentricity; much as I then dismissed Blake's dismissal of "Greece and Rome" (and specifically Virgil) as "destroyers of all Art."[61] (I attributed it in Milosz's case to his ambivalence about his Polish education in Wilno; in Blake's, to his resentment against the privileged classes of England.)

How wrong I was! I see now that Milosz's questioning of classicism, perhaps influenced by Simone Weil, constituted part of the most radical message of his lectures: namely, that poetry (like theology) was both a vehicle for change and redirection in cultural evolution, and simultaneously a flawed vehicle preserving vestiges of class privilege. In this way, Milosz both revived his 1930s quasi-Marxist criticism of our episteme, and also defined himself, more clearly here than before, as a futurist whose profound critique of the present is guided and disciplined by a full appreciation of the past. This stance, when so simply stated, now seems to me to be obvious, sane, generative, and unprecedented.

A dialectical pattern underlies the order of lectures in *The Witness of Poetry*; and the nostalgia in Milosz's "Biology" chapter for pre-scientific attitudes leads, in his next chapter, "A Quarrel with Classicism," to a closer and more critical view of the legacy of the more recent past.[62]

Milosz opens his lectures by describing how from childhood he was steeped in what I had to discover for myself: "In the gymnasium for several years I studied the history of the Roman Church.... Also ... Horace, Vergil, and Ovid, whom I read and translated in class" (WP, 5).

Recall that in his even-handed *History of Polish Literature*, Milosz had praised Kochanowski (with his Latin sources) for a "classical, limpid" style

(HPL, 60). Now, in *Witness*, Milosz clarified that "classicism [was] the subject of both my fascination and my dislike" (WP, 5); and that "the poetics of classicism" are "alien to a poet of today, but also intriguing in their strangeness" (WP, 62).

> For us, classicism is a paradise lost, for it implies a community of beliefs and feelings that unite poet and audience. No doubt the poet was not then separated from the "human family," though obviously that was a family of modest size [excluding] the illiterate rural populations. . . . Were classicism only a thing of the past, none of this would merit attention. In fact, it constantly returns as a temptation to surrender to merely graceful writing. (WP, 65)

Milosz thus linked "classicism" to the desire, taken from Mallarmé, to write "pure" poetry, which he had criticized in the poets of Young Poland and in his mentor Iwaszkiewicz (TP, 7, 16, 71n).

Milosz saw a contrast between his own fidelity to poetry as a "passionate pursuit of the Real" (WP, 66), and "the weakening of the faith in the existence of the objective reality situated beyond our perceptions [which] seems to be one of the causes of the malaise so common in modern poetry, which senses something like the loss of its raison d'être" (WP, 66).

To sustain his quarrel with classicism, Milosz quoted from Erich Auerbach's *Mimesis*:

> Auerbach pointed to a certain lack of reality whenever a convention is used: where the poet creates as beautiful a structure as possible out of topoi universally known and fixed, instead of trying to name what is real and yet unnamed. . . . In antiquity, Auerbach writes, "the question of style became really acute when the spread of Christianity exposed Holy Scripture, and Christian literature in general, to the aesthetic criticism of highly educated pagans. They were horrified at the claim that the highest truths were contained in writings composed in a language to their minds impossibly uncivilized and in total ignorance of stylistic categories." (WP, 62–63)

And Milosz added, paraphrasing Auerbach: "But it is precisely for this reason that we learn more of everyday life in the Roman empire from the Gospels than from the Latin poetry of the Golden Age. Horace and Vergil so filter and distill their material that we can only guess at some of the down-to-earth data hidden behind their lines" (WP, 63).[63] Like Auerbach, Milosz saw the classics as a literature shared only by a privileged class, one that is protected from experience, isolated from the audience of the general public and also from their sufferings.

This leads to an important passage where Milosz draws many important strands of his work together: his poetic Hegelianism, his cousin's concerns about social "schism" between artist and public (WP, 18; cf. TP, 20), his own privileged childhood, even his critical observations about competing forces in Poland's complex literary history:

> Mankind has always been divided by one rule into two species: *those who know and do not speak; those who speak and do not know*.[64] This formula can be seen as an allusion to the dialectic of master and slave, for it invokes centuries of ignorance and misery among serfs, peasants, and proletarians, who alone knew the cruelty of life in all its nakedness but had to keep it to themselves. The skill of reading and writing was the privilege of the few, whose sense of life was made comfortable by power and wealth. (WP, 66–67)[65]

This separation is one he remembered from his own childhood. Elsewhere he has written in prose how his "shame that I came from a family which had lived for generations off the labor of the common people" (ABC, 204). We have seen in how, in his important late poem "Treatise on Theology," Milosz described his uneasiness at being separated from "his fellow believers [in] a Catholic parish" by his study of "Latin, a language completely incomprehensible / to peasants in their sheepskin coats" (SS, 47–48). And Milosz had already noted in his *History* how the clash between Latin and vernacular had a special religious and political significance in Poland (HPL, xv–xvi).

All this leads to a more ambivalent attitude toward Oscar's target, the "schism . . . between the poet and the great human family" (WP, 26; cf. 18, 66, 75).[66] Instead of just blaming it for "the gloom of twentieth-century poetry" (WP, 37), Milosz now sees it as also corresponding to a doubleness in ourselves and in reality itself, between one level, that of "physical pain," and another, accessible through faith, "objective reality situated beyond our perceptions" (WP, 66).

This recalls his acknowledgment in the Nobel lecture of "another, hidden reality, impenetrable, though exerting a powerful attraction that is the central driving force of all art and science." He linked this in turn to his "longing for the end of the contradiction which opposes the poet's *need of distance* to his feeling of solidarity with his fellow men."[67]

In *Witness* Milosz linked this doubleness in reality to the doubleness within himself and other poets:

> All I want is to make clear . . . that, roughly described, a quarrel exists between classicism and realism. This is a clash of two tendencies independent of the literary fashions of a given period and of the shifting meanings of those two terms. These two opposed tendencies usually also coexist within one person. It must be said that the conflict will never end and that the first tendency is always, in one variety or another, dominant, while the second is always a voice of protest. (WP, 69)

Milosz then illustrated this doubleness in himself by his 1957 poem "No More," where he saw himself as an artisan "Who arranged verses about cherry blossoms," failing to find adequate words "In a graveyard whose gates are licked by greasy water" (NCP, 158). The poem accepted this inability at the end: "so, cherry blossoms must suffice for us" (WP, 72).[68] (Milosz later commented in an interview that "what we have [in this poem] is the desire to go beyond beauty, beyond aesthetic values—to reality.")[69]

Milosz concluded his lecture by observing that this ironical statement is "in fact a declaration of dissatisfaction with classicism."

> My aim here has been to indicate a contradiction that resides at the very foundation of the poet's endeavor. This contradiction was not clearly perceived by Kochanowski or other poets of the Renaissance. Today it is difficult to escape the awareness of an internal tension between imperatives. Such tension does not invalidate my definition of poetry as "a passionate pursuit of the Real." On the contrary, it gives it more weight. (WP, 75)

RUINS, POETRY, AND HOPE

In keeping with the dialectical progress of *Witness*, the next lecture, "Ruins and Poetry," looks more closely at what is meant by "the Real." It clarifies that "A hierarchy of needs is built into the very fabric of reality and is revealed when a misfortune touches a human collective, whether that be war, the rule of terror, or natural catastrophe" (WP, 79).

In such a time, "The fate of a city, of a country, becomes the center of everyone's attention," and "a great simplification ... occurs" (WP, 79–80). The effect of such "disintegration," as experienced in Polish poetry, is to draw the poet back from the escapism of pure poetry to history: "events burdening a whole community are perceived by a poet as touching him in a most personal manner. Then poetry is no longer alienated" (WP, 94–95). Milosz here is obviously describing the pattern of evolution in *A Treatise on Poetry*, but the examples he gives here are poems from his contemporaries like Świrsczyńska and Herbert. "From this perspective, nineteenth-century poems, like Mallarmé's 'Le tombeau d'Edgar Poe,' can be reproached 'for lacking a sense of hierarchy when appraising phenomena, or more simply put, for lacking realism'" (WP, 96).[70]

And he argued in his last chapter, "On Hope," for a return to a different poetry, one that will turn from the shortcomings of "a reductionist Weltanschauung" (WP, 109) to a new dimension of humanity grounded on "a newly acquired historical consciousness," seeing man as "that creature mysterious to itself, a being incessantly transcending its own limits" (WP, 110).

This "new dimension" of humanity, he argued, "the dimension of the past of our human race" (WP, 109), should be the source of hope. "'From where will a renewal come to us, to us who have devastated the whole earthly globe?' asks Simone Weil. And she answers, 'Only from the past, if we love it'" (WP, 114).

Admitting that Weil's utterance is "enigmatic," and that "it is difficult to guess what she has in mind," Milosz directs us to the melding of the beautiful and the mundane in literary works like *Pan Tadeusz*, "where the most ordinary incidents of everyday life change into a web of fairytale" (WP, 114–15).

But after years of puzzlement, I would say that the catastrophist urgency of Weil's dictum needs a more collective and less escapist answer: namely, that the disasters inflicted on our world by our culture—from war to oppression to environmental destruction—creates a need for *renewal* (not just revival) of the values at the heart of our same culture.[71]

I say this in the spirit of what Milosz himself saw, when he wrote that, in times of catastrophe, "The fate of a city, of a country, becomes the center of everyone's attention," and "a great simplification ... occurs" (WP, 79–80). It is in the spirit, also, of Milosz's wartime collection *Ocalenie* ("Rescue," "Salvation," or just "Making Whole"). There Milosz placed Faith, Hope, and Love at the center of his book, to reaffirm the basic perspective and core values of our civilization's history, as the necessary perspective from the past (e.g., to see oneself as "only one among many" [NCP, 50]) with which to deal with the calamities of the present.

It is in the spirit, again, of the "Treatise of Morals," where Milosz, using the "discipline of Elimination" (W 2:85) to discard current fashionable beliefs like existentialism, returned to "the common gift of modest wisdom"—"a healthy mind, and a balanced heart"—as the *ocalenie* ("Rescue," "Salvation," "Making Whole") that "is in you alone." (W 2:98–99). And it is in the spirit of "A Treatise on Poetry," where "a sense of history,"—like a plumb with a pure gold center—coupled with "a new tenderness," "are seen as the means of liberating man from [Stalinist] fatalism and determinism" (TP 52, 117, where "liberating" paraphrases the Polish word *ocalenie*, W 2:238).

I hope that my more extended treatment of *Ocalenie* and the two treatises has illuminated how Milosz sees our sense of history and the past should liberate us from the fashionable doctrines of our episteme that tell us we are governed only by impersonal fatalistic forces, like Marxism or neoliberalism. I have paused to emphasize this large argument, because of its relevance to my concluding chapter.

In other words, the Harvard lectures of Milosz open with Blake's romantic expectations for the future, and they conclude by tacitly agreeing with Eliot's critique of Blake for not being sufficiently grounded in the past. Thus, I see Milosz's work as achieving what the times badly need, a synthesis, or marriage, of Blake and Eliot. It is a marriage in another sense as well. Blake and Eliot, each in their own way, were mostly partisans for only one of the opposing forces—romanticist and classicist, radical and conservative, yin and yang—that exist (to greater or lesser extents) in most, perhaps all, great contemporary poets.

By acknowledging and validating both forces in himself and in society, by acknowledging his desire "to retain both sides of the contradiction" (TP, 122n), Milosz has helped move society away from partisan endorsements and toward a new post-secular level of reconciliation and "tenderness" (TP, 52), in both aesthetic and political discourse.

Both *The Land of Ulro* and *Witness* are open-ended: their richness and complexity permit many interpretations. Here is my own over-simplification, to support my case in my next chapter for Milosz's urgent contemporary relevance.

Milosz reminds us that at its core, our civilization contains at its heart a vision of an objective reality not yet attained (WP, 25; cf. WP, 37); that "the weakening of faith in the existence" of this objective reality is "one of the causes of the malaise so common in modern poetry (WP, 66);" the resulting schism between the poet and the "great human family" aggravates the social breakdown it reflects (WP, 27), and that, in the catastrophe induced by this breakdown the poet suffers with the community, "Then poetry is no longer alienated . . . the great schism in poetry is curable" (WP, 94–95).

Milosz illustrated this dialectical turn with the work of other postwar Polish poets. But he is accurately describing a trajectory in his own life. And not just poets, but all who care about the future of our culture, can profit from his example.

A CLOSER LOOK AT MILOSZ'S QUARREL WITH ELIOT

I am curtailing the many ideas in the Harvard lectures in order to highlight one in particular: the quarrel "between classicism and realism" that exists both in our culture and within ourselves ("These two opposed tendencies usually also coexist within one person" [WP, 69]). Though Milosz has through his life been constantly exemplifying and describing this doubleness within himself, I believe this is the first occasion in which he has acknowledged its universal historical importance, as a tension reflecting the way our divided psyches mirror the divided cultures we grow into.[72]

A "voice of protest" quarreling with one of refinement and affirmation: Are these not precisely Milosz's conflicting reactions during his existential crisis at Goszyce in 1944, followed by his later quarrels with first romanticism and then classicism? And today, in a postmodernist era when we no longer feel compelled to choose between one cause and the other, is it not now obvious that a serious poet should feel obligated to observe both? That is to say, first acknowledge this doubleness in oneself, and then seek both to preserve our precious self-criticizing heritage, and also to change it?

This is the moment for a deeper comparison between Milosz and Eliot. For Eliot has been described as a "reactionary modernist," sharing for some years with Georg Lukács a "position that was both modernist and anti-modern, revolutionary and conservative."[73] This was most true in the years after World War I, when Eliot, disillusioned with the prevailing liberal culture, praised the French syndicalist Georges Sorel and his translator T. E. Hulme (he called Hulme "classical, reactionary and revolutionary . . . the antipodes of the eclectic, tolerant, and democratic mind of the end of the last century.")[74]

Like most critics, Jesse Airaudi has stressed the similarities between Milosz and Eliot; he sees both as exemplars of modernism, defined as "a tradition-based protest against materialist values."[75] But the longer Milosz lived, the more importance he attached to the differences between them, in terms of style, religion, and politics.

The first real problem with Eliot noted by Milosz, who believed in "simple speech," had to do with his style: "The poetics he [Eliot] chose made him an 'obscure' poet. and some of his digressions, such as those in *Four Quartets*, are indecipherable without resort to the often dubious assistance of his commentators."[76]

And even here the real issue was not so much with Eliot himself as with his complex but powerful influence. In Eliot's shadow, Milosz wrote, "American poetry fell ill; excessive straining for high culture and a fear of simplicity of expression are not, as a rule, healthy for poetry."[77] This hostility to "highbrow" literature well-wrought is echoed in his comment that "theories of literature as *Écriture*, of speech feeding on itself," are conducive to "the growth of the totalitarian state."[78]

Milosz's difference from Eliot's elitism was not limited to style but extended to their different attitudes to spirituality and indeed society. Milosz's return to Catholicism was a reaffirmation of his links to the people he was born among; Eliot's Anglo-Catholicism, in sharp contrast, was a way of *distancing* himself from the Unitarianism of his family and surroundings in St. Louis. In Eliot's famous profession of his new values—"an Anglo-Catholic in religion, a classicist in literature and a royalist in politics"—all three terms stand out as deliberately, and provocatively, *un*popular.

Milosz, in life-long debt to Eliot's poetry, never discusses his criticism; and I suspect may have been offended by it. As one dependent on his own *daimonion*, he cannot have been pleased by Eliot's definition of "Romanticism" as inspiration from an "inner voice, which breathes the eternal message of vanity, fear, and lust."[79] Milosz had his own dialectical quarrel with romanticism; but he also "realized that I am a promethean romantic who has been inoculated with his special vocation, who attempts to 'remake breadeaters into angels'" (YH, 119, quoting from Słowacki, one of the last romantic poets from the Age of Raptures).

More Miloszian was Eliot's famous question in response to the shadow of an imminent Second World War: "was our society, which had always been so assured of its superiority . . . assembled round anything more permanent than a congeries of banks, insurance companies and industries, and had it any beliefs more essential than a belief in compound interest and the maintenance of dividends?"[80] But the setting for this question, Eliot's *The Idea of a Christian Society*, underlines the fundamental difference between the two poets. Eliot, here as in his earlier criticism, is seeking to *restore* the past; and Milosz, as always, to move forward.

Milosz once commented on the poetry of Philip Larkin, "That emptiness and cruelty, which is the basis of Larkin's weltanschauung, should be accepted as a basis upon which you work *towards* something light."[81] Intelligent critics have seen Eliot's work as a lifelong striving toward something light, indeed a "heart of light."[82]

But if poetry is to "change nations and people," Eliot's contorted and unhopeful spirituality, together with his idiosyncratic classicism, must be seen as too refined and elitist to be serviceable for a better society.

CONCLUSION: BLAKE, ELIOT, AND MILOSZ

In every generation, but especially in times of profound and traumatic change, great poets face the task of readjusting the relationship of the past to the future. Each great poet offers their own personal (and usually idiosyncratic) solution to the dilemma of reconciling the old and the new, as defined by correcting his or her antecedents.

I now see Milosz as a sane and important corrective to Eliot's important but decidedly idiosyncratic view of tradition, which itself can be seen as a sane corrective to the crazy idiosyncratic perspectives of Blake (who wrote how Milton came to him in Lambeth, in the form of a falling star, and entered his left foot).[83]

It is worth recalling Eliot's famous dissent from what he described in Blake as "the crankiness, the eccentricity, which frequently affects writers outside of the Latin traditions." What Blake's "genius required," Eliot continued,

and what it sadly lacked, was a framework of accepted and traditional ideas which would have prevented him from indulging in a philosophy of his own, and concentrated his attention upon the problems of the poet. Confusion of thought, emotion, and vision is what we find in such a work as *Also Sprach Zarathustra*; it is eminently not a Latin virtue. The concentration resulting from a framework of mythology and theology and philosophy is one of the reasons why Dante is a classic, and Blake only a poet of genius.[84]

Milosz, both a born Catholic and also even more of a geographic outsider from Latin Europe than Blake or Eliot, has, I think, achieved a far more balanced incorporation of Blake into the generative tradition. He recognizes, what the royalist classicist Eliot ignored, the importance of Blake's compassion for "those who know and do not speak": "William Blake combats the diabolic vassal of inertia responsible for the inhuman industrialization of England, or, as Allen Ginsberg calls it, 'Moloch whose name is the mind.'"[85]

In the close to his Nobel lecture of 1980, Milosz acknowledged Blake as one of three writers from whom he has received a mandate, as he concluded:

> Our century . . . has also been a century of faith and hope. A profound transformation, of which we are hardly aware, because we are a part of it, has been taking place, coming to the surface from time to time in phenomena that provoke general astonishment. . . . For we all who are here, both the speaker and you who listen, are no more than links between the past and the future.[86]

My own hope is that posterity will agree with Joseph Brodsky's judgment that "Czeslaw Milosz is one of the greatest poets of our time"; and will recognize his works as classics. I would make this claim in particular for *The Witness of Poetry*. Despite its Polish perspective, it is in the tradition of Schiller's *Letters on the Aesthetic Education of Mankind* and Shelley's *A Defence of Poetry*—with the difference that it is at present more relevant than they are for reviving "a sense of open space ahead" (WP, 14), and also for reconciliation between warring factions. Milosz's wisdom is badly needed in a new era of breakdown and depression, anxiety, even despair.

Chapter 16
Saning Insanity: Milosz as Healer of a Post-Secular Era

How to combine "transcendence" and "devenir" has always been my main question.

—Czeslaw Milosz[1]

Culture is the way out of the present human condition.

—Stanisław Brzozowski[2]

sane, v. *Obsolete. transitive.* To cure, to heal.

—*Oxford English Dictionary*[3]

I have been shamelessly selective in presenting the Milosz who has so inspired me and will, I hope, inspire future generations. Not to admit this would be dishonest. But, of course, everyone wrestling with Milosz's protean mind has done pretty much the same thing. With abundant data, Nathan and Quinn wrote persuasively of Milosz the Catholic, Kraszewski of Milosz the heterodox, Tischner of Milosz the moralist, Hass of Milosz the self-questioning skeptic.

Such critics have often preferred the Americanized Milosz who wrote in 1975, "I . . . have no ambition to save America or the world" (Visions, 218), or who ruthlessly admitted his own streak of Ketman: "One more of my disguises. In discussing literature, I pretend that I care about it, instead of proclaiming that it is a frivolous, godless occupation. Frivolous because, although it is supposed to turn reality into words, very little reality penetrates it" (YH, 73).

A more objective assessment of Milosz might have described how this praiser of gentleness could be severe in discounting others, as for example in his "aversion" to Robert Lowell (YH, 219), for which he later apologized (NCP, 722), or his angry dismissal of the "utterly senseless demands" of the Berkeley Free Speech Movement (Visions, 214), for which he did not.

I can only say that I have tried to be true to the Milosz I knew and loved in the early 1960s, the man who cared enough about literature to devote his life to it, and yet rejected the offer of a farm where he would not have had to do anything else.

"What is poetry, that does not change / Nations or people?" (NCP, 77). That question, not yet translated into English, electrified me in Milosz's home in 1961, when I first read it. It was my hope, then, that Milosz's poetry might help change not just American "poetry of the 'well-wrought urn'"[4] but America itself, indeed the world.

I believed, in short, in the efficacy and potential of Milosz's strategy for cultural evolution (ethogeny) or what Milosz called his "unpolitical politics" (NR, 247). When I began this book, as I noted in my first chapter, I was thinking of the power of poetry to enhance and advance politics, as I noted in the influence of *Paradise Lost*, described by historians, on the American Revolution.[5] Thus the doorway to my thinking was chapter 2, on the acknowledged contribution of Milosz's writings, both in poetry and prose, to the success of the Polish Solidarity Movement.

That is still my hope today. But writing this book has changed me, just as Milosz himself evolved. I now consider his role in Solidarity to be incidental, almost a footnote, to his global role in renewing shared values toward "an open space ahead," a revitalized mindset beyond conservatism, modernism, and postmodernism.

Hopefully all factions can learn from his role as a futurist whose profound critique of the present was guided and disciplined by a full appreciation of the past—a role played not just by Milosz but by great poets since the beginning of letters.

MILOSZ'S "UNPOLITICAL POLITICS" AND AMERICAN POLITICS

When I began this book over a decade ago, my friends of good will were appalled by the criminal folly of America's Iraq War and appalled also by their inability to stop it. Repeatedly, in my prose books since then, I have argued that America should learn from the ultimate success of Solidarity in Poland, with its initial strategy of promoting social rather than political change, and its appeal to two traditionally opposed factions, the Church and the Left.[6]

It was then that I first thought of writing this book, to promote in America the cultural evolution (or what Adam Michnik called "an almost two-decade effort" to change civil society) preceding Poland's Solidarity movement.[7] And I noted, as again in this book, that "This closely parallels John Adams' observation that the American Revolution was not the war: 'It was in the minds of the people . . . in the course of fifteen years, before a drop of blood was shed at Lexington.'"[8]

The American Revolution remains exemplary for Solidarność and other nonviolent movements. It exhibited successful empowerment from below ("in the minds of the people") against repressive enforcement from above. But America today is immensely larger than Poland or the Thirteen Colonies. Thus, a poetic effort to envision and effect a comparable change of heart today will be immensely more difficult. That does not mean it is impossible.[9]

Again, a foreign poet who wrote mostly in Polish might seem at first glance to be an unlikely candidate to change America. But though Milosz is unlikely ever to appeal to large numbers of people, he is already cited, sometimes reverently, by a wide spectrum of opinion-molders in this country, from Chris Hedges on the left to Russell Kirk on the right.

It is here, I believe, that Milosz's idea of an "unpolitical politics" shows us a way forward: to deal with such radical problems as climate or war-making, the nation must change culturally before it can change politically. Today's two-party politics, with both parties converging at best on an unsustainable status quo, cannot by itself begin to supply an answer.[10] If there is to be an answer, as I have suggested elsewhere, it might come from the cultural change inspired by Milosz and implemented just a generation ago in Solidarity: an alliance of social movements, including both Church and the Left, against a military-industrial complex at the center, dominated by the need to make profit and wage war.[11]

And if, as seems quite possible, there is no such alliance, the forces behind American interventions will continue. So will international forces opposing them: there is an increasing similarity between the decline of US power today and that of British power before 1914.[12]

There is an increasing chance, in short, of catastrophe. But here is where Milosz's larger views on catastrophe, and how to exploit its potential, would become even more relevant, as a guide for a bigger and more fundamental change.

MILOSZ'S CULTURAL POLITICS AND GLOBAL EVOLUTION

In the course of writing this book, I have come now to see Milosz as a guide to change, not just on a political level but, more broadly, on the level of culture itself. As Seamus Heaney expressed it, behind the "secular" Milosz, concerned with the troubles of his century, was a "millennial" Milosz who had experienced the span of culture from the "folk-belief and taboo" of Lithuania to the ideological extremes of Nazism and Stalinism.[13]

His experience of traumatic cultural disruption in 1945, combined with his poetic distance, gave him the spiritual strength to think about a deeper pattern beneath present chaos. He asked, in 1960, whether history, despite appearance, did not contain beneath its troubled surface a force worthy of our commitment:

> Is there any immanent force located in *le devenir*, in what is in the state of becoming, a force that pulls mankind up toward perfection? Is there any cooperation between man and a universe that is subject to constant change? So worded, the question is related to the quite recent discovery of the historical dimension, unknown to the rather immobile societies of the past. Curiously enough, Christian theologians are helpless when confronted with those issues.[14]

Milosz later put the same question more succinctly in his notes to the *Treatise on Poetry*: "Is history just a mass of facts, without traceable logic or direction? Or is it submitted to hidden laws?" (TP, 97). I shall suggest in a moment that this intuiting of pattern in cultural disruption derived from his having, in part by accident, been in the midst of it.

Milosz's "immanent force" is analogous to Eliot's concept of destiny, which "implies that the world, and the course of human history, have meaning."[15] But Eliot distanced destiny from the poet's "inner voice, which breathes the eternal message of vanity, fear, and lust." Milosz, in contrast, wrote of an affinity between the "immanent force" of history and the "unknown, impersonal voice" (NCP, 13) within him, dictating his own best work.

Milosz distinguished his question about history from "the providentialist philosophy propagated by Bossuet" (the Panglossian theologian, d. 1704), because of the latter's failure, with other Catholic theologians, to grasp the "historical dimension" of the human condition (i.e., to see the human condition as a developmental process rather than a settled state).[16]

And I would like to distinguish it also from nineteenth-century beliefs in Progress, because of the failure in that century to distinguish between the erratic surface events of socio-political development, and a deeper, steadier incremental pattern of dialectical cultural development, that I have called *ethogeny*.[17]

I agree with Wordsworth that "The world is too much with us"; we tend not to see that true history, the only meaningful history, is cultural history, not the political history that dominates our headlines.

Let me digress for a moment or two on the deep pattern of cultural development, the terrain of Milosz's greatest legacy.

HISTORY AS CULTURAL (NOT POLITICAL) EVOLUTION: A DIGRESSION

The difference between political and cultural development can be crudely compared to that between daily weather changes and global warming. Weather catastrophes, such as tornadoes and ice storms, are notoriously difficult to anticipate; and it is even more difficult to imagine their chaos as a continuous force toward perfection. On the other hand, climate trends measured over centuries show a more coherent pattern, even if a non-directional one.

A better, because more dialectical, analogy is the tectonic movement called subduction. This slowly builds up stored energy where one tectonic plate slides under another and then becomes locked, ultimately producing a catastrophic rupture and adjustment through volcanic and earthquake activity.[18]

Here is change that does not, in the short run, turn back on itself; the subductive forces lifting Mount Everest are, in our time frame, irreversible. There are also subductive forces at work in history, trending toward justice and well-being. And poets, at least poets attuned to the sufferings of common people, are in a position to detect, record, and thus strengthen them.

For example, Rousseau can be said to have composed anticipatory poetry when he wrote in 1762, three decades before the French Revolution, "Man is born free, but everywhere he is in chains." That memorable line in *The Social Contract* encapsulated and simplified an awareness of the rising middle-class frustration that would soon, like a tectonic plate, push up and topple the French *ancien régime* oppressing it.[19] And we can also say that what we now see as flaws in his vision—leading to the simplified claim that man must "be forced to be free"—also anticipated and sped the coming of the gulags of the Soviet Union and China.

Like Milosz, one can be ambivalent about Rousseau's legacy, but one can still see his lines as ethogenic activity, leading to a cultural victory of the mind over the forces of mere violence. We can say the same of the writings of Isaiah and Jeremiah, which converted the disaster of military annihilation by the Babylonians into an enduring spiritual victory. The Jewish prophets strengthened a faith that, more than any empires from that era, has changed human life on every continent of the world.

And we can see the same principle in John Adams's observation that the American revolution was not won by armies, but "in the minds of the people." He too saw the pattern anticipated in 1947 by Milosz in his "Treatise on Morals": that ethogeny is a deep current, outlasting tyranny.

Six years later, perhaps encouraged by the support he was receiving from Americans after his defection, Milosz wrote more confidently in *The Captive Mind*, "The war years taught me that a man should not take a pen in his hands merely to communicate to others his own despair and defeat. . . . Today the only poetry worthy of the name is eschatological, that is, poetry which rejects the present inhuman world in the name of a great change."[20]

CATASTROPHIC RENEWAL IN WESTERN CULTURAL DEVELOPMENT: A FURTHER DIGRESSION

Milosz cast light on aspects of the deeper dialectical pattern of cultural development, when he compared the Soviet destruction of prewar Poland to the barbarian overwhelming of Rome. He also noted how the disruption of the past—when "a great simplification of everything occurs and an individual asks" himself why he took to heart matters that now seem to have no weight" (WP, 80)—could also liberate minds to prepare for the future.[21]

The political collapse of Rome was not an unqualified disaster. On the contrary, it produced the collapse of the Roman slavery system and the break-up of the vast latifundia supporting it. This led directly to improvement in techniques of agriculture, including the development of a deeper plough. According to the eminent science historian Lynn White Jr., "In technology, at least, the Dark Ages mark a steady and uninterrupted advance over the Roman Empire."[22]

The traumatic political collapse of Rome also led to centuries of monastic withdrawal, and sustained contemplation there of human purpose, in the context of Western European culture's root texts: the Bible and Virgil. I believe this deepened meditative attention to life and literary symbols led to enhanced psychological awareness in general; in particular it helps explain the enormous cultural differences between Virgil and Dante.

The Dark Ages were not the first instance in our history of a traumatic political disaster, followed by creative response. Nor is Milosz's own extraction of hope from catastrophe, for example in *Ocalenie*, at all unique. Milosz himself in that one book both replicated and alluded to previous cultural breakthroughs in response to political catastrophes: Virgil's *Aeneid* at the end of the Roman republic, Milton's *Paradise Lost* after the English Civil War,

Blake's epics and Wordsworth's "Tintern Abbey" and "Prelude" after the demise of the original, nonviolent French revolution, and Eliot's *Waste Land* after World War I.[23]

Underlying all of these was the influence on his style of the Bible, shaped in large part by the destruction of the Jewish kingdoms and temple, and (in Milosz's words) supplying the "grain of our [Western] civilization" (WP, 37).

By pulling together all of these influences Milosz recapitulates, like no one else in his generation, the pattern of catastrophic disruption and renewal that is at the very heart of our culture. His works fall into line with the earlier root texts that embody this pattern and advance it, each referring back to its predecessors, and providing a kind of spine to the body of our literary canon. In particular, Milosz's poetry has aligned the Polish fate, of disappearance twice from the political map, with that of the Jews, whose Temple and kingdoms were also twice destroyed.

No other recent poet, not even Eliot, is as mindful of this legacy. This distinguishes Milosz in three respects, all related. The first is his emphasis on the relationship of catastrophe to renewal. The second is his notion that the highest creativity is not totally free but conforms to material arising from circumstances and *given* to the artist, not freely *selected* by him.[24]

The third is his conviction, expressed clearly only after his distancing himself from the nationalistic Polish Church, that our contemporary age is wrong to reduce religion to a social artifact; that there was merit to his cousin's concern about "an erroneous direction taken by science in the eighteenth century";[25] and that poets should sustain Blake's dream of a new Jerusalem "in England's green & pleasant Land." Because of these beliefs, and especially the third, I am tempted to see Milosz as a poet, perhaps even a bard, of a post-secular era that is already upon us.

Critics in the twentieth century have had much to say about literature as supplying an *alterity* or *Other* to our imperfect human condition.[26] This alterity can be non-dialectical and irrelevant to cultural change, as when Helen Vendler cited "what Richard Wilbur has called the '*mad instead*' of poetry."[27] But Milosz distinguished between the alterity of "pure poetry" outside the human crisis, "organized as a peculiar anti-world" (WP, 46), and that of the engaged poetry of postwar Polish poets, who "tend to view it [poetry] as a witness *and participant* in one of man's major transformations" (WP, 4, emphasis added).

I agree with Milosz that our civilization is eschatological, and that at its core is a tradition of visions, drawn, not just in our own time but repeatedly, from the anguish of catastrophe. Our culture, in both its classical and its Jewish roots, is grounded in a sequence of such catastrophes, from many of which have evolved and matured the mythic promise of a new society emerging from the destruction of the old.[28]

POETRY AND CULTURAL EVOLUTION: A FURTHER DIGRESSION

I agree with Milosz, furthermore, that poets like Virgil, Dante, and Wordsworth have contributed to major shifts in our Western cultural evolution, and that our current cultural distemper, sometimes diagnosed as a failure of imagination, calls for healing redirection by another such great poet.

I believe that cultural history proceeds from a series of pivotal moments of fundamental breakthroughs in consciousness that, once learned from, meet with resistance but are unlikely to be reversed. Like Milosz, I believe also that these breakthroughs are often initiated or consolidated in the visionary reassessments of major poetry, as the most concentrated, memorable, and sharable crystallization of them. ("One clear stanza can take more weight / Than a whole wagon of elaborate prose," NCP, 109; TP, 1.)

An example often given is Dante's revision of Virgil on the question of erotic love, seeing it as a force giving order to society rather than (as in the *Aeneid*) threatening it. The difference was set out well by Eliot:

> The term which one can justifiably regret the lack of in Virgil is *amor*. It is, above all others, the key word in Dante. . . . There is tenderness and pathos enough in the Aeneid. But Love is never given, to my mind, the same significance as a principle of order in the human soul, in society and in the universe that pietas is given; and it is not Love that causes *fatum*, or moves the sun and the stars. Even for intensity of physical passion, Virgil is more tepid than some other Latin poets, and far below the rank of Catullus. If we are not chilled we at least feel ourselves, with Virgil, to be moving in a kind of emotional twilight. Virgil was, among all authors of classical antiquity, one for whom the world made sense, for whom it had order and dignity, and for whom, as for no one before his time except the Hebrew prophets, history had meaning.[29]

It took Dante, however, to see that love (*amore*) for a woman could be a "sweet guide" (*Paradiso* 23:34) to that meaning rather than (as in the Dido episode of the *Aeneid*) a distraction from it.

We can track this evolution, of deepening psychological awareness and more coherent sensibility, in the progressive deepening of commentaries on the *Aeneid*. The story of Dido was treated lightly by the fifth-century grammarian Servius: "It's all about schemes and subtleties, so that it is virtually in the comic style—no wonder, as it deals with love (*paene comicus stilus est; nec mirum, ubi de amore tractatur*)."[30]

But inevitably, medieval commentators, as they became accustomed to allegorizing the Old Testament in search of truth, came to allegorize and deepen the Dido story as well. Thus, for example, John of Salisbury (d. 1180), wrote: "The fourth part [of the Aeneid] unites illicit loves and leads the fire unwisely conceived in the heart toward the unfortunate pyre of the lover."[31]

This deepening of the text set the stage for Dante's echo of Dido's lament when he sees Beatrice in the Earthly Paradise: *conosco i segni dell'antica fiamma* ("I recognize the signs of the ancient flame").[32] Dido, for Dante, has come to be the embodiment of an enduring love force that was merely secular in pagan times but can also be Christian, enlightening in a region where reason (as represented by his pagan guide Virgil) cannot penetrate. And Milosz's handling of love, albeit complex and often ironic, is ultimately Dantean rather than Virgilian.

After the tragic disruptions of the twentieth century, poets in unprecedented numbers tried to think and write about politics—as a rule, not very helpfully. Some (Yeats, Pound, Eliot) sought an alterity in their idiosyncratic conceptions of the past, while others, including Futurists like Mayakovsky, sought it by rejecting the past—"Throw Pushkin, Dostoevsky, Tolstoy, etc., etc. overboard from the Ship of Modernity."[33]

One historic function of poetry has been to preserve and reinforce the vision of alternative space. It can take many forms, ranging from the wholly personal (Rückert's "Ich leb' allein in meinem Himmel"—"I live alone in my Heaven") to the collective (Schiller's "Alle Menschen werden Brüder"—"All men will become brothers"). Alterity in other words may be less a fixed blueprint or Platonic archetype "laid up in heaven for him who has eyes to see it" (Plato, Republic 582ab, 402cd), than a dialectical *concordia discors*—a venue of vying dreams, diverse but ultimately synergistic. A pattern evolving, in other words, in the same chaotic but possibly patterned way as some see in the rest of the physical and biological universe.

Or else poetry may do nothing more than imply this alternative space negatively by its emphatic "Not this!"—its vigorous rejection of the status quo (as in Allen Ginsberg's *Howl*).

As I have noted throughout this book, I believe that Milosz served this function, both in his poetry and in his prose—as, for example, when he wrote that the social task of the inspired poet is "to transcend his paltry ego," and remind the "soul of the people" of "the open space ahead." (WP, 28, 25, 14).

CATASTROPHE AND HOPE

Milosz, shaped in part by his memory of the "lost paradise" of Szetejnie (YH, 84), never lost the sense, which we should share, that our civilization is in a protracted crisis, of which the catastrophe of the Second World War was merely a corollary (LU, 271). Using Heaney's terms, we can describe some aspects of the crisis as "secular," such as violent war and upheavals. But some are "millennial," such as (in Milosz's terms) "the dialectic of master and slave [between] *those that know and do not speak; those who speak and do not know*" (WP, 66). The catastrophes that issue periodically from this crisis, though threats to hope in the short run, are also what clear space for a better view of "the other shore" (LU, 270), a higher hope in the long run.

Milosz, for all his balancing of the classicist and romantic urges within himself, preserved the romantic hope that our future, even if falling short of the messianic Third Age contemplated by Joachim of Fiore, will offer a "renewed civilization," in which "dreams of an age of friendly cooperation between nations could still come true" (LU, 272, 274).

I have tried to show how Milosz's works have not just anticipated this better age, but advanced the world, and not just Poland, toward it. A true heir of the conflicting, more single-minded visions of Blake and Eliot (romantic and classicist), Milosz did more than just synthesize the two. With a saner view than they had of this doubleness in himself and others, Milosz developed a much-needed style of self-questioning gentleness—a key to more honest poetry, and hopefully also to a better world.

I believe that today it is even more urgent to learn from his *aperçu* that we reflect within ourselves a social quarrel between "opposed tendencies [that] usually also coexist within one person" (WP, 69). The decline of shared beliefs in our culture encourages us to foster one tendency at the expense of the other; questioning of self gives way to anger at others. Influenced by Milosz, I wrote back in 2006 that "The more there are individuals who can think of themselves as both liberal and conservative, the easier it will be to heal the artificial divisions in our civil society."[34] Poetry, but especially Milosz's poetry, by increasing our self-awareness and sensitivity, can help restore that inner dialectical equilibrium, or "balanced heart," that is so easily lost in polemics.

This conclusion has been influenced by McGilchrist's metaphoric distinction (in the spirit of Hegel) between "reason" and "rationality": "Reason is about holding sometimes incompatible elements in balance, a right-hemisphere capacity, whereas rationality is typically left-hemisphere. . . . Rationality imposes an 'either-or' on life which is far from reasonable."[35] That in turn has alerted me to the number of times that poets, and particularly exile poets, have been praised for their "dual vision." Among those so praised are Milosz himself, and two other Nobel Prize winners close to him: Joseph Brodsky[36] and Seamus Heaney.[37]

The Buddhist poet Jane Hirshfield has also praised Milosz's poem "Winter" for its "dual vision," but in a different way, for its "fully-felt fulcrum of balance." She singled out for praise the Milosz who "remained all his life a poet whose descriptions and affections were ultimately tuned to the small, the visibly near."[38] Milosz's search for balance, his desire "to retain both ends of the contradiction" (TP, 122), may offer a "way ahead" for the needed reconciliation of post-modernism and post-secularism.

But the Milosz of polemical prose, specifically the author of *The Captive Mind*, has also been praised by an Australian critic for his (and its) "dual vision."[39] She cites Milosz's epigraph to *The Captive Mind*, a quotation, attributed to "An Old Jew of Galicia": "When someone is honestly 55% right, that's very good and there's no use wrangling. . . . Well and what about 100% right? Whoever says he's 100% right is a fanatic, a thug, and the worst kind of rascal."[40] That simple piece of folk wisdom, so pertinent to the historic de-escalation of the Cold War, is no less relevant today. And hopefully we may proceed to a future culture and counterculture more respectful of their mutual debts, in which scientists can agree with Max Planck (and McGilchrist) that "Science cannot solve the ultimate mystery of nature";[41] and believers can accept the benefits of doubt, criticism, and tolerance to the advancement of religion.

Let me conclude with Brodsky's judgment that "Czeslaw Milosz is one of the greatest poets of our time; perhaps the greatest."[42] And let me add what Seamus Heaney wrote of the moreness in Milosz's life and work, how they embodied "loyalty to the ancient dream that human beings are on earth to transcend their worst selves, to create civilisation, to build the new Jerusalem in spite of all. . . . [His poems] fortify something in what might be called our spiritual immunity system."[43] The generative dialogue to which Milosz made so large a contribution, will, I believe, continue among great poets.

There already exists a strong American contribution, from Whitman through Allen Ginsberg to Leonard Cohen and Bob Dylan.[44] But the counterculture to which Ginsberg and Dylan contributed so much also has a streak of demotic anti-intellectualism in it. For a movement of change to mobilize support not just at the margins but at all levels of society, as Solidarność did in Poland, its popular appeal must I believe be grounded on the kind of thoughtful self-questioning that Milosz offers.

May we all learn from Milosz to look beyond the threatening divisions of today and work instead for a more tolerant hopeful world, with "dreams of an idyllic earth where 'the hay smells of the dream'; where tree, man, animal are joined in praise of the Garden's beauty" (LU, 275).

Appendix

Three Poems to Czeslaw Milosz: Introduced by a Personal Memoir

After years of pondering why Milosz chose in 1967 to drop me as his translator, I have come to suspect that a chief reason may have been my over-eager zeal to preserve the original meaning of the poem "Dedication," with its memorable question, "What is poetry which does not save / Nations or people?" I argued strenuously with Milosz, for example, that the lines "To, że późno pojąłem jej wybawczy cel, To jest i tylko to jest ocalenie" should be translated literally: "That I discovered, late, its [good poetry's] salutary aim, / This is, and only this is, salvation." Milosz insisted on a toned-down, less bardic and more subjective adaptation of the second line: "In this and only this *I find* salvation" (NCP, 77, emphasis added).

It would certainly not have been the only reason. In the fall of 1967, Milosz (as I noted earlier) attended a rally where I spoke on the same platform as Noam Chomsky. Since then, I have become more concerned by the divisions in American civil society to which left-wing fanatics have contributed, and also (though to a far lesser extent) by the imbalances in Chomsky's monochromatic denunciations of America.[1]

Earlier, in late 1964, I was caught up in the historical eddies of the Free Speech Movement (FSM), which I knew Milosz disapproved of, although he did not discuss this displeasure with me. Milosz and I had opposite reactions to an event we both attended, when UC President Kerr spoke to the entire student body in the campus Greek Theater. Milosz was appalled by the "utterly senseless demands of the students," reacting "with one great hostile shout at the speech."[2] Meanwhile I was appalled by the sight of the police wrestling the student leader Mario Savio roughly to the ground, when he tried also to address the crowd.[3] But I believe that for three years we managed never to discuss the FSM. And by early 1965 I was speaking out regularly against the Vietnam War. Obviously, Milosz's hostility to Communism was irreconcilable with my desire then for peaceful coexistence with Moscow. But for two

243

years at least, these differences did not trouble our relationship. For the most part, we did not discuss them either.

I take partial responsibility for the rift which began to develop between us. As a North American who had greatly enjoyed working at United Nations Assemblies and Conferences, I did not yet fully appreciate, to the extent that he did, the "fragility of those things we call civilization or culture," (WP, 97) and the "high cost of our growing consciousness of global interdependence."

Furthermore, he was far more aware than I of disturbing developments in the so-called Polish People's Republic, which in the 1960s began to clamp down on its citizens more severely than when I had been there, between 1959 and 1961, toward the end of the so-called Polish thaw. On my part, I think I became more aware than he of disturbing developments in American foreign policy.

This was particularly true after the US-encouraged massacre of a million or more Indonesians in 1965, when Sukarno was overthrown. I became obsessed with the Indonesian massacre in 1965, and less mindful of Stalin's crimes, such as the massacre of Polish officers at Katyń.

By this time, as noted in chapter 4, issues of translation were beginning to divide us, and not just over his own poetry. One major disagreement concerned the last lines of Zbigniew Herbert's famous poem "Pebble" ("Kamyk")—Milosz insisted on translating them as "to the end they will look at us / with a calm and very clear eye." I have always believed that we should have followed Herbert's carefully selected word order in Polish, which is "with an eye calm and very clear." I think that here Milosz followed his own personal preference for a continuous vernacular style, over the heightened resonance of Herbert's final word "clear."[4]

But the most dramatic example (as noted above) was over Milosz's own poem, "Dedication" ("Przedmowa")—whether to translate it literally, or (as Milosz quite reasonably preferred) to adapt it for a non-Polish audience. I see now that it was naïve of me to assume that I was on the same level with Milosz, with respect to his own poems, that I had been when we were both translating Kochanowski or Herbert. As I wrote later, the sharp edges of our critical tools, "turned / on the sensitive flesh of your own poems / could only draw blood."[5] Today my view of life is no longer so contrasted to his, but this is irrelevant. I took it as no less than a disaster that our sessions suddenly ended, contributing to a severe depression that lasted years.[6]

The first public sign of trouble between us was a memorable faculty meeting in 1973 or 1974, in which he opposed a plan for a new experimental college program, which I was proposing with two colleagues. As I remember it, the gist of his (misplaced, in my opinion) criticism was that we were the type of pedagogical positivists whom he had once described as being "from the point of view of literature . . . Romantic arsonists."[7]

He seemed to assume, from the fact that we were proposing an avowedly innovative program, that we would turn our backs on the traditions of European culture that were so important to him. But it was in this program that, for the first time, I began to teach Virgil, as I did for the remainder of my academic career.[8]

It was now clear that there was a major rift between us. I was, frankly, broken-hearted.

Things went from bad to worse. In 1982, I was surprised to see my translation of Herbert's poem "Two Drops," which I had completed before ever meeting Milosz, appear in an important poetic anthology, *The Rattle Bag*, ascribed to Milosz and not to myself.[9] Then new editions of our Penguin edition of Herbert's *Selected Poems* appeared, both in England and America, without any communication with, permission from, or recompense to me.[10] Milosz was very busy in these years of being famous, and his business was handled between his secretary and a powerful agent; so I attribute no malice to him in these details. But they indicate how far I had receded from his attention.

The denouement was after I had been invited to a conference in 1982 at Stanford, in order to participate in a panel with two other poets (Pinsky and Hass) on translating Milosz. I was looking forward eagerly to rejoining Milosz's world. Then a letter arrived telling me that my invitation had been withdrawn, and Milosz himself would be taking my place. I still have no idea who was responsible for this decision, but I was again shattered by it.[11]

My despair resulted in the long "Letter to Czeslaw Milosz" which follows.

> Now that I shall not see you at the weekend
> conference with your new translators,
> surprised, even hurt, to have been disinvited,
> I am also relieved: because we share no future,
> at last I am free to tell you, face
> to absent face, how much your gift,
> of loneliness inhabited, has meant.[12]

Someone gave the poem to him, and to my delight he phoned me to set up a reconciliatory meeting. He scheduled it for 2:30 p.m., a half-hour before the Commencement ceremony for Slavic Studies would begin. But instead, we talked non-stop for three-and-a-half hours, with a new and intense candor about our differences. I walked with him finally to the Commencement, to find workmen folding away the chairs and tables. I recall that we were able to salvage half a plastic glass of wine each from the last remaining bottle.

Our reconciliation was fated not to be total. I tried to suggest to him on this occasion that we were both fundamentally striving for the same cause—nonviolence—and that the influence on our campus of people like me had served to help spare Berkeley the anti-academic violence one had seen at Columbia and Yale. His unforgettable response is printed indelibly in my memory, as in my trilogy *Seculum*: "My dear Peter, of course you gave the enemy comfort!"—the enemy being the forces of violence that had, for example, set fire to Wheeler Hall where I maintained my office.[13] Equally memorable is the way he said it, with a fatalistic, almost despairing, but also—dare I say this?—ultimately friendly chuckle.

If I cannot report that our old intimacy was restored after that meeting, at least after that our occasional encounters were cordial and respectful. Whenever we met he would discuss the dramatic political developments of the 1980s in Poland. I took his detailed analyses as a compliment, a recognition that, whatever our differences, there were still certain interests that we two shared and most at the university could not.

I last saw him in 1998 at a memorial dinner for our mutual friend Denise Levertov. He was now in his late eighties, and his wife Carol sat me at the table next to his one good ear. For hours he proceeded to deconstruct the complexities of post-Solidarity Polish Catholicism with undiminished discrimination and ardor. It was clear that he was ambivalent about the forces which had uneasily replaced socialism in Poland.

And thankfully I was able to tell him how much I admired him, was grateful to him, had been changed by him, and loved him. He responded in a low voice with some self-deprecating and almost indecipherable comment about his difficult personality. But I deduced from his smile, and our subsequent long talk at dinner, that for a moment we had been united again.

POSTSCRIPT

Most of the above, though it follows the body of this book, was written before it, for an anthology of memories about Milosz that was published by Cynthia Haven in 2011.[14] It expresses the love and gratitude I was able to confess to him in 1998, at a memorial dinner for Denise Levertov.

But that love falls short of what I feel now, for the dead Czeslaw Milosz, after five years of learning, thinking, and writing more about him. I no longer regret the differences I had with him, or the separation that followed. I now see that he had to follow his tortuous path, and I mine; and that all this was good.

I will continue to treasure above all our collaboration in translating "Throughout Our Earth," which in 1964 became Milosz's first published poem in English.[15] As noted above, California at the time was in the beginning stages of a sexual revolution, which in its later, exploitative stages both of us came to question. But at that time the opening to sexuality was still relatively gentle, evoking similar poems in each of us. (Milosz's poem of ambivalence about civilized restraints in *Encounter*, "Throughout Our Lands" in 1964, was matched by my own poem, "The Forest of Wishing," one year later in the *Times Literary Supplement*.)[16]

In the course of time, I, as well as Milosz, would come to question the exploitative aspects of the Sexual Freedom League and the Summer of Love.[17] But for a brief period, we shared the utopian excitement we had for this climate of openness, as well as the foreboding that America was not yet ready for it.

In celebration of this shared spirit, after completing a draft of the present book in 2019, I composed the third poem.

Appendix B

Three Poems to Czeslaw Milosz

I. LETTER TO CZESLAW MILOSZ (1982)[1]

October 27, 1982

Dear Czeslaw,

        Dreams once of the future
become the past. I am not likely
ever to take you to the unsecret
exposed hill in the nearby Briones
where someone saw two golden eagles mating,
or collect and then make for you a soup
of cress from the small brooks where they empty
into the Pacific. And yet
I have never been more in need of a friend, a man
not to agree with—agreement
only makes me the more anxious—
but whom I can watch survive, far from
birthplace and original heroic causes.
I used to think of you as a giant
Jeffers-like lighthouse on its quirky secure crag
a lighthouse not much use
for reading small print by or exploring
the local landscape, but a beacon
reaching far out to sea, and into time,
punctuating the usual darkness with
occasional unnatural light
perhaps too bright close up, but a godsend
to ships foundering. and those whose life
seems over-menaced in small unaccustomed
lifeboats. Sometimes the pleasant
company I am seldom without

seems, when I look up and see waves,
a threat to our survival. Even my wife
after a quarter century, I begin to admit
has her own problems of another sex
to deal with, inscrutable. Thus alone
in the midst of friends, I need to know
what it is your strange eyes have seen
out there in the night.
   So I read your books. This is the way
it should be. Face to face
those years we translated Herbert
and so many others, word
by recalcitrant word, translation proved
a more intimate, because more demanding,
intercourse than mere natural speech
in a single language: the distance
between our tongues defined them
the more closely, a parallax
to peer beyond night's surface, give an edge
so sharp to our words that, handled by two,
they became dangerous; and, turned
on the sensitive flesh of your own poems,
could only draw blood.
   I have come to think
having watched others who also came close
it was that transgression
of your intimacy, which led
to my no longer seeing you—and not,
as I first thought, our hopeless disagreement
over the Vietnam War (although that hurt,
your pointed jibe at, not myself, but Chomsky,
on whose platform you had seen me sitting:
one of those intellectuals of no sense
who destroyed Weimar).
   I never expected
silence after that outburst. For me
divergence over "how to defend the west"
was a small matter, almost parochial.
I have always had trouble choosing sides.
That takes experience. I am tempted
even today, with fresh news of strikes
in Nowa Huta and Bydgoszcz, to wish compassion
for all those, including the oppressors,
who move from so little choice,
though I can see how much more severe

Three Poems to Czeslaw Milosz　　　　　　　251

I am in judging America's repressions.
Your defection from the diplomatic
came after friends had gone to jail, or
elegantly accommodated lies, while foreign
troops lurked in the western forests.
To you, my philosophizing
must seem demented, when the issue
is not just brute stupidity but enslavement:
just as, in this book, you scorn the unhappy
youth who asked how *life in Sacramento
differed from a concentration camp*.　　　　　Visions, 146
　　　In your book there is fear
or *orgies of masochism*, revolutionary　　　　Visions, 214
students with walkie-talkies (as if the police
could not jam those scratchy plottings at their will)
or *nearly suicidal freedom
of expression*. But then you wrote　　　　　Visions, 212
of that Catholic or Marxist in yourself
that wished to censor what you had written about,
de Sade, because words are important
(*Who has not dreamt of the Marquis de Sade's châteaux?*) NCP, 187
and the hellish aura of the ghettos burning
on the living-room TV, so toxic
that our escape is in *brutish
contemplation like a cow*. Your true fear　　　Visions 113
was of your own ferocity; in this
you spoke to the censorious libertine
in each of us, even if
some of us would not censor but correct.
And of something else (Vietnam!) your sense was tragic:
you wanted neither side to win.
　　　Strange, just yesterday
to find what you must have written
long before that final sunny noon
in Sproul Plaza we crossed by accident,
the first time in two years. The war
was going badly then, and you imputed
to me, with gruffness, some contrary opinion,
some joy I did not feel. I said *No,
my view of this was always tragic*, and you relented;
we talked for two hours on the terrace
over coffee, though I did not then dare
to tell you how much I missed
the long drinking nights of translation
at your house, overlooking the stars

and shiplights in the bay: Herbert, Wat,
Mandelstam, the peasants of Lithuania,
until you fell forward in your chair, and Janka,
at that exact moment, slipped from behind a door
to tell me to go home.
                                  Drunk myself,
I would inch homeward on the winding
crest of Grizzly Peak, through fog as dense
as my confusion. Strange single branches then,
that hung out of the swirling wet white,
the silhouette of a fawn above my headlights,
or the ping on my Peugeot roof
of a eucalyptus nut, would strike on my senses
the marks of a signed universe. Always
what I saw, after talking to you,
was like, only more than, what the door frames
as you leave an art museum.
And for the first time, in my mid-career,
anything seemed possible.
                      I did not tell you this
because we were face to face; and you
I believe are like what I have become,
perhaps what we all become,
someone you can only be close to
by keeping far enough away. If others
translate with you now, and are not rejected,
I would like to think they are too different
to be estranged, having lived
only in one country, being too much poets
to have, like us, wrestled the ideas
of Massis, Curtius, and Benjamin,
above all, too knowledgeable to wish,
any more than Horace would, to change the world.
You have *no ambition to save the world*,[2]
and yet, thank god, you grumble
continuously about salvation.
umysł ludzki jest wspaniały, usta potężne,
i wezwanie tak wielkie, że musi otworzyć się Raj
the human mind is splendid, lips powerful,
and the summons so great, it must open Paradise.   *NCP, 184*
      We are of course all aliens out here,
where, as you wrote, your accent made you normal.
This strangeness I am used to
from my so-called native land, yet nonetheless

it gave me unasked-for roots, and roots
(above all roots one is in flight from)
are what distinguishes the émigré.
I was the rustic who sat at your feet,
having come, as you did, out of the black north
to visit the huddled cities of Europe,
or even the soft vineyards of the Pacific,
as a querulous appreciative stranger.
And I thought of you at the salons
of your odd Parisian cousin, so jolted
by what you were only half prepared for:
no chance for you to fit in,
to grace a movement, your only alternative
was greatness.
        How human that was. Though I myself
am still engaged in various schools and causes,
only too innocent as I perceive them,
yet I will concede, the mind is most poetic
not in intimacy, but in reaching out:
real poetry is the invasion of darkness,
not settlement, not familiarity.
Now that I shall not see you at the weekend
conference with your new translators,
surprised, even hurt, to have been disinvited,
I am also relieved: because we share no future,
at last I am free to tell you, face
to absent face, how much your gift,
of loneliness inhabited, has meant.

II. FOR CZESLAW MILOSZ (1992)[3]

An old man contemptuous blackhearted
    dumbfounded that a short time ago
        he was twenty   *NCP, 362*

challenges my English self
    I am reading in bed
        the reason Denise was glad

to be single once again
    the Polish I once breathed
        stary człowiek wzgardliwy

kochał i pragnął
    but it turned out badly
    the world was faster than he was

and now he sees the illusion[4] *Milosz '84, 18–9; NCP, 362*
    we are past midsummer
    the song sparrow rarely sings

Maylie away again
    the goldfinch shakes the wire
    coming up under our eave

as the fog wanders through the elms
    while he high above us
    looks out like Issa or Wang Wei

through the dripping redwood *NCP, 349*
    on this sea of white fog
    with sirens in it

Słyszę twój śmiech w ogrodzie
    I hear your laughter in the garden *Milosz '84, 124–25;*
    could that have been my English *NCP, 82*

his Polish eye gleaming
    when after search for a phrase
    the shortcomings of our two tongues

shaping an aporia
    and to plug this blacked-out space
    some new word-shape worked

as if the universe
    had given birth to an atom
    and we knew we were pleased with our invention

and with language itself
    potential messenger
    to a few good people *Milosz '84 192; NCP, 245*

before he turned on me
    my not reflecting
    how cruel nature is, and so on[5]

Three Poems to Czeslaw Milosz

it was he who taught me
    what was to be preserved
    in the abandonment of cities

was it by some
    failure or transgression
    I had to forfeit

that inebriation of language
    or were we too similar
    I thought having arrived

at the solitude of one's fifties
    a poet would no longer care
    if we had been for the winning

or losing cause in Vietnam
    when desires for a stranger
    who happens to stoop

for a pencil on the carpet
    or the surge when crowded against
    the teen-aged siren

in a two-piece bathing suit
    her wet hair dripping chlorine
    on the hotel elevator floor

have become as if memories
    as bizarre and alien
    as quaggas at the city zoo

(What are we if not wanting
    when we grope for desire and find
    only contentment?)

I thought that having exhausted
    the furor of those barricades
    and arrived at the preparation of sauces[6]   *Milosz '84 200–201;*
                                                                                                                         NCP, 356

we would turn in gratitude
    to the clear speech of poets
    the cares of old angers

dim as the flattened
    world so far below
  I wrote to say this

and got back his great Polish chuckle
  my dear Peter of course
  you gave the enemy comfort

you cannot compare
  a lemon with a triangle[7]
this fragile culture

and all its faults
  with that which is a cancer
  I miss you you inveterate warrior

waging the last peace
  so much the maker of your world
  there is hardly room in it

for the voices of the young
  and writing out of your fierce heart
  precisely because there is no one

else left like you
  (*Should I really experience*
nature as alien

and heartless   Merton, 139
  as you would have me do
I read *Commentary*

the young Vietnamese student
  who like yourself stayed on
  after the revolution

All of us could see
  the brutality of Saigon
the other side remained hidden)[8]

We are divided
  by our separate gratitudes
  each wanting to atone

for years of well-meaning service
    with opposing governments
    in the name of peace

Can the poet Issa replace
    the valley of your childhood
    in which places and people have disappeared

For you everything grows smaller   *szystko zgęszcze się*
    meaning in turn that you   *Miłosz '84 198–99, NCP, 356*
    must grow smaller to me

though no less noble
    and what *is* poetry
    if not the salvation of all people?

an inner elixir?
    language's blind erasure
    of its human origins?

or a pair of jade discs? Can these surpass
    two men ploughing the southern fields[9]
    while the empire surges?   *Confucius Analects 18:6*

Her *sesshin* how long?   retreat
    Congress voting again tomorrow
    my mother busy

arranging about the books
    that were once my father's
    With whom if not humans

am I to associate?
    I cannot associate with birds   *Confucius Analects 18:6*
    I recite in bed

to the muttering window shades
    in my empty bedroom
    I wszędzie tutaj

przemiawają głosy
    And on all sides voices
    in such great numbers   *Miłosz '84 20–21, NCP, 363*

    the smooth circle
        on the back of my wrist
        where my watch

is missing.

III. TO CZESLAW MILOSZ (2019)

The hysterical howls of the Beat poets are the rebellion of a well-brought-up muse, a return to their native tradition [i.e., Whitman], somewhat vulgar but still authentic.

—Czeslaw Milosz[10]

i

Flight (Ucieczka)

Czeslaw   in your eight-line poem
    you and Janka
    were fleeing the burning city   *NCP 74*

with what you could carry on your back
    until on the road
    in a time of general starvation

you were robbed even of that
    now totally liberated
    from your entitled past

you had to dig
    potatoes for a week
    just so you could reach

that country manor outside Kraków
    right before it was looted
    by the Soviet armies

in a barbarism you compared
    to the sack of Rome by the Goths
    the world was all before you

you closed your eight-line poem
  we are fated to beget
  a new and violent tribe

and the earth was opened
  by a sword of flames   NCP 74
  years later you added

that from the death
  of the Republic
  Comes man, naked and mortal

Ready for truth, for speech, for wings   TP 54

                ii

Treatise on Poetry (Traktat poetycki)

From western Europe
  in the grip of its demonic forces   TP 113
  you wrote *I would like to be*

a poet of the five senses
  That's why I don't become one   NCP 170
  the *eternal moment*

did not attract you *as it should*   TP 58
  you wanted instead
  to raise *the dust of events*   TP 58

but after you left
  for America *and its eternal*
  rotation of seasons   TP 113

no longer in the shadow
  of a nationalist church
  and *that crazy St. Dominic*   Striving Towards Being 133

but where *the oaks*
  perfect the shadow of May leaves   NCP 184
  you wrote to the Trappist Thomas Merton

In spite of all my hatred for the Thomists
  I know that the only subject for a poet
  is the verb "to be"   Striving Towards Being 133

and in verse *Only this*
    is worthy of praise
Only this:

the day   NCP 184

iii

Throughout Our Lands (Po ziemi naszej)

Czeslaw we met in Berkeley
    when it was still newly aroused
    by a brief and gentle revolution

when for a very short while
    before they mass-marketed
    The Summer of Love

women walked braless in see-through blouses
    and your id acknowledged
    that beneath the sprinklered lawns

where the girls *came back from the tennis courts*
    devils *were turning somersaults*   NCP 184
    which you later confessed *To Allen Ginsberg*

were the *diabolic dwarfs* in yourself   NCP 611
    Like the shipwrecked Cabeza de Vaca   c.1488–1560
    among Gulf Coast tribes

on a *seven years march to California*   NCP 187
    you soon *adapted*
    to the lives of the indigenous   Wikipedia

not able thereafter
    to be a true European
    you for a very short while

dispensed with pessimism
    wrote *give them a few stones*
    and edible roots, and they will build the world   NCP 186

and skepticism *what if Pascal*
    had not been saved
    I shall never agree   NCP 184

adding *On all fours!* NCP 188
Who has not dreamt of naked nuns? NCP 187
Smear our thighs with war paint

Lick the ground. Wha ha, hu hu. NCP 188

    iv

    To jest i tylko to jest ocalenie

1964
    when our poem was published   *Encounter February 1964*
    your first poem ever to appear in English

(*translated* you wrote
    by Peter Dale Scott
    with my minor assistance)   *Postwar Polish Poetry vii*

was the year of the FSM   *Free Speech Movement*
    and the passionate faculty assembly
    to support the students' demands

which you later dismissed as *Maoist madness*   ABC 230
    a solemn event in which
    we voted on opposite sides

Was this the key
    to the end of our joyous years
    in drunken collaboration

or was it that meeting
    to oppose the Vietnam war
    where you had seen me on the panel

with Chomsky whom you called
    in a tone foreboding
    my imminent expulsion

one of those intellectuals
    who destroyed Weimar
    a charge which I disputed

or was it your Warsaw poem
    with its good question
    What is poetry that does not save   NCP 77

nations or people
    that I fought to *translate*
    That I wanted good poetry

without knowing it   NCP 77
    (like a lover able to see
    he is *only one among many*

who thus heals his heart *without knowing it*)   NCP 50
    this is and only this is salvation
    while you no longer a bard

in your communal culture
    but now just a poet
    in this new and softer *episteme*

insisted on blurring that line
    to make it personal
    In this and only this

I find salvation?   NCP 77

                v

    Orpheus and Eurydice

When Janka died in Berkeley   *Milosz's first wife*
    you wrote an American poem
    recalling your life together

campfires, fires of burning cities
    you confessed *I betrayed her with women,*
    though faithful to her only.   NCP 469

But now back in the Poland
    you had helped to save—
    those words you'd written *for your desk*   *in secret*

You who wronged a simple man
    Do not feel safe. The poet remembers   NCP 103
    now in steel on the Gdańsk memorial—

you were again that bard
    in the language surrounding him
    standing on the flagstones

> *of the sidewalk*
> > *at the entrance of Hades*
> > *responding to Carol's death* *Milosz's second wife*
>
> *with a nine-stringed lyre*
> > *he yielded to the dictation of a song*
> > *And so Hermes brought forth Eurydice*
>
> *A steep climbing path phosphorized*
> > *But under his faith a doubt sprang up*
> > *he turned his head*
>
> *and behind him on the path*
> > *was no one*
> > *And he fell asleep with his cheek*
>
> *on the sun-warmed earth.* Second Space, 99–102

> and soon you too were gone
> but still with us

behind you on the path

Permissions

Parts of this book appeared in earlier versions as follows:
Chapter 2: "Czeslaw Milosz and Solidarity; or, Poetry and the Liberation of a People," *Brick* 78 (Winter 2006): 67–74.
Chapter 14: "Poetry and the Open Space Ahead," lecture, at A Celebration Honoring Czeslaw Milosz, Claremont McKenna College, October 19–21, 2011.
Chapter 15: "Milosz and the Generative Canon: Virgil, Dante, and Blake," lecture, English Department, University of California Berkeley, February 21, 2017; "Czeslaw Milosz, T. S. Eliot, and Literature Past and Future," Claremont McKenna College, April 3, 2017; "Miłosz, Eliot, and the Generative Canon: Literature, the Past, and the Future," *Sarmatian Review*, 37, no. 3 (September 2017).
Appendix: "A Difficult, Inspirational Giant," in Cynthia L. Haven (editor), *An Invisible Rope: Portraits of Czeslaw Milosz* (Athens, OH: Ohio University Press, 2011).

POEMS

"Letter to Czeslaw Milosz," in Peter Dale Scott, *Crossing Borders: Selected Shorter Poems* (New York: New Directions, 1994), 34–39.
"For Czeslaw Milosz," in Peter Dale Scott, *Listening to the Candle: A Poem on Impulse* (New York: New Directions, 1992), 128–33.

Notes

CHAPTER 1

1. Michel Eyquem de Montaigne, "De la Gloire"; as quoted first by Charles Williams, *The Descent of the Dove: A History of the Holy Spirit in the Church* (New York: Pellegrini and Cudahy, 1939), 192; and thence by W. H. Auden, as an epigraph to *The Double Man* [alias "New Year Letter"] (New York: Random House, 1941). See chapter 9; Edward Mendelson, *Early Auden, Later Auden: A Critical Biography* (Princeton, NJ: Princeton University Press, 2017), 450.

2. Pascal, *Pensées*, quoted by Auden in an endnote to *The Double Man*, and many times also by Milosz, for example, in a conversation with Robert Faggen; "Pascal . . . was writing against the wolf of skepticism, Montaigne. Pascal personifies a man in crisis. So for a man of crisis as I am, Pascal is a spiritual brother in a way" (Czeslaw Milosz, in Cynthia L. Haven [ed.], *Czesław Miłosz: Conversations* [Jackson, MS: University Press of Mississippi, 2006], 179). See chapter 9.

3. Another poet with a comparable background was Seamus Heaney, whose interest in Milosz derived from their shared marginality. At the impressionable age of eighteen, I spent a summer working in a lumber camp amid Acadian loggers who shared their first- or second-hand experiences of miracles (e.g., of a priest invoking rain to save a burning haystack). Much later I read some almost identical miracles in Gregory of Tours.

4. Zbigniew Herbert, *Selected Poems*, translated by Czeslaw Milosz and Peter Dale Scott (Harmondsworth, Middlesex: Penguin Books, 1968; New York: Ecco Press, 1986).

5. See chapter 14.

6. Czeslaw Milosz, "A Semi-Private Letter about Poetry," in *To Begin Where I Am: Selected Essays* (New York: Farrar, Straus and Giroux, 2001), 351.

7. Clare Cavanagh, "Journal, Day Three," Poetry Foundation, https://www.poetryfoundation.org/harriet-books/2006/04/journal-day-three-56d34c7611bcb.

8. In his first book of poetry in exile, *Światło dzienne* [Daylight] (1953), Mikosz chose to reprint from his wartime collection *Ocalenie* [Rescue] only the idyllic central sequence "Świat" [The World]. For whatever reason, the rest of the book, including "Dedication," was omitted.

9. Czeslaw Milosz, "Nobel Lecture," December 8, 1980, http://nobelprize.org/literature/laureates/1980/milosz-lecture-en.html.

10. For my thoughts on ethogeny, see Peter Dale Scott with Freeman Ng, *Poetry and Terror: The Politics and Poetics of* Coming to Jakarta (Lanham, MD: Lexington, 2018), xv, 147–48, 185–86.

11. Though Milosz titled his Charles Eliot Norton lectures *The Witness of Poetry*, one should not deduce that Milosz considered himself to be (in Carolyn Forché's sense) a "poet of witness." When his sometime friend Al Alvarez described Milosz as "a poet of memory, a witness" (Al Alvarez, "Witness," *New York Review of Books*, June 2, 1988, 21). Milosz responded in an irritated letter that he was uneasy to see his work "encapsuled by Mr. Alvarez in the word 'witness,' which for him is perhaps a praise, but for me is not" (Czeslaw Milosz, "A Poet's Reply," *New York Review of Books*, July 21, 1988, 46). See chapter 6.

12. See Iain McGilchrist, *The Master and His Emissary: The Divided Brain and the Making of the Western World* (New Haven, CT: Yale UP, 2018), 461–62. Further discussion of this book in chapters 3 and 15.

13. See chapters 5 through 11.

14. See chapters 9 and 15. As late as *The Witness of Poetry* (1983), Milosz confessed to the "two tendencies" of "classicism and realism" in the world and within himself, "struggling with each other" (WP, 69, 72).

15. Czeslaw Milosz, letter to Thomas Merton of January 17, 1959, in *Striving Towards Being: The Letters of Thomas Merton and Czeslaw Milosz*, ed. Robert Faggen (New York: Farrar, Straus and Giroux, 1997), 9. In focusing on my preferred Milosz, I have done less than justice to related themes that keep recurring in these pages—above all, Milosz's antiquated attitudes toward women, love, and sex. In much of his writings, Milosz presents himself, I would say, as more a man of the past than of the future. I attribute this in large part to the permanent damage done to his first marriage, by the unforeseen separation of Milosz and Janka for three years after his defection, during which time he became involved with the Swiss philosopher Jeanne Hersch. But in my view, much I might have criticized is redeemed by the profundity of his loving elegy, "Orpheus and Eurydice," on the death of his second wife, Carol Thigpen (SS, 99–102).

16. Robert Hass, *Twentieth Century Pleasures: Prose on Poetry* (New York: Ecco Press, 1984), 191; Robert Hass, *What Light Can Do: Essays on Art, Imagination, and the Natural World* (New York: Ecco, 2012), 182.

17. A decade later, Milosz would publish some of the ideas that excited me, both in *The Land of Ulro* and in *The Witness of Poetry*.

18. Czesław Milosz, "Reflections on T. S. Eliot," in Czesław Milosz, *To Begin Where I Am*, 391. Originally published in *Kultura* (Paris), March 1965.

19. Cf. WP, 34: "In Eliot and to some extent in Pound a certain norm is placed in the past, the model of time is regressive, the future does not promise anything good."

20. Many European *emigré* professors had similar reactions, seeing (I think wrongly) an analogy with the often fascistic and anti-Semitic student protests of the 1930s in Europe, which Milosz had personally opposed in Wilno.

21. Thirty years later, Milosz would recall having thoughts at the time quite similar to my own: "that the Vietnamese were fighting a patriotic war against foreigners, and that foreigners could not win such a war" (ABC, 44).

22. If I am right in this memory, then Milosz was exhibiting considerable self-restraint. Already in 1961, he had expressed to Thomas Merton his "deep skepticism as to moral action which seems to me Utopian," and his "distrust of any peace movements," which he compared to the peace movement of Stalin in 1948 (*Striving Towards Being*, 138).

23. Peter Dale Scott, *The War Conspiracy: JFK, 9/11 and the Deep Politics of War* (New York: Skyhorse, 2013), 147–77.

24. "Milosz's attitude to America . . . was complex and not very favorable to the counterculture . . . charging it with political naivety, lack of historical memory, superficial religiosity, and, most importantly, hypocrisy" (Marcin Jaworski, "*Songs of Ecstatic Despair*: Miłosz and the Counterculture," *Przekładaniec* 25 [2011], 147).

25. In an interview, Milosz commented, "The indifference, even the anti-American posture, which I have observed while teaching at Berkeley is very shocking. It is very hard to understand. Probably it means that still I come from a very traditional world as far as values are concerned. I have been witnessing in America the subversion of the ethic of the working class which was God, my country, my family" (Czeslaw Milosz and Nathan Gardels, "An Interview with Czeslaw Milosz," *New York Review of Books*, February 27, 1986, http://www.nybooks.com/articles/1986/02/27/an-interview-with-czeslaw-milosz/).

26. Peter Dale Scott, *Listening to the Candle* (New York: New Directions, 1992), 131; reproduced in the appendix, poem II as "For Czeslaw Milosz."

27. Czeslaw Milosz, *The Captive Mind* (New York: Vintage International, 1990), 55. A belated comment: my subjective distaste for *The Captive Mind* had also to do with Milosz's dismissive treatment of Jerzy Andrzejewski's novel (and later film) *Ashes and Diamonds*, which I admired. But after finishing this book, I now realize that my opinion of *The Captive Mind*, as reported in this chapter, was grossly one-sided. In it, Milosz had clearly outlined, perhaps for the first time in prose, the eschatological role for poetry that inspired him from *Ocalenie* (1945) to his Harvard lectures (1982), and which I praise in my concluding chapter as his enduring achievement: "The war years taught me that a man should not take a pen in his hands merely to communicate to others his own despair and defeat. . . . Today the only poetry worthy of the name is eschatological, that is, poetry which rejects the present inhuman world in the name of a great change" (*Captive Mind*, 216, 237). The second sentence is highlighted in my copy of his book. I should have remembered it in writing this chapter.

28. All but the last two, incidentally, were either friends or correspondents with Milosz.

29. John M. Bates, "Heresy and Its Afterlives in Communist-era Poland," in Andrew P. Roach and James R. Simpson (Eds.), *Heresy and the Making of European Culture: Medieval and Modern Perspectives* (Abingdon, Oxon: Routledge, 2016), 437. At a public lecture organized by the young Andrzej Michnik in 1966, Kołakowski, then still a PZPR Party member, told a sympathetic audience that "In the present day . . . Party representatives tended to be chosen by the principle of 'negative selection,'

according to which 'fawning, cowardice, absence of initiative, [and] willingness to eavesdrop were qualifying factors. Poland suffered from 'spiritual pauperization'" (Glenn Dynner and François Guesnet [eds.], *Warsaw: The Jewish Metropolis: Essays in Honor of the 75th Birthday of Professor Antony Polonsky* (Leiden: Brill, 2015), 595. As a consequence of this speech, Kołakowski was expelled from the party; and two years later he was sacked from the University. The thaw was over.

30. The only clear exceptions were the sexagenarian Słonimski and the filmmaker Munk (who died in a car crash in 1966). Herbert never abandoned Poland, but from even before the thaw he spent much of his time abroad. He returned to Poland to support Solidarność, but later joined the Polish right in attacking Milosz, Michnik, and the Round Table Agreement.

31. Andrzej Walicki, *Zniewolony umysł po latach* (Warsaw: Czytelnik, 1993), 309–10; quoted in Franaszek, *Miłosz: A Biography* (Cambridge, MA: Harvard University Press, 2017), 306. *The Captive Mind* is remembered internationally as "brilliant" in *The Cambridge History of Twentieth-Century Political Thought*, edited by Terence Ball (Cambridge: Cambridge UP, 2003), 190, cf. 192, 196; it does not need to be celebrated here.

32. Christopher Lasch, quoted in Giles Scott-Smith, *The Politics of Apolitical Culture: The Congress for Cultural Freedom, the CIA, and Post-War American Hegemony* (London: Routledge, 2002), 223.

33. Looking back over the decade (2012–2022) that it took to write this book, I realize that at the outset I *forgave* Milosz for his years as a Cold Warrior; then I gradually began to understand and *appreciate* his role as a Cold Warrior, until, at last, I admired and *was grateful* for his role as a Cold Warrior. Although I realize that this will sound like normal progress on the road from engagement to senile acceptance, I still believe that my change in attitude was a result of cognitive progress, not hardening of the arteries. To put it another way: I am now grateful that France and Italy, widely expected in 1950 to vote in the Communists, did not have to undergo the agonies experienced in East Germany.

34. Milosz later wrote that "Looking back with hindsight, I have to say that the 'liberal conspiracy' was necessary and justified" (ABC, 87). I fully agree.

35. See also his late homage "To Allen Ginsberg": "Allen, you . . . persisting in folly attained wisdom" (NCP, 611). And no doubt he was thinking of Ginsberg when, in 1982, he commented favorably that "In the United States a new relationship between poet and audience was adumbrated by the youth revolt of the 1960s, which has had lasting effects and, to some extent, reduced the poet's isolation" (WP, 31).

36. See also Milosz to Adam Michnik: "In Berkeley, the young people worked themselves into a frenzy. At one time, I was giving a lift to some hippie or other, and he said, 'Revolution, there's going to be a revolution!'" (Cynthia L. Haven, *Czesław Miłosz: Conversations*, 123).

37. "A Semi-Private Letter about Poetry," in *To Begin Where I Am*, 348.

38. Czeslaw Milosz, "Throughout Our Lands," NCP, 184; see chapter 13. (The poem opens with a line from Whitman.) See below, "Letter to Czeslaw Milosz," in the appendix, where I preface these lines with another, contradictory Milosz quote:

You have *no ambition to save the world*,

and yet, thank god, you grumble
continuously about salvation.

In 1946, Milosz wrote of the importance of the "arcadian . . . dream about the happy life of the human race" (Milosz, "A Semi-Private Letter about Poetry," in *To Begin Where I Am*, 347).

39. Another symptom of Milosz's late arcadian revival is that the American poet who obsessed him in the mid-1960s was the bleak inhumanist Robinson Jeffers (the closest American equivalent to the Polish catastrophists). In his magnificent 1982 Harvard lectures, *The Witness of Poetry*, the dominating American poet is Whitman, a poet whose optimism had inspired Milosz throughout his career. In 1989, Milosz told Joseph Brodsky that his greatest love in poetry in English was for Whitman ("that gluttonous attitude, omnivorousness, toward reality"); Jeffers did not make the list (Haven, *Czesław Miłosz: Conversations*, 116). See also Marta Skwara, "The Poet of the Great Reality: Czesław Miłosz's Readings of Walt Whitman," *Walt Whitman Quarterly Review* 26 (Summer 2008): 1–22.

40. "Anima Hominis," *Essays* (1924). Milosz was also capable of great rhetorical poetry, such as "You Who Wronged," part of which now is on a statue in Gdańsk (NCP, 103).

41. I particularly regret that I did not respond to his suggestion that I read and edit with him the manuscript translation of his autobiographic *Native Realm*, a work I have read and re-read so many times since. At a time when I was struggling to gain tenure, it unfortunately seemed too huge a task.

42. Milosz and Gardels, "Interview."

43. Simone Weil seems to reach the same point differently: in her words, we need to focus our minds on "the rational in the Cartesian sense . . . so that we might bring to light that which lies outside its range" (quoted by Milosz, *To Begin Where I Am*, 254). Commenting on Weil, Milosz seems to identify his "sense of an open space ahead" with Providence, which he rephrases with the question whether there is an "immanent force located in *le devenir* . . . a force that pulls mankind up toward perfection" (Milosz, *To Begin Where I Am*, 247–48).

44. In 2017, the University of California at Berkeley Library had eighty-nine books about Milosz, the vast majority of them in Polish. Only twelve were in English, only eight were critical assessments of Milosz, only five of these were in any way comparable in format and scope to this one, and only three had been published (all by Poles) since 1991.

45. Robert von Hallberg, *Lyric Powers* (Chicago: University of Chicago Press, 2008), 49.

46. Robert Hass, "Milosz at Eighty," in *What Light Can Do: Essays on Art, Imagination, and The Natural World* (New York: Ecco/HarperCollins Publishers, 2012), 179.

47. In addition, Singer always wrote and published in Yiddish, although he edited the English translations of his works. Note that not one American WASP is in this list, though WASPs form a much larger part of the population. Morrison is black; Bellow was Jewish and the son of immigrants; both Dylan and Glück are Jewish and

the grandchildren of immigrants. The suffering that produced so much great postwar Polish and Jewish poetry is remote from the experience of most American WASPs.

48. Brodsky, born in Russia, is buried in Venice. Milosz, born in Lithuania, is buried in Kraków. Both Heaney and Walcott voluntarily ended their long sojourns in America. Walcott, who since 2009 has taught in England, has noted that he, Brodsky, and Heaney, were a group of poets "outside the American experience."

49. Some African American poets, such as Claudia Rankine and Robin Coste Lewis, draw on this international heritage. The critic Christopher Nealon has noted that, throughout her book *Don't Let Me Be Lonely*, "Rankine draws on what we might think of as her poetry's cousins and antecedents—Hegel, Celan, Milosz, Vallejo, and Césaire" (Christopher Nealon, *The Matter of Capital: Poetry and Crisis in the American Century* [Cambridge, MA: Harvard University Press, 2011], 51).

50. Milosz read Whitman (in a Polish translation) early in his career; and repeatedly the meditative long lines of his lyrics reflect Whitman's influence.

51. In 1987, Milosz himself wrote that when young, "I was convinced that we write for perhaps twenty or thirty individuals, for our fellow poets; that belief is returning" (YH, 5). I hope in this book to clarify the distinction between this belief, and Oscar Milosz's sarcastic dismissal of "aristocratic spirits and 'elitist souls,'" endorsed by Czeslaw Milosz in *The Witness of Poetry* (WP), 30.

(In a companion book to this one, discussed in the next chapter, I illustrate how the cultural-countercultural dialectical process characterizes all of ethogeny.)

52. See Eugene W. Holland, *Baudelaire and Schizoanalysis: The Socio-Poetics of Modernism* (Cambridge: Cambridge University Press, 1993).

53. "What is Sociopoetix?" http://sociopoetix.org/what-is-socio-poetix/.

54. Ethogeny is a *dialectical* process, in part because culture shapes individuals but is also shaped partly by individuals (and not, as dialectical Marxists believed, by impersonal objective forces alone). See chapters 9 and 11.

55. Scott with Ng, *Poetry and Terror*, 187; citing Robert Middlekauff, *The Great Cause: The American Revolution, 1763–1789* (Oxford: Oxford University Press, 2005), 51, 136ff.; Lydia Dittler Schulman, *Paradise Lost and the Rise of the American Republic* (Boston: Northeastern University Press, 1992).

56. Clearly the writings of Marx, Lenin, and Mao helped generate profound political revolutions. But they were not as focused on the issues of cultural change, which led to disastrous missteps in the early Chinese revolution, and which in the case of the Russian revolution may have proved to be a fatal defect.

CHAPTER 2

1. Quoted in Czeslaw Milosz, "A Semi-Private Letter about Poetry," in *To Begin Where I Am: Selected Essays* (New York: Farrar, Straus and Giroux, 2001), 345.

2. Adam Michnik, *Partisan Review* (Winter 1999): 19.

3. John Paul II was the first non-Italian pope since Adrian VI in the sixteenth century.

4. Adam Michnik, "In Search of Lost Sense," *Sign and Sight*, September 9, 2021, http://www.signandsight.com/features/373.html: "It was a time of three Polish miracles. Pope John Paul II visited Poland in June 1979. Then the August strike, Lech Walesa and Solidarity. Finally, the Nobel Prize was awarded to Czeslaw Milosz. For years we had been telling ourselves that waiting for a miracle was not enough, that it would take work for miracles to happen. In 1980 the Poles saw the results of their own work."

5. Adam Michnik, "The Montesinos Virus—Democracy, Dictatorship, Peru, Serbia, Poland," *Social Research* (Winter 2001).

6. John Adams, *The Works of John Adams*, vol. 10 (Boston: Little, Brown and Company, 1956), 85; quoted in Jonathan Schell, *Unconquerable World: Power, Nonviolence, and the Will of the People* (New York: Metropolitan Books, 2003), 160. Schell also quotes on the same page from page 180 of the Adams volume: "The revolution was in the mind of the people, and in the union of the colonies, both of which were accomplished before the hostilities commenced."

7. In *Enmindment—A History* (forthcoming) a companion volume to this one, I call such envisioners "minders," people who both have something in mind and also mind the world as they see it.

8. Michnik, "In Search of Lost Sense."

9. Michel Masłowski, "Czesław Miłosz," in Ewa Atanassow and Alan S. Kahan (eds.), *Liberal Moments: Reading Liberal Texts* (London: Bloomsbury Methuen Drama, 2016), https://www.bloomsburycollections.com/book/liberal-moments-reading-liberal-texts/ch23-czes-aw-mi-osz, 183.

10. Andrzej Franaszek, *Miłosz: A Biography* (Cambridge, MA: Harvard University Press, 2017), 426–28. "By 1980 . . . Nowa had published 2 editions of *Captive Mind, Miasto bez imienia, Król Popiel i inne wiersze, Światło dzienne, Traktat poetycki. Traktat moralny*; and *Gdzie wschodzi słońce i kędy zapada* (which also had been published by another publisher). His poetry also had appeared in *Zapis* and in smuggled copies of *Kultura*" (personal communication from a historian of postwar Poland).

11. Franaszek, *Miłosz: A Biography*, 427–28. At the height of Solidarność's power, Milosz's poetry was read at a major victory rally, and the underground Polish edition of *The Captive Mind* was publicly displayed on a notice board at Warsaw University (Timothy Garton Ash, *Solidarity: The Polish Revolution* [New Haven, CT: Yale University Press, 2002], 90, 94–95).

12. Adam Michnik, "A Farewell to Czesław Miłosz," New School, Transregional Center for Democratic Studies, *Bulletin*, October 2004. I can confirm from my own two years in Poland, from 1959 to 1961, that to possess anything by Milosz in that relatively relaxed period qualified a Pole for both membership in a special coterie, and special attention from the secret police.

13. Adam Zagajewski, *Partisan Review*, *Intellectuals and Social Change in Central and Eastern Europe*, Special Issue, 19, no. 4 (Fall 1992): 674, 675. American readers should understand that in the Polish context, "anti-nationalistic" means "antiracist."

14. Milosz recalls his isolation and some of these attacks on him in YH, 104, 116–18, and 146–47.

15. Jerzy Illg, "An Invisible Rope: Czeslaw Milosz in the Literary Underground in Poland," trans. Lillian Vallee, *Periphery* 4 (January 1999), http://www-personal.engin.umich.edu/~zbigniew/Periphery/No4/illg.html. Some of the Polish *émigrés* I met in Berkeley in 1961, eight years after the publication of *The Captive Mind*, warned me energetically not to be seen associating with Milosz. An FBI memo of 1960 uncritically forwarded the warning that "Since his break with the Polish government, Milosz has published a series of books. Each of these books at the time of publication was of great value to the Soviet government as evidence supporting the Soviet line of the moment" (Milosz FBI File, serial 100–358076–31, Hoover letter of September 2, 1960, to Office of Security, State Department; cf. YH, 243).

16. "My Faithful Mother Tongue," in Czeslaw Milosz, NCP, 245. But Milosz in the 1960s was also hearing from friends' letters that "Young people [in Poland] look up to you as if you were a star" (Letter to Milosz from Zbigniew Herbert, 1964; in Franaszek, *Miłosz: A Biography*, 428).

17. Michnik, "A Farewell to Czesław Miłosz." Though his emotion was no doubt sincere, Milosz was exaggerating his isolation from his Polish audience. Thanks to the "thaw" of 1955/1956, as he wrote to Thomas Merton in 1959, "Now I have friendly relations with a majority of my confrères over there" (*Striving Towards Being*, 7).

18. Jeffrey C. Isaac, "Adam Michnik: Politics and the Church," *Salmagundi* 103 (Summer 1994): 199.

19. Czeslaw Milosz, "Foreword," in Adam Michnik, *Letters from Prison and Other Essays* (Berkeley: University of California Press, 1985), x. This is also the opinion of Carl Tighe, "Adam Michnik: A Life in Opposition," *Journal of European Studies* 27, no. 3 (September 1997).

20. Response of April 2006 to my question, transmitted by a mutual friend, Robert Faggen. Asked also whether Milosz played a role in the publication of *Kościół, lewica, dialog*, Michnik replied that the key role was played by Konstanty Jeleński of *Kultura*, but that Milosz (who also knew Jeleński) would most probably have supported the idea.

21. "Czesław Miłosz, whose translation of Weil's writings was published in 1958 in the 'Kultura' Library, certainly contributed to the popularity of Simone Weil in Poland. The texts of the great Frenchwoman were suggested to him by Józef Czapski, himself fascinated by Weil's thoughts—he would often return to her in the pages of his famous diary" (Tadeusz Sławek, "Między herezją a wiarą. Simone Weil—Sokrates naszych czasów," Polskie Radio, August 24, 2021, https://www.polskieradio.pl/8/195/Artykul/424586,Simone-Weil-%E2%80%93-miedzy-herezja-a-swietoscia). Camus was a close friend of the Weil family, and introduced Milosz to them.

22. Czeslaw Milosz, "The Importance of Simone Weil," in *To Begin Where I Am*, 258. Milosz foresaw the potential alliance in chapter 8 of *The Captive Mind* (1953), where he wrote that "The workers . . . know that the goals of the state are far from identical with their own," and that the Church is the "last stronghold of opposition" (Czeslaw Milosz, *The Captive Mind* [New York: Vintage International, 1990], 186, 212). See Renata Gorczyńska to Milosz: "In the chapter 'Man, the Enemy,' you . . . mention the workers and the Church as the most likely sources of opposition. And that has proved true in the Polish situation." Milosz, "Yes indeed" (Ewa Czarnecka

and Aleksander Fiut, *Conversations with Czeslaw Milosz* [San Diego, CA: Harcourt Brace Jovanovich, 1987], 148).

23. Czeslaw Milosz, interviewed by Adam Michnik, in Czarnecka and Fiut, *Conversations,* 127. It appears that the impact of Weil in Poland has outlasted Solidarność: in 2010, the dramatic series "Personas" of Krystian Lupa studied "three iconic figures from the Twentieth Century: the American sex icon Marilyn Monroe, the French mystic Simone Weil and the Russian theatre reformer George Gurdjieff" ("The Polish Stage: Between Spirituality and Prank," Culture.pl, January 3, 2011, https://culture.pl/en/article/the-polish-stage-between-spirituality-and-prank, Lupa may have been introduced to Weil by the 1976 play "Apocalypsis cum figuris" of Jerzy Grotowski, which in Miloszian fashion mixed quotes from "the Bible, church songs, Dostoyevsky's writings, Eliot, and Simone Weil" (Culture.pl, July 2, 2014, https://culture.pl/en/article/grotowski-to-garcia-the-loudest-scandals-of-polish-theatre).

24. In addition, the monument has a quotation in Polish from Psalm 29, also translated by Milosz.

25. Jerzy Illg, "An Invisible Rope," *Partisan Review* 66, no. 1 (1999): 17. But in 1950 Milosz was still a Polish diplomat, and this poem had been written "for the drawer"—that is, with no prospects of it then being published.

26. See chapter 6.

27. This is Milosz's assessment in *The Captive Mind*, when he reproves "Alpha" (Jerzy Andrzejewski) for having inspired by his stories of loyalty the "disaster" of the Uprising, "that terrible example of what happens when blind loyalty encounters the necessities of history" (Czeslaw Milosz, *The Captive Mind*, 97; reprinted in Milosz, *To Begin Where I Am*, 129–30).

28. Milosz, "A Semi-Private Letter about Poetry," in *To Begin Where I Am*, 349. Later, in *Native Realm* (241–42, 244–49), Milosz clarified his dislike of the AK (Home Army) and its ill-fated uprising.

29. Dominik Horodyński, quoted in Franaszek, *Miłosz: A Biography*, 248. See chapter 8.

30. To get a sense of that unsettled postwar period, a Westerner can read *Ashes and Diamonds*, by Milosz's close friend Jerzy Andrzejewski (Harmondsworth, UK: Penguin Books, 1980), or see the movie version by Andrzej Wajda.

31. Tennent H. Bagley, *Spy Wars: Moles, Mysteries, and Deadly Games* (New Haven, CT: Yale University Press, 2008), 120–22.

32. Milosz, *The Captive Mind*, 103.

33. "Translators' Note," in Zbigniew Herbert, *Selected Poems*, translated by Czeslaw Milosz and Peter Dale Scott (New York: Ecco Press, 1986), 17. Though the "Note" was jointly written, the words quoted here are all by Milosz. Ironically, only two years after this encomium to Herbert's poetry appeared, Herbert, having drunk too much at a Berkeley dinner party, "viciously attacked Miłosz [and] reproached him for his lack of participation in the Polish resistance" (Cynthia Haven, "The Worst Dinner Party Ever: Czesław Miłosz, Zbigniew Herbert, and the Lady Who Watched the Fight," *The Book Haven*, March 30, 2011, https://bookhaven.stanford.edu/2011/03/the-worst-dinner-party-ever-czeslaw-milosz-zbigniew-herbert-and-the-lady-that-watched-the-fight/). In the 1980s, as the Polish People's Republic was collapsing,

Herbert renewed publicly, both in prose and in verse, his charge that Milosz, born in Lithuania, was a cosmopolitan and not a true Polish patriot.

34. See Milosz, "A Semi-Private Letter about Poetry," in *To Begin Where I Am*, 350–51: "When I wrote in the introduction to *Rescue* that I accepted the salvational goal of poetry, that was exactly what I had in mind, and I still believe that poetry can either save or destroy nations."

35. Hannah Arendt, *Crises of the Republic: Lying in Politics, Civil Disobedience, Thoughts on Politics and Revolution* (New York: Harcourt Brace Jovanovich, 1972), 24.

36. Arendt, *Crises of the Republic*, 30.

37. Czeslaw Milosz, "It is a Grave Responsibility to Kill Hope," *New York Times*, December 18, 1981, https://www.nytimes.com/1981/12/18/opinion/it-is-a-grave-responsibility-to-kill-hope.html; see Franaszek, *Miłosz: A Biography*, 437.

38. Franaszek, *Miłosz: A Biography*, 437.

39. Jerzy Illg, *Mój Znak* (Kraków: Znak, 2009), 53; quoted in Franaszek, *Miłosz: A Biography*, 437.

40. It is interesting to contrast Milosz's path through his century with that of his former close friend, Jerzy Andrzejewski, who was always much closer to the prevailing intellectual trends of the time. During the war, although both men helped Jews to escape, Andrzejewski wrote patriotic fiction that Milosz in *The Captive Mind*, where Andrzejewski was analyzed as "Alpha," reproached him for, since it inspired Poles to die in the Home Army (*The Captive Mind*, 97–98). After the war, Andrzejewski's novel *Ashes and Diamonds* won a state prize; soon Milosz attacked the novel for having "favorably compared the ethic of the New Faith [Communism] with the vanquished code [of the Home Army]" (*Captive Mind*, 105). But after the bloody repression of the Poznań riots in 1956, Andrzejewski left the PZPR Party, and in 1976 Andrzejewski became one of the most famous founding members of the Workers' Defense Committee (KOR) that helped inspire and coordinate Solidarność.

41. Ash, *Solidarity*, 24–27. Some of the KPN leaders, calling themselves "True Poles," also voiced the anti-Semitic hopes of the prewar Polish Republic and Church for an ethnically "pure" Poland.

42. Grzegorz Wąsowski, "Doomed Soldiers Memorial Day," The Doomed Soldiers, http://www.doomedsoldiers.com/doomed-soldiers-memorial-day.html.

43. Ibid; see chapter 6; Czeslaw Milosz: "[W]hat was said about the recurrence of Romantic patterns applies particularly to Baczyński's poetry, whose rich imagery served more and more overtly, as he developed, to point up his central theme of self-immolation for the sake of an ideal Poland" (Czarnecka and Fiut, *Conversations with Czeslaw Milosz*, 128).

CHAPTER 3

1. Czeslaw Milosz, *Beginning with My Streets: Essays and Recollections* (New York: Farrar, Straus and Giroux, 1991), 148.

2. Translated by Czeslaw Milosz into Polish as, "Don't ever forget / we walk over hell / gazing at flowers" (Czeslaw Milosz, *The Separate Notebooks* [New York: Ecco, 1984], 208, 209).

3. Czeslaw Milosz, "Happiness," in *To Begin Where I Am: Selected Essays* (New York: Farrar, Straus and Giroux, 2001), 20.

4. Andrzej Franaszek, *Miłosz: A Biography* (Cambridge, MA: Harvard University Press, 2017), 44.

5. Cf. Franaszek, *Miłosz: A Biography*, 18–19.

6. Franaszek, *Miłosz: A Biography*, 25. Late in life, Milosz denied this. He told Aleksandr Fiut that the farm hands lived either in their own small houses or in "a large servants' hall [which] was a separate building" (Czeslaw Milosz, in Ewa Czarnecka and Aleksander Fiut, trans. Richard Lourie, *Conversations with Czeslaw Milosz* [San Diego: Harcourt Brace Jovanovich, 1987], 8). But I find the evidence of the poem persuasive:

[downstairs] a room for each of the four families
I pronounce the names with surprise:
Tomaszunas, Sagatis, Osipowicz and Vackonis, the manager,
Though I felt embarrassed at being the young master.
("Do Natury," W 5:281)

7. Milosz, "The Nobel Lecture," in Milosz, *Beginning with My Streets*, 273; online at http://www.nybooks.com/articles/1981/03/05/the-nobel-lecture-1980/; emphasis in original.

8. Milosz, "The Nobel Lecture," *Beginning with My Streets*, 276–77. The child's privileged perspective of looking down "from above" may have been reinforced by his experience of reading (if Franaszek is correct) above another world with a different language.

9. Czeslaw Milosz, *Road-Side Dog* (New York: Farrar, Straus and Giroux, 1998), 59.

10. It also explains the more cosmopolitan perspective of their work. As Milosz wrote, "A complete liberation from the gravitational forces of the local and provincial condemns a poet to imitate foreign models" (*Road-Side Dog*, 58). All four also lived in exile (Herbert only sporadically); Mickiewicz and Słowacki both died there. (Herbert was born in 1924 in Lwów [in Polish, Lviv in Ukrainian, Lemberg in German], which then was assigned to Poland. Today part of Ukraine, it was always the capital of its Ukrainian-speaking region, and thus part of the *kresy*.)

11. Franaszek, *Miłosz: A Biography*, 45

12. Franaszek, *Miłosz: A Biography*, 47: "Like the majority of Poles in their area, she opted to settle in Wilno. The only possibility for former Polish inhabitants to re-visit their families and home region was by crossing the border illegally. In the course of Miłosz's summer breaks from secondary school, the family several times returned to Lithuania by means of illegal crossings, an activity fraught with danger: Because diplomatic relations between Poland and Lithuania had been broken off, it was impossible, legally, to get there."

13. Franaszek, *Miłosz: A Biography*, 38.

14. Oedipal considerations, though not part of this book, could be used to analyze many of Milosz's poems, starting with "Hymn" (NCP, 13).

15. Milosz, *Beginning with My Streets*, 25. Milosz's father, then in the army, had taken part in the uprising, with the consequence that thereafter he (and his family with him) could no longer live in the new state of Lithuania (Franaszek, *Miłosz: A Biography*, 44–45).

16. Milosz, in Czarnecka and Fiut, *Conversations with Czeslaw Milosz*, 124. Still later, Milosz identified one of his schoolmates, Alik Protasewicz, as "My first encounter with God's cruelty" (ABC, 19).

17. "I am a man of contradictions, and I do not deny that" (Czeslaw Milosz, in *Beginning with My Streets*, 148).

18. Milosz, in Czarnecka and Fiut, *Conversations with Czeslaw Milosz*, 114.

19. Anthony Day, "The Poet Remembers," *Los Angeles Times Magazine*, August 15, 1993, in Cynthia L. Haven (ed.), *Czesław Miłosz: Conversations* (Jackson: University Press of Mississippi, 2006), 147.

20. Cf. ABC, 203: "When I went to school in Wilno I was closer to poverty than to wealth."

21. *Striving Towards Being: The Letters of Thomas Merton and Czeslaw Milosz*, ed. by Robert Faggen, (New York: Farrar, Straus and Giroux, 1997), 80.

22. Franaszek, *Miłosz: A Biography*, 35–36.

23. Cf. ABC, 35, where he speaks of "my fate as a man born to class privilege, but always conscious of my advantages."

24. Robert Bideleux. *A History of Eastern Europe: Crisis and Change* (London: Routledge, 1998), 122.

25. An interesting survey of Milosz's gentry forbears is supplied by Franaszek, *Miłosz: A Biography*, 34–40.

26. Milosz also blamed on the teachings of Father Chomski "my almost unhealthy conviction that sexuality is evil" (NR, 272), which contributed to his self-reproving view of himself as a "fleshy . . . Caliban" (*To Begin Where I Am*, 258).

27. Thanks to his problems with Father Chomski, Milosz continued for years to have problems with confession. In 1959, while still in France, he told Thomas Merton, "I go rarely to confession, every few years." In America, more of a church-goer than before, he still, five years later, felt that "Confession is for me an obstacle, an absurdity" (*Striving Towards Being*, 44, 162; cf. 24).

28. According to Anthony Day, "Miłosz says that in his youth he came to take a 'scientific, atheistic position mostly'" (Anthony Day, in Cynthia L. Haven [ed.], *Czesław Miłosz: Conversations*, 145). But Milosz himself wrote of "my early fascination with the Manichaean heresy" (LU, 37); and one cannot deny his lifelong preoccupation with spiritual and theological matters, above all with theodicy.

29. Enda O'Doherty, "Apples at World's End," *Dublin Review of Books*, July 2018, http://www.drb.ie/essays/apples-at-world-s-end.

30. Franaszek, *Miłosz: A Biography*, 88–89. The attackers included Jerzy Putrament, later a prominent leader in the postwar Communist government.

31. Milosz's son Tony tells me that, "after my father's sight had almost completely failed, and he was mostly bedridden, I used to read to him, and one of the last books he had picked was *Magic Mountain*."

32. Czeslaw Milosz to Robert Faggen, in Haven, *Czesław Miłosz: Conversations*, 164. (Milosz said much the same in conversation with Adam Michnik, "I was always fascinated by Naphta, not Settembrini." (Adam Michnik, *Letters from Freedom: Post–Cold War Realities and Perspectives* [Berkeley: University of California Press, 1998], 2011.) But even Milosz's acknowledgment in 1994 of his doubleness does not do justice to his dialectical complexity. As we shall see, his *History of Polish Literature* (1969) praises both the Enlightenment and the romantic reaction to it; his *Land of Ulro* (1977) is a sustained account of Blakean attempts to escape the Enlightenment; and his *Witness of Poetry* (1982) praises what he calls "the Age of Raptures" (WP, 13) of authors like Schiller and Mickiewicz, embodying both Enlightenment and post-Enlightenment features.

33. As already noted, Milosz commented on the Poetic Treatise that "the struggle between the conservative force of *être* ('to be') and the revolutionary force of *devenir* ('to become') had been tearing Europe apart since the French revolution" (TP, 107n).

34. Peter Dale Scott, *Enmindment—A History: A Post-Secular Poem in Prose* (forthcoming).

35. Iain McGilchrist, *The Master and His Emissary: The Divided Brain and the Making of the Western World* (New Haven, CT: Yale University Press, 2018). In a review, Jacob Freedman wrote that "In essence, Iain McGilchrist's book is an exploration of the link between the brain's hemispheric asymmetry and the historical development of Western society. This is no small task: chronicling how the left brain's determined reductionism and the right brain's insightful and holistic approach have shaped music, language, politics, and art" (Jacob Freedman, "The Master and His Emissary: The Divided Brain and the Making of the Modern World," *American Journal of Psychiatry* 168, no. 6 (June 2011): 655–56.

36. McGilchrist, *The Master and His Emissary*, 461–62:

> The divided nature of our reality has been a consistent observation since humanity has been sufficiently self-conscious to reflect on it. That most classical representative of the modern self-conscious spirit, Goethe's Faust, famously declared that "two souls, alas! dwell in my breast" (*Zwei Seelen wohnen, ach! in meiner Brust*). Schopenhauer described "two completely distinct forms of experience" (*zwei völlig heterogene Weisen gegebene Erkenntniß*); Bergson referred to "two different orders of reality" (*deux réalités d'ordre différent*). Scheler described the human being as a citizen of two worlds (*Bürger zweier Welten*) and said that all great European philosophers, like Kant, who used the same formulation, had seen as much. What all these point to is the fundamentally divided nature of mental experience. . . . One puts that together with the fact that the brain is divided into two relatively independent chunks which just happen broadly to mirror the very dichotomies that are being pointed to.

37. Milosz, *Beginning with My Streets*, 15, 25.

38. Quoted in Franaszek, *Miłosz: A Biography*, 86. Many years later he would write of the "strong socialist leanings" he once had "from thinking about those millions of

human lives trampled [by nineteenth-century 'capitalism'] into the mud." In 1940, in Nazi-occupied Warsaw, he "joined the socialist organization Freedom" (ABC, 303); but this may have been his way of declaring his rejection of the mainstream Polish resistance movement, the nationalist Home Army.

39. Franaszek, *Miłosz: A Biography*, 367.

40. Franaszek, *Miłosz: A Biography*, 98. Commenting after the war on a reference to a knowledge "mobile" in time, in his "Treatise on Morals" [Traktat moralny; 1947], Milosz explained, "A mobile knowledge—just as the human being is mobile— seems correct to me here. This mobility does not have a psychological so much as a civilizational meaning. Such mobility—that is, historical variability dependent on the individual civilizations—has aroused my constant astonishment since the moment I landed in America. This is a very Marxist passage" (Łukasz Tischner, *Miłosz and the Problem of Evil* [Evanston, IL: Northwestern University Press, 2015], 95; citing Czeslaw Milosz, *Zaraz po wojnie: korespondecja z pisarzami 1945–1950* [Kraków: Znak, 1998], 275). In Tischner's thoughtful analysis, the reference is perhaps more Hegelian.

41. Franaszek, *Miłosz: A Biography*, 97.

42. Czeslaw Milosz, "On Oscar Milosz," in *To Begin Where I Am*, 77. The cousinship was remote. According to Oscar, their common ancestor was Oscar's great-great-grandfather (LU, 90). This is compatible with the information in Franaszek (*Miłosz: A Biography*, 39–40), but not confirmed by it.

43. Similarly, Duncan's theosophist parents told him that "Modern science, would come upon secrets of Nature . . . and . . . destroy America . . . in a series of holocausts, an end of Time that would come in my life time" (Robert Duncan, "The Truth and Life of Myth: An Essay in Essential Autobiography" *Robert Duncan: Collected Essays and Other Prose* [Berkeley: University of California Press, 2014], 142). Both Duncan's parents and Oscar Milosz belonged to Hermetic orders with a fixation on Luxor from their common roots in Rosicrucianism. See Robert Duncan, *Robert Duncan: Collected Essays and Other Prose* (Berkeley: University of California Press, 2014), 142, 399; Lynn Picknett and Clive Prince, *The Sion Revelation: The Truth About the Guardians of Christ's Sacred Bloodline* (New York: Simon & Schuster, 2006), 351–52.

44. *Żagary* is a word in Vilnius dialect for "brushwood" or "dry sticks," which perhaps expresses the group's anti-romanticism.

45. Czeslaw Milosz, "A Letter to Defenders of Culture," quoted in Franaszek, *Miłosz: A Biography*, 159. Original in *Poprostu* (1936), 147–54.

46. Czeslaw Milosz, "*Do księdza Ch.*," [1936], in Czeslaw Miłosz, W 1:108.

47. Milosz, in Czarnecka and Fiut, *Conversations with Czeslaw Milosz*, 107.

48. Milosz, in Czarnecka and Fiut, *Conversations with Czeslaw Milosz*, 108.

49. Milosz to Jadwiga Tomaszewicz, née Waszkiewicz, October 24, 19981, in Franaszek, *Miłosz: A Biography*, 123.

50. Milosz to Jadwiga Tomaszewicz, née Waskziewicz, September 17, 1987, in Franaszek, *Miłosz: Biografia* (Kraków: Znak, 2011), 184, 782n224. The date offered in translation, "September 17, 1935" (p. 120), is obviously wrong.

51. Cf. Franaszek, *Miłosz: A Biography*, 119: "It is beyond doubt, however, that Miłosz's abandonment of Jadwiga . . . had traumatic repercussions which affected him for the rest of his life."

52. Milosz, *Beginning with My Streets*, 110. Cf. WP, 37: "I think that . . . the two meanings of hope were interlaced and merged with each other."

53. Milosz told Gorczyńska that "various characters" speak in the poem, but then clarified that the poem is "far from polyphonic. . . . A great many voices really can emerge at times when a person has a great many conflicts and contradictions. A person is never all of a piece" (Milosz, in Czarnecka and Fiut, *Conversations with Czeslaw Milosz*, 114).

54. Milosz, in Czarnecka and Fiut, *Conversations with Czeslaw Milosz*, 115.

55. In 1987 Milosz discussed the poem's themes of alienation from self and urban society: "'Slow River' . . . begins, after all, with words of ecstasy: 'There has not been for a long time / A spring as beautiful as this one.' My attention was focused, however, on sensual detail, while the Wilno of the people of those days was no denser than fog. At that time, in 1936, I very much wanted to be capable of love and friendship, although I doubted that I had that capacity and was even in despair because of it" (YH, 64).

56. Milosz, in Czarnecka and Fiut, *Conversations with Czeslaw Milosz*, 115–16. To Gorczyńska's question, "A world government, with each nation preserving its identity?" Milosz replied, "Yes, a world government. A United States of Earth . . . I'd like to add that my work is very strongly marked by the expectation of a new era. That's very Romantic. The Third Epoch of the Spirit, the age of eschatology." The same hope is voiced, less expectantly, at the end of *The Land of Ulro*.

57. Czeslaw Milosz, "A One-Man Army: Stanisław Brzozowski," in Czeslaw Milosz, *Emperor of the Earth: Modes of Eccentric Vision* (Berkeley: University of California Press, 1977). Brzozowski died in 1911; many of Marx's most important early writings were not published until 1927 and 1932.

58. The two aphorisms are presented as similar in Władysław Tatarkiewicz, *A History of Six Ideas* (The Hague: Nijhoff, 1980), 194. But Milosz (HPL, 178) links the second to the passivity of Young Poland. In Warsaw, Milosz regularly attended a Tatarkiewicz seminar, with his friend Tadeusz Julius Kroński (Franaszek, *Miłosz: A Biography*, 207); and for the next few years, encouraged by Kroński, Milosz wrote vigorously against late romanticism (see chapters 5–7).

59. In his introduction to his *New and Collected Poems*, Milosz writes that in poetry, to handle "the weight of fact" without becoming "only a reporter . . . calls for a cunning in selecting one's means and a kind of distillation of material to achieve a distance to contemplate the things of the world as they are, without illusion" (NCP, xxiii).

60. Franaszek, *Miłosz: A Biography*, 167, quoting Milosz, *Beginning with My Streets* (Polish version). Cf. Milosz, *Land of Ulro*, 67–68: "Wilno, in all frankness, belonged to the provinces. . . . I suffered from the acute snobbery of a provincial fop. I was even awed by Warsaw, although it was an awe mixed with terror, as of a Babylon. I was to be severely punished for that snobbery, condemned to the life of an émigré from the time I left Wilno."

61. Czeslaw Milosz, "Anus Mundi," in *To Begin Where I Am: Selected Essays* (New York: Farrar, Straus and Giroux, 2001), 371–72.

CHAPTER 4

1. Czeslaw Milosz, "A Semi-Private Letter about Poetry," in *To Begin Where I Am: Selected Essays* (New York: Farrar, Straus and Giroux, 2001), 350.
2. *Ocalenie*, and its synonym *zbawienie*, both mean "salvation." They were frequently used by Milosz in both poetry (NCP, 19, 23, 77, 144, 541, 543), and prose. His second-to-last published poem was "To Salvation" ["O Zbawieniu," in Czesław Miłosz, "Wiersze ostatnie"]. But Milosz does not use these words in a narrowly Catholic or even religious sense. For example, Milosz tells us that his Marxist humanist friend Tadeusz Kroński "really only believed in one thing: Salvation" [Zbawienie] (NR, 267; cf. 289). Thus it was not surprising for Milosz to translate his book title *Ocalenie* as *Rescue* (NCP, vii, 23), and in the very late "Theological Treatise" (all three treatises use the word) he translates the plural as "escapes" (SS, 62). It is relevant that the verb *ocalić* in Polish is cognate with the word *cały*, "whole," and is sometimes explained as "to make whole." It is thus somewhat like the obsolete medieval English verb "to sane," meaning "to make sane."
3. Czeslaw Milosz, in Ewa Czarnecka and Aleksander Fiut, *Conversations with Czeslaw Milosz* (San Diego, CA: Harcourt Brace Jovanovich, 1987), 118.
4. Although it serves the argument of this book to see "The World" as Blakean, another important influence may have been that of the English mystic poet Thomas Traherne (d. 1674), who Milosz first ran across "in 1936, I think." Milosz later wrote of Traherne's poetry, "It means that suffering . . . can be avoided through a return to beginnings; that is, through the recovery of a lost naïve vision." And he praised "the simplicity of his style" (Czeslaw Milosz, "The Earth as Paradise," in Czeslaw Milosz, *Beginning with My Streets: Essays and Recollections* [New York: Farrar, Straus and Giroux, 1991], 137, 140).
5. Jan Błoński, *Miłosz jak świat* (Kraków: Znak, 1998), 94–95; Magda Heydel, "Czeslaw Milosz and T. S. Eliot," in Elisabeth Däumer and Shyamal Bagchee (eds.) *The International Reception of T. S. Eliot* (London: Continuum, 2007), 228.
6. Czeslaw Milosz, in Czarnecka and Fiut, *Conversations with Czeslaw Milosz*, 126.
7. ABC, 29; Andrzej Franaszek, *Miłosz: Biografia* (Kraków: Znak, 2011, 380; Clare Cavanagh, *Lyric Poetry and Modern Politics: Russia, Poland, and the West* (New Haven, CT: Yale University Press, 2009), 19.
8. Cavanagh, *Lyric Poetry and Modern Politics*, 248.
9. Milosz, in Czarnecka and Fiut, *Conversations with Czeslaw Milosz*, 127.
10. Milosz, in Czarnecka and Fiut, *Conversations with Czeslaw Milosz*, 128. Milosz wrote of Baczyński in *The Captive Mind* [New York: Vintage, 1990], 97) that "With him, the greatest hope of Polish poetry perished."
11. We see this for example in the untranslated poem "Morning" [Ranek]: "Under the steady drumming of rain, in the foggy morning, / Amid the crowing of cocks, the long scream of a goose, / A sleepy village and native country awaken" (W 1:285).

12. Later I shall use the literal translation, "This is, and only this is, salvation" [To jest, I tylko to jest, Ocalenie], in place of Milosz's more moderate and subjective "In this and only this I find salvation." See discussion in "Personal Memoir" (in the appendix).

13. "Love"'s next line, "A bird and a tree say to him: Friend," also points to this mystery, as do "Przedmowa"'s opening lines:
I swear, there is in me no wizardry of words.
I speak to you with silence like a cloud or a tree.

14. Adam Mickiewicz, "The Romantic," trans. W. H. Auden; in LU, 99.

15. "In [Mickiewicz], the philosophy of *les lumières* is both negated and accepted as a basic optimism toward the future" (WP, 13).

16. A clue to this is Milosz's decision to translate "Świat (Poema Naiwne)" as "The World: A Naïve Poem." The original is, unambiguously, "The World: Naïve Poems."

17. Czeslaw Milosz, in Czarnecka and Fiut, *Conversations with Czeslaw Milosz*, 127; emphasis added. The first editor to segregate these three poems in English, and publlish them out of context (in *Postwar Polish Poetry*), was Milosz himself.

18. Milosz frequently emphasized this presence of irony throughout, as in "We can say that *The World: A Naïve Poem*, which was written during the war, is a work of pure irony" (Milosz, in Czarnecka and Fiut, *Conversations with Czeslaw Milosz*, 118, cf. 127). The ironic effects are probably even greater in the Polish versions. "The subtitle 'naive poems' (*'poema naiwne'*)—with its archaic use of the plural *'poema'* in the original Polish—gives a clear sign of ironic distance, a peculiar abstraction from the historical here and now" (Łukasz Tischner, *Miłosz and the Problem of Evil* [Evanston, IL: Northwestern University Press, 2015], 24). In the quasi-apocalyptic "Song on the End of the World," Milosz later explained that he introduced the man busily tending his tomatoes "for purely humorous effects. It's ironic. In the original the humor is more pronounced than it is in the translation" (Milosz, in Cynthia L. Haven (ed.), *Czesław Miłosz: Conversations* [Jackson, MS: University Press of Mississippi, 2006], 50).

19. "I wrote a long work consisting of short poems, entitled 'The World: A Naive Poem,' . . . I considered the world so horrible that these childish poems were answers—the world as it should be, not as it was. *Written in view of what was happening*, 'The World' was a profoundly ironic poem" (Milosz, in Haven, *Czesław Miłosz: Conversations*, 156–57; emphasis added). Cf. Milosz, in Czarnecka and Fiut, *Conversations with Czeslaw Milosz*, 127: "Warsaw in 1943 . . . was the exact opposite of the world that I decided to depict—a rather ironic operation."

20. Milosz, in Czarnecka and Fiut, *Conversations with Czeslaw Milosz*, 132.

21. Cf. "Milosz, "Flight" (NCP, 74; Genesis 3:24: "So he drove out the man; and he placed at the east of the garden of Eden Cherubims, and a flaming sword which turned every way, to keep the way of the tree of life"). Discussion in chapter 7.

22. In addition, the frame included, after "Przedmowa," the poem "Flight" (discussed in chapter 7), a section of two very early poems, and another of six more from his prewar book *Three Winters*, including "Slow River." Then a fourth wartime section was introduced by "In My Homeland." The ensuing sections were "The World," "Voices of Poor People," and an unnamed seventh and final section.

23. Czesław Miłosz, *Wiersze* (Kraków: Znak, 2001), 1:142.

24. Hank Lazer also notes "Encounter"'s "dialectical movement. Flat, compressed observation in the past tense gives way to a consideration of mortality in the present" (Hank Lazer, "Poetry and Thought: The Example of Czeslaw Milosz," *VQR* (Summer 1988), https://www.vqronline.org/essay/poetry-and-thought-example-czeslaw-milosz.

25. Czeslaw Milosz, "A Semi-Private Letter about Poetry," in *To Begin Where I Am*, 349; quoting from "Ranek," W 1:185.

26. Milosz, in Czarnecka and Fiut, *Conversations with Czeslaw Milosz*, 118.

27. In the last line, there is an allusion to Słowacki's "No time to grieve for roses when the forests are burning" [Nie czas żałować róż, gdy płoną lasy]—the line a Polish friend persuaded me to use as an epigraph for my translation of Herbert's poem "Two Drops" [Dwie krople], another very different poem about the destruction of Warsaw. Milosz quotes the line more directly in his next poem "Morning" [Ranek]: "And again there is no time, *no time to grieve for roses*" [I znów nie czas, nie czas żałować róż] (W 1:185), emphasis added.

28. Milosz, "A Semi-Private Letter about Poetry," in *To Begin Where I Am*, 346; quoting *Walc*, W 1:190. We shall discuss later Milosz's complex feelings about his uses of irony, with which he was not always reconciled. Cf. TP, 20, 89–90n.

29. The word "greenwood" of course suggests Shakespeare's lyric

    Under the greenwood tree
    Who loves to lie with me,
    And turn his merry note
    Unto the sweet bird's throat,
    Come hither, come hither, come hither:
    Here shall he see
    No enemy
    But winter and rough weather

from *As You Like It*, a play which Milosz translated in 1943, in the midst of Warsaw's misery. But the allusion is so obvious only in Milosz's English translation. The Polish original of "greenwood" in Milosz's poem is *radosne gaje*, or "joyful groves," just as in Milosz's translation of Shakespeare's lyric the first line is translated only as *w zielonej*, or "in the green." However, this translation probably inspired the reference to "The green of England" [zieleń Anglii] we noted earlier in the 1942 poem "Morning."

30. In America Milosz did much to eschew a bardic image for a less outlandish democratic one.

31. Aleksander Fiut, *Czesława Miłosza autoportret przekorny* (Kraków: Wydawnictwo Literackie, 1988), 334–36; quoted in Jerzy Illg, "Invisible Rope," *Periphery* 4/5 (1999), http://www-personal.engin.umich.edu/~zbigniew/Periphery/No4/illg.html.

Neither "To a Politician" [Do polityka] nor "To Lech Wałęsa" appear in his *New and Collected Poems*. Cf. Czarnecka and Fiut, *Conversations with Czeslaw Milosz*, 130: "The poems chosen for some anthologies make me appear noble, the bard of the nation. That's not in the least to my taste."

CHAPTER 5

1. NR, 125.
2. Timothy Garton Ash, *The Polish Revolution: Solidarity* (New Haven, CT: Yale University Press, 2002), 216.
3. A second influence, as Milosz acknowledged, is Thomas Traherne (1636–1674), who lived through the English Civil War (Czeslaw Milosz in Ewa Czarnecka and Aleksander Fiut, trans. Richard Lourie, *Conversations with Czeslaw Milosz* [San Diego: Harcourt Brace Jovanovich, 1987], 127).
4. Late in life, Milosz told a journalist, "I didn't know at the time that I was repeating the procedure of Blake, who had written Songs of Experience and Songs of Innocence. It was very difficult to liberate myself from prewar patterns and tastes and styles, but I knew when I wrote these poems that it was a turning point in my poetry" (Czeslaw Milosz, in Nicholas Wroe, "A Century's Witness," *The Guardian*, November 9, 2001). But "in wartime Warsaw . . . I came across a few of Blake's poems . . . and in that landscape so unhospitable to a child's awe before the miraculous, Blake restored me to my earlier raptures, perhaps to my true vocation, that of lover" (Milosz, LU, 31). My memory from talking to him is as follows: he was quite conscious at the time he wrote of the similarities between "Songs of Innocence" and "The World." Only later did he become more aware of "Songs of Experience," and their correspondence in *Ocalenie* to "Voices of Poor People."
5. "The Excursion to the Forest," NCP, 51; cf. "The Bird Kingdom," NCP, 52.
6. NCP, 36. The perspective is reversed in the final quatrain, when "father, leaning on a hoe . . . from his flower bed inspects the whole region."
7. Franaszek, *Miłosz: A Biography*, 211.
8. Cf. 1 Corinthians 13:13; Łukasz Tischner, *Miłosz and the Problem of Evil* (Evanston, IL: Northwestern University Press, 2015), 33: "It is no coincidence that these three poems appear precisely where they do in the cycle."
9. Milosz, "The Nobel Lecture," Stockholm, December 8, 1980, in Czeslaw Milosz, *Beginning with My Streets: Essays and Recollections* (New York: Farrar, Straus and Giroux, 1991), 281; http://www.nobelprize.org/nobel_prizes/literature/laureates/1980/milosz-lecture.html.
10. Peter Dale Scott, *Enmindment—A History: A Post-Secular Poem in Prose* (forthcoming).
11. Tischner, *Miłosz and the Problem of Evil*, 33–34. Nathan and Quinn also rationalize "Faith"'s second stanza, as meaning "we are certain" that the "garden in Hope" "(is it paradise?) . . . is there, just ahead" (Leonard Nathan and Arthur Quinn, *The Poet's Work: An Introduction to Czeslaw Milosz* [Cambridge, MA: Harvard University Press, 1991], 20).
12. Perhaps the most authoritative effort at a Thomistic reading of "The World" is that of Aleksander Fiut:

> In *Visions from San Francisco Bay* Milosz declares: "My imagination is not like that of someone who lived when Thomas Aquinas's world view was reflected in Dante's symbols" (V[isions] 30) . . . Milosz adds: "What is worse, time, always strongly spatial, has

increased its spatiality; it has stretched infinitely back out behind us, infinitely forward into the future toward which our faces are turned" (V[isions] 31). Perhaps, then, even at the cost of naivete, we should attempt a re-creation of the universe according to the models inherited from Aquinas. "The World" is just such an attempt. (Aleksander Fiut, *The Eternal Moment: The Poetry of Czeslaw Milosz* [Berkeley: University of California Press, 1987], 28–29).

He develops his argument by referring to two poems, "A Parable of the Poppy" and "By the Peonies" from what I view as the "horizontal," "spatial," or "Thomistic" first half of "The World"; he is silent about the "vertical," "temporal," or "historicist" second half.

13. Milosz, in Czarnecka and Fiut, *Conversations with Czeslaw Milosz*, 182.

14. In Polish, "pewnika, że ludzkie rzeczy stają się, a nie tylko są," more literally, "the certainty that human things become, and not only are" (Czesław Miłosz, *Rodzinna Europa* [Warsaw: Czytelnik, 1990], 88).

15. For example, Milosz, "Esse," NCP, 249; TP, 35, 106–8.

16. Andrzej Franaszek, *Miłosz: Biografia* (Kraków: Znak, 2011), 212, emphasis added. The douple meaning given by Franaszek in this sentence to the word "reality" reflects the double meaning conferred on the word by Milosz himself.

17. Franaszek, *Miłosz: Biografia*, 211.

18. St. Thomas, *Contra Errores Graecorum*, c. 32: "*Ostenditur etiam quod subesse Romano Pontifici sit de necessitate salutis*; It is also shown that to be subject to the Roman Pontiff is necessary for salvation." Cf. "*Unam Sanctam*" (Papal bull of Pope Boniface VIII, 1302): "*Porro subesse Romano pontifice omni humanae creaturae declaramus, dicimus, definimus et pronuntiamus omnino esse de necessitate salutis.*" Boniface VIII is the pope that Dante described as destined for Hell (*Inferno* 19.52–54); but "*Unam Sanctam*" was endorsed by the *Catholic Encyclopedia*, at least until Vatican II (Johann Peter Kirsch, "Unam Sanctam." *The Catholic Encyclopedia*, 15 (New York: Robert Appleton, 1912), http://www.newadvent.org/cathen/15126a.htm.

19. St. Thomas, *Summa Theologiae*, 1.1.9

20. Franaszek, *Miłosz: A Biography*, 347; citing Czesław Miłosz, *Rozmowy polskie*, (Kraków: Wydawnictwo Literackie, 2011), 588: "My principal argument here is that we cannot get stuck in the *esse* state, by digging in our heels and shouting 'No' to change."

21. Milosz in Czarnecka and Fiut, *Conversations with Czeslaw Milosz*, 176.

22. Commenting on this passage to Gorczyńska, Milosz said: "The process of shifting to the so-called new reality has already begun—the reality of People's Poland, in a word. 'Becomes' is the opposite of 'to be' . . . 'esse,' a fundamental concept in Thomistic ontology and for the whole philosophy of being in general . . . ['Becomes' is] pure Hegelianism" (ibid.).

23. Czeslaw Milosz, "The Importance of Simone Weil" (1960), in Milosz, *To Begin Where I Am: Selected Essays* (New York: Farrar, Straus and Giroux, 2001), 247–48.

24. Milosz, *To Begin Where I Am*, 247–48.

25. Milosz may be thinking of the nineteenth-century Bohemians of whom he later wrote, "These rebels against the Establishment had no programs except negation" (HPL, 323; cf. WP, 27).

26. Adam Mickiewicz, "The Romantic," trans. W. H. Auden; in Czeslaw Milosz, LU, 99. The poem is over two pages long, but Milosz reproduced all of it twice, first in his *History of Polish Literature* (211–13), and then in *The Land of Ulro*. Cf. Milosz, LU, 31: "My conversion to Blake was, at that time, an emotional one, for my understanding failed me. . . . And yet that obscurity, so unlike that cultivated in the poetry of my contemporaries, was part of the magic." Auden generally made a point of translating only from languages he himself knew, yet he did not know Polish. I suspect that Milosz may have collaborated on the project with him—perhaps as early as 1947, when they were both in New York.

27. Tischner aptly compares "The World" to a passage in Oscar Milosz's poem "Storge": "And though lunacy or madness may dictate this to me, I assert that within this indefinite, unlocatable universe, I know one certain place where reason is lost— and that place is my love" (Tischner, *Miłosz and the Problem of Evil*, 28).

28. Joel Burnell, *Poetry, Providence, and Patriotism: Polish Messianism in Dialogue with Dietrich Bonhoeffer* (Eugene, OR: Pickwick Publications, 2009), 234. The "scholar" in the poem is modeled on the Enlightenment rationalist, Jan Śniadecki, who had attacked romanticism as "a school of treason and plague" (Milosz, HPL, 207; cf. 213).

29. Czeslaw Milosz, "On Oscar Milosz," in *To Begin Where I Am*, 82.

30. Milosz, LU, 97–99 ("The Romantic"), 104, 284 ("polemic"); Milosz, *To Begin Where I Am*, 84 ("schism"). Cf. WP, 13.

31. In *The Land of Ulro*, Milosz noted that Mickiewicz "sprang from a hinterland untouched by the skepticism of the Age of Reason"; and that "Mickiewicz's imagination never divested itself of pre-scientific cosmologies" (LU, 103).

32. Gražina Krivickas, "Relations Between the Living and the Dead in Lithuanian Folklore," *Lituanus: Lithuanian Quarterly Journal of Arts and Sciences* (Summer 1995), http://www.lituanus.org/1995_2/95_2_03.htm.

33. Milosz, "The Importance of Simone Weil" (1960), in Milosz, *To Begin Where I Am*, 247.

34. Nathan and Quinn, *The Poet's Work*, 21.

35. William Blake, edited by Geoffrey Keynes, *Poetry and Prose of William Blake* (London: Nonesuch Press, 1948), 118.

36. *A Treatise on Poetry* (see chapters 11 and 12) expands on this return, so important to Milosz. It reflects the role of art as defined by Staniszlaw Brzozowski: "Art is not an accidental entertainment, an escape from the painful problems of a real life. On the contrary, anticipating life as it should be . . . art brings man back to reality, summons him to reform the world here and now (Tadeusz Szkolu. "Polish Aesthetic Axiology in the Twentieth Century (1890–1999)," in Stanisław Jedynek [ed.], *Polish Axiology The 20th Century and Beyond* [Washington, DC: Council for Research in Values and Philosophy, 2005], 14). Milosz credits Brzozowski (who died in 1911) for discerning "the Romantic crisis in European culture" before Erich Heller did in *The Disinherited Mind* (Milosz, LU, 94; cf. Milosz, *To Begin Where I Am*, 83).

37. Cf. WP, 69, 72: "These two opposing tendencies [classicism and realism] usually coexist within one person . . . struggling with each other."

38. "Esse" was the poem selected for the program of Milosz's Nobel Prize ceremony in 1980.
39. Milosz, "The Importance of Simone Weil," *To Begin Where I Am*, 254.

CHAPTER 6

1. Helen Vendler, *The Music of What Happens: Poems, Poets, Critics* (Cambridge: Harvard University Press, 1988), 210.
2. Milosz, "Nobel Lecture," Stockholm, December 8, 1980, in Czeslaw Milosz, *Beginning with My Streets: Essays and Recollections* (New York: Farrar, Straus and Giroux, 1991); http://www.nobelprize.org/nobel_prizes/literature/laureates/1980/milosz-lecture.html, 276–77.
3. As we shall see, Milosz called faith in this world the "raison d'être of poetry."
4. In *Ocalenie*, and again in the Polish edition of Milosz's collected poems (W 1), the "Songs of Adrian Zieliński" are included at the end of "Voices of Poor People." In the English edition (*New and Collected Poems* [Ecco, 2001]), they are not, but follow after.
5. Cf. T. S. Eliot, "The Hollow Men": "This is the way the world ends / This is the way the world ends" (https://www.shmoop.com/hollow-men/poem-text.html).
6. I have departed here from the NCP translation by Robert Hass and Renata Gorczyńska, which is distorted to meet the constraints of a strict ABCB rhyme scheme.
7. In 1944, with the imminent arrival of the Russians, Milosz's poetry (as we shall see shortly) became markedly more apocalyptic in tone.
8. Aleksander Fiut, *The Eternal Moment: The Poetry of Czeslaw Milosz* (Berkeley, CA: University of California Press, 1987), 79.
9. Czeslaw Milosz in Ewa Czarnecka and Aleksander Fiut, trans. Richard Lourie, *Conversations with Czeslaw Milosz* (San Diego: Harcourt Brace Jovanovich, 1987), 126.
10. Magda Heydel, "Ceslaw Milosz and T. S. Eliot," in Elisabeth Däumer and Shyamal Bagchee (eds.) *The International Reception of T. S. Eliot* (London: Continuum, 2007), 231.
11. Ecclesiastes 9:4: "For to him that is joined to all the living there is hope: for a living dog is better than a dead lion."
12. Fiut compares "Songs of Adrian Zielinski": "Even the dead cannot be found. / They lie like cramped, black ants/ In the sandy, amber-colored ground, / And no eye can pick them out." (NCP, 68).
13. Fiut, *The Eternal Moment*, 42
14. Milosz, in Czarnecka and Fiut, *Conversations with Czeslaw Milosz*, 135.
15. Milosz, in Czarnecka and Fiut, *Conversations with Czeslaw Milosz*, 135; quoting "The Poor Poet," NCP, 59.
16. Milosz, in Czarnecka and Fiut, *Conversations with Czeslaw Milosz*, 135–36; quoting "The Poor Poet," NCP, 59. This reading of the "revenge" is quite opposite to that of Helen Vendler, who claims the poem "sees the creating of the symbolic order a

form of revenge against the horrors of life" (Helen Vendler, *The Music of What Happens: Poems, Poets, Critics* [Cambridge, MA: Harvard University Press, 1988], 128). There is no such affirmation of art here; the "poor poet" says clearly that the tree his pen created is "like an insult/ To suffering humanity."

17. *The History of Polish Literature*, 461–62.

18. NCP, 33–35; 63–64. Milosz himself wrote later that he considered the "Voices of Poor People" sequence in *Ocalenie*, of which "A Poor Christian" is one, "to be among the most complex poems I have written" (*To Begin Where I Am: Selected Essays* [New York: Farrar, Straus and Giroux, 2001], 347).

19. Milosz later explained that the *karuzel* in question, often translated "carousel . . . was actually a chairoplane, with couples soaring into the sky" (YH, 4).

20. Some right-wing Polish nationalists have recently claimed the two poems are a libelous attack on wartime Poland. But the perspective of "A Poor Christian" is obviously far older and broader, that of "a Jew of the New Testament / Waiting two thousand years for the second coming of Jesus." I see the self-questioning here as addressed not just to Poland in particular but also to Christianity itself.

21. Milosz, in Czarnecka and Fiut, *Conversations with Czeslaw Milosz*, 132.

22. See Czeslaw Milosz, "Adders and Other Reptiles," *New York Review of Books*, May 11, 1995, https://www.nybooks.com/articles/1995/05/11/adders-and-other-reptiles/; and a relevant exchange of letters, *New York Review of Books*, June 22, 1995, https://www.nybooks.com/articles/1995/06/22/enigma/.

23. Milosz, in Czarnecka and Fiut, *Conversations with Czeslaw Milosz*, 130; emphasis added. The Polish for "guardian" in this poem, *strażnik*, can mean either "watchman" or "guardian." I suggest that the strong overtones of guilt here make "watchman" a better translation; "guardian" connotes a quite alien protective role. Instead, I see the mole as gnawing at him internally, in the depths of his shattered consciousness. Note that the mole in "Throughout Our Lands" (NCP, 182; see chapter 13) is once again a *watcher*, not a protector.

24. Milosz, in Czarnecka and Fiut, *Conversations with Czeslaw Milosz*, 134.

25. Ibid; cf. Czesław Miłosz, "Niemoralność sztuki," in Czesław Miłosz, *Ogród nauk* (Paryż, Instytut Literacki, 1979), 161–68. Again, if we think of the mole as a "watchman," the second poem reverses the "immoral" gaze of the first: not the ghetto now but the poor Christian is being watched.

26. Robert Alter, "Milosz: Poetry and Politics," *Commentary*, April 1, 1983, https://www.commentarymagazine.com/articles/milosz-poetry-and-politics/.

27. The impact of Błoński's essay was so significant in the history of Polish-Jewish relations that it is customary to distinguish between pre-Błoński and post-Błoński periods. Cf. Piotr Forecki, *Reconstructing Memory: The Holocaust in Polish Public Debates* (Frankfurt am Main: Peter Lang, 2013), 117: "The significance of the article can be proven by the fact that, as Daniel Błatman noted, "it has long been a landmark in the examination of Polish-Jewish relations."

28. Jan Błoński, "Biedni Polacy patrzą na getto," *Tygodnik Powszechny*, January 11, 1987, translated as "The Poor Poles Look at the Ghetto," *Polin: A Journal of Polish-Jewish Studies* (1987), 321–35.

Cf, Monika Adamczyk-Garbowska, "Czesław Miłosz (1911–2004)," in S. Lillian Kremer (ed.), *Holocaust Literature: An Encyclopedia of Writers and Their Work* (New York: Routledge, 2003): "The most frequent reading of the poem is as a manifestation of the sense of guilt and bad conscience of Polish Christians for not helping enough or being indifferent to the plight of the Jews in the Warsaw ghetto in particular, and Jewish victims of the Nazis in general."

29. Czeslaw Milosz to Paul W. Rea; in *Czesław Miłosz: Conversations*, edited by Cynthia L. Haven (Jackson, MS: University Press of Mississippi, 2006), 92.

30. Aleksander Szumański, "The Truth about the Nobel Prize winner," Dziennik Związkowy (Chicago), December 20 –22, 2002, https://www-rodaknetcom.translate.goog/rp_szumanski_0.htm?_x_tr_sch=http&_x_tr_sl=pl&_x_tr_tl=en&_x_tr_hl=en&_x_tr_pto=sc Cf. Adam Kuz, "Karuzela na Campo di Fiori," Salon24, https://www.salon24.pl/u/adamkuz/772306,karuzela-na-campo-di-fiori; Orzeł może "bawić się na karuzeli podczas powstania," https://blogpress.pl/node/16562.

Another who attacked Milosz, "calling him a man devoid of patriotism and an opportunist," was his former protege Zbigniew Herbert, in his late years of declining mental health. See "Like two gods. Herbert and Miłosz: An interview [by Grzegorz Nurek] with Andrzej Franaszek, biographer of both Zbigniew Herbert and Czesław Miłosz," *New Eastern Europe*, September 1, 2018, https://neweasterneurope.eu/2018/09/01/like-two-gods-herbert-milosz/.

31. Fiut, *The Eternal Moment*, 11.

32. Compare Adrian Zieliński's "The round ass of a girl passing by," previously noted.

33. The use of specific verbal reminiscence, as opposed to general allusion, is much less common in Polish poetry than in English. We saw already, for example, that the repetition of "without knowing it," in Milosz's English translations of "The World" and *Przedmowa,* does not occur in the Polish originals.

34. In *Ocalenie*, as in the Polish edition of Milosz's collected poems (W 1), The "Songs of Adrian Zieliński" are included in "Voices of Poor People." In the English edition of "Rescue," (*New and Collected Poems* [Ecco, 2001]), they are not.

35. Cf. "A Treatise on Poetry" on the same event: "Amid thunder, the golden house of is / Collapses, and the word becoming ascends" (TP, 35; NCP, 132). The best evidence for this reading is that Milosz has told us to think of the poems in the book as part of a single process; and the next poem in date of composition is "Flight," which begins, "When we were fleeing the burning city" (NCP, 74). As noted, "Flight" was used by Milosz, along with "Przedmowa," to open *Ocalenie*. In the English sequence "Rescue," the sequence is "Songs of Adrien Zieliński," "Farewell" [to the city], and then "Flight" [from the city]; but the poems are dated, and "Farewell" is later than the others.

36. Franaszek, *Miłosz: A Biography*, 219. Milosz commented later why he cared little about money: "I had walked out of too many burning cities (literally or figuratively) without looking back: *omnia mea mecum porto* [Everything I own I carry with me]" (NR, 264).

37. Czeslaw Milosz, *The Captive Mind* (New York: Vintage, 1990).

38. Peter Dale Scott, *Minding the Darkness: A Poem for the Year 2000* (New York: New Directions, 2000), 6; quoting from the famous 1929 debate between Ernst Cassirer and Martin Heidegger (Rudiger Safranski, *Martin Heidegger: Between Good and Evil* (Cambridge, MA: Harvard University Press, 1998), 187.

39. Writing in *The New York Review of Books*, Al Alvarez once described Milosz as "a poet of memory, a witness; his real heroes are the dead to whom his poems make reparation" (Al Alvarez, "Witness," *New York Review of Books*, June 2, 1988, 21). Milosz responded in a letter, with some vehemence, that he was uneasy to see his work "encapsuled by Mr. Alvarez in the word 'witness,' which for him is perhaps a praise, but for me is not. . . . Poetry should not freeze, magnetized by the sight of evil perpetrated in our lifetime. . . . a poet repeatedly says farewell to his old selves and makes himself ready for renewals" (Czeslaw Milosz, "A Poet's Reply," *New York Review of Books*, July 21, 1988, 46). I have chosen Milosz's last sentence here as an apt epigraph for the next chapter.

CHAPTER 7

1. Friedrich Hölderlin, "Patmos," in *Poems of Friedrich Hölderlin: The Fire of the Gods Drives Us to Set Forth by Day and by Night*, selected and translated by James Mitchell (San Francisco: Ithuriel's Spear, 2007), 70–71.

2. Czeslaw Milosz, "A Poet's Reply," *New York Review of Books*, July 21, 1988, 46.

3. Cf. NR, 251; Andrzej Franaszek, *Miłosz: A Biography* (Cambridge, MA: Belknap Press/ Harvard University Press, 2017), 218.

4. Franaszek, *Miłosz: A Biography*, 219.

5. It would be months before they returned to their ruined home in Warsaw.

6. Milosz, NCP, 74. The compactness of this rapid escalation is enhanced by relatively tight metrics and rhyme (ABABCDCD). The last line, in Polish, is, "A miecz płomieni otwierał nam ziemię." Cf. Genesis 3:24: "So he drove out the man; and he placed at the east of the garden of Eden Cherubims, and a flaming sword which turned every way, to keep the way of the tree of life."

7. Cf. Franaszek, *Miłosz: A Biography*, 223: "The advance of the Red Army through Polish territory left large estates, modest-sized towns and small villages devastated. Plunder, arson, and rape were commonplace. . . . A month later, the owners of Goszyce were thrown off their property, but the Ghost of History was merciful: no-one got shot, and in order for them to gather their things, they were generously given twenty-four hours."

8. Auschwitz, then still active, was in fact not far from the New Year's Eve party at Goszyce.

9. Franaszek, *Miłosz: A Biography*, 251. Later in the same year, when Milosz was leaving Poland to be a diplomat in Washington, he asked "Turowicz, the only person he could trust not to censor any of his poems, to oversee the . . . editing and correction" of *Ocalenie* (Franaszek, *Miłosz: A Biography*, 249). Three decades later, Turowicz and the Catholic journal he founded, *Tygodnik Powszechny*, would also play a crucial role in forging the postwar church-labor-intellectual alliance that produced

Solidarity (Timothy Garton Ash, *Solidarity: The Polish Revolution* [New Haven, CT: Yale University Press, 2002], 22, 177, 374). In the 1960s Cardinal Wyszynski, the senior prelate of Poland, smuggled tapes of Milosz reading his poems into Poland for Turowicz to distribute (Franaszek, *Miłosz: A Biography*, 417–18). Meanwhile Milosz wrote to Turowicz that "the task of *Tygodnik Powszechny* should be to prevent the 'quite primitive Voltairean tendencies of the Polish intelligentsia'" (Franaszek, *Miłosz: A Biography*, 386).

10. Czeslaw Milosz, "Nobel Lecture," Stockholm, December 8, 1980, in Czeslaw Milosz, *Beginning with My Streets: Essays and Recollections* (New York: Farrar, Straus and Giroux, 1991), 281; http://www.nobelprize.org/nobel_prizes/literature/laureates/1980/milosz-lecture.html.

11. "It even amazes me that that acute consciousness of the end was registered so inadequately by me and by others" (YH, 238).

12. Franaszek, *Miłosz: A Biography*, 233.

13. Franaszek, *Miłosz: A Biography*, 233.

14. Cf. Genesis 3:24: "So he drove out the man; and he placed at the east of the garden of Eden Cherubims, and a flaming sword which turned every way, to keep the way of the tree of life"; Matthew 8:22: "Let the dead bury their dead." The syntax of the original—"A miecz płomieni otwierał nam ziemię"—is, "'Let us go'—and a sword of flames opened the earth for us."

15. That the tribe he and Janka are fated to beget is "new and violent" may suggest a hint of guilt in their expulsion from Eden. Cf. my remarks in chapter 3 about Milosz's expulsion from what he called the "lost paradise" (YH, 84) of Szetejnie.

16. Blake, "The Marriage of Heaven and Hell," in *Poetry and Prose of William Blake*, ed. Geoffrey Keynes (London: Nonesuch Press, 1927), 197. See below.

17. George Gömöri, "'Truth' and 'Beauty' in Miłosz's Poetry," *World Literature Today*, Summer, 1978, 414. Cf. Franaszek, *Miłosz: A Biography*, 221, where the poem is given its earlier title, "Farewell." There is also a difference: at Troy, Aeneas is separated forever from his wife Creusa (Aeneid 2.740), while Milosz and Janka are escaping together. Erotic love is a more creative force in *Ocalenie* than in the Aeneid.

18. Aleksander Fiut, *The Eternal Moment: The Poetry of Czeslaw Milosz* (Berkeley: University of California Press, 1987), 66. As a Pole, he overlooks the obvious echo of Milton.

19. Milton, *Paradise Lost* 12:645–46.

20. The nineteen lines which at this time Milosz translated from the end of *Paradise Lost* follow at pp. 17–18.

21. Blake, "The Marriage of Heaven and Hell," in *Poetry and Prose of William Blake*, ed. Geoffrey Keynes (London: Nonesuch Press, 1927), 197. Milosz began to read "a few of Blake's poems" in wartime Warsaw (LU, 31), but there were already signs of a Blakean take on history, which Milosz was exposed to in the works of his cousin Oscar, in his earlier catastrophist poems like "Slow River."

22. Eric Pyle, *William Blake's Illustrations for Dante's Divine Comedy: A Study of the Engravings, Pencil Sketches and Watercolors* (Jefferson, NC: McFarland & Company, 2014), 236.

23. WP, 33: "Oscar Milosz did not know Blake, and the affinities between them may be explained by their common indebtedness to Swedenborg." Cf. LU, 136.

24. This sense of liberating possibility in disaster, of beginning anew, probably explains why Milosz in 1945 chose "Flight," immediately after "Przedmowa," to introduce his book *Ocalenie*.

25. Though the exalted tone of "Flight" is startlingly new, it is not wholly unanticipated: We saw a premonition of it earlier, first in "Hymn" ("I have no wisdom, no skills, and no faith / but I received strength, it tears the world apart"); and again in the "Envoy" to the early wartime poem "A Day of Generation" ("It is your destiny so to move your wand, / To wake up storms, to run through the heart of storms, / To lay bare a monument like a nest in a thicket, / Though all you wanted was to pluck a few roses," NCP, 32).

26. Ewa Czarnecka and Aleksander Fiut, *Conversations with Czeslaw Milosz* (San Diego: Harcourt Brace Jovanovich, 1987), 137.

27. Andrzej Franaszek, *Miłosz: Biografia* (Kraków: Znak, 2011), 380.

28. *William Wordsworth*, ed. Seamus Heaney (London: Faber & Faber, 2011), 15–16; discussed in Peter Dale Scott with Freeman Ng, *Poetry and Terror: Politics and Poetics in* Coming to Jakarta (Lanham, MD: Lexington Books, 2018), 182.

29. R. L. Brett and A. R. Jones, eds., *Lyrical Ballads: Wordsworth and Coleridge; the text of the 1798 edition with the additional 1800 poems and the prefaces*. (New York: Barnes & Noble, 2013), 287. In 1848 the Duke of Argyle heard from Wordsworth that in fact he had taken "four days to compose it, the last 20 lines or so being composed as he walked down the hill from Clifton to Bristol" (Ernest de Selincourt, ed., *Poetical Works of William Wordsworth* [Oxford: Clarendon Press, 1954] vol. 2, 517).

30. Valerie Eliot, "Introduction," in T. S. Eliot, *The Waste Land: A Facsimile and Transcript of the Original Drafts Including the Annotations of Ezra Pound* (New York: Harcourt Brace, 1971), xxi. When applying for leave from the bank, Eliot wrote as his reason, "nervous breakdown."

31. See also my chapter, "Trauma, Poetry, Politics, and the Mystery of Hope," in Peter Dale Scott with Freeman Ng, *Poetry and Terror*, 179–87.

32. Three more were later consolidated by Milosz into one and translated as "A Frivolous Conversation" (NCP, 169), Here too the poem's close magnificently transcends the catastrophic context in which it was written, though in a more personal, less bardic way:
—The earth, the sky, and the sea, richly cargoed ships,
Spring morning full of dew and faraway princedoms.
At marvels displayed in tranquil glory
I look and do not desire for I am content.
(NCP, 169)
In addition, at least three more poems were written at this time but published later: "Przyrodzie—Pogróżka" ("Nature: A Threat"; Goszyce, 1944; W, 1: 244, untranslated), "Mid-Twentieth-Century Portrait," Kraków, 1945 (NCP, 88), and "A Nation," Kraków, 1945 (NCP, 89). Milosz "composed many poems during his time

[in Goszyce], and a sole copy of a booklet comprising ten handwritten poems was produced and presented to Jerzy" [Turowicz, his host] (Franaszek, *Miłosz; A Biography*, 221).

33. One can ask if Milosz in his title was also perhaps thinking of Blake's Los, the prophet who, "because he is conscious of the fall of Eden . . . can guide mankind to it" (David V. Erdmann, Blake, *Prophet Against Empire: A Poet's Interpretation of the History of His Own Times* [Princeton, NJ: Princeton University Press, 1977], 253).

34. Czeslaw Milosz in Czarnecka and Fiut, *Conversations with Czeslaw Milosz*, 139. Cf. 140: "The poem you're asking about is a joyful one—a turning away from the past, an affirmation of life masked as a stylistic exercise, as was done during the Baroque."

35. Milosz, in Czarnecka and Fiut, *Conversations with Czeslaw Milosz*, 137–38.

36. For example, it was claimed that "in the city of Olsztyn in March 1945, practically no woman survived without being violated by the Soviet rapists 'irrespective of their age.' Their ages were estimated to range from 9 to 80." (Joanna Ostrowska and Marcin Zaremba, "*Kobieca gehenna*," *Polityk*a, October 16, 2013); Cf. Anthony Beevor, "'They raped every German female from eight to 80,'" *The Guardian*, May 1, 2002, https://www.theguardian.com/books/2002/may/01/news.features11. (The title quote is from a Soviet female observer, a friend of Sakharov.) Cf. also note 17.

37. In "Przedmowa," one of Milosz's greatest poems, I have to regret the unnecessary last line of the stanza
What is poetry which does not save
Nations or people? . . .
Readings for sophomore girls.
(NCP, 77)
Might not the third line ("Czytanką z panieńskiego pokoju") in fact be stronger, if "translated" as "Readings for sophomores"? (With the stress now on "readings," rather than "girls.")
I have the same reaction to Milosz's final words about the "Complaint" to Gorczyńska: "There's even a certain sense of resignation here: tough luck, bid the ladies farewell, there's nothing you can do about it" (Czarnecka and Fiut, *Conversations with Czeslaw Milosz*, 138). See also chapter 14.

38. Czarnecka and Fiut, *Conversations with Czeslaw Milosz*, 137–38.

CHAPTER 8

1. Their order of composition is "Farewell," "In Warsaw," and "Przedmowa." This is also their order in "Rescue." In *Ocalenie*, as mentioned, "Przedmowa" introduces the book, along with "Flight." *Ocalenie* also contains a brief undated fourth poem, titled simply "* * *." It is similar to "Farewell" in its admixture of despair and equanimity:
They fell into the darkness of contempt
where wormwood and hemlock are growing. . . .
The messenger prefers the unrighteous. . . .

And the trial of violence is over,
The most terrible of all trials.
(W 1:226).

2. Ewa Czarnecka and Aleksander Fiut, *Conversations with Czeslaw Milosz* (San Diego: Harcourt Brace Jovanovich, 1987), 138. In 1944 to 1946, over a million Poles were displaced from their birthplace in Lithuania, Belarus, and Ukraine. There was also a compensating reverse migration of Ukrainians and others out of Poland eastward. About twelve million *Volksdeutsch* Germans were also displaced, along with most surviving Jews. Social services were almost nonexistent at the time, and many died. But Milosz does not mention rape, even though "In Kraków, Soviet entry into the city was accompanied by the wave of rapes of women and girls, . . . this behavior reached such a scale that the Polish communists installed in the city by the Soviet Union, composed a letter of protest to Joseph Stalin himself. At the Kraków Main station, Poles who tried to rescue the victims of gang rape were shot at" ("Rape during the liberation of Poland (1944–1947)," citing Rita Pagacz-Moczarska "Okupowany Kraków—z prorektorem Andrzejem Chwalbą rozmawia Rita Pagacz-Moczarska" [Prof. Andrzej Chwalba talks about the Soviet-occupied Kraków]. *Alma Mater*, no. 4. Jagiellonian University, (2004).

3. In "A Poor Christian," for example, the speaker talks of "Waiting two thousand years for the second coming of Jesus"; but he expects only to be counted "among the helpers of death."

4. Warsaw is said to have been 96 percent destroyed by the Nazis, in revenge for the 1944 Uprising. The Party seriously considered, but rejected, a proposal to simply rebuild a new city elsewhere. Much of Warsaw was still not rebuilt when I was there from 1959 to 1961.

5. "That is not it" [To nie to], exclaims the speaker, echoing Prufrock's "That is not it, at all." The echo of Eliot is strengthened a few lines later: "children's laughter in the garden." Cf. *East Coker*, "The laughter in the garden"; *Burnt Norton*: "Go, said the bird, for the leaves were full of children, / Hidden excitedly, containing laughter."

6. The Polish word *ziarno* (grain or seed) will play an important metaphorical role, as a kernel of the future, in Milosz's major poems "A Treatise on Morals" (1947) and "A Treatise on Poetry" (1957). See chapters 9 and 12.

7. This last two lines—"tylko trud / nie więcej" [only toil, nothing more] echo in Polish, perhaps accidentally, a bitter joke I heard very frequently in Warsaw:"In Moscow, there used to be two newspapers, *Prawda* [Truth] and *Trud* [Labor]. Now there is only *Trud* [tylko Trud]."

8. Czarnecka and Fiut, *Conversations with Czeslaw Milosz*, 139.

9. I am not alone in my esteem for "In Warsaw." It was the only poem from *Ocalenie* selected by Edward Balcerzan for his important textbook *Poezja polska w latach 1939–1968* (Warsaw: Wydawnictwa Szkolne i Pedagogiczne, 1998, 265–66.

10. Czarnecka and Fiut, *Conversations with Czeslaw Milosz*, 137. Cf. "An image arises. . . . And then you have to work and be stubborn. . . . The daimonion and hard work go hand in hand" (133).

11. Franaszek, *Miłosz: A Biography*, 233.

12. Milosz, in Cynthia L. Haven (ed.), *Czesław Miłosz: Conversations* (Jackson, MS: University Press of Mississippi, 2006), 18.

13. Czarnecka and Fiut, *Conversations with Czeslaw Milosz*, 137.

14. As noted before, I have restored here the literal translation, "This is, and only this is, salvation" [To jest, i tylko to jest, Ocalenie], in place of Milosz's more moderate and subjective "In this and only this I find salvation."

15. See chapter 2. The Warsaw Uprising was the work of the Home Army [Armija Krajowa, or AK], directed by the right-wing Polish government-in-exile in London. Milosz in contrast was a member of Organizacja Socjalistyczno-Niepodległościowa "Wolność" [The "Freedom" Socialist Pro-Independence Organisation]. In his activity with "Wolność," Milosz helped protect Jews, for which he, like his brother Andrzej, later received the medal of the Righteous Among the Nations in Yad Vashem,

16. Milosz, LU, 147; HPL, 447. In both passages, Milosz associates this twofold legacy with the influence in particular of Juliusz Słowacki: "Today I am of the opinion that Słowacki has nothing to offer the religiously minded person, that he has inflicted great harm . . . under Słowacki's pen and those of other Messianists, the language turns flaccid, mushy" (LU, 147). Yet late in life Milosz quoted Słowacki when defining himself: "I am a promethean romantic who has been inoculated with his special vocation, who attempts to 'remake bread-eaters into angels'" (YH, 119).

17. Czarnecka and Fiut, *Conversations with Czeslaw Milosz*, 128.

18. Milosz, HPL, 445–47. Self-sacrificial revolt was celebrated by all three of the nineteenth-century romantic bards: Krasiński, Mickiewicz, and Słowacki. *Przedmowa* was composed after Milosz had had a serious argument at Goszyce with a partisan, Jan Josef Szczepański, in which he "explained with great conviction that he had no intention of fighting, because it was essential for him to survive the war: his duty was to write, not to fight. The possible loss of his life would be of no use, but his writing was very important to the country" (Adam Boniecki, in *Czesław Miłosz in memoriam* [Kraków: Znak, 2004], 76; quoted in Franaszek, *Miłosz: A Biography*, 221.)

19. Milosz, HPL, 447. In addition, Baczyński has been seen, then and since, as preeminent among his generation of poet-martyrs in the Warsaw Uprising. His poetry shows the influence of Milosz's *Three Winters*, and Franaszek (*Miłosz: Biografia*, 807) speculates that Milosz may have attended Baczyński's wedding.

20. Mickiewicz, *Dziele*, 1:41–44; translation in Koropeckyj, *Adam Mickiewicz*, 23 (adapted). Cf. Adam Mickiewicz, "Digression," in Wacław Lednicki, *Pushkin's Bronze horseman: the story of a masterpiece* (Berkeley: University of California Press, 1955), 122.

21. Mickiewicz, "Ode to Youth," translated by Helen N. Fagin, *South Atlantic Bulletin*, November 1977, 105–6.

22. The Polish is "Szaleństwo tak żyć bez uśmiechu I dwa powtarzać wyrazy Zwrócone do was, umarli, Do was, których udziałem Miało być wesele Czynów myśli i ciała, Pieśni, uczt. Dwa ocalone wyrazy: Prawda i sprawiedliwość" (W 1:230). A more literal translation might be:
Madness to live so without a smile
And to reiterate two words
Returned to you, the dead,

To you whose part
Should have been a wedding
Of actions of thought and flesh,
Songs, feasts.
Two saved [*ocalone*] words:
Truth and justice.

23. Adam Kirsch, "Czeslaw Milosz's Battle for Truth," *New Yorker*, May 29, 2017, https://www.newyorker.com/magazine/2017/05/29/czeslaw-miloszs-battle-for-truth: "Certainly, there is no ground for believing that truth or reason will ultimately prevail in human life."

24. Czeslaw Milosz, "Anus Mundi," in *To Begin Where I Am: Selected Essays* (New York: Farrar, Straus and Giroux, 2001), 371–72.

25. Adam Mickiewicz (trans. Krystyn Lach-Szyrma), *The Books and The Pilgrimage of the Polish Nation* (London: James Ridgway, 1833), 4:
And at last said Christ: "He that follows me, shall be saved, because I AM TRUTH AND JUSTICE." And hearing this doctrine of Christ, the judges were terror-struck; for they had judged in the name of the Emperor of Rome; and they said to each other: "We have expelled Justice from the earth, and behold, she is returned. Let us kill her, and bury her in the earth." They then crucified the holiest and most innocent of men; and after having laid his body in the tomb, they exclaimed: "Truth and Justice are no more on earth; who now will dare to rise against the Emperor of Rome?" But by thus exclaiming, they only betrayed their folly.

CHAPTER 9

1. Czeslaw Milosz, *The Captive Mind* (New York: Vintage, 1990), 67–68.

2. Czeslaw Milosz, in Ewa Czarnecka and Aleksander Fiut, *Conversations with Czeslaw Milosz* (San Diego: Harcourt Brace Jovanovich, 1987), 205. Franaszek argues (Andrzej Franaszek, *Miłosz: A Biography* [Cambridge, MA: Belknap Press/ Harvard University Press, 2017], 275) that one can recognize the figure of Milosz also in his 1945 poem "Mid-Twentieth Century Portrait": "Keeping one hand on Marx's writings, he reads the Bible in private. . . . In his hand: a memento of a boy 'fascist' killed in the Uprising" (NCP, 88).

3. The original Latin meaning of *persoaa* (*per* [through]) + *sona* [make sound]) was of course "mask."

4. Cf. Tony Judt, "Captive Minds, Then and Now," *New York Reiew of Books*, *NYR Daily*, July 13, 2010, https://www.nybooks.com/daily/2010/07/13/captive-minds-then-and-now/: "Recall the Ketman-like trance of those intellectuals swept up in George W. Bush's hysterical drive to war just a few years ago. Few of them would have admitted to admiring the President, much less sharing his worldview. So they typically aligned themselves behind him while doubtless maintaining private reservations. Later, when it was clear they had made a mistake, they blamed it upon the administration's incompetence."

5. Kazimierz Wyka, "Ogrody lunatyczne i ogrody pasterskie" [Lunatic Gardens and Pastoral Gardens], *Twórczość,* 1946; Milosz, "A Semi-Private Letter about Poetry," in *To Begin Where I Am,* 348; Franaszek, *Miłosz: A Biography,* 248.

6. Quoted in Franaszek, *Miłosz: A Biography,* 248.

7. According to Łukasz Tischner, Milosz composed *Traktat moralny,* in response to Horodyński's review (Łukasz Tischner, *Miłosz and the Problem of Evil* [Evanston, IL: Northwestern University Press, 2015], 93). See below.

8. Fransazek, *Miłosz: A Biography,* 208.

9. Milosz twice reproduces Auden's translation into English of Mickiewicz's two-page long poem, "The Romantic," which was important to him (HPL, 211–13; LU, 97–99). As I noted earlier, Auden generally made a point of translating only from languages he himself knew, yet he did not know Polish. I suspect that Milosz may have collaborated on the project with him—perhaps as early as 1947, when they were both in New York.

10. Milosz, "A Semi-Private Letter about Poetry," in *To Begin Where I Am,* 341–42.

11. Milosz, "A Semi-Private Letter about Poetry," in *To Begin Where I Am,* 345.

12. Milosz, "A Semi-Private Letter about Poetry," in *To Begin Where I Am,* 351, emphasis added; quoting from Mickiewicz, "Digression" [in "Forefather's Eve"], in Milosz, HPL, 224.

13. Both in *The Captive Mind* and in "A Treatise on Poetry," Milosz comments on the ease with which the poet Konstanty Ildefons Gałczyński transitioned from being a racist right-wing nationalist to becoming "the bard of Communist Poland" (TP, 21, 90n).

14. Milosz, "A Semi-Private Letter about Poetry," in *To Begin Where I Am,* 344–45, 351; emphasis added.

15. Milosz, "A Semi-Private Letter about Poetry," in *To Begin Where I Am,* 350–51.

16. Milosz, "A Semi-Private Letter about Poetry," in *To Begin Where I Am,* 338.

17. For example, consider that in "A Treatise on Morals," a far more Christian poem than *Ocalenie,* the only overtly Christian reference is in one couplet: "Raising children, making laws, / Man stands before the Almighty" (W 2:90; cf. Tischner, *Miłosz and the Problem of Evil,* 102).

18. W. H. Auden, *The Double Man* (New York: Random House, 1941). *The Double Man* actually consists of five parts: "Prologue" (11–12), "New Year Letter" (15–71), "Notes" (75–162), "The Quest" [a sonnet sequence] (165–84), and "Epilogue" (187–89). My discussion of *The Double Man* will be confined to the Letter and its Notes. Auden had arranged for a British edition of *The Double Man* to be published by John Lehmann at the Hogarth Press, but Eliot claimed the MS for Faber under a prior contract. Because the Hogarth Press had already advertised *The Double Man* as forthcoming, Eliot, "without asking Auden. . . . changed the book's title to *New Year Letter*. He also noticed that the words 'the double man' appeared in [the] verse prologue to the volume, so, again without asking Auden . . . he changed the phrase to 'the invisible twin'" (Humphrey Carpenter, *W. H. Auden: A Biography* [London: George Allen & Unwin, 1981], 303). This desecration by an aging Eliot of another poet's major work shows him thinking as a businessman, not as a poet.

19. Czeslaw Milosz, "Wprowadzenie w Amerikanów," *Twórczóść* 5 (1948): 19.

20. That magic lamp which looks so dull
And utterly impractical
Yet, if Aladdin use it right,
Can be a sesame to light.
(vv. 829-32)

21. Auden, *The Double Man*, 116: "The Truth is one and incapable of self-contradiction; / All knowledge that conflicts with itself is Poetic Fiction." Cf. Yeats, "We make out of the quarrel with others, rhetoric, but of the quarrel with ourselves, poetry" (*Per Amica Silentia Lunae Anima Hominis*, Part V).

22. Stan Smith, *Poetry and Displacement* (Liverpool: Liverpool University Press, 2007), 15.

23. "Introduction," in Joseph P. Natoli and Linda Hutcheon (Eds.), *A Postmodern Reader* (Albany, NY: State University of New York, 1993), xi; quoted in Peter Dale Scott with Freeman Ng, *Poetry and Terror: Politics and Poetics in* Coming to Jakarta (Lanham, MD: Lexington Books, 2018), 180. Compare this excerpt from the definition in the *Oxford English Dictionary*: "any of various styles, concepts, or points of view involving a conscious departure from modernism, esp. when characterized by a rejection of ideology and theory in favour of a plurality of values and techniques."

24. Aidan Wasley, *The Age of Auden: Postwar Poetry and the American Scene* (Princeton, NJ: Princeton University Press, 2011), 37.

25. The burning of churches and murder of priests and nuns by the Republicans left Auden "shocked and disturbed," a feeling "far too intense to be the result of a mere dislike of intolerance" (Humphrey Carpenter, *W. H. Auden: A Biography* [Boston: Houghton Mifflin, 1981], 209-10; cf. 215; citing an unpublished Auden interview for *Time* by T. G. Foote, 1963.)

26. W, H. Auden, *The Collected Poetry of W. H. Auden* (New York: Random House, 1941), 181. Cf. John Fuller, *W. H. Auden: A Commentary* (Princeton, NJ: Princeton University Press, 1998), 285.

27. Auden, *The Collected Poetry*, 57-59.

28. Edward Mendelson, *Early Auden, Later Auden: A Critical Biography* (Princeton, NJ: Princeton University Press, 2017), 450; from Charles Williams, *The Descent of the Dove: A History of the Holy Spirit in the Church* (New York: Pellegrini and Cudahy, 1939), 192; Michel Eyquem de Montaigne, "De la Gloire."

29. We have already seen that Milosz began after the forties to talk of his own "doubleness" or "double awareness."

30. "The Lame Shadow was Auden's name for the ideal figure that the wounded ego seeks in the world of the Alter Ego . . . to have learned the name from his early psychological mentor John Layard, who had apparently adapted it from Jung" (Mendelson, *Early Auden, Later Auden*, 423n). Compare the casting of the Devil as Nick Shadow in the Auden/Kallman libretto to Stravinsky's opera, "The Rake's Progress."

31. I suspect that by 1946 the two poets had already met in New York, where Milosz was soon speaking to American writers about Swift and Voltaire (Tischner, *Miłosz and the Problem of Evil*, 92). How else to explain that Auden, who spoke no Polish and was said to never translate from a language he did not speak, translated the whole of Mickiewicz's poem "The Romantic?" Or that Milosz reproduced all of the

poem, which is over two pages long, twice, first in his *History of Polish Literature* (211–13), and then in *The Land of Ulro* (97–99)?

32. In a Note, "Rousseau's falsehood of the flesh" is explained by a quotation from Blake: "Rousseau thought men good by nature: he found them evil and made no friend" (Auden, *The Double Ma*n, 139; quoting Blake, "Jerusalem," 52; William Blake, ed. Geoffrey Keynes, *Poetry and Prose of William Blake* [London: Nonesuch Press, 1948], 498).

33. In his endnotes, Auden supplemented this line with one of Pascal's *Pensées*: "*Nier, croire, et douter bien sont à l'homme ce que le courir est au cheval*" ["Denying, believing and doubting are to man what running is to a horse"]. This quote was repeated many times by Milosz, never more passionately (if inaccurately) than in a conversation with Robert Faggen; "Pascal . . . was writing against the wolf of skepticism, Montaigne. Pascal personifies a man in crisis. So for a man of crisis as I am, Pascal is a spiritual brother in a way. Pascal said that 'to believe and to doubt, and to gain this belief [*sic*] is for man what running is for a horse.' Every hour, I believe this one hundred times" (Czeslaw Milosz, in Cynthia L. Haven [ed.], *Czesław Miłosz: Conversations* [Jackson, MS: University Press of Mississippi, 2006], 179).

34. Writing under a pseudonym when a diplomat in America, Milosz expressed what I see as a concurrent view of disruption in history: "Human life is governed by the avalanche rule. The aberration of the center is slowly created, and, believe me, one day it will express itself by means of some kind of madness, incomprehensible for people from beyond and who are not subject to the central infection" (J. M. Nowak [Czeslaw Miłosz], *Życie w USA* [Living in the USA], "Odrodzenie" 1947, no. 31).

35. Tischner, *Milosz and the Problem of Evil*, 99; citing *Traktat moralny, Traktat poeticzny: Lekcja literatury z Czeslawem Miloszem, Aleksandrem Fiutem I Andrzejem Franaszkiem* (Kraków: Wydawnictwo Literackie, 1996), 15.

36. "'A Treatise on Morality' came about as a result of the direct influence of Kroński, and some passages were changed according to the latter's instructions" (Franaszek, *Biography*, 275).

37.The term is from Pascal: "Le cœur a son ordre, l'esprit a le sien qui est par principe et démonstration. Le cœur en a un autre, on ne prouve pas qu'on doit être aimé en exposant d'ordre les causes de l'amour, cela serait ridicule" (Pascal, *Preuves de Jésus-Christ* [fragment; cf. Louis Lafuma, "L'ordre de l'esprit et l'ordre du cœur," *Recherches des sciences religieuses*, XLVI, 1958, 416–20]). In the background is the medieval notion of *caritas ordinata*, first used by Augustine in *De doctrina christiana*, and derived from Jerome's translation of the Septuagint Song of Songs 2:4, "ordinavit in me caritatem."

38. Mendelson, *Early Auden, Later Auden: A Critical Biography*, 428.

39. Much of the content was mined from an earlier unfinished collection of Blake-inspired *Pensées* "called 'The Prolific and the Devourer,' taking its title from Blake's anatomization of human identity in *The Marriage of Heaven and Hell* into warring halves, the creator and the consumer" (Wasley, *The Age of Auden*, 11).

40. Jonathan Swift; (ed.) Dutton Kearney, *Gulliver's Travels: With an Introduction and Contemporary Criticism* (San Francisco: Ignatius Press, 2010), 165–244. A decade later, in Paris, Milosz could speak more directly: "Poland's economy, a

captive of ideological requirements, made one's hair stand on end. It brought to mind Gulliver's observations about the land of the Balnibarbi, administered by the enlightened Academy of Projectors, where 'the people [at the top] are too much taken up in their own speculations to have regard to what passed here below,' and where 'the people in the streets walked fast, looked wild, their eyes fixed, and were generally in rags'" (NR, 281).

41. Edith L. Blumhofer (ed.), *Religion, Education, and the American Experience: Reflections on Religion and American Public Life* (Tuscaloosa: University of Alabama Press, 2002), 67.

42. Roger Lundin, *Believing Again: Doubt and Faith in a Secular Age* (Grand Rapids, MI: W. B. Eerdmans, 2009), 59.

43. Edward Mendelson, *Early Auden, Later Auden: A Critical Biography* (Princeton, NJ: Princeton University Press, 2017), 9.

44. Mendelson, *Early Auden, Later Auden*, 5.

45. For example, Stanislaw Beres, "Milosz's Apocalypse," in Edward Mozejko (ed.), *Between Anxiety and Hope: The Poetry and Writing of Czeslaw Milosz* (Edmonton: University of Alberta Press, 1988), 41.

46. Delighted with the stylistic innovations of *The Double Man*, Milosz singled out this passage in particular for praise and translated it: "The logical construction is clear, fast rhythm, driven by the property that the English call *wit*, the French *esprit*, and we are somewhat inaccurately translating as a joke—it contributes to easy reading. No other language has ever had such a poetic achievement in recent times" (Czeslaw Milosz, "Wyprowadzenie w Amerikanów," *Kontynenty* [Kraków: Znak, 1999], 107).

47. Tischner, *Miłosz and the Problem of Evil*, 92. Cf. Milosz, NR, 267: [For Tiger] "Romanticism was Enemy Number One. . . . Thus Heraclitus's maxim 'A dry flame is the best and wisest soul' seemed to contain the future of the earth." Cf. Heraclitus, frag. 118 D-K: "The dry soul is wisest and best."

48. Czeslaw Milosz, in *Traktat moralny, Traktat poetyczny: Lekcja literatury z Czeslawem Miloszem, Aleksandrem Fiutem I Andrzejem Franaszkiem*, 16–17; quoted in Tischner, *Miłosz and the Problem of Evil*, 94.

49. Cf. Genesis 8:11: "And the dove came in to him in the evening; and, lo, in her mouth was an olive leaf pluckt off."

50. Tischner, *Miłosz and the Problem of Evil*, 98.

51. Cf. vv. 1704–7: "'Our life and death are with our neighbor' adapts Saint Athanasius's 'Your life and death are with your neighbor,' . . . which [Auden's source, the Christian author Charles] Williams also quotes in *The Descent of the Dove*" (Arthur Kirsch, *Auden and Christianity* [New Haven, CT: Yale University Press, 2005], 36). Auden was free to quote liberally from the Church Fathers; Milosz, facing Communist censorship, could not.

52. Franaszek tells us that a *nagan* was a revolver used by the NKVD (Franaszek, *Miłosz: A Biography*, 275).

53. Franaszek, *Miłosz: A Biography*, 274.

54. Czeslaw Milosz, Letter to Tadeusz and Zofia Breza; in Czeslaw Milosz, *Zaraz po wojnie: Korespondencja z pisarzami 1945–1950* (Kraków: Znak, 2007), 169.

55. E.g., "The images preserved by a cultural elite undoubtedly also have political significance as they influence the decisions of the groups that govern, and it is no wonder that the statesmen who signed the Yalta agreement so easily wrote off a hundred million Europeans from these blank areas in the loss column" (WP, 7; cf. 83: "Poland . . . a country betrayed by its allies").

56. Milosz could be similarly outrageous, as when he referred to French existentialists as "Pośmiertna czkawka Heidelbergu" [The posthumous hiccups of Heidelberg, i.e. Heidegger,] (W 2:90).

57. Czeslaw Milosz, in Haven (ed.), *Czesław Miłosz: Conversations*, 15.

58. Adam Zagajewski, "The Poet at Ninety," *Los Angeles Times*, July 1, 2001, http://articles.latimes.com/2001/jul/01/books/bk-17554/2.

59. This assessment in terms of cultural development is quite independent of an assessment of the poetic value of the three poems. I have written elsewhere that certain ninth-century Anglo-Latin poems represented a cultural development beyond Vitgil's Eclogues, without suggesting that they were in any way *poetically* superior.

60. Czeslaw Milosz, "The Importance of Simone Weil" (1960), in Milosz, *To Begin Where I Am*, 247–48.

61. Milosz, "A Semi-Private Letter about Poetry," in *To Begin Where I Am*, 350–51.

62. Czeslaw Milosz, "Letter to Jerzy Andrzejewski," in *Legends of Modernity* (New York: Farrar, Straus and Giroux, 2005), 205. As we have seen, Milosz admired Pascal, and this remark echoes Pascal's "le cœur a ses raisons que la raison ne connaît point" [the heart has its reasons, which reason knows nothing about].

63. Cf. Henri Bremond. *La poésie pure: avec Un débat sur la poésie, par Robert de Souza* (Paris: B. Grasset, 1926).

64. Oscar Milosz, "A Few Words on Poetry," quoted in WP, 28.

65. Bogdana Carpenter, *The Poetic Avant-Garde in Poland, 1918–1939* (Seattle: University of Washington Press, 1983), 197.

66. Czesław Miłosz, "Kłamtswo Dzisiejszej o Poezji," *Orka na Ugorze*, 5, 1938; in Carpenter, *The Poetic Avant-Garde*, 197–98.

67. Czeslaw Milosz, "The Boundaries of Art," in *Legends of Modernity*, 130–31; emphasis added.

68. Czeslaw Milosz, "The Boundaries of Art," in *Legends of Modernity*, 133–35; emphasis added.

69. Milosz, in Czarnecka and Fiut, *Conversations*, 190, emphasis added. Cf. 191; "Because, as I say here, out of love for contemplation in poetry, I turned against contemplation in poetry, and toward the immediate, time, fluidity." Cf. chapter 12.

70. Milosz, "A Semi-Private Letter about Poetry," in *To Begin Where I Am*, 341.

CHAPTER 10

1. Witold Gombrowicz, "Introduction" to *The Marriage Ceremony*.
2. Czeslaw Milosz, *The Captive Mind* (New York: Vintage, 1990), xii.
3. Andrzej Franaszek, *Miłosz: A Biography* (Cambridge, MA: Harvard University Press, 2017), 265, 268.

4. Franaszek, *Miłosz: A Biography*, 266.

5. Milosz had approached Einstein earlier on another matter, which had illuminated the issues at stake. "When Milosz first contacted Einstein back in 1948, he invited the physicist through strictly official channels to take part in the World Congress of Intellectuals in Poland. Einstein . . . agreed to write an address. . . . The Russians did not allow the delegates to hear Einstein's address, in which he appealed for international control of access to atomic energy" (Franaszek, *Miłosz: A Biography*, 271).

6. Cf. TP, 124n: "The last passage of the poem describes travel by ship to Europe in 1950. For the author, this was a very difficult option, slightly insane from a practical point of view, but not without a hidden existential logic."

7. In 1987, Milosz recalled: "Janka was terrified of the Russians. This was rooted in her childhood experiences during World War I; she had a recurring dream from that period and it was the background against which she experienced January 1945 in Goszyce. For her, America was not first and foremost a land of well-being and wealth; rather, it signified security and a homeland for the children" (YH, 120; cf. 239).

8. Franaszek, *Miłosz: A Biography*, 255.

9. Letter from Janina Milosz to Secretary of State, February 9, 1951; in Cynthia Haven (Ed.), *Czesław Miłosz: A California Life* (Berkeley: Heyday, 2021), 53; from Milosz's FBI file.

10. Letter of January 15, 1951, from Czeslaw to Janka, intercepted and translated in US intelligence files; Haven, *Czesław Miłosz: A California Life*, 49–50.

11. Franaszek, *Miłosz: A Biography*, 283 (undated Milosz letter); 280 (article by Natalia Modzelewska).

12. Eric Karpeles, *Almost Nothing: The 20th-Century Art and Life of Józef Czapski* (New York: New York Review Books, 2018), 287. Milosz himself confirms his great uncertainty in his "trials" at that time (NR, 285–86), as does Franaszek (*Miłosz: A Biography*, 282).

13. Franaszek, *Miłosz: A Biography*, 280–81.

14. *Striving Towards Being: The Letters of Thomas Merton and Czesław Miłosz*, ed. Robert Faggen, (New York: Farrar, Straus and Giroux, 1997), 48–49.

15. Zygmunt Modzelewski's adopted son Karol would eventually become one of the founders of Solidarność, and the man who gave the movement its name.

16. After asking his monitor for some tea from the kitchen, Milosz slipped out quickly through the back door. A friend, Aniela Micińska, was waiting in a taxi. Fearing for his life, he remained in hiding for six months.

17. Cf, YH, 227: "I met with [Micińska] immediately afterward [after returning to Paris from Poland] in an obscure cafe." According to Franaszek (281), Micińska was by prearrangement waiting for him outside the embassy in a taxi.

18. Franaszek, *Miłosz: A Biography*, 294."

19. Karpeles, *Almost Nothing*, 272.

20. Cf. Hugh Wilford, *The Mighty Wurlitzer: How the CIA Played America* (Cambridge, MA: Harvard University Press, 2008), 74–75: "Burnham was OPC's main point of contact with the group of Polish exiles gathered around the Paris-based journal *Kultura*, including the charismatic Joseph Chapski [*sic*, i.e., Czapski], with whom he developed a proposal for a refugee institute that would eventually become

the . . . Free Europe University in Strasbourg. He also intervened on behalf of Czeslaw Milosz with the American immigration authorities, liaising with the exile relief organization the International Rescue Committee to expedite the Polish writer's visa application (but only after having interviewed Milosz personally to satisfy himself that rumors he was a Soviet agent were baseless)."

21. FBI Serial 100–358076–1. The file included a 1948 letter from the Office of Naval Intelligence, with the claim of a woman that Milosz was a "rabid Communist." I am grateful to Cynthia Haven for giving me access to her redacted copy of Milosz's FBI file, which she obtained under the Freedom of Information Act.

22. Karpeles, *Almost Nothing*, 273.

23. Franaszek, *Miłosz: Biografia*, 480; cf. Franaszek, *Miłosz: A Biography*, 298: "The evidence for this is an extensive correspondence between Giedroyc, Czapski and Burnham, kept in the Archives of the Literary Institute in Paris, where Milosz is referred to as 'M.'"

24. Franaszek, *Miłosz: Biografia*, 447.

25. Cynthia Haven, *Czesław Miłosz: A California Life* (Berkeley: Heyday, 2021), 48; Confidential Memorandum from FBI Washington Field Office to FBI Director J. Edgar Hoover, September 21, 1950; under 100–358076–4. The opinion of Milosz's colleagues was that he would "rather remain in the United States and ask for political asylum."

26. Franaszek, *Miłosz: A Biography*, 285–87.

27. Giles Scott-Smith, "The Congress for Cultural Freedom, the End of Ideology and the 1955 Milan Conference: 'Defining the Parameters of Discourse,'" *Journal of Contemporary History*. (July, 2002), 238. Cf. Saunders, *Cultural Cold War*, 363: "When news reached [CIA officer and Congress organizer Michael] Josselson in 1956 that the Communists planned 'to make a big push' at the PEN conference in Japan the next year, he easily persuaded [PEN Secretary David] Carver that the Congress's 'top battery' (listed as 'Silone, Koestler, Spender, Milosz etc.') should be brought out in opposition." Once again, Milosz's later talk of "my only casual relations with the Congress" should be taken as a cover story (ABC, 88). Cf. Eric Thomas Chester, *Covert Network: Progressives, the International Rescue Committee, and the CIA* (Armonk, NY: M. E. Sharpe, 1995). 71: "From the time of his defection, Milosz was aided by the CIA-funded Congress for Cultural Freedom."

28. Joanna Mazurska, "Making Sense of Czeslaw Milosz: A Poet's Formative Dialogue with His Transnational Audiences," PhD Dissertation, Vanderbilt University. August, 2013, 104.

29. Introductory statement in *Kultura* (May, 1951), in Franaszek, *Miłosz: A Biography* 287.

30. Michael Warner, "Origins of the Congress of [*sic*, i.e., 'for'] Cultural Freedom," *Studies in Intelligence* 38, no. 5 (Summer 1995), https://www.cia.gov/library/center-for-the-study-of-intelligence/csi-publications/csi-studies/studies/95unclass/Warner.html. Indeed, Frances Stonor Saunders cites the "Nie" press conference as a CIA/CCF coup: "[CCF Secretary-General Nicolas] Nabokov threw himself into his new career as impresario of the cultural Cold War. In May, the Congress 'presented' a prize intellectual defector at a press conference in Paris. He was . . . Czeslaw Milosz.

... Brilliantly stage-managed by Nabokov, Milosz's appearance on the side of the angels was an early coup for the Congress" (Saunders, *The Cultural Cold War*, 100). But the event was one of intellectual importance, not a mere political *coup de théâtre*.

31. Franaszek, *Miłosz: A Biography*, 306.

32. Mazurska, "Making Sense of Czeslaw Milosz," 104; citing Archive of the Congress for Cultural Freedom, Special Collections, Regenstein Library, University of Chicago. International Association for Cultural Freedom, series II, box 187, f.3. In another footnote (104n226), she notes that "The CCF periodicals mentioned above, in which Milosz published upon his exile included: *Preuves, Encounter, Tempo Presente, Der Monat, Cuadernos,* and *The Twentieth Century*." As late as 1960, Milosz published a CIA-funded selection of essays on the 1956 Hungarian uprising (Czesław Miłosz, with Pierre Kende, Sándor Fekete, *Węgry [Hungary]* [Paris: Instytut Literacki, 1960]; cf. Franaszek, *Miłosz: A Biography*), 332.

33. Franaszek, *Miłosz: A Biography*, 298. From declassified CIA documents we learn that their "foundation type proprietary" QKOPERA (the Congress for Cultural Freedom) "supported individuals [as well as] international organizations involved with cultural matters":

QKOPERA/DTGODOWN "This foundation type proprietary supported individuals and international organizations involved with cultural matters. To give the entity substance and provide funds for day-to-day administration, the Agency started the organization with a substantial grant [$50,000, more like $1 million today] which was invested in income producing securities (Miscellaneous Records of the Church Committee, US National Archive, RIF #157 10014 10144, 92–93).

34. Franaszek, *Miłosz: A Biography*, 326: "At times Janka felt uneasy going to the local shop, where they were given credit, because the debt they had amassed was getting out of hand."

35. RFE did however "broadcast excerpts from Milosz's writings on Communism" (Chester, *Covert Network*, 72). And in April 1952 Janka told the FBI that "the State Department ... has been using for some time Mr. Milosz's writings on the Voice of America Program, yet would not grant him entry into this country" (FBI Washington Field Office Memo to DIR FBI, April 1, 1952, 100–358076–28).

In the same period, Milosz received some support from wealthy, government-connected American friends, Mac [and Sheba] Goodman and Joseph [and Muriel] Buttinger (Franaszek, *Miłosz: A Biography*, 327, 328–29). Franaszek writes that Milosz met the Buttingers through a mutual friend who was a Czech refugee (328), but this is almost certainly wrong. Sheba Goodman and Joseph Buttinger together ran the Paris office of the International Rescue Committee, which at this time was working along with one part of the CIA to get Milosz to America. In 1956 Buttinger and the IRC tried again to get a US visa for Milosz; and failed, despite getting written assurance from Allen Dulles that, "once given the appropriate information, 'he would do everything he could to help'" (Chester, *Covert Network*, 72).

36. Franaszek, *Miłosz: A Biography*, 294–95.

37. Originally founded by socialists in the 1930s, the International Rescue Committee by the 1950s "had been absorbed into the American foreign policy establishment [and became] deeply involved in ... an array of sensitive clandestine operations.

The IRC thus evolved from a small organization of committed activists to a global operation functioning as one link in the CIA's covert network" (Book description, Chester, *Covert Network* [London: Routledge, 1995], https://www.routledge.com/Covert-Network-Pro[ressives-the-International-Rescue-Committee-and-the/Chester/p/book/9781563245510).

In this period, Milosz "spent time sitting in the Paris branch of the International Rescue Committee . . . and became a frequent guest" of Sheba Goodman, an IRC employee, and her husband Mac, an Embassy employee (Franaszek, *Miłosz: A Biography*, 327; cf. YH, 242–44).

38. "According to one internal Office of Policy Coordination memorandum, Polish social democrats were among those calling for their compatriot, the famous anti-Stalinist writer Czeslaw Milosz, to be denied a visa to enter the United States because they objected to his continuing to call Poland's economy 'socialist'—they interpreted this as a slander on socialism" (Hugh Wilford, *The Mighty Wurlitzer* [Harvard University Press, 2008], 37).

39. Franaszek, *Miłosz: A Biography*, 298–300. Milosz clarifies that "a certain woman of Russian descent" in the US Paris Embassy relied on the opinions of a pre-war Polish intelligence chief ["blindly devoted to Piłsudski"], who "was absolutely convinced that I was an exceptionally dangerous agent who . . . was actually working for my eastern handlers" (YH, 243).

40. "Sooner or later I will have to end my life" (letter to Stanislaw Vincenz, 1952; quoted in Franaszek, *Miłosz: A Biography*, 301). Cf. earlier letters to Vincenz, at Franaszek, *Miłosz: A Biography*, 296 ("How can one get rid of this feeling that one is a traitor and a swine?"); 310 ("By thinking I become unwell, nauseous, and physically drained. . . . I can't do anything").

41. Franaszek, *Miłosz: A Biography*, 301–2. Milosz's life of indigence was occasionally punctuated by moments of high living. Stephen Spender's journal for April 11, 1960, records, "Arrived in Paris for lunch with [Belgian Baroness] Hansi [Lambert], [Czeslaw] Milosz, [Constantin] Jelenski and Mme. Philippe de Rothschild" (Stephen Spender, *New Selected Journals, 1939–1995* [London: Faber & Faber, 2012], 283).

42. Franaszek, *Biography*, 313–15.

43. Milosz letter to Stanisław Vincenz, probably 1954, Franaszek, *Biography*, 313.

44. "To Albert Einstein" (1948), partially translated in YH, 122.

45. Cf. NR, 293: "The classic result of all sudden ruptures and reversals is the rumination on one's own worthlessness and the desire to punish oneself, known as *delectatio morose*. I would never have been cured of it had it not been for the beauty if the earth. The clear autumn mornings in an Alsatian village surrounded by vineyards . . . or the sharp light of early spring on the Lake of the Four Cantons near Schiller's rock . . . —all this reconciled me with the universe and with myself."

46. Giles Scott-Smith, *The Politics of Apolitical Culture: The Congress for Cultural Freedom, the CIA, and Post-war American Hegemony* (London: Routledge, 2002), 86.

47. As late as 1955, Milosz, given funds to attend a CCF conference in Milan, "cashed in his first-class ticket and [took] a coach down from Paris, sitting up all

night" (Frances Kiernan, *Seeing Mary Plain: A Life of Mary McCarthy* [New York: W.W. Norton & Company, 2000], 396).

48. "There were moments when I envied Lowell. I would say: 'Ah, he is clever; he has a breakdown, and they take him to a sanatorium where he can write peacefully; while when I go through a crisis I have to function normally'" (Czeslaw Milosz, in Cynthia L. Haven [ed.], *Czesław Miłosz: Conversations* [Jackson, MS: University Press of Mississippi, 2006], 82). Later, Milosz repented, and wrote in his poem "To Robert Lowell": "I had no right to talk of you that way, / Robert. An émigré's envy/ must have prompted me to mock / Your long depressions, weeks of terror, / Presumed vacations in the safety of the wards" (NCP, 722).

49. Two further sections of Milosz's important poem have never been translated (W 2:296–97).

50. Spender was embarrassed and widely discredited after his years of CIA collaboration were exposed in 1967 (Frances Stonor Saunders, *The Cultural Cold War* [New York: New Press. 1999], 382–90).

51. This distinction in "The World" was experiential; here it, following Brzozowaki, is ontological. Milosz seems unaware of the seminal work *Process and Reality* by Alfred North Whitehead, where the cosmos is analyzed as composed, not of material *substance* (as in Newton), but (like history) of *events*.

52. The discussions with Kroński during Milosz's 1949 Paris visit were "heated . . . invariably voices were raised" (Franaszek, *Miłosz: A Biography*, 268).

53. Czeslaw Milosz, "Letter to Pawel Hertz"; in Czeslaw Milosz, *Zaraz po wojnie: Korespondencja z pisarzami 1945–1950* (Kraków: Znak, 2007), 497.

54. Cf. Psalm 137:1: "By the waters of Babylon we sat and wept when we remembered Zion"; Eliot. *The Waste Land*, v. 182: "By the waters of Leman I sat down and wept."; Randy Malamud, "Frankenstein's Monster: The Gothic Voice in *The Waste Land*," *English Language Notes* (1988), 41: "It was by the waters of Lake Leman (Lake Geneva), at Lausanne, that Eliot composed and organized most of his poem. He spent two months in Switzerland recovering from nervous collapse, under the care of the nerve specialist Dr. Roger Vittoz. Eliot's treatment under Vittoz was the catalyst, as he might have said himself, for the organization and ordering necessary to create *The Waste Land*."

55. This version follows, with my modifications, the translations by Theodosia S. Robertson, assisted by Milosz (Aleksander Fiut, *The Eternal Moment* [Berkeley: University of California Press, 1987], iii; and by Clive Wilmer, *New and Selected Poems* (Manchester: Carcanet, 2012), 426–27.

56. Franaszek, *Miłosz: A Biography*, 324.

57. Randy Malamud, "Frankenstein's Monster: The Gothic Voice in *The Waste Land*," *English Language Notes* (1988), 41.

58. Milosz, in Ewa Czarnecka and Aleksander Fiut, *Conversations with Czeslaw Milosz* (San Diego: Harcourt Brace Jovanovich, 1987), 181.

59. Although published in 1957, the *Treatise on Poetry* is dated 1956, and (as we shall see) was completed before the Polish uprising of that year.

60. Czeslaw Milosz, "The Boundaries of Art," in *Legends of Modernity*, 130–31; emphasis added. Cf. Postscript to chapter 9.

61. Fiut, *The Eternal Moment*, 4.
62. Cf. Milosz's comment on his line in the Treatise, "For contemplation fades without resistance" (TP, 59): "This line is . . . a polemic with the T. S. Eliot of *The Four Quartets*. By renouncing the world for the sake of the 'still point" of perfect stillness outside time, we may deprive contemplation of its intensity" (TP, 123).
63. Czeslaw Milosz, "A One-Man Army: Stanisław Brzozowski," in Czeslaw Milosz, *Emperor of the Earth: Modes of Eccentric Vision* (Berkeley: University of California Press, 1977), 228.

CHAPTER 11

1. *A Treatise on Poetry* [*Traktat poetyczny*] is a poem of 123 pages in its American edition, in which, as in Auden's *The Double Man*, the extensive prose notes, added decades later in Milosz's case, are longer than the poetic text. There are occasional divergences between the Polish original and English translation of both the text and the notes. What follows is an analysis drawing on all four of these sources, as well as on Milosz's helpful comments in his conversations with Renata Gorczyńska (Czeslaw Milosz, in Ewa Czarnecka and Aleksander Fiut, *Conversations with Czeslaw Milosz* [San Diego: Harcourt Brace Jovanovich, 1987], 173–92).
2. Milosz, in Czarnecka and Fiut, *Conversations with Czeslaw Milosz*, 187.
3. Helen Vendler, "A Lament in Three Voices," *New York Review of Books*, May 21, 2001, https://www.nybooks.com/articles/2001/05/31/a-lament-in-three-voices/.
4. Karl Marx, *Capital: A Critique of Political Economy* (ed.), Frederick Engels (New York: Modern Library, no date, first published 1906), 25: "With [Hegel] it is standing on its head. It must be turned right side up again, if you would discover the rational kernel within the mystical shell."
5. The word which Milosz translated as "tenderness" in "Bobo's Metamorphosis," is "tkliwość," not "czułość." But the underlying antithesis of tenderness to Marxist necessity is the same in both poems.
6. Cf. Czeslaw Milosz, "A One-Man Army: Stanisław Brzozowski," in Czeslaw Milosz, *Emperor of the Earth: Modes of Eccentric Vision* (Berkeley: University of California Press, 1977), 207, 225.
7. Milosz, in Czarnecka and Fiut, *Conversations with Czeslaw Milosz*, 182. Cf. Milosz's discussion of Cyprian Norwid's "sensitivity to history as a system to be deciphered," whose "writing is full of historicism, the *storicismo polacco*, as Brzozowski called it, that characterizes Polish literature" (YH, 28).
8. The proof of the last audacious couplet was I believe demonstrated during Solidarność. A poem by Milosz, even if banned from libraries and bookstores, could (unlike a novel) be learned by heart and shared by a movement. See chapter 2.
9. Here Milosz follows the critique of Young Poland poets for their decadence and aestheticism by Stanislaw Brzozowski, summarized by Milosz as "they took flight into their souls" (HPL, 378). However, in pursuit of a larger argument, I am not doing justice to the complexity of Milosz's detailed poetic judgments. A Western reader who wants a better feel of the poem's texture would do well to compare the treatment

of specific poets like Kasprowicz in the Treatise (7), and Milosz's *History of Polish Literature* (HPL, 338–40).

10. In an endnote, Milosz adds, "his story 'Heart of Darkness' (1902) has been called (by Thomas Mann) the work that opens the twentieth century" (TP, 76).

11. Quoted in Czeslaw Milosz, "A Semi-Private Letter about Poetry," in *To Begin Where I Am: Selected Essays* (New York: Farrar, Straus and Giroux, 2001), 345.

12. In fact, Słonimski was born to a converted Jewish father and a Polish Catholic mother; he was baptized a Catholic.

13. Cf. WP, 80–81: "Polish poetry began to move away. . . . To define in a word what had happened, one can say: disintegration. People always live within a certain order and are unable to visualize a time when that order might cease to exist. The sudden crumbling of all current notions and criteria is a rare occurrence and is characteristic only of the most stormy periods of history."

In chapter 15, I will present arguments from neuroscience that lend support to Milosz's argument in this passage of the Poetic Treatise.

14. The Horst Wessel Lied was of course a Nazi song. Milosz comments: "One may well ask how, in Poland, directly endangered by Germany, such an imitative movement was possible, Were these people blind? They were" (TP, 90n).

15. The lines prove Milosz is not introducing himself here to settle personal issues. He chooses to overlook the fact that after his defection, at a Polish government conference convened to denounce him, Słonimski had dutifully attacked Milosz's writings as "an enemy to every worker and peasant"; and Milosz's old mentor Iwaszkiewicz condemned him for writing in *Kultura*, which he called a "neo-Nazi paper" (Franaszek, *Miłosz: A Biography*, 292). Gałczyński meanwhile attacked Milosz in "A Poem for a Traitor" (YH, 104–5). Elsewhere Pablo Neruda, a former friend of Milosz who had translated his work, now denounced him in an article entitled "The Man Who Ran Away."

16. See chapter 9.

17. Where the English has "I do not know," the Polish (*Nie wie*) is "He does not know." The narrator uses the first person for the first time here in English. In Polish, it is not used by the poet-narrator (as opposed to a Jewish persona, TP, 37) until the narrator's very comparable closure to Part III, followed by the poet's personal response to the rowboat experience in Part IV: "I know I'll die. / I remember everything" [wiem że umrę. / Wszystko pamiętam] (TP 49).

Compare the "pretty girl" and "barren field" [jałowe pole] of "Outskirts," in "Voices of Poor People" (NCP, 66).

18. Cf. Genesis 2:9: "And out of the ground made the Lord God to grow every tree that is pleasant to the sight, and good for food; the tree of life also in the midst of the garden, and the tree of knowledge of good and evil."

19. Czesław Miłosz, "Wprowadzenie w Amerikanów," *Twórczość*, 1947; in Czesław Miłosz, *Kontynenty* (Kraków: Znak 1999), 132–36; cf. Robert Lowell, "The Quaker Graveyard in Nantucket." In addition, a passage in Part IV ("Let him visit the graveyard of the whalers / Who drove spears into the flesh of leviathan / And looked for the secret in guts and blubber" [NCP, 141; TP, 48]) appears to imitate, almost to the point of pastiche, the same Lowell poem (speaking "gracelessly and roughly").

20. Something significant but untranslatable happens here. The Polish for "Angelus"—a prayer recited three times a day at the tolling of the Angelus bell—is "Anioł Pański," The Angel of God." (The name of the prayer is its *incipit*, or opening word[s].) So, in Milosz's two lines. the "Angel of God" is set against the "Spirit of History." These represent the two modes of being that will shortly be introduced into the poem as *"is"* [JEST] and *"becoming"* [STAJE SIĘ,] NCP, 132; TP, 35), and in the notes as *être* and *devenir*" (TP, 107n).

More importantly, God is named here, but only in the same oblique way that God was first named in Part Two: "'God and country' had ceased to be a lure" (NCP, 121; TP, 20). In this poem about history, Gałczyński's "gods the nation worshipped" and now the "inferior god" of history appear as the topics of discussion. God is named only in aspects of Polish culture.

This antithesis will become explicit at the end of Part III, with the first overt reference to God—"Christ the Lord" [Panu Bogu Christu Boigu], NCP, 138–39; TP, 43—in the folk Christmas carols that survived, unaffected by the imposition of Communism.

21. Milosz refers here to "myths and legends" in general; not specifically to poetry. But in his "Preface" he has already claimed that "Novels and essays serve but will not last. / One clear stanza can take more weight/ Than a whole wagon of elaborate prose" (NCP, 109; TP, 1).

22. Einstein alluded to this correspondence in his famous (and often misquoted) dictum. "The eternal mystery of the world is its comprehensibility. . . . The fact that it is comprehensible is a miracle" (Walter Isaacson, *Einstein: His Life and Universe* [New York: Simon & Schuster, 2007], 628n46). Because of its focus on history, Milosz's passage is perhaps closer to my idea of the "prevailable will" in politics. Cf. Peter Dale Scott, *The Road to 9/11* (Berkeley: University of California Press, 2007), 25, 270.

23. G. W. F. Hegel, *Philosophy of Right* (1820), "Preface."

24. Czeslaw Milosz, "A Semi-Private Letter about Poetry," in *To Begin Where I Am*, 350–51.

25. Łukasz Tischner, *Miłosz and the Problem of Evil* [Evanston, IL: Northwestern University Press, 2015], 124. Cf. Revelation 9:11: "And they had a king over them, which is the angel of the bottomless pit, whose name in the Hebrew tongue is Abaddon, but in the Greek tongue hath his name Apollyon." The Destroyer here (*Tępiciel* in Polish) suggests this destroying angel, whose Hebrew name Abaddon is from the verb stem *abad* ("perish" or "destroy"). Cf. Job 26:6: the grave [Sheol] is naked before Him, and destruction [Abaddon] has no covering." Apollyon (Ἀπολλύων) in Greek means "the destroyer" (or place of destruction)," from the present participle of Greek *apollumi* (ἀπόλλυμι), "to destroy utterly").

26. Milosz, in Czarnecka and Fiut, *Conversations with Czeslaw Milosz*, 174. Milosz went on to apply Brzozowski's distinction between materialistic Marxists, who view "history as a continuation of nature, everything is determined," and dialectical Marxists, who attempt "to view nature and history as opposites" (175).

27. "In Goethe's Faust the Spirit of the Earth [*Erdgeist*] was Nature, which governed with the law of universal necessity. If the Spirit of History is just another name

for the Earth Spirit, then the law of necessity, of strict determinism, applies to history as well" (TP, 102n; cf. NCP, 757n).

28. Czeslaw Milosz, "Treatise on Theology," SS, 51; cf. 57; ABC, 61: "When he published *On the Origin of Species* in 1859, he announced with regret that his work proclaimed the devil's theology. This can only mean that he had succumbed to his own observations, and they pointed to a structure of life that was no less repellent to him than to the churches which fought against his theories." In conversation with Robert Faggen, he recalled how, as an adolescent, he had been "entranced" by Darwin's theories while also learning about the church's dogmatics at school: "Eventually I turned away from Darwinism because of its cruelty, though at first I embraced it" (Cynthia L. Haven [ed.], *Czesław Miłosz: Conversations* [Jackson, MS: University Press of Mississippi, 2006], 152).

29. Milosz, *Emperor of the Earth*, 227.

30. Cf. *Native Realm*, 275: "Whoever commits himself to movement alone will destroy himself. Whoever disregards movement will also destroy himself."

31. "STAJĘ SIĘ" was translated by Milosz as "becomes" in the original quite different Milosz-Hass translation of this stanza in his *Collected Poems: 1931–1987* (New York: Ecco, 1988), 115. And he uses "becomes" orally, in a third different version, in Czarnecka and Fiut, *Conversations with Czeslaw Milosz*, 176.

32. Cf. Milosz, *History of Polish Literature*, 262–63. According to Jan Kott, Hoene-Wroński may also have spoken of "the omnipresence of the devil in history" (Jan Kott, *Still Alive: An Autobiographical Essay* [New Haven, CT: Yale University Press, 1994], 66); cf. Michał Wieczorek, "A Madman on Trial: Józef Maria Hoene-Wroński and the Price of Truth," Culture.pl, November 16, 2018, https://culture.pl/en/article/madman-on-trial-jozef-maria-hoene-wronski-truth. If true, this fact might further complicate the narrator's invocation of hellish spirits at the opening of Part IV, "Natura."

33. Czeslaw Milosz, "Speaking of a Mammal," in Milosz, *To Begin Where I Am*, 211.

34. Tischner also compares the grovelers to "the wild devotees of Conrad's Kurtz" (*Milosz and the Problem of Evil*, 126).

35. The adjective for "hope" in the second line is "martwą," which means "dead," not "hidden." So Milosz's version of the lines in conversation is more accurate, if more puzzling: "And everyone kept / A dead hope that time's domains / Had an expiration date" (Milosz, in Czarnecka and Fiut, *Conversations with Czeslaw Milosz*, 177). Milosz comments on these lines that the period of terror in Poland lasted only until Stalin's death in 1953, after which "poets were the first to . . . deviate from Stalinist dogma" (TP, 108–9n).

36. Milosz, in Czarnecka and Fiut, *Conversations with Czeslaw Milosz*, 177.

37. Adding to the chaos of this sequence is the fact that the fourth stanza of the Jew's song has been omitted in the English editions. Here it is as translated in Tischner (*Milosz and the Problem of Evil*, 128): "Apart from my heart, which will stop, / Apart from my word, which will stop, / I know neither father, nor son, nor home." Cf. W 2:223.

38. Milosz to my knowledge had only one connection to Skierniewice. It was the town near the village where, on his escape from Warsaw to Kraków, he spent a week digging potatoes for a farmer named Kijo (NR, 253; Franaszek, *Milosz: A Biography*, 219). This experience is remembered a few pages later, at the end of Part III. And his memory of it in *Native Realm* elicits a thought similar to this passage of the poem: "No matter what happens, the plow must till the soil; wheat and potatoes must be harvested" (NR, 253).

39. I have modified the translation of the first two lines, which in Polish are *Pagrków leśnych, jasnych wód potrzeba./ Nigdy się tutaj nie obroni człowiek* (W 2:227). Milosz and Hass have "What we do need are forests, clear waters. / For there's nothing here to defend a man." But in the Polish, the hills of the first line emphasize the contrast between "Plains, empty and misty" stretching from Poland to the Urals (TP, 40), and the (Lithuanian) narrator, "not born on these level plains." They also refer to the line from Mickiewicz in the line before ("A castle sits on the Nowogródek hill" (*góry*), which Milosz explained as "a luxury now ... because there's nothing but a plain" (Milosz, in Czarnecka and Fiut, *Conversations with Czeslaw Milosz*, 178).

40. Tischner, *Milosz and the Problem of Evil*, 130; citing Jan Błoński, *Miłosz jak świat*, (Kraków: Znak, 1998), 45ff.

41. Milosz, in Czarnecka and Fiut, *Conversations with Czeslaw Milosz*, 178. The Milosz-Hass translation reads, "Mickiewicz is too difficult for us. / Ours is not a lordly or a Jewish knowledge" (NCP, 137; TP, 42). The word *szlachta* occurs not in the poem but in an explanatory note (W 2:228; TP, 112n).

42. Milosz will say more about this cultural gap in his "Quarrel with Classicism" (WP, 59–75), where he speaks of "two species: *those who know and do not speak; those who speak and do not know*" (WP, 66; emphasis in original).

43. Milosz, in Czarnecka and Fiut, *Conversations with Czeslaw Milosz*, 178.

44. Milosz's climax of a sophisticated worldly section with breath-taking spiritual naiveté reminds me of Mahler's climax of his Fourth Symphony with childlike lyrics from *Des Knaben Wunderhorn*. Dennis O'Driscoll makes a similar comparison of Milosz's naïve poetic novel *The Issa Valley* to Mahler's Third Symphony (Dennis O'Driscoll, "Czeslaw Milosz: The Optimistic Catastrophist," *The Crane Bag* 7, no. 1 [1983]: 60).

45. Gracjan Kraszewski, "Catalyst for Revolution: Pope John Paul II's 1979 Pilgrimage to Poland and Its Effects on Solidarity and the Fall of Communism," *The Polish Review* 57, no. 4 (2012): 30; Timothy Garton Ash, *Solidarity: The Polish Revolution* (New Haven, CT: Yale University Press, 2002), 31–33. As previously noted, the three men commemorated on the Gdańsk memorial to martyred workers are Lech Wałęsa, Milosz, and Pope John Paul.

46. In a note on the tinderbox, Milosz explains, "Perhaps, in the midst of general devastation and a return to the primitive, a tinderbox would be more appropriate than matches. The narrator is taking a rest from his agricultural occupation: digging potatoes" (TP, 112n).

47. I identify the "she ... snapping her garter" with the "she ... who wears a veil." (In English, but not in Polish, the words "And she" introduce both passages.)

48. In *Native Realm*, Milosz recalls that during his dramatic escape from Warsaw to Goszyce, he spent time "digging potatoes for a peasant named Kijo. A return to an elementary existence. And yet what was Poland, after all, if not thousands of villages and that hard indifference to history's upheavals?" (NR, 253). This occurred near Skierniewice, in the landscape of "potato fields" remembered in the Treatise a few pages earlier (TP, 40; cf. Franaszek, *Milosz: A Biography*, 219).

CHAPTER 12

1. Czeslaw Milosz, YH, 117.
2. A case could be made for dating the Part Four "(1948–1950)," not "1949." Though Milosz returned to Europe in both years, the poem clearly ends with his return by ship in 1950. The return in 1949 was by plane, and to check on developments in Poland. Thus it did not carry the same symbolic meaning of "starting one's life . . . anew" (NCP, 149, TP, 58).
3. Milosz, in Ewa Czarnecka and Aleksander Fiut, *Conversations with Czeslaw Milosz* (San Diego, CA: Harcourt Brace Jovanovich, 1987), 179.
4. "The sudden shift from the 'earth of destruction' and the Spirit of History to the 'enchanted' land of the Spirit of the Earth partly suggests a desperate (and ultimately unsuccessful) attempt to repeat the beginning of Goethe's *Faust, Part II*" (Łukasz Tischner, *Miłosz and the Problem of Evil* [Evanston, IL: Northwestern University Press, 2015], 133). Milosz's earlier invocation of the Earth-Spirit (TP, 31) has been compared to Goethe's in *Faust I*, vv. 461–515: in his PhD Dissertation, "The Catholic Imagination of Czeslaw Milosz" (University of Washington, 2014), 70), Artur Rosman sees Milosz's invocation of the Spirit of the Earth—"Who are you, Powerful One? The nights are long. / Do we know you as the Spirit of the Earth?" (TP, 31)—as "an almost verbatim recapitulation" of the invocation in Goethe's *Faust I*. I see no such recapitulation.
5. Mann's novel, like Milosz's poem, looks at a larger pattern of degeneration in European history, and attacks aestheticism as a precursor to totalitarianism. This is in keeping with Mann's confession earlier that "I must regretfully own that in my younger years I shared that dangerous German habit of thought which regards life and intellect, art and politics as totally separate worlds" (*Life* April 17, 1939, 76). Mann's hero is modeled partly on Nietzsche's increasing madness; in it an observer summarizes Nietzsche's thoughts on the duality in art of the Apollonian and Dionysian (or as Milosz would say, classicism and realism, *esse* and *devenir*).
6. Milosz, commenting on the different voices in his poem "Slow River," recalled Bakhtin's use of the term "polyphony" to describe the different voices in Dostoevsky, and commented that "a great many voices really can emerge when a person has a great many conflicts and contradictions" (Czarnecka and Fiut, *Conversations with Czeslaw Milosz*, 114). This condition is certainly that of Milosz in "Natura." Milosz's ambivalences and inner turmoil resembled those of his new acquaintance Robert Lowell. How fitting that Milosz should allude here without acknowledgment to Lowell's "The Quaker Graveyard in Nantucket": "Let him visit the graveyard of

the whalers / Who drove spears into the flesh of leviathan / And looked for the secret in guts and blubber" (TP, 48).

7. Czeslaw Milosz, *The Issa Valley* (New York: Farrar, Straus and Giroux, 1978), 6–7.

8. Czeslaw Milosz, *The Land of Ulro* (New York: Farrar, Straus and Giroux, 1985), 103.

9. Wallace Stevens, "The Comedian as the Letter C," *The Collected Poems of Wallace Stevens* (New York: Knopf, 1955), 27: "Nota: man is the intelligence of his soil, / The sovereign ghost. As such, the Socrates / Of snails, musician of pears, principium / And lex." Cf. John Gould Fletcher, "The Revival of Estheticism," *Freema*n 8, no. 10 (December 1923): 355: "The artist can do nothing else but select out of life the elements to form a 'fictive' or fictitious reality. But this is not necessarily a higher reality. . . . It is merely the artist's reality."

The question *Wikipedia* sees in the poem (s.v. "The Comedian as the Letter C") seems very relevant to Milosz's situation in "Natura": "Can Crispin (the artist, the poet, Stevens) hope to be something more than 'the intelligence of his soil'? Can the 'Socrates of snails' leave . . . for the sea, and refocus his imagination?"

10. A philosophical emphasis on "where, amidst thunder / The golden house, the word *is*, collapses / And the word *becoming* ascends to power" also marks the six-page translation of excerpts from "Treatise on Poetry" in the 1987 *Collected Poems* of Milosz (p. 115).

11. Milosz, in Czarnecka and Fiut, *Conversations with Czeslaw Milosz*, 184.

12. The Milosz-Hass translation has "He binds," but this substitution of the third for the first person (*Zwijałem*) is an awkward transition to the choice of "My boat" just five lines later. I will take issue at various moments with the translation of Section Four, done later when Milosz and Hass were both famous and thus more preoccupied with other matters. It is relevant that the translation of Section Four was mostly done remotely: Hass would simply edit drafts that he received by mail from Milosz.

Thus there are even errors—mostly trivial, like "bufflo" (TP, 58) for "buffalo" (NCP, 148), "Karmomama" (TP, 115n) for "Karomama" (cf. W 2:236), "black thorn" for "blackthorn" ("tarniny," NCP, 140; TP, 47). One is embarrassingly anachronistic: when British soldiers during the American revolution are described as "Moving soundlessly up the Appalachian trail" ("szlakiem Appalachów," NCP, 148; TP, 57), a well-known trail which dates from 1923. There is of course no "the" in the Polish. At times I will use Milosz's oral recollection of this Part IV, as translated by Richard Lourie in Czarnecka and Fiut, *Conversations with Czeslaw Milosz*.

13. The "mosquitoes" ("komary") are obviously fireflies.

14. Milosz, in Czarnecka and Fiut, *Conversations with Czeslaw Milosz*, 181.

15. Czeslaw Milosz, "The Hooks of a Corset," NCP, 410; Cynthia L. Haven (ed.), *Czesław Miłosz: Conversations* (Jackson, MS: University Press of Mississippi, 2006), 82. The speaker in the poem identifies himself as historical: "In the Quartier Latin, when bells ring for the New Year 1900, I am the one who walks uphill on rue Cujas" (NCP, 409–10).

16. Milosz, in Czarnecka and Fiut, *Conversations with Czeslaw Milosz*, 181.

17. Cf. "Only through time, time is conquered" (T. S. Eliot, *T. S. Eliot, Collected Poems, 1909–1962* [New York: Harcourt Brace Jovanovich, 1991], 178).

18. In a note, Milosz explained that "'A new diction' and 'a new tenderness' are seen as the as the means of liberating man from fatalism and determinism, from the presumed law of historical necessity" (TP, 117n).

19. Milosz, in Czarnecka and Fiut, *Conversations with Czeslaw Milosz*, 182–83; I prefer Lourie's re-translation of TP, 52: "to gather in an image / The furriness of the beaver, the smell of rushes, / And the wrinkles of a hand holding a pitcher / From which wine trickles."

20. Milosz, in Czarnecka and Fiut, *Conversations with Czeslaw Milosz*, 183.

21 "La réflexion saisit donc la temporalité en tant qu'elle se dévoile comme le mode d'être unique et incomparable d'une ipséité, c'est-à-dire comme historicité" (Jean-Paul Sartre, *L'Être et le Néant* [Paris: Gallimard, 1943], 205). Milosz's use of "historicity," recalling its meaning in French, does not conform to the usages listed in the Oxford English Dictionary. As I understand it, his definition might be in the order of "a fuller autonomy and liberation that comes from a fuller consciousness of our situation in history." This would imply, for example, liberation from restrictive self-definition as either radical or conservative, traditionalist or Marxist.

22. Asking himself who the "we" in Part IV were, Milosz speculated that "Perhaps I'm writing about Kroński and me here" (Milosz, in Czarnecka and Fiut, *Conversations with Czeslaw Milosz*, 191), This is corroborated by his statement that "the highest of awards" for the poem was an approving letter from Kroński in Warsaw, who was once a member of the Communist Party in France (NR, 296).

23. *Striving Towards Being: The Letters of Thomas Merton and Czeslaw Milosz*, ed. Robert Faggen, (New York: Farrar, Straus and Giroux, 1997), 9.

24. In a lengthy digression on "Rhetorical Abstraction in Auden," Shapiro faulted him in particular for his use of "The Word 'History.'" Though Auden at first used abstractions humorously and as metaphor, Shapiro wrote, soon "The capital letter moved across his lines / As ponderously as German nouns,"—spreading "malignant vapors" among his imitators (Karl Shapiro, *Essay on Rime* [London: Secker & Warburg, 1947], 40–41). Milosz was interested in this passage and singled it out for translation into Polish (Czeslaw Miłosz, *Kontynenty* [Kraków: Znak, 1999], 125–26). But what Shapiro intended as a warning against abstraction became for Milosz a model. "A Treatise on Poetry," especially in Polish, is littered with abstractions like *hystoryczność*, many of them—for example, *Postęp* (Progress) and *Rozum* (Reason)—capitalized. This break with the post-romantic precepts of modernist prosody is what chiefly distinguishes the style of *Treatise on Poetry* from that of *Ocalenie*, as well as most American poetry.

25. Milosz's use in translation of the stronger and less tentative verb "anticipate" echoes his earlier assertion in *The Witness of Poetry* (109) that the poetic act "both anticipates the future and speeds its coming."

26. The wings here recall the lines in Mickiewicz's "Ode to Youth": "O Youth! Pass me thy wings. . . . Mighty as an eagle's is Thy flight" (https://en.wikisource.org/wiki/Ode_to_Youth).

27. Czeslaw Milosz, "Who is Gombrowicz?" in Czeslaw Milosz, *Beginning with My Streets: Essays and Recollections* (New York: Farrar, Straus and Giroux, 1991), 230. Milosz is actually comparing the passage to Kołakowski in the light of another author, Witold Gombrowicz.

28. Milosz, in Czarnecka and Fiut, *Conversations with Czeslaw Milosz*, 185, emphasis added.

29. Milosz, in Czarnecka and Fiut, *Conversations with Czeslaw Milosz*, 185, emphasis added.

30. Edmund Burke, ed. Peter J. Stanlis, *Edmund Burke: Selected Writings and Speeches* (New York: Doubleday, Anchor, 1963), 494; discussion in Peter Dale Scott with Freeman Ng, *Poetry and Terror: The Politics and Poetics of* Coming to Jakarta (Lanham, MD: Lexington, 2018), 184–88.

31. Why does the poet leave the rowboat with only one of its oars, leaving the other? A possible explanation: This line (in English) echoes the instruction of Teiresias to Odysseus to "take a well-made oar and carry it," in order, after a long journey to a distant land, to have peace and long life at home (Odyssey 11:119–33; 23:266–81). This comment pertains only to the English translation. In the original, as we might expect, he is carrying "oars" ("wiosłami," W 2:241).

32. "Amerika ma dla mnie sierść racoona," W 2:241. Note that Milosz here, as if to emphasize his remoteness here from Poland, uses "racoona" (not in Polish dictionaries), rather than the available Polish *szop*, or *szop pracz*.

33. Goethe, *Zahme Xenien*, ix.

34. W. H. Auden, *The Double Man* (New York: Random House, 1941), 63, 146–47.

35. The idea of living on a farm continued to tempt Milosz. At the press conference in 1980 when he received the Nobel Prize, "Milosz said that he may buy a farm with the prize money" (Joseph McLellan, "Poet Czeslaw Milosz Wins Nobel Prize for Literature," *Washington Post*, October 10, 1980.

36. Milosz, in Czarnecka and Fiut, *Conversations with Czeslaw Milosz*, 187. Milosz later confirmed in *Year of the Hunter* that he spoke "frankly with people whom I included in my own, that is, my intellectual, circle—Thornton Wilder, for example. . . . Wilder thought that I ought to remain in America and he promised to set me up on a farm where I could write in peace" (YH, 121). In 1946 Milosz had met Wilder for dinner in New York; a year later he wrote Wilder to propose cultural exchange visits of writers between Poland and the US (Letter of May 23, 1947 from Czesław Miłosz to Thornton Wilder; New Haven, CT: Yale University, Beinecke Library, Call Number YCAL MSS 108).

37. Milosz, in Czarnecka and Fiut, *Conversations with Czeslaw Milosz*, 187.

38. Tischner, *Milosz and the Problem of Evil*, 139. Tischner rightly recalls also "the warning from the *Treatise*'s second section—'Young reader, you won't live inside a rose' [NCP, 125; TP, 24]—which foretells the tragedy of the 'twenty-year-old poets of Warsaw'" (Milosz, in Czarnecka and Fiut, *Conversations with Czeslaw Milosz*, 187).

39. Milosz, in Czarnecka and Fiut, *Conversations with Czeslaw Milosz*, 187–88.

40. His first mention of love was also dismissive, when he ended his catalog of historic memories prompted by the beaver with the couplet: "Perhaps this is only my own love speaking / Beyond the seventh river. Grit of subjectivity" (TP, 50). The only

other mention of the word "love" is by the Jewish persona in Part III: "On the wall of my cell for a whole night I carved / A word of love, so that syllables survive, / And roll with this prison around the sun" (TP, 38). There "love" is just that, a word. But we shall discuss how Horace writes of Venus in the treatise's last line.

41. Letter from Janina Milosz to Secretary of State, February 9, 1951; in Cynthia Haven, *Czesław Miłosz: A California Life* (Berkeley: Heyday, 2021), 53; from Milosz's FBI file.

42. Even so, she accepted Milosz's decision to return. Cf. Andrzej Franaszek, *Miłosz: Biografia* (Kraków: Znak, 2011), 447: "She did not want him to leave her alone, but she knew that if she forced him to emigrate, it would destroy their love."42.

43. In the Milosz-Hass translation of the Treatise, there is no visible reference to this painful aspect of Milosz's crisis. However, I shall argue below that it is the crux explaining the poem's closing lines.

44. Milosz wrote this ode to an October without history before the outbreak of the October 1956 uprisings in Hungary and Poland, the latter instantly celebrated as the "Polish October." Milosz later commented on this irony: "In October 1956 people said that I had predicted those events" (Milosz, in Czarnecka and Fiut, *Conversations with Czesław Miłosz*, 188).

45. Franaszek, *Miłosz: Biografia*, 448.

46. Rightly or wrongly, I take this note as corroboration of my suspicion that the October ode, along with the city and rose lyrics, may have been written at the time of his departure, and indeed may have contributed to his decision to leave.

47. This is confirmed by the fuller Franaszek biography in Polish: Milosz "really wanted to avoid "choosing freedom" in the United States. He even preferred to be "caught," but alone—without Janka. She did not want him to leave her alone, but she knew that if she forced him to emigrate, it would destroy their love (Franaszek, *Miłosz: Biografia*, 447). Cf. ABC, 31: "Janka loved America; she wanted me to stay, but she was afraid that I would hold it against her."

48. The self-questioning "(?)" occurs only in the English translation, not the Polish ("moralnego," W 2:246).

49. This suggests that the notes in Polish, in contrast to the poem itself, are a back-translation from the English, not the original text.

50. Again, this anguish in Part IV (bracketed as it is before and aft by diabolic and Faustian allusions) is so intense that I suspect that sections of it may have been originally drafted before Czeslaw and Janka were reunited in 1953.

51. In a note, Milosz clarifies:

Who are the accused? Who are the accusers? Roughly speaking, the first are all those who have chosen movement, *devenir* or becoming, and accept therefore the flux of things, including the idea of truth. These are the disciples of Marx, Nietzsche, Dewey, etc. The narrator, despite his reservations about Marxism, belongs to this group. There are, however, people attached to a conservative vision of immutable essences. For them the partisans of flux and universal movement undermine, with their materialism and determinism, a divine order. This division into two camps has political implications. The peculiar situation of the author, who was not himself a Communist, who was in the employ of a Communist government, exposed him to attacks from the political right. They are, perhaps, the accusers. (TP, 122n)

52. Milosz, *Emperor of the Earth*, 228.
53. Czeslaw Milosz, *The Captive Mind* (New York: Vintage, 1990), 68.
54. NR, 269. See chapter 9.
55. In making this difficult decision "to be of use," rather than write poetry on a farm, Milosz may have been influenced by the example of his model Mickiewicz, who in 1848 "went to Italy and organized a Polish legion there to fight for the liberation of the northern Italians from Austria" (HPL, 230).
56. Earth (*ziemia*), the fourth of the elements, is the one most suggestive of that natural American landscape Milosz is renouncing. It is also a term he chose for no less than three of his related titles: "Po naszej ziemi" [Throughout Our Lands], *Ziemia Ulro* [The Land of Ulro], and *Nieobjęta ziemia* [Unattainable Earth].
57. This line in Polish ("Mijamy strefę mewy i delfina," W 2:250) is not translated by Milosz and Hass.
58. In a note, Milosz explains, "The ocean is Nature and the frail ship civilization" (TP, 125n). Milosz may be evoking for Polish readers Norwid's use of a ship in his short story "Civilization," see HPL, 272.
But Milosz's note is not the whole truth. As the narrator reflects, the nothingness of the endlessly repetitive ocean also contains "the bones / Of pirates, the silky eyebrows of governors / On which the crabs feast—in other words, of those who were part of the historical process without changing it" (NCP, 141; TP 60–61). Perhaps the ocean should be construed as "nature" in the sense of what the poem calls "the repeatable pattern of things" (NCP, 114; TP, 48), as distinguished from meaningful historical change. The line not translated by Milosz and Hass ("We pass the zone of gulls and dolphins") might seem to confirm that he is leaving a realm of "nature" beyond that of beavers.
59. Karpeles, *Almost Nothing: The 20th-Century Art and Life of Józef Czapski* (New York: New York Review Books, 2018), 272. It was at this time that, for a while, Milosz thought of "going to Primavera . . . a commune founded by the Hutterites in the forests of Paraguay. They wanted to practice a kind of basic Christianity, with a life of hard work and simplicity. I used to meet the delegates from that sect in Washington. Fortunately, my wife, who was more sober than I, was opposed to that idea" (Czeslaw Milosz, in Haven [ed.], *Czesław Miłosz: Conversations*, 180; cf. ABC, 224–25).
60. Andrzej Franaszek, *Miłosz: A Biography* (Cambridge, MA: Harvard University Press, 2017), 252.
61. This recalls the open-endedness of "Flight," as Milosz walked away from the ruins of his past life in Warsaw.
62. The thinking in these paragraphs again makes me suspect that part of "Natura" was composed in 1950—that is, before Milosz knew the outcome of his trip—and that it was only expanded into the Treatise in 1956.
63. "W tobie i we mnie" (W 2:250).

64. This reading of the poem as an address to Janka is also *possible* with the "us" in the Milosz-Hass translation, but such a reading never occurred to me until I read the Polish original; nor could I find any relevance for the final line until then.
65. Milosz, in Czarnecka and Fiut, *Conversations with Czeslaw Milosz*, 192. The logic of this alleged "reason" escapes me.
66. 1980 is also the year if "Bypassing Rue Descartes," which Milosz also discussed with Gorczyńska, more candidly, but not then for publication.
67. This complementing of the historical with the personal (and romantic) is a movement that I discuss in *Enmindment—A History*, the companion book to this one. I see it there as a dialectical shift from yang to yin, a deep cultural pattern that is not alien to epic: it can be seen, for example, in complementing of the *Iliad* by the *Odyssey*, and of the *Mahabharata* (a social account of a great battle) by the *Ramayana* (a love story about the God Rama). Among other examples I give are (1) the complementing of the *Shih Ching* [Shījīng, The Chinese Book of Odes] by the later *Chu Ci* [Songs of Chu], a collection of more personal, autobiographical, and often sorrowful poems, (2) the complementing of the Torah and Prophets in the Jewish bible by the Psalms and Song of Songs.

CHAPTER 13

1. Czeslaw Milosz, letter to Thomas Merton of October 30, 1960, in *Striving Towards Being: The Letters of Thomas Merton and Czeslaw Milosz* (New York: Farrar, Straus and Giroux, 1997), 93.
2. Czeslaw Milosz, *Visions from San Francisco Bay* (New York: Farrar, Straus and Giroux, 1982), 51.
3. Czeslaw Milosz, "Discreet Charm of Nihilism," *The New York Review of Books*, November 19, 1998, https://www.nybooks.com/articles/1998/11/19/discreet-charm-of-nihilism/.
4. Czesław Miłosz, *Postwar Polish Poetry: An Anthology* (Garden City, NY: Doubleday, 1965), v.
5. Also in 1965, Milosz would defend the same primitivism in the Beat revolt against the decaying academicism of the Eliot tradition: "The hysterical howls of the Beat poets are the rebellion of a well-brought-up muse, a return to their native tradition [i.e., Whitman], somewhat vulgar but still authentic" (Czeslaw Milosz, "Reflections on T. S. Eliot" [*Kultura*, March 1965], in Czeslaw Milosz, *To Begin Where I Am* [New York: Farrar, Straus and Giroux, 2001], 397). In 1975, Milosz, while defending censorship, mocked "the censors making fools of themselves," including "the judges who order literary works confiscated for immorality, precisely those works which subsequently enter the classical canon of required school reading" (Visions, 103; cf. 66, 126).
6. My interest in this poem sequence is partly subjective. It was our first major collaboration, and also, I believe, the first of his poems to be published in English (in *Encounter*, February 1964, 46–49). One year later, while I was still in Milosz's good graces, six sections of the poem were republished in *Postwar Polish Poetry* as

"translated by Peter Dale Scott with my minor assistance" (Czeslaw Milosz, ed. and trans., *Postwar Polish Poetry: An Anthology* [Garden City, NY: Doubleday, 1965], vii, cf. 54–56).

7. *Ziemi* in Polish, whether meaning "land" or "earth," is clearly singular. But I now think I was wrong in 1961. Though I hope the poem will be ultimately remembered in English as "Throughout Our Earth," America was clearly not ready in 1961 for such a sweeping erasure of its national sentiments.

A Polish-American critic, Charles Kraszewski, sees a *double entendre* in the title: "It can mean '[we walk] over our land,' or in a geographical sense, 'all over our land,' as well as the despairing "it's all over for our country" (Charles S. Kraszewski, *Irresolute Heresiarch: Catholicism, Gnosticism and Paganism in the Poetry of Czesław Miłosz* [Newcastle upon Tyne: Cambridge Scholars Publishing, 2012], 120). But I reject Kraszewski's third reading; Milosz is thinking globally in this poem, no longer just as a Pole.

Czeslaw Milosz, in a letter to Thomas Merton of October 5, 1961, in *Striving Towards Being*, 132. The same letter sends Merton two sections in French of "Throughout Our Earth," not yet translated by Milosz and myself into English. The letter describes the sections as "a certain number of pure, I hope, poems" (139). But Milosz soon realized he these "poems" were in fact all focused, however disjointedly, on a single unifying concern.

8. A decade later, Milosz, echoing his poem, discussed his ambivalent respect for Miller: "Despite my awe of Miller, for who does not dream of being freed from all controls to sit at the typewriter and bang out whatever the saliva brings to the tongue, I never trusted him" (Visions, 138–39).

9. In the first lines of the poem, Milosz rhymes his own movements in America with those of his model Whitman, whom he first read in Polish translation around 1930: "When I pass'd through a populous city / (as Walt Whitman says, in the Polish version)" (NCP, 182). Both the openness and the capacious range of Milosz's poem can be called Whitmanesque.

10. *New and Collected Poems* has "drawn up in line for footrace," which I take to be a typo. I have reproduced the line as we translated it and as it first appeared in *Encounter* (February 1964, 46–49).

11. Just over a decade later, a more conservative Milosz expressed his alienation from California's easy acceptance of de Sade: "The works of the Marquis de Sade, including his *Philosophy in the Bedroom*, are also available [here] in paperback, and what is of interest to me is my instinctive opposition" (Milosz, Visions, 106). But his detailed paraphrase of Sade's works, plus his misquotation of Weiss's play *Marat/Sade* ("There is no universal revolution without universal copulation," Visions, 230; cf. the *Marat/Sade* lyric "What's the Point of a Revolution Without General Copulation") demonstrates that Sade was a matter of interest to both aspects of his conflicted ego: the moralist ("Naphta") and also the liberationist ("Settembrini"). In 1997, long after the disappearance of the New Left and his return to Poland, Milosz confessed more openly to this personal ambivalence:

Seeing the demagogues who were the leaders in Berkeley, I felt not the slightest temptation to join them; at the same time, I can understand Kot Jelenski, who approved of the Paris revolt, a more radically liberating universal revolution, and universal copulation. Unfortunately, one's assessment of those events depended on one's age, it seems. I was fifty-seven at the time [1968], and I suspected that, at best [?], I envied the students. (ABC, 6)

12. Only two years earlier, in 1959, Milosz wrote to Thomas Merton from partially Catholic France, "I have always been crypto-religious and in conflict with the political aspect of a Polish Catholicism" (*Striving Towards Being*, 11). There was less reason to disguise his spirituality in secular America.

13. About this time, in a letter of May 30, 1961, Milosz wrote to Thomas Merton, "I am preoccupied with religious problems and I strive hard" (*Striving Towards Being*, 117).

14. Milosz, *Striving Towards Being*, 134.

15. Milosz, *Striving Towards Being*, 133. In his notes to the Treatise on poetry, Milosz wrote of "Being, which to medieval thinkers was another name for God" (TP, 122n). One is of course reminded of the poem "Esse" (NCP, 249), quoted earlier, which was written in 1954 but apparently not published until later, perhaps in the same year 1961.

16. "Hell no" translates "No nie" ("No, never"). I may have suggested the more colloquial and contemporary "Hell no," but Milosz endorsed it. Every aspect of this poem, particularly the title, was meticulously discussed.

17. In 1965, Milosz would defend the same primitivism in the Beat revolt against the decaying academicism of the Eliot tradition: "The hysterical howls of the Beat poets are the rebellion of a well-brought-up muse, a return to their native tradition [i.e., Whitman], somewhat vulgar but still authentic" (Czeslaw Milosz, "Reflections on T. S. Eliot" [*Kultura*, March 1965], in Milosz, *To Begin Where I Am*, 397).

18. Cf. Milosz in 1975: "For me the human labyrinth is splendid, spellbinding. Besides, it matters little what I think of it; what I am in relation to it is important" (Visions, 195).

19. Contrast for example the regretful tone of his 1980 poem, "Account" (NCP, 395): "alas, / . . . I was afraid of what was wild and indecent in me."

20. Czeslaw Milosz, "Who is Gombrowicz?" in Czeslaw Milosz, *Beginning with My Streets: Essays and Recollections* (New York: Farrar, Straus and Giroux, 1991), 230.

21. Nina Witoszek, *The Origins of Anti-Authoritarianism* (Abingdon, Oxon: Routledge, 2019), 58..

22. Letter of January 17, 1959, in *Striving Towards Being*, 11.

23. In the same period, Milosz also wrote more than once to Merton about his discomfort, dating back to his struggles with Farther Chomski, with confession to a priest (e.g., *Striving Towards Being*, 162: "Confession is for me an obstacle, an absurdity"; cf. 24, 44).

24. Czeslaw Milosz, undated letter of 1960/1961 to Thomas Merton, *Striving Towards Being*, 101.

25. Note that these natives, ignorant of *becoming*, inhabited the same world of *being* as the beaver (in the Treatise on Poetry), which also "does not know time" (TP, 49).

26. Seamus Heaney, *Finders Keepers: Selected Prose 1971–2001* (New York: Farrar, Straus and Giroux, 2002), 444.

27. Andrzej Franaszek, *Miłosz: A Biography* (Cambridge, MA: Harvard University Press, 2017), 69. In *New and Collected Poems*, this poem is dated "1963." But in an essay on the poem, Milosz explains that "'Elegy for N. N.' was written in 1962, but for a long time it remained in manuscript, as I hesitated whether to publish it at all" (Czeslaw Milosz, "Elegy for N. N.," in Czeslaw Milosz, *Beginning with My Streets*, 59).

28. Milosz later offered three hints to the reader who the beloved might be: "a husband? a brother? a son?" (Czeslaw Milosz, "Elegy for N. N.," in Milosz, *Beginning with My Streets,* 60). In the context of the poem itself and of Franaszek's commentary, it seems likely to me that it was her husband.

29. Milosz, "Elegy for N. N.," in Milosz, *Beginning with My Streets.*

CHAPTER 14

1. The bias also reflected a personal disappointment. After I had excitedly prepared a draft translation of "Foreword" [Przedmowa], Milosz asked me to translate his American poem "Bobo's Metamorphosis." I don't think I got very far; I was too shocked by the difference in voice and intention. I had to write this book before overcoming my distaste.

2. See Peter Dale Scott, "Greek Theater," in *Walking on Darkness* (Rhinebeck, NY: Sheep Meadow Press, 2016), 28–35; https://www.comingtojakarta.net/2014/09/07/greek-theater/#comment-42167.

3. Andrzej Franaszek, *Miłosz: A Biography* (Cambridge, MA: Harvard University Press, 2017), 89. In 1964, Milosz's former CIA patron James Burnham, by now at William Buckley's *National Review*, published *Suicide of the West* (New York: John Day, 1964), which attacked the dominant "ideological syndrome" of liberalism with its irrational guilt over evils for which no one was responsible. In the 1970s, Milosz wrote to Burnham, applying his analysis to the "not very edifying experience" of Berkeley "frolics": "Your diagnosis has been confirmed by the whole 'Movement' of the young generation. I agree with you as to the transfer of guilt—though never probably one could see such as a display as today—perhaps only among the Russian intelligentsia of the second half of the XIXth century" (undated letter, in Daniel Kelly, *James Burnham and the Struggle for the World: A Life* [Wilmington, DE: ISI Books, 2002], 289). The letter, in which Milosz stressed that his esteem for Burnham "does not mean . . . I could become a conservative," was published on February 9, 2002, in *The American Interest* (https://www.the-american-interest.com/2020/02/09/a-letter-discovered-an-admonishment-delayed/).

4. Letter of December 31, 1964; *Striving Towards Being: The Letters of Thomas Merton and Czeslaw Milosz*, ed. Robert Faggen (New York: Farrar, Straus and

Giroux, 1997), 165–66. By choosing to repeat this excerpt from a personal letter, I clearly wanted to belittle Milosz's concern about the counterculture. But some years later, on a last review of this manuscript, I have begun to question my own stance as well as his. By endorsing a student movement with mindless slogans like "Never trust anyone over thirty" (or "Flower Power," putting a stolen rose on a bayonet) did I perhaps also contribute to the erosion of comity in US politics, leading to the January 6, 2022, occupation of the US Capitol?

5. Berkeley certainly had more than its share of Maoists, and even for some years a Maoist bookshop (subsidized, I suspect, by Beijing). But the Maoists were very marginal to the nonviolent Berkeley "Movement" and frequently at odds with it. A key example was the People's Park episode of 1969, a short-lived movement project to turn a vacant lot into a park. This was opposed by the Maoists (we suspected on orders from Beijing) on the grounds that the park would deprive the working class of needed parking space. Cf. YH, 220, where Milosz dismisses the Free Speech Movement as, for him, a "pitiable spectacle. Could it be that the grownups felt the same about our Dembiński 'movement' in Wilno? Here, there was Mario Savio working the mass of students into a fanatical, hysterical trance." (According to Milosz, Dembiński, originally a member of Milosz's Żagary group, was a Communist by the time of the 1930s protests; YH 288). Bettina Aptheker, an old-line Communist, was indeed one of the FSM's informal leaders; but it was common knowledge on campus that "Communists exercised a restraining influence on the more militant elements in the FSM, Savio included" (Christopher Powell, [a review of] Robert Cohen, *Freedom's Orator: Mario Savio and the Radical Legacy of the 1960s* [New York: Oxford University Press, 2009], *Labour/Le Travail*, December 2, 2011] 218.)

6. Daniel Bourne, "A Conversation with Czeslaw Milosz," *Artful Dodge* (1982), https://artfuldodge.spaces.wooster.edu/interviews/czeslaw-milosz/.

7. Milosz, ABC, 254.

8. Milosz, ABC, 6: "True, the Berkeley students tried to burn books, but they didn't destroy trees like the French students—standing for 'universal copulation.' . . . I was fifty-seven at the time, and I suspected that, at best, I envied the students."

9. Cf. Milosz, Visions, 127: "The students in the Greek Theater [at Berkeley] were united by the tacit and, for them, obvious premise that any authority issuing from an evil system and protecting that system was itself pure evil."

In an interesting epilogue to the second edition of his *History of Polish Literature* ([Berkeley: University of California Press, 1983], 533), Milosz noted the "completely different causes" distinguishing the 1968 student riots in Poland from those in Paris and Berkeley: they were "provoked by an order of the authorities to suspend theatrical performances of Mickiewicz's *Forefathers' Eve* (an anti-Tsarist, i.e., anti-Russian, play)." In other words, Polish students were objecting to the kind of separation from the past that Western students were campaigning for.

10. Such as the blackthorn spike, on which a shrike has impaled a grasshopper in the Treatise (NCP, 140; TP, 47), and a caterpillar in "Three Talks" (NCP, 204).

11. Metternich was a major architect of the 1815 Treaty of Vienna that ratified the partition of Poland.

12. A commentary to this poem in Polish, not translated, confirms that the speaker is Metternich, while "the name Hermantia is chosen randomly and does not signify any historical person age" (Aleksander Fiut, *The Eternal Moment* [Berkeley: University of California Press, 1987], 174).

13. A decade later Milosz would write that "Rousseau . . . opposed the views of Hobbes, which were shared by the sober disciples of Reason" (Visions, 115).

14. Fiut, *The Eternal Moment*, 174.

15. Fiut, *The Eternal Moment*, 194. I can agree with this conclusion, but only if we recognize the continuous self-opposition that energizes Milosz's poems, in which now one side, and now another, prevails. I do not see Fiut doing this.

16. Particularly in his prose, Milosz frequently distanced himself from his youthful sense of bardic mission. "Yesterday, a visit from a sweet couple from Poland. . . . It's only during such encounters that I learn that I am a bard. Which is to say, on one level, I am aware that that's how I'm thought of over there, but it's a theoretical awareness which dissipates in the face of my different life over here; nothing here nourishes it." Or again: "Didn't [Gombrowicz], despite his rejection of Polish literature as weak . . . take from it the romantic myth of the bard, anointing himself as a genius, a leader in the spiritual sphere? And didn't my early belief that I was called also derive from that myth?" (YH, 108, 154).

17. John Updike, "Survivor/ Believer," *New Yorker*, December 24, 2001, https://www.newyorker.com/magazine/2001/12/24/survivor-believer.

18. See chapter 15.

19. Seamus Heaney, *Finders Keepers: Selected Prose 1971–2001* (New York: Farrar, Straus and Giroux, 2002), 444.

20. Brodsky called this poem "perhaps the *magnum opus*" of Milosz (George Gomori, "Czeslaw Milosz," *Independent*, August 16, 2004, https://www.independent.co.uk/news/obituaries/czeslaw-milosz-5384655.html).

21. A middle section is titled "Lauda," which looks liturgical but is actually the name of a former district in Lithuania. The section is a gallimaufry of genealogical and other details; it is reminiscent of the Sarmatian genre *Silva Rerum*, a multi-generational chronicle, kept by many Polish and Lithuanian noble families, and including diary-type entries on current events, memoirs, letters, etc.

22. Milosz liked a quote from his "spiritual brother" Pascal, which he had read in Auden's *The Double Man*: "Denying, believing and doubting are to man what running is to a horse." "Every hour," Milosz added in an interview, "I believe this one hundred times" (Czesław Milosz, in Cynthia L. Haven [ed.], *Czesław Miłosz: Conversations* [Jackson, MS: University Press of Mississippi, 2006], 179).

23. Milosz said later to interviewer Robert Faggen that "writing religious poetry in the twentieth century is very difficult. [Pope John Paul II] commented on some of my work. . . . 'You make one step forward, one step back.' I answered: 'Holy Father, how in the twentieth century can one write religious poetry differently?' [The Pope] smiled" (Czesław Milosz, in Haven, *Czesław Miłosz: Conversations*, 153).

24. Milosz later clarified that he was rejecting enchantment only as a motive to write, not as a result: "'Not to enchant' is a concentration upon my own struggles,

not upon my contact with the readers" (Milosz, in Haven, *Czesław Miłosz: Conversations*, 85).

25. Jane Hirshfield, Letter to the Editor, *Poetry* (Chicago), October 30, 2005, https://www.poetryfoundation.org/poetrymagazine/articles/68313/letter-to-the-editor-56d247dd14507.

26. If the poem had been written a few years later, Phnom Penh might have been added to the capitals from which the youthful barbarians arrived. Both Pol Pot and his deputy, Ieng Sary, studied together in Paris; under their regime, between 1.5 and 2 million people, approximately a quarter of Cambodia's population, died.

27. Suzanne Bacon, "Nobel Poet Reads at Library: Milosz Appears Before a Packed House," *The Library of Congress Information Bulletin*, April 21, 1997, https://www.loc.gov/loc/lcib/970421/milosz.html.

28. Czeslaw Milosz, Letter to Jósef Czapski, 1978, in Andrzej Franaszek, *Miłosz: A Biography*, 409.

29. Franaszek, *Miłosz: A Biography*, 410. Franaszek cites also a letter of 1978 to Lillian Vallee, which wrote of "a terrible guilt about my existence, partly justified, partly pathological" (ibid.).

30. Czeslaw Milosz, "Odstąp ode mnie" [Get away from me], in Czeslaw Milosz, *Wiersze* (Kraków: Znak, 2001), W 3:213, Franaszek, *Miilosz: A Biography*, 410. The poem is one of a group called "Ciemne i zakryte" [Dark and hidden things]; the previous poem is "Do mojej natury" [To my nature]."

31. In the same decade, as we saw in chapter 3, Milosz would refer to this abandonment as "you might say . . . the greatest sin of my life" (Milosz to Jadwiga Tomaszewicz, née Waskziewicz, September 17, 1987, in Franaszek, *Miłosz: Biografia* [Kraków: Znak, 2011], 184, 782n224).

32. Franaszek, *Miłosz: A Biography*, 440–41.

33. Milosz letter to Stanisław Vincenz, probably 1954, Franaszek, *Biography*, 313.

34. The clear echo here of Roman and Polish indifference in "Campo dei Fiori" may have been deliberate.

35. Franaszek, *Miilosz: A Biography*, 410

36. Some scientists corroborate this suspicion: "Psychopathology during pregnancy has physiological consequence for the foetus. However, the mechanism through which maternal depression affects foetal brain development and function is unknown. In the absence of direct neural connections between the mother and foetus, it is thought to be mediated by hormones; specifically, stress hormones" (Kristin L. Leight, Elizabeth M. Fitelson, Christi A. Weston, and Katherine L. Wisner, "Childbirth and Mental Disorders," *International Review of Psychiatry* 22, no. 5 [2009]: 453–471; citing, inter alia. E. V. Cosmi, G. Luzi, F. Gori, and A. Chiodi, "Response of Utero-Placental Fetal Blood Flow to Stress Situation and Drugs," *European Journal of Obstetrics Gynecology and Reproductive Biology* 36 [1990]: 239).

37. Not to be confused with his youthful catastrophist poem "To Father Ch.," which, as noted earlier, says "a stream of boiling lava / will extinguish the cities and Noah will not escape in his ark" (W 1:108).

38. Franaszek, *Miłosz: A Biography*, 440; cf. "At Noon," NCP, 26. That Corsica encounter generated a remarkable poem about a casual affair in Houston, from which Milosz learned

> Some compassion for us people, some goodness,
> And, simply, tenderness, dear Y. Z.. . . . .
> I would like everyone to know they are the king's children
> And to be sure of their immortal souls.
> (NCP, 442–43)

39. Franaszek, *Miłosz: A Biography*, 118–19.
40. Letter to Jadwiga Waszkiewicz of June 24, 1984; in Franaszek, *Miłosz: A Biography*, 440.
41. In *Native Realm* Milosz illustrates this enthusiasm by his childhood hero, the fictional bachelor Dr. Catchfly, who on the way to what would have been his wedding had instead climbed a tree in his tails to catch "a rare species of beetle" (NR, 272; cf. NCP, 286).
42. And then wrote to his mentor Iwaszkiewicz, "I am far away from thinking about marriage and could not imagine myself being part of a society preoccupied just with earning a living" (Franaszek, *Miłosz: A Biography*, 118–91; letter to Iwaszkiewicz of December 7, 1935).
43. See chapter 7. I cannot think of any Milosz poem from Berkeley with this kind of a mythic voice. Heaney also notes Milosz's development in the 1990s of "a voice somewhere between the Orphic and the Tiresian" (Seamus Heaney, *Finders Keepers: Selected Prose 1971–2001* [New York: Farrar, Straus and Giroux, 2002], 444).
44. In the Polish original edition of *Druga Przestrzeń*, there is a final untranslated Part V, with translations into Polish of some of Ovid's *Metmorphoses*.
45. Milosz writes that he and Ignacy Święcicki were "in the same secret organization 'Pet'" (ABC, 277). Franaszek, more tentatively, concludes from "biographical hints dispersed in different texts," that Milosz himself may have "joined a Masonic lodge" called PET, with "roots in the nineteenth-century": "The PET chapter in Wilno maintained a progressive, tolerant outlook on most issues and was hostile to nationalist fanaticism. Its members did not regard themselves as part of a political group (Franaszek, *Miłosz: A Biography*, 70).
46. Like most scholars, Milosz regretted Mickiewicz's eventual messianic "obsession with the occultism of [Andrzej] Towiański, which caused him to lose his chair at the Collège de France and ruined his course" (LU, 100).
47. "*Homo ritualis*. Aware of it, I do what is prescribed for a one day's master" (SS, 59). Cf. Visions, 224: "At the same time, ritual, which had been a dead letter for the rationalistically inclined generations, begins to acquire more value. . . . A ritual constructs a sacred space among those present at it."

CHAPTER 15

1. Czeslaw Milosz, "Nobel Lecture," Stockholm, December 8, 1980, in Czeslaw Milosz, *Beginning with My Streets: Essays and Recollections* (New York: Farrar,

Straus and Giroux, 1991), 281; http://www.nobelprize.org/nobel_prizes/literature/laureates/1980/milosz-lecture.html.
2. Simone Weil, quoted in WP, 114.
3. T. S. Eliot's two efforts at synoptic prose works—*The Idea of a Christian Society* and *Notes Towards the definition of Culture*—have in my opinion added little to his otherwise significant legacy.
4. Thus for example, the chapter on "Romanticism" disposes of the disastrous Third Partition in a half-sentence ("the *Respublica* disappeared from the map of Europe," HPL, 195), but spends eighty-four pages on the three "national bards" who emerged in response to this crisis (Mickiewicz, Słowacki, and Krtasziński) as well as the general cult of the poet as "charismatic leader" which filled the vacuum: "Byron's fame in his native country was insignificant if we compare it to the near worship surrounding him in the Slavic countries" (HPL, 203).
5. As noted earlier, Milosz liked to tell me of the Polish intellectuals like Samuel Hartlib who, at the time of the Counter Reformation, migrated to London (where Hartlib befriended both Milton and Robert Boyle of the future Royal Society). Milton's 1644 pamphlet, "On Education," is addressed to Samuel Hartlib.
6. As with the Wycliffites in England, "Hussitism was a considerable factor contributing to the development of [Polish] literature in the vernacular" (HPL, 17).
7. "In one of their records from 1569, "the word 'communist' was used for the first time in the Polish language" (HPL, 33).
8. In *The Land of Ulro*, Milosz describes a similar condition of protective bilingualism in himself: in America, "My Polish served my pride by erecting a protective barrier between myself and a civilization in the throes of puerility (*qui sombre dans l'idiotie*), just as my 'Westernness,' my 'universality,' served me as a faithful ally in my revolt against 'Polishness'" (LU, 8).
9. "New rationalist trends were . . . reaching Poland from abroad, and a parallel can be drawn between that phenomenon and the fruitful borrowing from the humanism of Erasmus in the sixteenth century (HPL, 159).
10. The lodges "provided a meeting ground for various layers of society . . . including some Jews" (HPL, 160).
11. Cf. above, chapter 9; Czeslaw Milosz, "A Semi-Private Letter about Poetry," in Czeslaw Milosz, *To Begin Where I Am* [New York: Farrar, Straus and Giroux, 2001], 344–45, 351.
12. For example, Rocco Buttiglione, *Karol Wojtyla: "The Thought of the Man Who Became Pope John Paul II"* (Grand Rapids, MI: Eerdmans, 1997), 26: "Norwid, perhaps through the mediation of [Pierre-Simon] Ballanche, who was also an important influence upon him, came into contact with Vico's thought."
13. Peter Dale Scott, *Enmindment—A History: A Post-Secular Poem in Prose* (forthcoming).
14. Iain McGilchrist, *The Master and His Emissary: The Divided Brain and the Making of the Western World* (New Haven, CT: Yale University Press, 2019).
15. McGilchrist, *The Master and His Emissary*, 2.
16. McGilchrist, *The Master and His Emissary* 4, 46–47.
17. McGilchrist, *The Master and His Emissary*, 350, 352–53.

18. McGilchrist, *The Master and His Emissary*, 332.
19. McGilchrist, *The Master and His Emissary*, 1.
20. McGilchrist, *The Master and His Emissary*, 107: "After much cogitation, Kekulé seized the shape of the benzene-ring, the foundation of organic chemistry, when the image of a snake biting its tail arose from the embers of his fire. . . . The structure of the periodic table of the elements came to Mendeleyev in a dream."
21. McGilchrist, *The Master and His Emissary*, 330–31.
22. Czeslaw Milosz, in Ewa Czarnecka and Aleksander Fiut, *Conversations with Czeslaw Milosz* (San Diego: Harcourt Brace Jovanovich, 1987), 250.
23. Czeslaw Milosz, *The Land of Ulro* (New York: Farrar, Straus and Giroux, 1985), 32.
24. "Swedenborg merits scrutiny. It is a fact that the greatest poets and prose writers have borrowed liberally from him. The list is long: first Blake, as his direct spiritual descendant; then Goethe, a fervent reader of Swedenborg (as was Kant!); followed by Edgar Allan Poe, Baudelaire, Balzac, Mickiewicz, Emerson (who placed him between Plato and Napoleon in his temple of the great), and [n.b.] Dostoevsky" (LU, 136). A decade later, Milosz, now less marginal than he had been, wrote, "I would not want . . . to encourage anyone to read Swedenborg, because he will be disenchanted. As pedantic prose, it has potent soporific qualities" (ABC, 276–77).
25. Cf. chapters 8 and 12.
26. "That Mickiewicz's wife was a Frankist is well known" (LU, 119). Jacob Frank was a follower and self-declared reincarnation of the seventeenth-century false messiah Sabbatai Zevi and, like him, was excommunicated by orthodox Jewish authorities. Scholars have argued that Frank influenced Blake's "Marriage of Heaven and Hell"; see Marsha Keith Schuchard, "From Poland to London: Sabbatean Influences on the Mystical Underworld of Zinzendorf, Swedenborg, and Blake," in Glenn Dynner, *Holy Dissent: Jewish and Christian Mystics in Eastern Europe* (Detroit, MI: Wayne State University Press, 2011), 250–80.
27. Cf. LU, 239: "God had mercy on Oscar V. de L. Milosz and spared him from having to wait for the year 1944. . . . That which was fulfilled, the exploding of the first atomic bomb in 1945, has signaled, even to this day, neither a rebirth of Nature nor the end of an eon."
28. A theosophist commonplace dating back to Gabriel Rossetti in the nineteenth century; cf. René Guénon *L'ésotérisme de Dante* (Paris: Ch. Bosse, 1925).
29. Milosz, Visions, 103; cf. his description on p. 85 on California as a "mecca for . . . consciousness-expanding drugs, ecstatic sects, publications devoted to Hinduism and Zen Buddhism, for prophets preaching wisdom provided by Tibetan monks."
30. Eric Ziolkowski, "[Review of] The Land of Ulro." *The Journal of Religion* 67, no. 1 (1987): 141–42.
31. Cf. Milosz's extended notes on D. T. Suzuki and the "Mindfulness" of Thich Nhat Hanh (ABC, 274–77, 196–200). Milosz quotes a long passage by Thich Nhat Hanh on "Interbeing" ("You cannot just *be* by yourself alone. You have to be with every other thing," ABC, 1999), which could be used in a commentary on Milosz's central poem "Love" ("For you are only one thing among many," NCP, 50).

32. Jaroslaw Anders, "Voice of Exile," *New York Review of Books*, February 27, 1986, https://www.nybooks.com/articles/1986/02/27/voice-of-exile/.

33. Cf. LU, 7–8: "There was a time when I dreamed of an international role for myself, of world renown—guiltily, hesitantly so. . . . How glad I am now that I clung to my native language."

34. Although Milosz's concept of a *wieszcz* or bard is profoundly Polish, it can also be found in the *Democratic Vistas* of Walt Whitman, whom Milosz read at an early age in a Polish translation: "I demand races of orbic bards, with unconditional uncompromising sway. Come forth, sweet democratic despots of the west!" (*Democratic Vistas*, 407).

35. Milosz, "Nobel Lecture," 281.

36. Milosz, "Nobel Lecture," 277.

37. T. S. Eliot, "Tradition and the Individual Talent," in T. S. Eliot, *Selected Essays* (London: Faber & Faber, 1951), 15.

38. Octavio Paz, *Children of the Mire: Modern Poetry from Romanticism to the Avant-garde* (Cambridge, MA, Harvard University Press, 1974), 1. Cf. Michael Palmer, *Active Boundaries: Selected Essays and Talks* (New York: New Directions, 2008), 106, etc.

39. Eliot, *Selected Essays*, 16.

40. Milosz, "Nobel Lecture," 280–83.

41. I dare to say "correction," because so many of Eliot's early attention-getting critical assessments were not only idiosyncratic but untenable. For example, Eliot himself revised his earlier downplaying of Milton and Goethe, just as his decade of efforts to define himself as "a royalist in politics" ended when in 1935 he approved of Edward VIII's forced abdication. For details, see Peter Dale Scott, "The Social Critic and His Discontents," in A. David Moody (ed.). *The Cambridge Companion to T. S. Eliot* (Cambridge: Cambridge University Press, 1994), 70. Milosz also could modify his assessments. As we have just seen, although he once paid considerable attention to Swedenborg, to whom Blake, Dostoevsky and his cousin Oscar Milosz were indebted, he himself later discounted Swedenborg's "pedantic prose" (ABC, 276–77).

42. Czeslaw Milosz, "Reflections on T. S. Eliot" (*Kultura*, March 1965), in Czeslaw Milosz, *To Begin Where I Am*, 388–98.

43. Here Milosz was reversing himself. In his earlier "Reflections on T. S. Eliot," he had assessed Eliot's work as a hopeful "attempt at learning that the imagination, and also religious poetry, can regain [their] privileges," lost since the age of Dante (Czeslaw Milosz, "Reflections on T. S. Eliot" [1965], in Milosz, *To Begin Where I Am*, 398): "This is an almost unbelievable undertaking; he built out of impossibility, absence, ruins. If, however, he achieved his aim to some extent, it would mean that people in the twentieth century need not be too pessimistic about their own potency."

44. Cf. YH, 211: "I am still the poet who knows and struggles against the subjectivism of contemporary poetry."

45. WP, 14: "While the list of dreaded apocalyptic events may change, what is constant is a certain state of mind. This state precedes the perception of specific reasons for despair, which come later." He finds the same sense of authorial responsibility in

Simone Weil: "I believe that writers of the period which just ended are responsible for the miseries of our time" (quoted at WP, 54).

46. In his Nobel Laureate lecture, as we have seen, he also contrasted the irrelevancy of "autonomous" poetry with the power, "like a pistol shot," of poetry "in search of reality," or what the American poet Robert Duncan has called "the truth of things" (Czeslaw Milosz, "Nobel Lecture,").

47. The full passage is, "Polish poetry became a home for incorrigible hope, immune to historical disasters." This can be read as a tribute to the steadfastness of the Polish people, who endured two centuries before regaining their freedom. But it can also be seen as an implied rebuke to poets like Mickiewicz, whose influence led Poles more than once into hopeless confrontations from which nothing was learned. Milosz, in contrast, might be seen as a poet of corrigible hope.

48. Milosz, "Reflections on T. S. Eliot," in Milosz, *To Begin Where I Am*, 397.

49. In my opinion, this substitution of Whitman for the obvious choice of Mickiewicz weakens Milosz's argument. Whitman, unlike Mickiewicz, was not only not grounded in a collectively united consciousness, like Ginsberg in our time; he was a voice of opposition. Cf. Peter Dale Scott, "Changing North America," Asia-Pacific Journal, June 27, 2011, http://japanfocus.org/site/view/3553.

50. Cf. WP, 95: "Whereas in romanticism a poet had to prophesy, to lead, to move hearts, here [with Mallarmé] we have the idea of purity and defensiveness, opposed to vulgarity and dirt."

51. Cf. Tibor Iván Berend, *History Derailed: Central and Eastern Europe in the Long Nineteenth Century* (Berkeley: University of California Press, 2003), 47: "When the German romantic F. W. J. Schelling (following Herder) explained the romantic notion that poets or painters may understand the spirit of their age more profoundly and express it in a more vivid and lasting manner than academic historians" (Berlin, 1978, 140), his view was taken at face value in Russia, Poland, and throughout the region."

52. Martin Heidegger (trans. William McNeill and Julia Davis), *Hölderlin's Hymn "The Ister"* (Bloomington, IN: Indiana University Press, 1996), 138–39.

53. Augustine, *City of God*, VIII, xviii. Augustine's actual target is Apuleius in his work *De deo Socratis*; he concedes that Plato is the greatest of the natural theologians.

54. St. Thomas Aquinas, *Summa Theologiae*, 1.1.9

55. The revolutionaries of 1848 failed to establish a constitution for a United Europe, a goal postponed until after World War II. But the setback of 1848 was in no sense a closure: we should recall, for example, how the American anti-slavery movement was strengthened after 1848 by such radical German exiles as Longfellow's friend and fellow-poet Ferdinand Freiligrath, and Lincoln's friend and political ally Carl Schurz. The ideas of Goethe and Schiller lived on in Thomas Carlyle, who in turn helped inspire both Emerson and Whitman. The visions of Blake and Shelley were revived and underscored by Yeats.

56. Milosz was far more affirmative in 1965 about Baudelaire's (and Eliot's) nostalgia: "yearning for the past and yearning for the future are interconnected: if industrial and scientific civilization deprived man of his innate, relative equilibrium, this means that an *optimum* exists and can be restored" (*To Begin Where I Am*, 389).

57. With respect to "catastrophe," I believe that the desperateness of the Polish condition in the 1940s created a special opportunity for poetry. As before 1918, there was no Polish state: so it again fell to authors to determine whether Poland would sink into acquiescence, or devise a strategy for its liberation. Milosz's poetry helped the Polish to see the need for change, the possibility for change, and the role of words as a vehicle for change. In short, it was the depth of the crisis that made poetic salvation possible.

58. Czeslaw Milosz, *The Captive Mind* (New York: Vintage International, 1990), 237.

59. Though in *Witness* Milosz defined poetry as "a passionate pursuit of the Real" (25), he recognized elsewhere that *Pan Tadeusz*, written with the goal "to fortify the heart," "is a fairy tale, an idyll, an embellishment" (YH, 363). "The Real," for Milosz, is Platonic rather than scientific.

60. Right after World War II, Milosz had similarly argued with a pro-Soviet realist critic that the social function of poetry was to sustain an Arcadian dream of "universal happiness." "Sometimes the world loses its face. It becomes too base. The task of the poet is to restore its face, because otherwise man is lost in doubt and despair. It is an indication that the world need not always be like this, it can be different" (Milosz, "A Semi-Private Letter about Poetry" [1946], in Czeslaw Milosz, *To Begin Where I Am: Selected Essays*, 348, 350).

61. Wlliam Blake, "Appendix to the Prophetic Books, On Virgil," https://www.bartleby.com/235/343.html: "Virgil and Ovid confirm this opinion, and make us reverence the Word of God, the only light of antiquity that remains unperverted by War. Virgil in the Æneid, Book vi, line 848, says: 'Let others study Art: Rome has somewhat better to do, namely War and Dominion.'" I discuss this often-repeated charge in *Enmindment—A History: A Post-Secular Poem in Prose* (forthcoming).

62. He may however have been influenced by his work translating Simone Weil. Weil, he told Merton, "considered Lucretius the only Roman poet, redeeming, to some extent, Roman (worthless) literature. A similar view in our poet of the 1st half of the XIX c, Mickiewicz" (*Striving Towards Being: The Letters of Thomas Merton and Czeslaw Milosz*, ed. Robert Faggen [New York: Farrar, Straus and Giroux, 1997], 150).

63. Cf. Erich Auerbach, trans. Willard Trask, *Mimesis: The Representation of Reality in Western Literature* (Princeton, NJ: Princeton University Press, 1968), 154.

64. Cf. *Tao Te Ching*, 56: "Those who know do not speak; those who speak do not know."

65. Cf. YH, 135: "Poland is a country of unheard-of caste differences, from heights such as are rarely met with elsewhere, to depressing lower depths, and perhaps the most powerful strata are the two extremes."

66. Milosz had echoed Oscar's concern in the Poetic Treatise: "This was a time of schism . . . a poet without community / Rustles in the wind like dry grass in December" (TP, 20; cf. Eliot's "Hollow Men"), Oscar himself has been criticized for exemplifying the split. In translating Lithuanian myths, he made allusions "to such masters of literary representation as Homer, Virgil, Dante Alighieri, Johan von Goethe, William Shakespeare, Edgar Allan Poe, Henry Wordsworth Longfellow, Daniel Defoe,

Voltaire, and others. Thus, the [Oscar] Miloszean texts restructure the picture of the Lithuanian audience from ancient rural (i.e. peasant/primitive) into elite (i.e. aristocratic/learned)" (Jadvyga Krūminienė, "Oscar Miłosz as Translator: Playing Games with Memory," *Respectus Philologicus*, April 2010.)

67. Milosz, "Nobel Lecture," 280 (emphasis added).

68. After winning the Nobel Prize, Milosz embraced the disjunction less ironically in his poem "Dante." Looking at a woman sitting at the edge of a bathtub ("Theodora, / Elvira, or Julia, whatever the name / Of her with whom I sleep and play chess"), he concluded by addressing Dante, and quoting from the *Paradiso*:

. . . . only, as once for you, this remains real:
La concreata e perpetua sete,[Dante, *Paradiso*]
The inborn and the perpetual desire
Del deiformo regno—for a God-like domain,
A realm or a kingdom. There is my home.
I cannot help it. I pray for light,
For the inside of the eternal pearl. *L'eterna margarita*.
(NCP, 567–68)

In thus grounding a vision of a "second space" in a setting of sordid casual sex, Milosz, once again, was thinking of Eliot's *Waste Land*.

69. Milosz, in Ewa Czarnecka and Aleksander Fiut, *Conversations with Czeslaw Milosz*, 202.

70. Cf. WP, 104: "[A] poet, as I have said, should be faithful to reality, evaluating it with a sense of hierarchy."

71. I believe it is no accident that the word "renewal" itself (παλινγενεσία, *renovatio*) dates from the period of widely perceived secular and religious disaster and renewal, at the beginning of the Common Era (see Titus 3:5).

72. As Plato once wrote, "You cannot be both powerful in the state and unlike it in character" (*Gorgias*, 513B); Peter Dale Scott, *Minding the Darkness: A Poem for the Year 2000* [New York: New Directions, 2000], 43).

73. Michael North, "Eliot, Lukács, and the Politics of Modernism," in Ronald Bush (ed.), *T. S. Eliot: The Modernist in History* (Cambridge: Cambridge University Press, 1991), 170.

74. *Criterion* 2 (1924): 231.

75. Jesse T. Airaudi, "Eliot, Milosz, and the Enduring Modernist Protest," *Twentieth Century Literature* (Winter, 1988): 453.

76. Czeslaw Milosz, "Reflections on T. S. Eliot" (1965), in Milosz, *To Begin Where I Am*, 391. As noted earlier, this charge could be laid against Milosz himself.

77. Milosz, "Reflections on T. S. Eliot," 397.

78. Milosz, "Nobel Lecture."

79. T. S. Eliot, "Tradition and the Individual Talent," in *Selected Essays*, 17. This immature jibe at the decadent romanticism of Dowson and J. M. Murray was irreconcilable with Eliot's later respect for Dante, who defined his *dolce stil nuovo* with the speech of his purgatorial pilgrim Bernart de Ventadorn: "I'mi son un che, quando / Amor mi spira, noto, e a quel modo / ch'e'ditta dentro" [I am one who, when Love

breathes in me, takes note, and goes affirming what he dictates to me inwardly] (*Purgatorio* 24:52–54).
80. T. S. Eliot, *The Idea of a Christian Society* (New York: Harcourt Brace, 1940), in T. S. Eliot, *Christianity and Culture: The Idea of a Christian Society, and Notes towards the Definition of Culture* (New York: Harcourt, Brace & World, 1968), 50–51.
81. Czeslaw Milosz, interviewed by Robert Faggen, "The Art of Poetry No. 70," *Paris Review* (Winter 1994), http://www.theparisreview.org/interviews/1721/czeslaw-milosz-the-art-of-poetry-no-70-czeslaw-milosz, emphasis in original.
82. See e.g., Lyndall Gordon, *T. S. Eliot: An Imperfect Life* (New York: Norton, 1998). Milosz in his autobiography writes, "Nothing could stifle my inner certainty that a shining point exists where all lines intersect." This seems to recall "Eliot's 'heart of light,' just as a later reference to his "contemplation of a motionless point" seems to echo Eliot's "still point of the turning world" (NR, 87, 125; T. S. Eliot, *Four Quartets* [New York: Harcourt Brace, 1943]. 14, 18).
83. "William Blake combats the diabolic vassal of inertia responsible for the inhuman industrialization of England, or, as Allen Ginsberg calls it, 'Moloch whose name is the mind'" (Czeslaw Milosz, "The Rebirth of Utopia: Herbert Marcuse," in Visions, 185).
84. T. S. Eliot, *The Waste Land and Other Writings* (New York: Modern Library, 2001), 185.
85. Czeslaw Milosz, "The Rebirth of Utopia: Herbert Marcuse," in Visions, 185; quoting from Allen Ginsberg, "Howl": "Moloch whose fate is a cloud of sexless hydrogen! Moloch whose name is the Mind! Moloch in whom I sit lonely! Moloch in whom I dream Angels! Crazy in Moloch!"
86. Milosz, "Nobel Lecture."

CHAPTER 16

1. Czeslaw Milosz, letter to Thomas Merton of January 17, 1959, in *Striving Towards Being: The Letters of Thomas Merton and Czeslaw Milosz* (New York: Farrar, Straus and Giroux, 1997), 9. In focusing on my preferred Milosz, I have done less than justice to related themes that keep recurring in these pages—above all, Milosz's attitudes toward women, love, and sex. In much of his writings, Milosz presents himself, I would say, as more a man of the past than of the future. I attribute this in large part to the permanent damage done to his marriage, by the involuntary separation of Milosz and Janka for three years after his defection, during which time he became involved with the Swiss philosopher Jeanne Hersch. But in my view, much I might have criticized is redeemed by the profundity of his loving elegy, "Orpheus and Eurydice," on the death of his second wife, Carol Thigpen (SS, 99–102).
2. "Kultura jest wyjściem poza człowieka aktualne" (Stanisław Brzozowski, *Pamiętnik* [1913] [Kraków: Wydawnictwo Literackie, 1985], 165; in Małgorzata Zemła, "Tygrys: Gnoza polityczna," *Postscriptum Polonistyczne* [2011], 184).
3. The *Oxford English Dictionary* gives as example, "CHAUCER Parson's Tale 973 For, as seith Ierom, by fasting be saned [Skeat prints saved; Pseudo-Jerome

(Migne xxx. 616) has sanandæ] the vices of flesh, and by prayere the vices of the soule."

4. Marjorie Perloff, *Poetic License: Essays on Modernist and Postmodernist Lyric* (Evanston, IL: Northwestern University Press, 1990), 2.

5. Robert Middlekauff, *The Great Cause: The American Revolution, 1763–1789* (Oxford: Oxford University Press, 2005), 51, 136ff; Lydia Dittler Schulman, *Paradise Lost and the Rise of the American Republic* (Boston: Northeastern University Press, 1992).

6. For example, *The Road to 9/11* (Lanham, MD: Rowman & Littlefield, 2007), 250–53; cf. *The American Deep State* (Lanham, MD: Rowman & Littlefield, 2017), 180–81.

7. Adam Michnik, "The Montesinos virus—Democracy, Dictatorship, Peru, Serbia, Poland," *Social Research* (Winter, 2001), http://www.looksmarttrends.com/p/articles/mi_m2267/is_4_68/ai_83144752.

8. Peter Dale Scott, "Czeslaw Milosz and Solidarity; or, Poetry and the Liberation of a People," *Brick* 78 (Winter 2006): 67–74. Cf. Peter Dale Scott, *The Road to 9/11* (Berkeley: University of California Press, 2007), 257.

9. When I first finished this book, I knew of no other thinker with a notion of "unpolitical politics." But it turns out there is one: Jacques Ellul's very relevant advocacy of Christian anarchism as "the only 'political anti-political' position in accord with Christian thinking" (Jacques Ellul, "Anarchism and Christianity," *Katallagete* 7, no. 3 [Autumn 1980]: S. 20–21; https://www.jesusradicals.com/uploads/2/6/3/8/26388433/anarchism-and-christianity.pdf). Although Ellul's paradoxical summation is not identical with Milosz's, the future he advocates is very compatible with that envisioned in Milosz's *The Land of Ulro*, precisely because both men escape the confines of present politics to project a less violent notion of power.

10. Let me spell this out a little for the unconvinced. If an American party becomes too clearly committed to change, as the Democrats did in 1972 with McGovern, the result is defeat. And if progressives group instead behind a third-party candidate, like Ralph Nader in 2000 or Jill Stein in 2016, the result will again be defeat.

11. Peter Dale Scott, *The Road to 9/11: Wealth, Empire, and the Future of America* (Berkeley: University of California Press, 2007), 250–53.

12. Discussion in Peter Dale Scott, *The American Deep State: Wall Street, Big Oil, and the Attack on US Democracy* (Lanham, MD: Rowman & Littlefield, 2015), 168–73.

13. Seamus Heaney, *Finders Keepers: Selected Prose 1971–2001* (New York: Farrar, Straus and Giroux, 2002), 444.

14. Czeslaw Milosz, "The Importance of Simone Weil" (1960), in Czeslaw Milosz, *To Begin Where I Am: Selected Essays* (New York: Farrar, Straus and Giroux, 2001), 247–48.

15. T. S. Eliot, "Virgil and the Christian World," in T. S. Eliot, *On Poetry and Poets* (London: Faber & Faber, 1957), 128.

16. Milosz, *To Begin Where I Am*, 248. Cf. Czeslaw Milosz, *Striving Towards Being*, 49–50: "I cannot get rid of hostility towards the idea of Providence in history. . . . Dislike Bossuet."

17. Peter Dale Scott with Freeman Ng, *Poetry and Terror: The Politics and Poetics of* Coming to Jakarta (Lanham, MD: Lexington, 2018), xv, 147–48, 185–86. Failure to make this elementary distinction was the problem with Shelley's overstated dictum in his *Defence of Poetry*, "Poets are the unacknowledged legislators of the world." Poets are leaders who advance us in the realm of culture, after which it falls to politicians to legislate.

18. Dogs and other animals are said to be able to anticipate earthquakes, because they can hear the high-frequency compressional soundwaves preceding them that are undetectable by human ears.

19. Compare Hölderlin's homage in his poem "Rousseau":
In the first sign he sees the final meaning,
And flies, this bold spirit, as eagles do,
Ahead of thunderstorms, to warn
Of the gods' approach.
(Friedrich Hölderlin, ed. D. E. Sattler, *Sämtliche Werke: Frankfurter Ausgabe* [Basel: Stroemfeld/Roter Stern, 1999], 5:787. Trans. by Maxine Chernoff).

20. Czeslaw Milosz, *The Captive Mind* (New York: Vintage 1990), 216, 237.

21. Adam Zagajewski has written how the writers under Communism "contributed to some degree to the collapse of the totalitarian Soviet system"; whereas today, facing "the dark sides of capitalism . . . they are probably more helpless than before, in the old times" (Adam Zagajewski, "The closing of an open society," *Eurozine*, March 1, 2016, https://www.eurozine.com/the-closing-of-an-open-society/). I would paraphrase this important insight by observing that the condition of free intellects is no longer as dialectical as before.

22. Lynn White Jr., *Technology and Invention in the Middle Ages* (Cambridge, MA: Mediaeval academy of America, 1940), discussion in Peter Dale Scott, *Enmindment— A History: A Post-Secular Poem in Prose* (forthcoming).

23. Elsewhere Milosz also quotes from Dante, witness to the chaos between the Great Interregnum in the Holy Roman Empire (1245–1312) and the so-called Babylonian Captivity of the Papacy (1309–1376); and from Plato, who wrote in response to the decisive defeat of Athens and loss of its empire.

24. For my thoughts on the unfashionableness of this belief in America, see my essay "Donna Brookman: Artist of Evolutions," in Donna Brookman, *Palace of Memory* (Berkeley: Gray Heron Press, 2017), 7–11.

25. Milosz, "Nobel Lecture," in Czeslaw Milosz, *Beginning with My Streets: Essays and Recollectios* (New York: Farrar, Straus and Giroux, 1991), 282.

26. For example, Theodor W. Adorno, "Commitment," *New Left Review* I/87–88, September–December 1974; in Terry Eagleton and Drew Milne, *Marxist Literary Theory: A Reader* (Oxford: Blackwell Publishers, 1996), 202: "Even in the most sublimated work of art there is a hidden 'it should be otherwise'. . . . As eminently constructed and produced objects, works of art . . . point to a practice from which they abstain: the creation of a just life."

27. Helen Vendler, *The Harvard Book of Contemporary American Poetry* (Cambridge, MA: Belknap Press/ Harvard University Press, 1985), 8; citing Richard Wilbur's sonnet "Praise in Summer." For Vendler, there is a radical disconnect between

the other world of poetry and this one, and if poetry teaches, it teaches the individual only. "We live in the poem's world, not it in ours."

28. One can perhaps see a parodic correlative to Isaiah's vision of non-martial peace in Homer's comically fanciful vision of a peaceful Phaeacia, the land which gave a temporary home and restoration to the warrior Odysseus, after a disastrous shipwreck in which all his companions were lost. The Phaeacians are not only kind but nonviolent and flagrantly antiheroic, as their king explained: "We may not be the greatest boxers or wrestlers, but we run fast in the race, and we are the finest sailors: and ever the feast is dear to us, the dancing and the lyre, fresh clothes, warm baths, and bed. . . . We excel not only in swiftness of foot, and seamanship, but in dancing too, and in song" (Odyssey 8:246–49, 252–53). Horace made a derogatory comparison of this unheroic androgynous life to the urban Rome of his era (Epistle 2). But in other respects, Phaeacia was transcendentally otherworldly, as King Alcinous explained: "For the Phaeacians have no pilots; their vessels have no rudders as those of other nations have, but the ships themselves understand what it is that we are thinking about and want; they know all the cities and countries in the whole world" (Odyssey, 8:557–59).

29. T. S. Eliot, "Virgil and the Christian World," in T. S. Eliot, *On Poetry and Poets* (London: Faber & Faber, 1957), 147–48.

30. Carlo Caruso and Andrew Laird (eds.) *Italy and the Classical Tradition: Language, Thought and Poetry 1300–1600* (London: Duckworth, 2009), 145.

31. John of Salisbury, *Policraticus*. in Marilynn Desmond, *Reading Dido: Gender, Textuality, and the Medieval Aeneid* (Minneapolis: University of Minnesota Press, 1994), 93. Cf. Bernardus Silvestris (twelfth century) on *Aeneid* 4:641–77: "Eneas speaks to the shade of Dido as the rational spirit, through hesitation, contemplates the natures of desire" (ibid., 91).

32. *Purgatorio*, 30:48; cf. *Aeneid*, 4:23, *agnosco veteris vestigia flammae*.

33. Vladimir Mayakovsky, "To the readers of our New First Unexpected," https://www.marxists.org/subject/art/literature/mayakovsky/1917/slap-in-face-public-taste.htm.

34. Peter Dale Scott, *The Road to 9/11* (Berkeley: University of California Press, 2007), 250. Political events since the Capitol intrusion of January 2021 have only increased the need for musual understanding, or what Milosz called "a new tenderness" (czułość); NCP, 144; TP, 52.

35. Iain McGilchrist, *The Master and His Emissary: The Divided Brain and the Making of the Western World* (New Haven, CT: Yale University Press, 2018), 331: "The highest achievements of the Enlightenment, those for which eighteenth century culture is widely admired, express harmony and balance. . . . But built into the foundations of e Enlightenment thought are precepts that are bound to lead eventually to a less flexible and humane outlook, that of the left hemisphere alone" (331–32).

36. David Bethea, *Joseph Brodsky and the Creation of Exile* (Princeton, NJ: Princeton University Press, 1994), 39.

37. Nicoleta Stanca, *Duality of Vision in Seamus Heaney's Writings* (Constanța: ExPonto, 2009).

38. "Jane Hirshfield on Czesław Miłosz (California Poet)," *Reader's Almanac*, October 12, 2012, http://blog.loa.org/2012/10/jane-hirshfield-on-czesaw-miosz.html.
39. Gillian Valladares Castellino, "The Captive Mind by Czeslaw Milosz," Read-Nobels, September 29, 2015, http://readnobels.blogspot.com/2015/09/the-captive-mind-by-czeslaw-milosz.html: "Emigration gave Milosz the gift of penetrating dual vision, i.e., the capacity to see and understand simultaneously, the inner workings of two widely disparate cultures, the Communist East and the democratic West." Of course, this book traces Milosz's doubleness, like that of Mickiewicz, back to the accident of birth in a region. Lithuania, where two discrete cultures were prevalent.
40. Czeslaw Milosz, *The Captive Mind* (New York: Vintage, 1990), v.
41. Max Planck, trans. J. Murphy, *Where Is Science Going?* (London: Allen & Unwin, 1933), 217.
42. Joseph Brodsky, "Presentation of Czeslaw Milosz to the [Neustadt Award] Jury," *World Literature Today* 3 (1978): 364.
43. Quoted in Michael Richard Parker, "Past Master: Czeslaw Milosz and His Impact on the Poetry of Seamus Heaney," *Textual Practice* 27, no. 5 (2013): https://www.tandfonline.com/doi/full/10.1080/0950236X.2012.751448. I see a greater homage in Heaney's book *Station Island*, where the magnificent central poem of that title, ending in a sea-side cloudburst, reads like a Joycean counter-argument to Milosz's kindred "Treatise on Poetry." (Evidence for this reading of "Station Island" can be seen in its framing between "Away from It All," which quotes Milosz ["I was stretched between contemplation / of a motionless point / and the command to participate / actively in history," cf. NR 125], and "The Master," in which Parker has discerned "an accurate portrayal of key facets of Miłosz's history and personality" [Parker, "Past master"].)
44. Nina Simone played a similar role among African Americans. See Scott with Ng, *Poetry and Terror*, 186, 200.

THREE POEMS TO CZESLAW MILOSZ: INTRODUCED BY A PERSONAL MEMOIR

1. Peter Dale Scott, *The Road to 9/11: Wealth, Empire, and the Future of America* (Berkeley and Los Angeles: University of California Press, 2007), 253, 265, etc.
2. Visions, 214, 127. The chief student demand was for the right to speak and organize politically on campus in support of the civil rights movement, a demand soon endorsed (with restrictions as to time, place, and manner) by the faculty (including myself), and eventually the university.
3. See my poem "Greek Theater," *Walking on Darkness* (Rhinebeck, NY: Sheep Meadow Press, 2016), 28–35; *The American Deep State* (Lanham, MD: Rowman & Littlefield, 2014), 183–90.
4. The issue is an open-ended and subtle one. What comes off in English as poetic inversion is in Polish a not unusual reversal of the adjective-noun word order at the end of the preceding stanza. See my note, "Translating 'Pebble' with Czeslaw Milosz," https://www.peterdalescott.net/pebble/.

Another issue between us was how to translate the title of *Po ziemi naszej*. I wanted a literal equivalent: "Throughout Our Earth," Milosz settled for the less radical "Throughout Our Lands."

5. Peter Dale Scott, "Letter to Czeslaw Milosz," in Peter Dale Scott, *Crossing Borders: Selected Shorter Poems* (New York: New Directions, 1994), 35. It is significant to me that whereas at first his collaborators all spoke Polish to some extent, increasingly with the passage of time most of them did not.

6. Peter Dale Scott with Freeman Ng, *Poetry and Terror: The Politics and Poetics of* Coming to Jakarta (Lanham, MD: Lexington, 2018), 23–24.

7. Miłosz, *To Begin Where I Am* (New York: Farrar, Straus and Giroux, 2001), 345.

8. It developed later that it was Milosz, not I, who had a "quarrel" with Virgil and classicism (WP, 59–75).

9. Ted Hughes and Seamus Heaney (eds.), *The Rattle Bag* (London: Faber & Faber, 1982), 498. Contains "Two Drops" by Zbigniew Herbert, translated by Peter Dale Scott, 441. (Translation erroneously attributed in first edition to Czeslaw Milosz.) The 2007 Ecco edition of Herbert's *Collected Poems* says that the opening epigraph for "Two Drops" from Słowacki "was added by Milosz and Scott." In fact, it was contributed by my language tutor in Poland, a friend of Herbert's.

10. Zbigniew Herbert. *Selected Poems*, translated from the Polish by Czeslaw Milosz and Peter Dale Scott. (Manchester: Carcanet Press, 1985; New York: Ecco Press, 1986).

11. When I called Stanford to ask for an explanation, I was told that "We understand that there is some kind of antagonism between you and Milosz."

12. "Letter to Czeslaw Milosz," in Scott, *Crossing Borders*, 39.

13. Scott, *Listening to the Candle*, 131; reproduced as "For Czeslaw Milosz." Milosz had brought up the torching of Wheeler Hall, the building containing my office. What actually burned was a large assembly room used regularly for meetings by student protesters. At the time, forces in the administration, perhaps acting in conjunction with Governor Reagan's terrorism advisor, Louis Giuffrida, were systematically eliminating these potential meeting-places for radical assemblies, and in my view the responsibility for this act of arson remains unknown. (For more on Giuffrida, see Scott, *The American Deep State*, 32.)

14. Cynthia L. Haven (editor), *An Invisible Rope: Portraits of Czeslaw Milosz* (Athens, OH: Ohio UP, 2011).

15. In *Encounter*, February 1964, 46–49. One year later, while I was still in Milosz's good graces, six sections of the poem were republished in *Postwar Polish Poetry* as "translated by Peter Dale Scott with my minor assistance" (Czeslaw Milosz, ed. and trans., *Postwar Polish Poetry: An Anthology* [Garden City, NY: Doubleday, 1965], vii, cf. 54–56).

16. "The Forest of Wishing," *Times Literary Supplement* (London) 3, 316 (September 16, 1965), 798.

17. Visions, 108, 130; Peter Dale Scott, *Coming to Jakarta* (New York: New directions, 1989), IV.ii, 104.

THREE POEMS TO CZESLAW MILOSZ

1. Peter Dale Scott, "Letter to Czeslaw Milosz," *Crossing Borders: Selected Poems* (New York: New Directions, 1994), 33–38.
2. Visions, 218: "I have never considered myself a political writer and have no ambition to save America or the world."
3. Peter Dale Scott, *Listening to the Candle* (New York: New Directions, 1989), IV.v, 128–33.
4. Czeslaw Milosz, *The Separate Notebooks* (New York: Ecco Press, 1984), 18–19. Henceforth "Milosz '84."
5. Thomas Merton, *Confessions of a Guilty Bystander* (New York: Doubleday 1968), 139.
6. Czeslaw Milosz, *The Separate Notebooks* (New York: Ecco Press, 1984), 200–201.
7.Czeslaw Milosz and Nathan Gardels, "An Interview with Czeslaw Milosz," *New York Review of Books*, February 27, 1986, 34.
8. Doan Van Toai, "Vietnam: How We Deceive Ourselves," *Commentary*, March 1986, 43.
9. Pauline Yu, *The Poetry of Wang Wei: New Translations and Commentary* (Bloomington Indiana: Indiana University Press, 1980), 198.
10. "Reflections on T. S. Eliot" (*Kultur*a, March 1965), in Czeslaw Milosz, *To Begin Where I Am*, 397.

A Short Milosz Bibliography

The volume *Czeslaw Milosz: An International Bibliography 1930–1980* (Ann Arbor, MI, 1983) ran to 162 pages. The Franaszek biography in Polish has seven pages of short titles by Milosz; in English three and a half. What is supplied here is a very short list of titles, primarily those used in preparing this book.

WORKS BY CZESLAW MILOSZ

Milosz, Czeslaw. *Beginning with My Streets: Essays and Recollections*. New York: Farrar, Straus and Giroux, 1991.
———. *The Captive Mind*. New York: Vintage, 1990 (1953).
———. *Emperor of the Earth: Modes of Eccentric Vision*. Berkeley: University of California Press, 1977.
———. *The Issa Valley*. New York: Farrar, Straus and Giroux, 1978 (1955).
———. *Kontynenty*. Kraków: Wydawnictwo Znak, 1999 (1958).
———. *The Land of Ulro*. New York: Farrar, Straus and Giroux, 1985 (1977).
———. *Legends of Modernity*. New York: Farrar, Straus and Giroux, 2005 (1996).
———. *Milosz's ABC's*. New York: Farrar, Straus and Giroux, 2001 (1997).
———. *Native Realm: A Search for Self-Definition*. New York: Farrar, Straus and Giroux, 1968 (1958).
———. *New and Collected Poems, 1931–2001*. New York: Ecco, 2003.
———. *Second Space: New Poems*. New York: Ecco, 2004 (2002).
———. *Selected and Last Poems*. New York: Ecco, 2006.
———. *Striving Towards Being: The Letters of Thomas Merton and Czeslaw Milosz*, ed. Robert Faggen. New York: Farrar, Straus and Giroux, 1995.
———. *To Begin Where I Am*. New York: Farrar, Straus and Giroux, 2001.
———. *A Treatise on Poetry*. New York: Ecco Press/ HarperCollins, 2001 (1957).
———. *Visions from San Francisco Bay*. New York: Farrar, Straus and Giroux, 1982 (1969).
———. *Wiersze*. Kraków: Wydawnictwo Znak, 2001–2003. Volumes 1–3.
———. *The Witness of Poetry*. Cambridge, MA: Harvard University Press, 1983,

———. *A Year of the Hunter*. New York: Noonday Press/Farrar, Straus and Giroux, 1995 (1990).

SECONDARY MATERIALS: BOOKS

Carpenter, Bogdana. *The Poetic Avant-Garde in Poland, 1918–1939*. Seattle: University of Washington Press, 1983.
Cavanagh, Clare. *Lyric Poetry and Modern Politics: Russia, Poland, and the West*. New Haven, CT: Yale University Press, 2009.
Czarnecka, Ewa, and Aleksander Fiut. *Conversations with Czeslaw Milosz*. San Diego, CA: Harcourt Brace Jovanovich, 1987.
Davie, Donald. *Czeslaw Milosz and the Insufficiency of Lyric*. Knoxville: University of Tennessee Press, 1986.
Eile, Stanislaw, and Ursula Phillips, eds. *New Perspectives in Twentieth-Century Polish Literature: Flight from Martyrology*. Basingstoke: Macmillan, 1992.
Fiut, Aleksander. *The Eternal Moment: The Poetry of Czeslaw Milosz*. Berkeley: University of California Press, 1990.
———, ed. *Poznawanie Miłosza 2*. Kraków: Wydawnictwo Literackie, 2000.
Franaszek, Andrzej. *Miłosz: Biografia*. Kraków: Znak, 2011.
———. *Miłosz: A Biography*. Cambridge, MA: Harvard University Press, 2017.
Golubiewski, Mikolaj. *The Persona of Czesław Miłosz: Authorial Poetics, Critical Debates, Reception Games*. Berlin: Peter Lang Edition, 2018
Grudzinska Gross, Irena. *Czesław Miłosz and Joseph Brodsky: Fellowship of Poets*. New Haven, CT: Yale University Press, 2009.
Hass, Robert. *Twentieth Century Pleasures: Prose on Poetry*. New York: Ecco Press, 1984.
———. *What Light Can Do: Essays on Art, Imagination, and the Natural World*. New York: Ecco, 2012.
Haven, Cynthia L. *Czesław Miłosz: A California Life*. Berkeley, CA: Heyday, 2021.
———, ed. *Czesław Miłosz: Conversations*. Jackson, MS: University Press of Mississippi, 2006.
———, ed. *An Invisible Rope: Portraits of Czeslaw Milosz*. Athens, OH: Ohio University Press, 2011.
Heaney, Seamus. *Finders Keepers: Selected Prose 1971–2001*. New York: Farrar, Straus and Giroux, 2002.
Kołodziejczyk, Ewa. *Amerykańskie powojnie Czesława Miłosza*. Warsaw: Instytut Badań Literackich, 2015.
———. "Czesław Miłosz's American Experience in *Światło dzienne* (Daylight)." *Acta Universitatis Lodziensis: Folia Litteraria Polonica* 8, no. 38 (2016): http://dx.doi.org/10.18778/1505-9057.38.07.
Kraszewski, Charles S. *Irresolute Heresiarch: Catholicism, Gnosticism and Paganism in the Poetry of Czesław Miłosz*. Newcastle upon Tyne: Cambridge Scholars Publishing, 2012.

Levine, Madeline G. *Contemporary Polish Poetry, 1925–1975*. Boston: Twayne Publishers, 1981.
Możejko, Edward, ed. *Between Anxiety and Hope: The Poetry and Writing of Czeslaw Milosz*. Edmonton: University of Alberta Press, 1988.
Nathan, Leonard, and Arthur Quinn. *The Poet's Work: An Introduction to Czeslaw Milosz*. Cambridge, MA: Harvard University Press, 1991.
Tischner, Łukasz. *Miłosz and the Problem of Evil*. Evanston, IL: Northwestern University Press, 2015.
Vendler, Helen. *The Music of What Happens: Poems, Poets, Critics*. Cambridge, MA: Harvard University Press, 1988.

PERIODICALS

Kołodziejczyk, Ewa. "Miłosz's American Alphabet." *Przekładaniec* ("Between Miłosz and Milosz") 25 (2011): 7–25.
Vendler, Helen. "A Lament in Three Voices." *New York Review of Books*, May 21, 2001.

Index

abandonment, transcendence and, 62–63
absence, of transcendence, 53
Adam Kadmon, 204
Adams, John, 18, 24, 233, 236
adolescent years of Milosz, 7, 177, 198
Aeneid (Virgil), 86, 236, 238, 239
Age of Raptures, 203, 218–220, 219, 229
Age of Reason, 63, 100, 157, 214, 219
Airaudi, Jesse, 228
Albigensians, 60, 184
alienation of Milosz: from class, 31, 34; from contemporary culture, 71; from East and West, 117, 129; from nationality, 34, 83; at school, 30; from Stalinism, 125
Alter, Robert, 74, 75
ambivalence of Milosz: about class, 30–32, 83; about nationality, 30–32, 83, 94–95; about nature, 10, 50–51; toward romanticism, 40
America: acceptance and support in, 9; adjustments to life in, 6; arrival in, 6; Chomsky on foreign policy of, 9; fame in, 15; lessons to learn from Milosz, 14–16, 233; Milosz's unpolitical politics and politics of, 232–233. *See also* Berkeley, University of California at; Vietnam

American poets: contemporary, 15; Milosz on, 200, 228. *See also specific poets*
American Revolution, 16, 18, 232–33, 236
Anders, Jaroslaw, 215–16
Andrzejewski, Jerzy, 35, 118, 120
Antigone (literary character), 101
anti-nationalist views of Milosz, 19, 30, 32
anti-Semitism, 30, 190
apocatastasis doctrine, 193
Arendt, Hannah, 24, 76
Arnold, Matthew, 221
Art and the Nation (journal), 98–99
As You Like It (Shakespeare), 46, 97
attainable/unattainable, in Milosz's poetry, 132; in "Esse," 66; in "Mittelbergheim," 130, 132; in "To Allen Ginsberg," 182
Auden, W. H.: *The Double Man*, 46, 107, 109–10, 113–14, 136, 139, 162, 166; influence of, 6, 16; "Letter," 110–13, 116–18
Auerbach, Erich, 223
"Auguries of Innocence" (Blake), 65
Augustine of Hippo, Saint, 60, 220

Bacon, Francis, 14

345

Baczyński, Krzysztof Kamil, 26, 47, 71, 98–99
balance: between being and becoming, 65–66; Milosz on, 122, 173, 226; of opposites, 136, 173; poetry and restoration of, 240; reason and, 213, 214, 240; salvation and, 107, 117–18; search for, 110–13, 240–41; theme of, 131
bard (*wieszcz*): defined, 5; goal of, 194; Mickiewicz as, 23, 216; in post-secular era, 237; role of global bard, 129, 185–86, 189, 216; role of national bard, 23, 55–56, 218; tradition of, 5
bardic voice of Milosz: in Goszyce poems, 85–89; movement away from, 6, 11, 55, 113–16, 191, 193; in *Ocalenie*, 79; revival of, 194
Baudelaire, Charles, 220
Bauman, Zygmunt, 11
becoming: balance and, 65, 183; choice between *being* and, 8, 132–36, 148, 160–62; eternal moment and, 160–62; as history, 138, 159, 234; in *Ocalenie*, 61, 62; poetic Hegelianism and, 119; transcendence and, 57; in "The World," 61, 65. *See also devenir*
Beethoven, Ludwig von, 13, 219
being (*esse*): balance and, 183–84; choice between *becoming* and, 8, 132–36; eternal moment and, 160–62, 171; history and, 185; in *Ocalenie*, 61; reflected being and, 66; in *A Treatise on Poetry*, 33, 160–62, 171; in "The World," 61, 62, 65
Bellow, Saul, 15
Berkeley, University of California at: in 1961, 181–88; author's years with, 3–16; counterculture at, 9, 12–13, 190, 241; Milosz at, 181–82, 183; self-reflexive poetry in Berkeley, 192–94; student revolution at, 190; "Throughout Our Lands," 182–87

Bierut, Boleslaw, 125
Blake, William, 4, 6, 8, 14, 16, 35, 40, 45, 46, 86, 87, 89, 96, 105, 109, 110, 113, 134, 161, 185, 193, 199, 209, 214–16, 218–19, 220, 221–22, 226–27, 229–30, 237, 240
Błoński, Jan, 46, 75
Boehme, Jakob, 35, 202, 214
Bolshevik Revolution, 82, 169
"A Book in the Ruins" (Milosz), 53, 67
Bossuet, Jacques-Bénigne, 234
brain, bilateral, 33–34, 79, 146, 204, 212, 268n12, 279nn35–36, 325n36
Brémond, Henri, 120
Brodsky, Joseph, 15, 192, 230, 240, 241
Browning, Robert, 46
Bruno, Giordano, 76, 198
Brzozowski, Stanislaw, 14, 40–41, 55, 135, 138, 147, 160, 161, 173, 207, 211–12, 214, 231
Buddhism, 194, 206, 215, 240
Burke, Edmund, 165
Burnham, James, 125, 126, 127, 128
"Burnt Norton" (Eliot), 160
"Bypassing Rue Descartes" (Milosz), 177, 194–98
"By the Peonies" (Milosz), 54, 65, 167

Cabeza de Vaca, Álvar Núñez, 184, 187
"Campo dei Fiori" (Milosz), 46, 47, 49, 53, 68, 73–74, 76
Camus, Albert, 20
capitalism, 8, 35
The Captive Mind (Milosz), 3, 11, 12, 15, 18, 23, 34, 105, 106, 127, 127–29, 134, 156, 173, 175, 236, 241
catastrophism, 7, 36, 37, 39, 183, 215
Catholicism, 186, 209, 230, 234; Catholic Counter-Reformation, 4; Polish Church, 4, 17, 20, 21, 32, 139, 152, 203, 210. *See also* Thomas Aquinas, Saint; Thomism
Catholicism in Milosz's poetry: in "A Poor Christian Looks at the Ghetto," 73–75; in "Przedmowa," 50; in

"From the Rising of the Sun," 192–93; in "Throughout Our Lands," 183, 186, 187; in *A Treatise on Poetry*, 152; in "The World," 60–63, 65–66
Catholicism of Milosz, 7, 20–21, 30, 32, 34, 35, 183, 187, 220, 224, 230, 293n20
Catholic theologians, 234. *See also specific theologians*
Celan, Paul, 15
"Central Park" (Milosz), 117, 129
Chiaromonte, Nicola, 12, 131
Chomski, Father, 32, 33, 36, 163, 199
Chomsky, Noam, 9, 20
Church, Left, Dialogue (Michnik), 20
Church Fathers, 8
CIA (Central Intelligence Agency): Burnham and, 125, 126, 127; Congress for Cultural Freedom (CCF) and, 125, 127, 174; *Encounter* (journal) and, 3; funding by, 12, 125, 126, 127, 128, 174; mistrust of Milosz by, 127, 128
Civitas Dei (City of God) (Augustine of Hippo), 220
class, Milosz's ambivalence about, 30–32, 134–35
classicism: ambivalence of Milosz toward 18th century classicism, 210; Eliot's reactionary classicism, 217, 227–29; neoclassicism of Swift, 118; "Quarrel with Classicism," 166, 206, 222–25, 227; realism and, 114, 227
classicist (satiric) voice, 46, 84, 109, 113–16, 118, 221, 227, 228, 230, 240
closure: of "Beautiful Times," 153; of "Complaint," 91; of "Flight," 91, 178; of "Natura" and Mickiewicz, 177–78; of *Ocalenie*, 168; open closure of "Natura," 174–75; open closure of "The Capital," 143, 153; of "The Sun," 65; of "Treatise on Morals," 116–17; in *The Waste Land* (Eliot), 150, 152
Cohen, Leonard, 241

Cold War: concerns for Poland/Polish intellectuals during, 4; cultural cold war, 12, 155, 174; de-escalation of, 241
Cold Warriors, 6, 175
Coleridge, Samuel Taylor, 40
"Comedian as the Letter C" (Stevens), 157
Commission of National Education, 210
Committee for Workers' Defense (KOR), 17–19
Communism: CIA operations against, 128–29; containment of, 12; Doomed (Cursed) Soldier(s) and, 101; Iron Curtain, 8, 12, 117, 149; Michnik and, 17, 26; Milosz on, 146, 152, 175; westward spread of, 124, 126. *See also* Solidarność (Solidarity)
Communist Party: fall of government in Poland, 200; Jędrychowski and, 34; Modzelewski and, 125; Putrament and, 34; Rakowski and, 11; Wcil and, 8
"Complaint of Ladies from a Bygone Time" (Milosz), 55, 90–91
Confederation for an Independent Poland (KPN), 25–26
Congress for Cultural Freedom (CCF), 6, 12, 126, 127, 130–31, 174, 304n27, 304n30; CIA and, 12
counterculture: defined, 16; disagreements over, 9–11; retreat from condemnation of, 12–13
Cuban Missile Crisis, 12
cultural change, as precursor to political change, 233, 272n56
cultural evolution: in America, 233; catastrophic renewal in Western, 236–37; continuity of Poland's, 208; great poetry and, 165; history as, 235–36; history of, 33, 165; human agency's role in, 112; human doubleness and, 34; human liberation and, 165; Milosz's strategy for, 232; poetry and, 24, 238–39;

political development and, 235–36;
  redirection in, 222; as tending
  toward emancipation, 6; "A Treatise
  on Morals" (Milosz) and, 111,
  113, 118–19; *A Treatise on Poetry*
  (Milosz) and, 137, 139; "Treatise on
  Theology" (Milosz) and, 205. *See
  also* ethogeny
cultural history, 235
cultural identity, 5
cultural politics, 234–35
culture: advancement of, 16; alienation
  from, 71, 83, 86; breakdown of, 112,
  240; class and, 166; concerns over,
  93, 108, 110; correcting culture, 89;
  cultural politics, 234–35; culture
  conflicts of 1930s, 33; defined, 16;
  derision of urban culture, 39; desire
  to save the, 84; divided cultures,
  227; furthered by Enlightenment,
  210; gap between two cultures, 187;
  generative culture, 16; global literary
  culture, 15, 34; human condition
  and, 231; intellectual culture of
  Solidarność (Solidarity), 5; interwar
  Polish culture, 68; isolation of poet
  of high culture, 218; liberal culture,
  228; Metternich on expense of,
  191; Mickiewicz as, 151; Milosz
  as shaper of, 222; Milosz's desire
  to save the, 84; Milosz's quarrel
  with elite culture, 155; nationalistic
  Polish culture, 87; non-Russian folk
  culture, 177; poets' role in evolution
  of, 5, 119; Polish culture in *Treatise
  on Poetry*, Part I, 139–40; pre-
  Enlightenment culture of Lithuania,
  7; redesigning of Polish culture, 21;
  renewal of, 237; restoring Polish
  culture, 22, 55; romantic notion of,
  221; traditional defense of, 182;
  values of, 226; Western cultural
  development, 236–37. *See also*
  cultural evolution
Czapski, Jósef, 20, 125, 126

daimonion of Milosz, 37–38, 88, 95,
  100, 119, 186, 228, 295n10; "Hymn"
  (Milosz) and, 37–38; Milosz on, 38,
  95, 295n10; "In Warsaw" (Milosz)
  and, 88–89, 95, 97–102
Dante Alighieri, 6, 220, 236, 238, 239
Davie, Donald, 189
"Day of Generation" (Milosz), 52, 53
decay: Eliot and oppositional stance to,
  8; in legacy of Enlightenment, 40;
  in Polish romanticism, 40; in *The
  Waste Land*, 134
"Dedication" ("Przedmowa") (Milosz),
  21, 47, 48, 50, 55, 61, 96–100, 108–
  9, 119, 146, 148
defection to West of Milosz, 123–25;
  clandestine background in decision
  on, 126–27
The Descent of the Dove (Williams), 110
détente, 9, 12
devenir: Milosz on, 8; in "Natura," 172;
  in *Ocalenie*, 61–62; transcendence
  and, v, 8, 57, 162, 231; in "The
  World," 62–65. *See also* becoming
dialectical materialism (diamat),
  7, 138, 163
dialectics, in *Ocalenie*, 61–62
The Dismissal of the Greek Envoys
  (Kochanowski), 166
Doctor Faustus (Marlowe), 156
Doomed (Cursed) Soldier(s), 23,
  25–26, 93, 101
Dostoevsky, Fyodor, 147, 149, 214, 239
doubleness: acceptance and exploration
  of, 7; ambivalence about class,
  nationality, and religion, 30–32;
  ambivalence about youthful
  leftist radical identity, 32–35; of
  ambivalence at Goszyce, 182;
  argument for, 131; Auden and,
  109–13; author/Milosz disagreements
  and, 8; balancing of, 13; Brzozowski
  and, 40–41; childhood in Lithuania,
  27–29; between classicism and
  realism, 227–28; as congenial, 7–8;

defined, 4; double focus, 109–10; "Hymn" (Milosz) and, 36–38; move to Poland, 29–30; "Natura" and, 157; neuroscience on human duality and, 212; in "No More," 225; in *Ocalenie*, 57, 61, 65, 66; search for balance and, 110–13; in *Second Space*, 201; "Slow River" (Milosz) and, 38–40; "Song of a Citizen" (Milosz) and, 51; "Three Winters" (Milosz) and, 36–40; in "Throughout Our Lands," 183; tradition and, 218; in *A Treatise on Poetry*, 203; in "The Voices of Poor People," 66, 73; war and, 40–41; wartime poems and, 45, 49; in *Witness*, 224
The Double Man (Auden), 46, 107, 109–10, 113–14, 136, 139, 162, 166
Dylan, Bob, 15, 241
Dziady (*Forefathers' Eve*) (Mickiewicz), 100, 131, 151, 157, 164, 177–78

Eastern Europe: bard (*wieszcz*) meaning in, 5; democratic movement in, 24–25; reminiscences of, 187–88; return to, 189; Soviet Union and, 9. *See also* Poland
Eastern Germany, 12
Eclogues (Virgil), 191
ecstatic pessimist, self-description as, 7, 13, 218
Einstein, Albert, 124, 307n5
"Elegy to N. N." (Milosz), 187–88
Eliot, T. S., 6, 8, 15, 16, 89, 209, 220, 229–30, 239; "The Hollow Men," 69; quarrel with, 227–29; reactionary classicism of, 217, 227–29; *The Waste Land*, 46, 88
emigration of Milosz: ambivalence over, 127–29; being/becoming choice, 132–36; Burnham and, 127; *The Captive Mind*, 127; clandestine background to decision, 126–27; Congress for Cultural Freedom and, 127; defection to West, 123–25; nature/history choice, 132–36; new poetic role's evolution, 129–32; of Polish intellectuals and poets, 11–12; private despair, 127–29; public success, 127–29. *See also* defection to West of Milosz
Encounter (journal), 3
"Encounter" (Milosz), 51, 53
Engels, Friedrich, 40
English Civil War, 236–37
Enlightenment: aging insights of the, 6; conflicting critiques of liberalism of, 8; legacy of materialism/secularism, 7; prose critique of, 14
Enmindment—A History (Scott), 33, 34, 212
Erasmus, 209, 210
Eros, 185, 219
erotic love: Dante and, 238; in *A Treatise on Poetry*, Part IV: "Natura," 159; *Unattainable Earth*, 199–200
Essay on Rime (Shapiro), 107
esse (being): conflicting claims of, 8; in *Ocalenie*, 61–62; in "The World," 62–65. *See also* being (*esse*)
"Esse" (Milosz), 62, 66
eternal moment, 121, 133, 135, 157–58, 160–61, 171
The Eternal Moment (Fiut), 15, 171
ethogeny, 6, 16, 33, 112, 119, 137, 165, 208, 212, 232, 235, 236. *See also* cultural evolution
"Eve," 199
"The Excursion to the Forest" (Milosz), 54, 65
exile of Milosz: in America, 6, 19–20, 200; dual vision and, 240; Milosz on situation after, 105–6; moral leadership after, 75; national bard role after, 55–56; poems after, 121; Polish exiles, 19, 177; Polish government in London in, 145–46, 149. *See also* America; Paris
existentialism, 117, 132, 175, 214, 226, 227

existentialists, 111, 161
Faggen, Robert, 32–33
"Faith" (Milosz), 49, 54, 58, 59, 60, 62, 65, 67, 196, 226
family of Milosz, 27, 31, 280n42. *See also specific family members*
"Farewell" (Milosz), 49–50, 55, 93, 96–97
Faust II (Goethe), 156
"Fear" (Milosz), 54, 57, 58, 64, 65
Fessard, Gaston, 62
Fiut, Aleksandr, 15, 69, 71, 77, 86, 118, 171, 191
"Flight" (Milosz): background of, 30; composition of, 95–96; inspiration in, 164; open closure of, 91, 178; order of, 47, 50, 53, 55; vatic voice of, 85–89, 116, 144. *See also Ocalenie* Part IV
Forefathers' Eve (*Dziady*) (Mickiewicz), 100, 131, 151, 157, 164, 177–78
Foucault, Michel, 6
The Four Quartets (Eliot), 135, 171, 172, 173, 228
Franaszek, Andrzej, 28, 125, 126
France: Catholicism in, 186, 192, 198; Communism and, 126, 155; comparison to America, 40; departure from, 3; Janka and, 129, 169; lack of acceptance and support in, 9, 19; Milosz on, 115; Polish culture and, 84; remote from, 192; Wordsworth and, 88; works published in, 175, 177. *See also* Paris
Frank, Jacob, 214
freedom: of America, 126; Auden and, 109–10, 112; authoritarianism and, 7; cultural freedom campaign, 12; Doomed (Cursed) Soldier(s) and, 26; Fund for Intellectual Freedom, 128; Mickiewicz on, 108, 177; Milosz on, 111, 164–65, 170, 182–83; necessity and, 147–48; neoliberalism and, 7; in "Ode to the City" (Milosz), 190–91;
in "O October," 169–70; Sartre on, 161; in "The Voices of Poor People," 71. *See also* Congress for Cultural Freedom (CCF)
Free Speech Movement (FSM), 9, 190, 232
French Revolution, 62, 88, 149, 178, 210, 235, 237
Freud, Sigmund, 6
"From the Rising of the Sun" (Milosz), 192
Frost, Robert, 155
Fund for Intellectual Freedom, 128
future, poetic act and, 6

Galczyński, Konstanty, 142
"The Gate" (Milosz), 54, 58, 62, 65
generative culture, 16
gentry (*szlachta*), 27, 31, 83–84, 85–86, 178, 210
"Gerontion" (Eliot), 93, 94
Gide, André, 112
Giedroyc, Jerzy, 20, 125, 126
Ginsberg, Allen, 15, 182, 218, 230, 239, 241
global evolution, 234–35
global security, 7, 49
Goethe, Johan von, 51, 156, 166, 214
Gömöri, George, 86
Gorczyńska, Renata, 30, 37, 39, 40, 74, 88, 89, 90, 95, 98, 135, 138, 147, 151, 160–61, 164, 168, 177, 194, 197
Goszyce poems, 82–91; bardic voice in, 85–89, 144–45; existential crisis and, 227; "Flight," 164; minor Goszyce poems, 89–91; as turning point, 82–83. *See also* "Flight" (Milosz)
Gramsci, Antonin, 40
"The Grand Inquisitor" (Dostoevsky), 147, 149
"Greek Portrait" (Milosz), 106
Gregory of Nyssa, Saint, 8
guilt of Milosz: abandonment of women by, 38, 125, 129, 196–98; in "Bypassing Rue Descartes," 194–98;

in "Café," 73; in "Campo dei Fiori," 49, 76; in "A Poor Christian Looks at the Ghetto," 49, 73–76
Gulliver's Travels (Swift), 113

Habermas, Jürgen, 7
Hallberg, Robert von, 15
Harvard lectures, 217, 218, 219, 226, 227
Hass, Robert, 6, 8, 15, 175, 189, 194, 196, 231
Heaney, Seamus, 6, 15, 88, 187, 189, 192, 234, 239, 240, 241
Hegel, Georg Friedrich, 6–7, 62, 145, 146, 147, 173, 240
Hegelianism: *Ocalenie* and, 137–39; prewar Poland's need for "new diction," 147–50; and salvational goal of poetry, 137–39, 146; *A Treatise on Poetry* and, 137–43
Heidegger, Martin, 117, 144, 220
Heller, Erich, 14
"Heraclitus" (Milosz), 170
Herbert, Zbigniew, 4, 11, 23, 29, 129, 225
Herodotus, 161, 162, 166
Hersch, Jeanne, 129, 134, 199
Hertz, Pawel, 132
Hertz, Zygmunt, 128, 132
Heydel, Magda, 46, 69, 70
Hirshfield, Jane, 194, 240
The History of Polish Literature (Milosz), 4, 36, 72, 74, 85, 178, 192, 207, 208, 208–12, 222–23, 224; translation of poems for, 4
Hoene-Wroński, Józef Maria, 149, 152
Hölderlin, Friedrich, 81, 178
"The Hollow Men" (Eliot), 69
Home Army (Armia Krajowa) (AK), 23, 24, 98–99, 107, 145–46
Homer, 220
"The Hooks of a Corset" (Milosz), 159
hope: catastrophism and, 239–41; for liberation, 217–21; poets as repositories and promoters of, 5; ruins, poetry, and, 225–27; "Three Winters" and, 38–40
"Hope" (Milosz), 49, 54, 58, 59–60, 62, 65, 67, 196, 226
Horace, 172, 175, 176, 177, 222, 223
Horodyński, Dominik, 107
Howl (Ginsberg), 182, 239
Hulme, T. E., 228
human duality, 33, 65, 191
Humanists, 8, 33, 72, 107–8, 209, 210, 213
Hungarian uprising of 1956, 152

idealism, 6, 13, 30, 60, 137
The Idea of a Christian Society (Eliot), 229
identity of Milosz: cultural identity, 5, 82–84, 205; prewar social identity, 32, 81–84
"Incantation" (Milosz), 100–101
incantation, Milosz on, 100–101, 156, 220
Indomitable Soldiers, 26. *See also* Doomed (Cursed) Soldier(s)
"In Salem" (Milosz), 199
Internal Security Act of 1950 (McCarran Act), 128
International Rescue Committee, 128
"In Warsaw" (Milosz), 48–50, 53, 88, 95, 97–102; daimonion and, 88, 95; incantation and, 100; last stanza of, 100–102
Iron Curtain, 8, 12, 117, 149. *See also* Communism
irony: in Milosz, 38, 47, 53, 100–102, 121, 142, 168, 220, 287n18; in *Ocalenie*, 49; in Oscar Milosz, 35
The Issa Valley (Milosz), 157
Iwaszkiewicz, Jaroslaw, 35, 86, 141, 142, 223

Jędrychowski, Stefan, 34
Jeffers, Robinson, 4, 9
Jesus Christ, 75, 152

Jewish influences, 20–21, 30, 32, 35, 74–75, 141, 204, 214, 235–36, 237
Joachim of Fiore, 240
John of Salisbury, 238–39
John Paul II, Pope, 17–18, 21, 152
justice: forces tending toward, 235; Milosz on, 207; truth and, 100–102, 108

Ketman practice, 11, 105–6, 108, 109, 122, 173, 231
Kirsch, Adam, 101, 102
Kisielewski, Stefan, 11
Kochanowski, Jan, 4, 166, 209–10, 222–23, 225; *The Dismissal of the Greek Envoys*, 166
Koestler, Arthur, 12, 128
Kołakowski, Leszek, 11, 164, 185
KOR (Committee for Workers' Defense, 17–19
Krasicki, Ignacy, 210
Kraszewski, Gracjan, 231
Kroński, Julius, 107, 115, 117, 119, 132, 138, 162, 163, 174
Kultura (journal), 18, 19, 125, 126, 128, 132, 134, 217–18
Kunat, Gabriela, 187–88

Lagerlöf, Selma, 28, 59
The Land of Ulro (Milosz), 14, 25, 34, 36, 48, 62, 63, 68, 100, 102, 149, 178, 192, 199, 207, 209, 210, 212, 213, 214, 214–16, 215–16, 220, 221–22, 227
Larkin, Philip, 229
Lasch, Christopher, 12
Law and Justice (PiS) Party, 25, 102
Lechoń, Jan, 127, 142
Legends of Modernity (Milosz), 112
The Leman Notebook, 121, 131, 133–35
"The Lesson of Biology" (Milosz), 222
liberalism, 8, 226
liberation of a people, 6, 10, 17, 90, 164–65, 170, 177. *See also* Solidarność (Solidarity)

"The Lie of Poetry" (Milosz), 120, 143
"Lines Written a Few Miles Above Tintern Abbey" (Wordsworth), 46, 88, 89, 237
Lithuania: border fluctuations of, 5, 27–28; childhood of Milosz in, 13, 27, 46, 100, 151, 184, 195; class-defining languages of, 166; comparisons to Poland, 31; folklore of, 31, 63, 99–100, 157, 196, 206, 214, 234; as homeland, 50, 196; memories of, 202; move to Poland from, 29–30; Polish language in, 4, 28; pre-Enlightenment culture of, 7, 29
"The Little Boy Found" (Blake), 57
"The Little Boy Lost" (Blake), 57
Locke, John, 4, 14, 209
"Lot" (Milosz), 90
Lourie, Richard, 121
love: in *Ocalenie*, 168; in *A Treatise on Poetry*, Part IV: "Natura," 166–69; in "The World," 168
"Love" (Milosz), 49, 54, 58, 60, 62, 65, 67, 196, 226
"The Love Song of J. Alfred Prufrock" (Eliot), 69, 77–78, 94
Lowell, Robert, 131, 144, 167, 232
Lukács, Georg, 40, 228
Lyrical Ballads (Wordsworth), 88

Macdonald, Dwight, 12, 20
Magic Flute (Mozart), 219
The Magic Mountain (Mann), 8, 33, 191, 192, 279n31
Mahler, Gustav, 167
Mahon, Derek, 15
Mallarmé, Stephane, 139, 219, 223, 225
"A Man from Detroit" (Milosz), 174–75
Mandelstam, Osip, 4
Manicheanism, 10, 13, 60, 193, 203
Mann, Thomas, 8, 33, 34, 156, 191, 192
Marx, Karl, 6, 40, 62, 137, 173
Marxism, 11, 35, 135, 137, 138, 220, 226

Masonic lodges, 203, 210
The Master and His Emissary (McGilchrist), 33–34, 212–13
materialism, 7, 14, 128, 144, 147
Mayakovsky, Vladimir, 239
McCarran Act (Internal Security Act of 1950), 128
McCarthy, Mary, 12, 131
McDonald, Dwight, 131
McGilchrist, Iain, 33–34, 212–13, 240, 241
McLachlan, H. L., 209
medievalism, 8, 61, 173, 238. *See also* Thomas Aquinas, Saint
Mendelson, Edward, 113, 114
Merton, Thomas, v, 8, 31, 125, 162, 183, 186
Metternich, Klemens von, 190–91
Michnik, Adam, 17, 18, 20–21, 24, 26, 233
Micińska, Nela, 125
Mickiewicz, Adam, 14, 31–32, 40, 118, 151, 177–78, 202
Międzyrzecki, Artur, 11
Miller, Henry, 182
Miłosz, Aleksander (father), 28, 29–30, 31
Miłosz, Andrzej (brother), 3, 23
Milosz, Janina "Janka" (wife): death of, 157, 168, 169, 200, 201; escape from Warsaw, 78, 81, 85, 90; in France, 129, 134; illness of, 196; marriage of Milosz with, 197, 199, Milosz's guilt over, 129, 157; pregnancy difficulties, 197; on return to Europe, 123, 124, 126, 169, 171–72
Milosz, Oscar (distant cousin/mentor): criticism of, 120; influence of, 7, 8, 40, 62, 63, 86, 87, 161, 214, 218, 219; in *The Land of Ulro*, 214–16; Milosz's visits to, 35–37, 118; predictions by, 35, 40, 87, 214–15, 220; relationship to Milosz, 284n42; theosophy and, 284n43

Milosz, Peter (Piotr) (son), 196, 197, 198
Milosz, Tony (son), 124, 169
Miłosz, Weronika Kunat (mother), 27, 29–30
Miłosz and the Problem of Evil (Tischner), 15
Milosz's ABC's (Milosz), 12–13, 31, 128, 131, 183, 190, 215, 224, 261
Milton, John, 16, 46, 85, 86, 87, 89, 229, 236
Mimesis (Auerbach), 223
Minding the Darkness (Scott), 79
"Mittelbergheim" (Milosz), 130–32, 134, 184
modernism, 6, 34, 114, 228, 232
modernists, 6, 228
Modzelewski, Zygmunt, 125
Montaigne, 110
"Morning" (Milosz), 52, 53
Mozart, Wolfgang Amadeus, 219
Munk, Andrzej, 11
Murry, J. Middleton, 217
"My Faithful Mother Tongue" (Milosz), 19
Myszeis (The Mouseiad) (Krasicki), 108

Nabokov, Nicolas, 127
Naphta (literary character), 8, 33. *See also The Magic Mountain* (Mann)
Nathan, Leonard, 64, 231
nationalism, 30–32, 94, 97, 99, 101, 102, 142, 237
Native Realm: A Search for Self-Definition (Milosz), 23, 30, 33, 83, 107, 121, 123–24, 132, 138, 147, 167, 173, 175, 197
"Natura." *See A Treatise on Poetry,* Part IV: "Natura"
nature: after emigration, 132–136; ambivalence about, 10, 50–51; in *A Treatise on Poetry,* Part IV: "Natura," 157–58
Nazism: in Germany, 145; ideological extremes of, 234; neo-Nazis, 19;

occupation of Poland, 45, 62, 93, 120; resistance to, 101
neoclassicism, 118
neoliberalism, 7, 226
Neruda, Pablo, 93
neuroscience on human duality, 33–34, 212–13
Neustadt Prize for Literature, 192, 196
New and Collected Poems: 1931–2001 (Milosz), 133–34, 192
Newman, John Henry Cardinal, 40, 136
Newton, Isaac, 14, 214
"New Year Letter" (Auden), 109, 110–13, 116–18
Nietzsche, Friedrich, 112, 173, 322n55
nihilism, 72–73, 173, 207
Nobel Prize for Literature: "Bypassing Rue Descartes" and, 194, 196, 198; effects of winning, 199, 216; emboldening by, 14, 38, 91, 192; fame after receiving, 15, 194; invitation from Poland after, 24
Non-Communist Left (NCL), 34, 128
Norwid, Cyprian, 17, 84, 141, 207, 211–12
"Notebook: Banks of Leman" (Milosz), 121, 131, 133–35, 157, 161, 171

Ocalenie ("Rescue") (Milosz), 45–56; about, 45–47, 67–68, 81–84, 93–95; anger and self-division within, 71–73; climax of, 76–79; composition in, 95–100; deep structure in poem order of, 50–53; dialectics in, 61–62; different arrangements in Polish and English, 55–56; *esse* and *devenir* in, 62–65; Hegelianism and, 137–39; integrity and development within, 48–50; Milosz's desire to save the culture, 84; *ocalenie* (term), 6; order of poems in, 53–55; partly unexplained in 1946, 119–22; poems framing, 68–71; "A Poor Christian" and, 73–76; post-war defense of, 107–8;

on truth, justice and madness, 100–102; "The World" as hub, 57–66. *See also* "Flight"; "Rescue"; "Voices of Poor People"
"O City," 162–65, 170
"Ode to Joy" (Beethoven), 13, 219
"Ode to Youth" (Mickiewicz), 23, 99
Office of Policy Coordination (OPC), 127
"On Parting with My Wife Janina" (Milosz), 200
"O October," 169–70, 176
Origen, 193
"Orpheus and Eurydice" (Milosz), 200–201
Orwell, George, 110
"Outskirts" (Milosz), 54, 76–77, 86
Ovid, 4, 222

Pan Tadeusz (Mickiewicz), 85, 177, 178, 221, 226, 227
Paradise Lost (Milton), 16, 46, 86, 236
Paradiso (Dante), 121, 205, 238–39
Pascal, Blaise, 3, 8, 183
Paz, Octavio, 217
Perse, Saint-John, 124
"Pictures" (Milosz), 54, 65, 67
Piłsudski, General Józef, 140, 142
PiS (Law and Justice) Party, 25, 102
Planck, Max, 241
Plato, 15, 111, 170, 190, 219–20, 239; use of, 219–20
Poe, Edgar Allan, 122
poetry: cultural evolution and, 238–39; freedom and, 169–70; global postmodern, 185–87; liberation of a people and, 17; Milosz on social function of, 4–5; "Reductionist Weltanschauung" of science and, 221–22; as "unpolitical politics," 5, 16, 24, 194, 232, 338n9
Poetry and Terror (Scott), 16
poet(s): American poets, 5, 7; as bard (*wieszcz*), 5; early poets, 4; influence on other, 15; Polish contemporaries,

4; role of, 14–15; theories about, 4; transnational poets, 15–16. *See also specific poets*
Poland: Catholic Church in, 17–18, 32, 186; "Golden Age" of, 4; *kresy* (outlying regions) of, 29; liberation of, 6; Polish thaw, 11, 12. *See also* Solidarity
Polish October, 152
Polish Revolution, 17, 23–24, 152
Polish Solidarity movement. *See* Solidarność (Solidarity)
Polish thaw, 11, 12
Polish uprisings of 19th Century, 23, 178
political evolution, 16
political history, 235
politics: American politics, 232–33; Milosz's cultural politics, 234–35; Milosz's unpolitical politics, 232–33; poetry and, 1
Politics (journal), 20
"A Poor Christian Looks at the Ghetto" (Milosz), 46, 49, 54, 73–76, 77, 87
"The Poor Poles Look at the Ghetto" (Błoński), 75
postmodernism: poetic development toward, 16; post-secular critique of, 6; of "Throughout Our Earth," 185–87
post-secularism: about, 6, 7, 231–32; catastrophic renewal in, 236–37; catastrophism in, 239–41; contribution of poetic energy to, 7; cultural evolution, 235–36; cultural politics, 234–35; global evolution, 234–35; hope and, 239–41; Milosz's unpolitical politics, 232–33; poetic development toward, 16; poetry and, 238–39; post-secular enlightenment, 8
postwar era: about, 105–6; Auden and doubleness, 109–10; bardic voice in, 113–16; cultural evolution and "Treatise on Morals" in, 118–19;

differences between "Letter" and "Treatise on Morals," 110–13; *Ocalenie* as unexplained in 1946, 119–22; satiric (classicist) voice in, 113–16; search for balance, 110–13
Postwar Polish Poetry, 4
Pound, Ezra, 218, 239
Poznań riots, 152
Prelude (Wordsworth), 87, 237
Preuves (journal), 127
"The Priest and the Jester" (Kołakowski), 185
prose, mature: about, 207; Blake and, 214–16, 229–30; contemporary episteme, 217–21; Eliot and, 216–17, 229–30; generative canon, 216–17; global evolution of, 6; *The History of Polish Literature*, 208–12; hope and, 217–21, 225–27; *The Land of Ulro* (Milosz), 214–16; neuroscience on human duality and, 212–13; poetry and, 225–27; post-secular critique in, 6; "Quarrel with Classicism," 222–25; quarrel with Eliot, 227–29; "Reductionist Weltanschauung" of science, 221–22; ruins, poetry, and hope, 225–27; *The Witness of Poetry* (Milosz), 216–17, 222–25. *See also specific works*
Protestantism, 4, 209; Catholicism and, 208; Kochanowski and, 210
Przedwiośnie (Early Spring) (Żeromski), 84
public success, after emigration, 127–29
Pushkin, Alexander, 239
Putin, Vladimir, 7
Putrament, Jerzy, 34, 155

"Quarrel with Classicism" (Milosz), 166, 206, 222–25
Quinn, Arthur, 64, 231

Radio Free Europe (RFE), 128
Raków School, 4, 209
Rakowski, Mieczysław, 11

"Recovery" (Milosz), 54, 57, 64, 65
Reid, Thomas Mayne, 142
Renaissance, 4, 213, 214, 225
Republic (Plato), 15, 170, 190, 220, 239
"Rescue" (Milosz): challenge of, 196; introduction of, 108; introduction to, v; order of poems in, 53–55; perspective in, 45; spirit of, 226; translation of *Ocalenie*, 47, 93. *See also Ocalenie* (Milosz)
Rilke, Rainer Maria, 114, 117
"The Road" (Milosz), 54, 57–58
romantic (vatic) voice: movement away from, 113–16; reformulation after Nobel Prize, 6
"The Romantic" (Mickiewicz), 210–11
Romeo and Juliet (Shakespeare), 94–95, 97
Rousseau, Jean-Jacques, 111, 210, 235
Różewicz, Tadeusz, 72, 208
Rückert, Friedrich, 239
Russian Revolution, 28, 169

Sadzik, Jósef, 198
Saint-Martin, Claude de, 214
salvational goal of poetry, v, 5, 6, 137–39
Sartre, Jean-Paul, 111, 161
satiric (classicist) voice, 113–16
Savio, Mario, 9
Schiller, Friedrich, 13, 219, 230, 239
Second Space: New Poems (Milosz), 189, 200–205, 263
"The Second Coming" (Yeats), 118, 213
"Secretaries" (Milosz), 116
secularism, 7, 16, 241
Seculum (Scott), 10
The Seizure of Power (Milosz), 129, 134, 175
"A Semi-Private Letter about Poetry," (Milosz), v, 107, 109, 114, 141, 146
Serra, Junipero, 186–87
Settembrini (literary character), 8, 33. *See also The Magic Mountain* (Mann)

sexual revolution, 182
Shakespeare, William, 46, 48, 97
Shapiro, Karl, 107, 109, 162
Shelley, Percy Bysshe, 6, 15, 230
Skamander group, 86, 141, 142, 211
Słonimski, Antoni, 11, 141, 142
Słowacki, Julisz, 29, 84, 151, 229
"Slow River," 30, 38–40, 46, 50
Smith, Stan, 109
Śniadecki, Jan, 210, 213, 214
The Social Contract (Rousseau), 235
Socinianism, 4, 209
socio-poetics, defined, 16
Solidarność (Solidarity), 12; in 1980/1981, 24–26; authoritarianism and, 7; contributions to, 5, 12; influence of Milosz on, 6, 17–18; as tripartite alliance, 17. *See also* Wałęsa, Lech
Solzhenitsyn, Aleksandr, 190
"Song of a Citizen" (Milosz), 51, 71
"Song of Myself" (Whitman), 27
"Songs of Adrian Zieliński" (Milosz), 54, 68, 69, 70, 73, 77–78, 93
"Songs of Experience" (Blake), 57
"Songs of Innocence" (Blake), 57
"Songs of Poor People" (Milosz), 51
Sorel, Georges, 228
Soviet Union: break up of, 6; Eastern Europe and, 9; hatred of, 9, 10, 12; uprisings and, 152; Vietnam and, 9. *See also* Communism; Solidarity
"Spain 1937" (Auden), 110
Spanish Civil War, 110
speaking "with silence," in Milosz's poetry, 119–20
in "Przedmowa," 119Spender, Stephen, 131
Spinoza, Baruch, 209
Spirit of History, 82, 138, 144–45, 147, 149
"The Stairs" (Milosz), 54, 58, 65
Stalin, Joseph, 17, 21, 123, 125
Stalin era, 11, 28, 62, 93, 101, 150

Index 357

Stalinism: Burnham's hatred of, 127; dialectical materialism of, 7; ideological extremes of, 234; Ketman practice under, 106; liberation from, 226; "Treatise on Morals" (Milosz) and, 118
Stalinist Poland: breaking from, 155; defecting from, 158; Janka and, 169; returning to, 157, 175
Stanislaw August Poniatowski, King of Poland, 210
Stevens, Wallace, 157
Stoicism, 210
Summa Theologiae (Thomas Aquinas), 60, 191
"The Sun," 54, 64, 65, 69
Swedenborg, Emanuel, 35, 183, 193, 214
Swift, Jonathan, 109, 113, 118
Świrsczyńska, Anna, 225
Sydney, Philip, 15
Symposium (Plato), 219–20
Szetejnie (birthplace), 27, 30, 31, 239
szlachta (gentry), 31, 83–84, 85–86, 178, 210
Szumański, Aleksander, 76
Szymborska, Wisława, 15

"A Task" (Milosz), 184
Taylor, Charles, 7
Tennyson, Alfred Lord, 192
Thigpen, Carol (second wife of Milosz), 200
Thomas Aquinas, Saint, 60, 61, 62, 138, 148, 191, 220
Thomism, 61–62, 65, 138, 184
"Three Winters" (Milosz), 36, 38–40, 53
"Throughout Our Lands" (Milosz), 3, 164, 182–87, 246
Thucydides, 110, 114, 115, 162
Tintern Abbey (Wordsworth), 46, 88, 89, 237
Tischner, Łukasz, 15, 60, 114, 147, 151, 156, 167, 231
"Toast" (Milosz), 130

"To Father Ch" (Milosz), 36, 163
Tolstoy, Leo, 239
"To Raja Rao" (Milosz), 9–10
"Tradition and the Individual Talent" (Eliot), 217
Traherne, Thomas, 46
"A Treatise on Morals" (Milosz), 24, 46, 102, 105, 107, 109, 110–11, 110–13, 114, 116–19, 139, 162, 236
A Treatise on Poetry (Milosz), 12, 33, 82–83, 118, 119, 132–33, 135, 137–53, 190, 197, 207, 211, 225, 226; close of "Natura" and Mickiewicz, 177–78; Hegelianism and, 137–53, 140–43; historic vision of, 12; open closure of "Natura," 174–75; "Part IV, "NATURA / Pennsylvania, 1948–1949," 155–78; personal closure of 1956, 176–77; second thoughts on decision to return, 170–74; "In You and In Me," 176–77
A Treatise on Poetry, Part I, "Beautiful Times," 139–40
A Treatise on Poetry, Part II, "The Capital," 143–47
A Treatise on Poetry, Part III, 150–53
A Treatise on Poetry, Part IV: "Natura," 155–78; beaver quest, 158–60, 170, 172–73; being and becoming in, 160–62, 171, 172, 173, 176; choice between history or love, 156, 158, 167–68, 171, 177, 178; differences between Polish and English versions, 157–58, 171–72, 176; doubleness in, 159, 164, 168, 171–72; "the eternal moment" and, 157–58, 160–62, 171; farm offer to settle on, 167, 169, 170, 173, 174, 177; historicity in, 161–62; history and nature opposed in, 155, 158, 163; irony in, 168; Janka (wife) and, 155, 157–58, 160, 169, 171–72, 176–77; nature in, 156–57, 158–60, 167, 171; "O City," 162–65; "O October," 169–70; open closure of, 175, 178; as path of hope, 162–64,

169, 178; poetry as path to liberation, 165, 175, 178; "The Rose . . . symbol of love and superterrestrial beauty," 165–66; seed of unnamed future, 162–63; version in English (2001), 157, 171; version in Polish (1956), 157, 176–77. *See also* "Natura"
"Treatise on Theology" (Milosz), 29, 177, 189, 202, 205–6, 224
Tuwim, Julian, 141
"Two Poems" (Milosz), 31
Tyrmand, Leopold, 11

Ulro, Blake's, 14, 68, 87, 214. *See also The Land of Ulro* (Milosz)
Unattainable Earth, 193, 199–200
Underground Theater Council, 97
United States. *See* America
unpolitical politics, 5, 16, 119, 338n9; American politics and, 232–33; "Bypassing Rue Descartes" and, 194; defined, 24; poetry to serve as, 5, 24; as strategy for cultural evolution, 232
Updike, John, 192
utopianism, 11, 13, 20, 52, 99, 158, 220

vatic (bardic) voice, 6, 144, 199; movement away from, 113–16; reformulation after Nobel Prize, 6, 189
Vendler, Helen, 6, 67, 137, 189, 237
Vico, Giovanni Batista, 138, 207, 211
Vietnam War, 9–11
Vincenz, Stanisław, 132
Virgil, 6, 85, 86, 191, 220, 222, 223, 236, 238
Visions from San Francisco (Milosz), 13, 183, 186, 190, 231–32
"Voices of Poor People" (Milosz), 46, 47, 49, 54, 61, 66, 67–79, 93. *See also Ocalenie* Part III
Voltaire, 210

Wajda, Andrzej, 21, 93
Wałęsa, Lech, 12, 17, 18, 24, 56

Walicki, Andrzej, 12
"Waltz" (Milosz), 52, 53
Warsaw Ghetto Uprising, 46, 76, 107
Warsaw Uprising of 1944, 22, 23, 78, 81, 89, 98, 107, 148
Wasley, Aidan, 109–10
The Waste Land (Eliot), 8, 46, 86, 88, 237
Waszkiewicz, Jadwiga, 38, 197, 199
Weil, Simone, 8, 20, 31, 62, 66, 119, 161, 207, 222, 226
Weimar Republic, 9, 33
Western Europe, 12, 209, 236
White, Lynn, Jr., 236
Whitehead, Alfred North, 14
Whitman, Walt, 13, 15, 16, 27, 31, 182, 183, 190, 219, 241
wieszcz (bard). *See* bard (*wieszcz*)
Wilbur, Richard, 5, 237
Wilder, Thorton, 167
Williams, Charles, 110
Wilno (Vilnius): as childhood city, 4, 27–28, 30; feelings of contempt in, 32; Jewish population of, 4
"Winter" (Milosz), 194, 240
"A Wish" (Milosz), 90
The Witness of Poetry (Milosz), v, 14, 15, 34, 108, 120, 189, 191, 192, 207, 216, 216–17, 217, 219, 220–25, 227, 230
Wonderful Adventures of Nils (Lagerlöf), 28, 59
Wordsworth, William, 9, 16, 46, 87–89, 155, 192, 235, 237, 238
"The World" (Milosz), 30, 196. *See also Ocalenie* Part II
World War I, 27, 89, 140, 150, 228, 237
World War II, 23, 28, 64, 143, 214, 220, 229
Wyka, Kazimierz, 36, 107
Wyspiański, Stanisław, 161

A Year of the Hunter (Milosz), 125, 168–69

Yeats, William Butler, 13, 109, 118,
 213, 220, 239
yin/yang duality, 33, 34, 59–60, 113,
 212, 216, 227
Young Poland, 40, 139, 173,
 174, 211, 223

Zagajewski, Adam, 18, 118
Żagary (literary group), 36
Żeromski, Stefan, 84

About the Author

For five years in the 1960s, **Peter Dale Scott** translated Polish poetry with Czeslaw Milosz, and with him produced the first book in English of the poetry of Zbigniew Herbert (Penguin, 1968, reissued by Carcanet and Ecco). His own books of poetry include his trilogy *Seculum*: *Coming to Jakarta* (1989), *Listening to the Candle* (1992), and *Minding the Darkness* (2000), and also *Mosaic Orpheus* (2009), *Tilting Point* (2012), and *Walking on Darkness* (2016). A Canadian, a former Canadian diplomat, and a professor in the UC Berkeley English Department from 1966 to 1994, he was also a co-founder of the Peace and Conflict Studies Program at UC Berkeley. In 2002, he was awarded the Lannan Poetry Award.

The poet and critic John Peck said of his trilogy that "Scott's *Seculum* is one of the essential long poems of the past half century" (John Peck, "Seeing Things as They Are," *Notre Dame Review* 31 [Winter/Spring 2011]: 239–52). Of *Coming to Jakarta*, James Laughlin wrote, "Not since Robert Duncan's *Groundwork* and before that William Carlos Williams' *Paterson*, has New Directions published a long poem as important as Peter Dale Scott's."

With Freeman Ng, he has written *Poetry and Terror: Politics and Poetics in* Coming to Jakarta. His published literary criticism includes a chapter, "The Social Critic and His Discontent," in A. David Moody (ed.), *The Cambridge Companion to T. S. Eliot*; as well as uncollected essays on Alcuin, Mary Shelley, Ezra Pound, F. R. Scott, and others. He is also the author of books on American deep politics, including *The Road to 9/11* (2007) and *The American Deep State* (2014, revised 2017).

www.ingramcontent.com/pod-product-compliance
Lightning Source LLC
Chambersburg PA
CBHW022008300426
44117CB00005B/81